Part of Our Lives

Part of Our Lives

A PEOPLE'S HISTORY OF THE AMERICAN PUBLIC LIBRARY

Wayne A. Wiegand

OXFORD
UNIVERSITY PRESS

OXFORD
UNIVERSITY PRESS

Oxford University Press is a department of the University of
Oxford. It furthers the University's objective of excellence in research,
scholarship, and education by publishing worldwide.

Oxford   New York
Auckland   Cape Town   Dar es Salaam   Hong Kong   Karachi
Kuala Lumpur   Madrid   Melbourne   Mexico City   Nairobi
New Delhi   Shanghai   Taipei   Toronto

With offices in
Argentina   Austria   Brazil   Chile   Czech Republic   France   Greece
Guatemala   Hungary   Italy   Japan   Poland   Portugal   Singapore
South Korea   Switzerland   Thailand   Turkey   Ukraine   Vietnam

Oxford is a registered trademark of Oxford University Press
in the UK and certain other countries.

Published in the United States of America by
Oxford University Press
198 Madison Avenue, New York, NY 10016

Library of Congress Cataloging-in-Publication Data
Wiegand, Wayne A., 1946–
Part of our lives : a people's history of the American public library / Wayne A. Wiegand.
pages cm
ISBN 978–0–19–024800–0 (hardback)
1. Public libraries—United States—History.   2. Libraries—United States—Public opinion—
History.   3. Public opinion—United States—History.   4. Library users—United States—
Attitudes—History.   5. Public libraries—Social aspects—United States—History.   6. Libraries
and community—United States—History.   7. Libraries and society—United States—History.
8. Books and reading—United States—History.   I. Title.
Z731.W734 2015
027.473—dc 3
2015014209

1 3 5 7 9 8 6 4 2
Printed in the United States of America
on acid-free paper

To Shirl:
Who introduced me to a world of love
I never would have discovered by myself.
June 19, 2015
Our Fiftieth Wedding Anniversary

Contents

So Much More Than Information

It's an indisputable fact—Americans love their public libraries. They always have, and evidence to support this statement abounds. First, the rhetoric: "The three most important documents a free society gives," wrote author E. L. Doctorow in 1994, "are a birth certificate, a passport, and a library card." "In this room," Pulitzer Prize–winning historian David McCullough said as he swept his arm around the Tulsa Public Library's auditorium in 1995, "we are at dead center in the absolute heart of the best institution in our society—the free library." "The America I loved still exists," said Kurt Vonnegut in 2005, albeit not in government or the media. "The America I love still exists at the front desks of our public libraries."[1]

Next, the research: A 2013 report by the Pew Research Center's Internet and American Life Project noted that in the previous decade "every other major institution (government, churches, banks, corporations) has fallen in public esteem except libraries, the military, and first responders." The study also found that 91 percent of those surveyed who were more than sixteen years old said libraries are "very" or "somewhat" important to their communities, and 98 percent identified their public library experience as "very" or "mostly positive." Another Pew study found that 94 percent of parents believe libraries are important for their children, and 84 percent said this was because libraries develop a love of reading and books.[2]

Although in the 1980s many evangelists of information technology predicted the demise of public libraries by the turn of the century, as of this writing their numbers have not dropped. In fact, in 2012 the United

States had 17,219 public libraries (including branches and bookmobiles). Nearly 300 million Americans—96 percent of the population—lived in a public library service area. While the number of visits declined slightly in 2012 from 1.52 to 1.5 billion (a recession forced public libraries to reduce hours of opening by 1.7 percent; more patrons were visiting "virtually" and downloading library e-books from home computers), the decade nonetheless showed a 21 percent increase. In 2012, 93 million Americans attended a public library program, a one-year increase of 4.1 percent and an eight-year increase of 37.6 percent. Sixty-five million program attendees were children, a 3.5 percent increase from the previous year and a 24.2 percent increase in the previous decade. In 2012, public libraries circulated 2.2 billion items (including audio and video materials and e-books)—a 28 percent increase from 2003; circulation per capita showed a ten-year increase of 16.8 percent. Public libraries also provided users with access to 250,000 Internet-ready computers, 100 percent more per capita than a decade earlier. And in 2012, the American Library Association (ALA) reported that 62 percent of public libraries were the only source of free access to computers and the Internet in their communities, where more than half of young adults and seniors living in poverty used them. "For all this," one *Forbes* journalist noted in 2013, "public libraries cost just $42 per citizen each year to maintain."[3]

Americans love their public libraries, but why? Despite the fact that the American public library has been strongly identified with the concept of equal educational opportunity, it is difficult to prove that these civic institutions are essential to democracy—the cornerstone of the narrative the profession uses to justify their existence. For the most part its alumni are anonymous and invisible, and because of the voluntary nature of public library usage, efforts to measure the impact of public library service have largely depended on soft data.[4]

This book is an attempt to bolster these soft data by tracing the American public library's history—not so much by analyzing the words of its founders and managers but mostly by listening to the voices of its users. To identify my perspective, I have adopted two phrases my former University of Wisconsin–Madison colleague Doug Zweizig used regularly. Rather than analyzing the "user in the life of the library"—a top-down view that largely mirrors the library profession's perspective—*Part of Our Lives* adopts a bottom-up "library in the life of the user" perspective that allows me to follow Howard Zinn, whose pioneering *People's History of the United States* (1980) takes this approach. It also invites me to feature in my narrative the voices of generations of public library users. As a humanist, I am most concerned with what Andrew Piper calls "the production of subjectivity"—how a human develops into a social being.[5] In *Part of Our Lives* I offer an analysis of how the American public library contributed to that process in so many ways.

Because of recent technologies, uncovering these voices was easy. Some are in published memoirs, autobiographies, and biographies of the famous; some are in archives across the country. The vast majority, however, are fixed in hundreds of US newspapers and periodicals digitized since the 1990s into huge databases. By using "public library" as a search term I found thousands of voices in letters to the editor, and thousands more quoted in stories reporters wrote about their local libraries. Combined, they revealed additional reasons the public library has been such a success over the generations and help explain why citizens have consistently reacted to threats of public library closures. But another fact struck me as I mined these databases: there is a relative lack of complaints about and protest against these libraries. By its eloquent silence, that absence strongly supports the conviction that Americans have always loved their public libraries.

As I pondered ways to arrange a historical narrative teeming with examples of users whose lives were changed and shaped by the American public library, I was surprised at how quickly the evidence organized into three major categories. History shows that the reasons Americans have loved their public libraries fit into three broad categories: for the useful information they made accessible; for the public spaces they provided; and for the power of reading stories they circulated that helped users make sense of phenomena in the world around them. In this book I analyze "information," "reading," and "place," but although library literature does a good job analyzing the first from a "user in the life of the library" perspective, it does little to explain from that view the roles public libraries have played as community places, and the power of reading libraries provided to fulfill essential needs in patrons' everyday lives.

For example, for many Americans (and probably most of my readers) the public library constituted the first place in the public sphere where they enjoyed adult privileges, and by obtaining a public library card as a child they formally accepted a civic responsibility to respect public property. In addition, over the generations many benefited from this place by having a piece of childhood artwork posted on a public library wall, by participating in a library puppet show, by reading at the library with a friend, or by telling a story. From a "library in the life of the user" perspective, knowing how and why patrons used library spaces and what they learned there is essential to discovering why people love public libraries.

And to demonstrate the power reading can have on public library patrons, two celebrities provide moving testimony. In a 2008 interview, eighty-eight-year-old Pete Seeger recalled an early life reading experience. "At age 7, a librarian saw that I could read fairly well and recommended me a book. . . . The one I got was 'Rolf in the Woods,' about a teenager who runs away from his stepfather—who's beating him—and is adopted by a middle-aged Indian whose tribe was massacred, and whose wife was sold into slavery, and is living alone." That he remembered this so vividly eight decades later is testimony to the power of reading, and in Seeger's case, a *New York Times* editor noted at his death in 2014, "fitting for someone who went on to engage issues of conscience."[6]

For Oprah Winfrey, reading was "an open door for freedom in my life" that "allowed me to see . . . a world beyond my grandmother's front porch" in Mississippi, "that everybody didn't have an outhouse, that everybody wasn't surrounded by poverty, that there was a hopeful world out there and that it could belong to me." To Winfrey, reading became her "comfort," her "solace, to commune with and learn something about myself, to learn something about other people, to learn something about the world." In a small Milwaukee apartment she shared as a nine-year-old with her half-brother and half-sister, she read *A Tree Grows in Brooklyn*—her "first all-night book—the story of Francie Nolan whose life was full of humiliation and whose only friends were in books lining the public library shelves. . . . I felt like my *life* was hers." Seven years later Winfrey read Maya Angelou's *I Know Why the Caged Bird Sings*. "I read it over and over. I had never before read a book that validated my own existence."[7]

Throughout their history, American public libraries have operated as local institutions (85 percent of their funding still comes from local government) that serve communities where the multiple groups who founded, funded, and managed them, and ultimately the millions who used them, interacted in numerous ways. On the one hand, these groups crafted libraries as comfortable places to celebrate commonalities in their cultural value systems. On the other, they also used libraries as sites to mediate differences occasioned by clashes in these systems. Naturally, public library managers functioned as players in the construction of many cultures whose heritage was addressed in one form or another by the libraries' collections and services. Sometimes the professionalism these library managers practiced facilitated cultural connections between groups; sometimes it slowed—even prevented—connections from forming. But that is also part of the story.

Before the latter part of the twentieth century, choices public librarians made about what to collect, how to organize, what to circulate, and what to preserve tended to favor dominant cultures. Public libraries can certainly take credit for educating their patrons through collections and services, but because these collections and services largely reflected values of locally powerful groups, on many occasions public libraries functioned as obstacles to cultural democracy by perpetuating the racism, sexism, classism, and homophobia their collections supported. At the same time, however, users heavily influenced the choices librarians made. Yes, American public libraries shaped the cultures they served; perhaps even more important, however, the cultures they served shaped American public libraries. To show this phenomenon, I have—where possible—let public library users of varied ethnicities, young and old, male and female, speak for themselves to tell their own stories.

Although Americans loved more than criticized their public libraries, in this book I pay some attention to the complaints precisely because they reveal issues this civic institution arbitrated—an important community service the public library has been performing for generations. Showing how public libraries have dealt with controversial materials and situations demonstrates that reading and library spaces have been transformative for patrons. It also helps identify the acceptable boundaries of a community's literary and cultural values—boundaries that public libraries sometimes openly mediated, more often intuitively recognized from traditions and demands inherited from previous generations of public library users.

By focusing on the American public library in the life of the user, this book attempts to show that since the mid–nineteenth century the public library has provided its users with information, reading, and places that have fused them into communities and have given them a sense of belonging. From a bottom-up perspective I also try to shift the focus from issues of information access to include analysis of the competencies and skills public libraries helped users develop that fostered sociability and invited community involvement. This book is primarily about people who in multiple ways used the spaces American public libraries provided, and about the reading these patrons obtained at their public libraries, reading that to cultural authorities often seemed unimportant, on occasion even harmful.

The average patron knows little (and often cares less) about what goes on behind the circulation desk of an American public library. She may not know how it is governed, managed, or funded. She may not know anything about the systems used to select materials and prioritize services. If she is a regular user, however, she does know what she wants and why she is there. Sometimes this involves contact with a librarian, sometimes not. Most often it involves a need for information, stories, and places that brings her to this civic institution—again and again. This does not diminish priorities librarians have held dear for generations; instead, it views them in a larger context, one the library profession has had to share with its publics because, after all, those publics are not required to use libraries.

I hope that this approach will create greater understanding of the multiple roles these ubiquitous institutions have played in their host communities over the generations and that it will deepen our understanding of why Americans love their public libraries. In my research the phrase "part of our lives" was voiced frequently by public library users. For example, because it had become so much a "part of our lives," lamented a New York Public Library (NYPL) branch patron in 1982, she had to turn down an invitation to attend the symbolic locking of the front door for renovation. "I would only cry," she said.[8] Given statistics on library usage I cite earlier, selecting my title proved not only easy but also historically accurate. In the chapters that follow I show from a people's perspective the multiple ways the American public library became for so many millions a "part of our lives."

CHAPTER ONE

"Improv'd the General Conversation of Americans"

Social Libraries before 1854

When Benjamin Franklin sent his first order to a London bookseller in 1732 to begin the Library Company of Philadelphia, he did not include any fiction or theology books. "Filled instead with dictionaries, grammars, an atlas, histories, and books on science and agriculture," one historian noted, the forty-six titles were "suited to the tastes and purses of young tradesmen." Franklin wanted his Library Company to nurture the "Self-Made Man" he had celebrated in his *Poor Richard's Almanac*, and fiction had no role in that process. By placing greater importance on information than on stories, Franklin reflected a priority that professional librarianship has followed to the present day.[1]

Eighteenth-century colonial social libraries were modeled after British institutions and made possible by an expanding transatlantic commerce that brought to American shores an ample supply of books and pamphlets. But libraries existed not just to collect and disseminate printed texts; they were also rooted in voluntary associations established for group activity. As a result, they functioned as places where people could develop social networks and participate in local culture. In Salem, Massachusetts, for example, a social library established in 1760 grew directly from a Social Evening Club begun at a tavern ten years earlier.[2]

Franklin obviously desired group activity; his idea for the Library Company grew from a wish to improve the Junto, a debating society he and his colleagues had organized earlier. The Junto modeled itself on societies advocated by leading Puritan clergyman Cotton Mather, who encouraged communities to organize meetings around predetermined questions. Franklin altered this model by suggesting that members drink a glass of wine between questions—perhaps to increase sociability. For these discussions, members "hired a Room to hold our club in" (initially in a tavern), but to stimulate discussion, Franklin recalled, "I propos'd that we should all of us bring our Books to that Room, where they would not only be ready to consult in our Conferences, but become a common Benefit, each of us being at Liberty to borrow such as he wish'd to read at home." When he recognized "the Advantage of this little Collection, I propos'd to render the Benefit from Books more common by commencing a Public Subscription Library."[3]

Junto meetings were clear manifestations of a public sphere institution that social reading facilitated. For the Library, Franklin drew up articles of agreement in 1731 and persuaded fifty friends to contribute forty shillings each and ten shillings per annum to buy books they would hold in common. He often referred to it as "the Philadelphia public library," and later bragged that it was the "mother of all N[orth] American subscription libraries." In two respects the Library Company served as a forerunner of the American public library. First, it assumed a position in a colonial public culture with older social institutions like the church, and newer social institutions such as bookstores, taverns, post offices, and coffeehouses where colonists began to develop a public interest. Second, by collecting materials "suited to the tastes and purses of young tradesmen," Franklin identified value in the Library with work, not leisure. In 1732, information addressing work was commonly referred to as "useful knowledge."[4]

All his life Franklin touted the value of social libraries. They "improv'd the general Conversation of the Americans," he argued, "made the common Tradesmen and Farmers as intelligent as most Gentlemen from other Countries, and perhaps have contributed in some degree to the Stand as generally made through the Colonies in Defense of their Privileges." Like other public sphere agencies, the Company provided self-selected influential citizens with a central gathering site where they could discuss and form "public opinion." The books it collected, however, were carefully selected. Although Franklin defied Mather's model for gatherings by serving wine, he did follow Mather in shunning fiction—the clergyman worried his children would someday "poison themselves with foolish

Romances, or Novels, or Playes, or Songs, or Jests."[5] Once they arrived, Library Company books were cataloged by size, then subject, and placed in a subscriber's home. In 1734 the Library contained 239 volumes, 25 periodicals, and sundry pamphlets. Six years later the Company moved to the Pennsylvania State House and in 1769 it merged with three other social libraries established between 1747 and 1757. In 1787 it served as a reference library for the men who drafted the Constitution.

Before the American Revolution, New England colonies hosted more than fifty social libraries; most used the Library Company as an organizational model; all looked to England for new titles. In 1733, eight founders subscribed twenty shillings each to establish the Book Company of Durham (Connecticut), a social library intended to "enrich our minds in useful and profitable knowledge by reading." In 1747 Abraham Redwood of Newport, Rhode Island, gave money for "a collection of useful Books suitable for a Publick Library . . . having nothing in View but the Good of Mankind." Directors ordered 751 titles "propagating Virtue, Knowledge & useful Learning." Three years later the collection moved into a building many claim as the continent's first to be used solely as a library. A 1764 catalog listed 700 titles; 33 percent high culture literature, 19 percent science, 16 percent history, 13 percent theology, and 8 percent law. The remaining 11 percent consisted of biography, travel, and the agricultural and military sciences. In its 1771 constitution, founders of the Social Library of Salisbury, Connecticut, identified reasons for organizing: the "promotion of Virtue, Education and Learning, and . . . the discouragement of Vice and Immorality."[6]

Social libraries in colonial America experienced some competition from "circulating libraries," which made books available for a fee. They were generally run out of newspaper offices, bookstores, and coffeehouses in towns with enough readers to constitute a market. A circulating library owner usually fronted the capital necessary to acquire a collection, then rented it by the book or time period (or combination of the two) to anyone willing to pay. Because profits depended on circulation, owners stocked books that circulated most. As a result, they preferred novels, a rapidly growing category of reading. Where social libraries avoided stories depicting romance, murders, hangings, and scandals of popular interest that papers like the *Boston Gazette* regularly reported, circulating libraries embraced them.[7]

As eighteenth-century novel-reading became more commonplace, it helped divest the printed word of "a sacramental aura" it inherited from

The first circulating library in Boston was established by John Main in November 1765.
Photo courtesy of Library of Congress, LC-USZ62-99619

previous centuries.[8] That women novel readers were central to this shift may explain why the patriarchal culture steeped in religious orthodoxy worried so much about the novel's effect on what it perceived as women's delicate sensibilities; perhaps that is also why white middle-class women who felt constrained by that religious orthodoxy found novels so compelling. Novels certainly provoked emotions and stimulated discussion among women. The novel reader "will probably be found more live to distress, more refined, more *companionable*, than the wholly unlettered

A 1787 newspaper article announced the opening of a new circulating library in Boston. *Massachusetts Centinal, December 29, 1787*

rustic," wrote one circulating library proprietor in a catalog preface.[9] "Pray, my dear," wrote one female to another after reading Samuel Richardson's novel *Pamela* in the 1750s, "how could Pamela forgive Mr. B all his Devilish conduct so as to consent to marry him?" Her query reflects the sense of shared identity and moral improvement the act of reading such stories fostered.[10]

And because non-alcoholic establishments ran most circulating libraries, women were welcome. In 1762, William Rind of Annapolis, Maryland, opened what may have been colonial America's first circulating library. He charged customers (including women) an annual fee to check out two books per circulation. In 1769 a Philadelphia printing firm opened a 300-volume circulating library, including multiple copies of popular works. In April 1772, there were as many women borrowers as men borrowers, but the men took out more books (perhaps for family members), and of 617 books borrowed that month, 86 percent were fiction. Although the library did not survive the Revolution, it pointed to major changes in the culture of print.[11] Because they opened longer hours and provided inexpensive access to more books, circulating libraries allowed more members of the middle class—particularly its increasingly literate females—to participate in shared reading.

Colonial America's media—mostly newspapers and pamphlets—played a major role in the American Revolution, and as public sphere institutions, social libraries participated. For example, many held copies of James Otis's *Rights of the British Colonists Asserted* (1764), Samuel Adams's *A Statement of the Rights of the Colonies* (1772), and Thomas Jefferson's *Summary View of the Rights of British America* (1774). Also common to many was John Locke's *Second Treatise on Government*, which fit the concept of a self-made man celebrating the virtues of talent, industry, and grit that Franklin and others promoted. After the Revolution gave way to constitutional forms of government at the federal and state levels, many states passed enabling legislation fostering even more social libraries. During the crucial years when new states ratified the Constitution (1787–1789), social libraries helped stimulate the public interest and resolve disputes through print and oral communication.

Public Libraries in the United States of America—a survey the federal government published for the nation's centennial—notes that twenty social libraries formed between 1775 and 1800 (more than double the number established before 1775), 179 in 1820–1825, 551 in 1825–1850, and 2,240 in 1850–1875.[12] Many did not survive long, but their existence helped communities mark themselves as friendly toward culture, and especially the culture of print that celebrated the moral values of dominant groups. Regional differences were obvious. New England chartered more than 500 social libraries between 1790 and 1815; by 1850 that number had doubled. Social libraries also followed the country's restless citizens as small towns west of the Appalachians established hundreds more. The same situation prevailed in the South. Fifty-nine Baltimoreans formed a Library Company in 1795. Five years later it had 345 members, all given access to its 3,300-volume collection. In 1798, a few Alexandria, Virginia, friends formed a subscription library; an 1856 catalog listed 4,481 volumes.[13]

In the new nation, citizens placed a high priority on education. "Religion, morality and knowledge being necessary to good government and the happiness of mankind," read the Northwest Ordinance of 1787, "schools and the means of education shall forever be encouraged." Not only education but also improved communication systems were encouraged. The Post Office Act of 1792 reflected the new government's commitment to the ideal of an informed citizenry and extended the world of mixed media for Early Republic citizens—which at the time included word-of-mouth communication, public speeches and performances, and signs in public spaces.[14]

Social libraries facilitated all these forms of communication. Improvements in publishing technologies, expanded availability of printed materials and their methods of dissemination, artificial lighting, and the increased availability and improvement of eyeglasses also influenced the spread of social libraries, which for these locally controlled associations reflected a faith in reading, social responsibility, community pride, and self-improvement. Social library founders expected the materials they collected to mold the kind of "character" they emulated. Although they remained intensely local (membership was self-selected), social libraries had a binding effect on their groups and across communities and the nation as the members were all reading and discussing the same texts.

Social libraries needed several conditions to prosper. They had to be in areas transitioning from frontier to populated settlements, gain a footing in the community during good times with adequate per capita income, build on enabling legislation, and offer lecture series and support lyceums. These lyceums had become an important component in American cultural life. Besides lectures, members also recognized the social nature of reading that libraries facilitated. Although books are the "easiest, the cheapest and most effectual mode of diffusing knowledge among the people," argued the Reverend Jeremy Belknap in 1792, their greatest "advantage" rested "in the social intercourse of persons who have read the same books by their conversing on the subjects which have occurred in their reading and communicating their observations one to another."[15]

As social libraries grew in number, attempts by cultural authorities to homogenize their collections followed. In 1793 Thaddeus Mason Harris published *Selected Catalogue of Some of the Most Esteemed Publications in the English Language Proper to Form a Social Library*. It cited 277 books Harris divided into three classes—"memory" (87 titles, including history, travel, and biography), "reason" (109 titles, including science, religion, and philosophy), and "imagination" (81 titles, including poetry, drama, art, and 11 fiction titles, or 4 percent of the total). The pamphlet sold well. Book publishers and dealers soon began cultivating social libraries by offering them special discounts.[16] Within decades, social libraries constituted an attractive fraction of the domestic book market.

After the Revolution, rhetoric justifying social libraries did not change. On petitioning the Massachusetts legislature to incorporate their Lunenburg Social Library in 1798, its organizers cited their "great utility . . . in diffusing useful knowledge among the People." But private communications show shifting priorities as subscribers demanded more novels. Some libraries resisted. "Though we would wish to mix the *utile* with the *dulce*," the Library Company of Philadelphia wrote its London agent in 1783, "we should not think it expedient to do to our present stock anything in the *novel* way."[17] Others bent to member pressure. "The bulk" of the Charleston (South Carolina) Library Society's latest catalog, its president acknowledged in the 1790s, contains "Books of much lighter reading than our last, but in a Society such as ours, we are obliged to consult all tastes and to have many books of mere amusement as well as books of instruction and science." In *The Algerine Captive* (1797), author Royall Tyler returns his protagonist to the new nation after a seven-year absence. Among things he noticed was the "extreme avidity with which books of mere amusement were . . . perused by all ranks of his countrymen," and where a "surprising alteration of taste" was obvious in the spread of social libraries "composed of books designed to amuse." As a result, "all orders of country life, with one accord, forsook the sober sermons and practical pieties of their fathers, for the gay stories and splendid impieties of the traveler and the novelist."[18]

Although the plots in many novels opposed the consumption of alcohol, lotteries, slavery, working conditions for women, and imprisonment for debt, cultural authorities who assumed responsibility to determine textual meanings and literary quality continued to disparage fiction reading. "Evergreen trees of diabolical knowledge," some called them; "greasy combustible duodecimos," said others. One condemned them as "puerile," and another said they inculcated "disgust for all serious employments" and nurtured "impure desires," "vanity," and "dissipation."[19]

Recent research analyzing these novels through readers' eyes, however, shows a different reception. After reading one 1806 novel, for example, a shy young Vermont male found there words and phrases he used to woo his future bride, who then bonded with him as they read the text together. Readers used novels for multiple purposes: as filters for their experiences, to jointly experience similar emotions, to make sense of their daily lives, to develop and strengthen social networks, to form and maintain a sense of identity, to provide a subject for conversation that connected people face-to-face and in written correspondence, and to effect a sociability that the act of reading nurtured. About the chief protagonist of *Clarissa,* a novel by Samuel Richardson, one mother wrote in 1784, "her letters are full of sentiment—I must adopt some of her excellent rules." "I delight to see flow from another pen the sensations I feel but am unable to express," wrote another in 1792 about a novel she recently read. "I cannot agree with her that Women are only born to suffer & to obey," said a third in 1800 about another novel's protagonist. These books "unconsciously reveal all the little household secrets," wrote Elizabeth Gaskell, herself a novelist. "We see the meals as they are put on the table, we learn the dresses which those who sit down to them wear, . . . we hear their kindly family discourses, we enter into their home struggles, and we rejoice when they gain the victory."[20]

Because they provided customers with novels they wanted, circulating libraries—"slop shops in literature," some critics called them—did a better job of addressing newer reading practices and experiences. In New York, for example, Hocquet Caritat's Circulation Library had more than 5,000 volumes seven years after it opened in 1797. From it "novels were called for by the young and the old," recalled an observer. "From the tender virgin of thirteen, whose little heart went pit-a-pat at the approach of a beau; to the experienced matron of three score, who could not read without spectacles." New circulating libraries popped up in places women frequented. In 1802, Mary Sprague added one to her Boston millinery shop. "She has spared no pains to make her collection deserving circulation," reported a local newspaper, "by mingling the useful with the amusing." Across the East Coast, between 1780 and 1820 fiction increased from a fourth to half of most circulating library collections.[21]

An early-nineteenth-century publishing revolution increased the number of printed texts. Technical innovations made paper cheaper, and the rapid rotary press pumped out thousands of inexpensive books. With diversity and choice expanded, reading habits shifted from primarily intensive (concentrating on a few texts read over and over) that characterized reading in previous centuries to extensive (absorbing more texts) more characteristic of today's reading behaviors. "Reading is now a sort of fashion & the great object is," author Richard Henry Dana wrote his publisher in the century's first decade, "to be first in the fashion, & in order to do that, to be the first in getting a new publication, the first in getting thro it, the first to talk about it, & the first in talking about it." The shift from intensive to extensive reading particularly evident in the novel's popularity was essential to the birth of the American public library a half-century later. More immediately, however, it led to a culture of reading that became a necessity in which social and circulating libraries played a major role.[22] In a variety of ways, they shaped the civic culture evolving around them.

West of the Appalachians, social library history reflects a pioneering spirit of cultural desire. In Cincinnati, for example, several men met at a tavern in 1802 to establish a social library. Thereafter twenty-five men purchased shares of stock, all for a library that opened a month later. In Ames, Ohio, residents pooled money and animal pelts (especially raccoons) in 1803 to send east with one member, who carried with him letters of introduction to Thaddeus Mason Harris. He returned months later. A fellow subscriber described his arrival: "He brought the books . . . in a sack. I was present at . . . the pouring-out of the treasure. There were about sixty volumes [mostly history and religion]; . . . there never was a library better read." Although organized as the Western Library Association, local lore dubbed it the "Coonskin Library."[23]

One of the nation's most venerable social libraries—the Boston Athenaeum—traces its roots to the Boston Anthology Society, which in 1805 voted "that a Library of periodical publications be instituted for the use of the Society." Eighteen months later the Massachusetts legislature incorporated the Boston Athenaeum to build an "extensive collection of such rare and valuable works, in ancient and modern languages, . . . which are deemed indispensable to those who would perfect themselves in the sciences." The Athenaeum organized in 1807, and by selling 150 shares of stock (no one could own more than three shares) it quickly raised $45,000.

Social libraries tried to regulate member behavior. In many, patrons generally spent hours poring over books with heads tilted, sitting silently upright at desks with both feet planted on the floor. In 1812 the Sterling (Massachusetts) reading room banned "unnecessary conversation" and "party disputes." In 1820, the New York's Apprentices' Library allowed "no conversation" in the reading room "under any pretense whatsoever," and insisted "all boys must have clean hands, face, shoes, and sit with their hats off." Others were not so strict. In 1810 the Boston Athenaeum not only allowed evening "conversation" in the reading room but trustees even ordered that "rooms be made convenient for that purpose." When the Athenaeum moved into a three-story building in 1823, the second floor contained a 500-seat lecture hall and reserved the top floor for artist exhibitions. Women could visit the gallery without male escorts. "Ladies will experience no embarrassment or difficulty in visiting the gallery without the attention of gentlemen," a flyer assured readers.[24]

Several communities also experimented with community-controlled libraries, many aimed at youth. In 1803, Caleb Bingham offered 150 books if Salisbury, Connecticut, established a library for youths nine to sixteen. Salisbury accepted the gift and supported the Bingham Library for Youth with public funds, probably making it the first instance of municipal government support for public library service. In 1833, citizens of Peterborough, New Hampshire, used part of a state literary fund to purchase books for a town library housed at the post office. Four years later the collection totaled 465 titles. In 1835, Ebenezer Learned's will provided West Cambridge, Massachusetts, with funds for a children's library. While each of these "public" libraries started auspiciously, communities generally failed to provide annual funds for new materials, adequate quarters, and competent staffing. Collections in these partially public-supported libraries ranged from several hundred to a few thousand volumes.[25]

If sales are any indication, however, most literate adults in the early nineteenth century wanted novels. America published one novel between 1770 and 1779, 25 between 1800 and 1809, 128 between 1820 and 1829, and 765 between 1840 and 1849. These numbers continued to perplex cultural authorities. "A great obstacle to good education is the inordinate passion prevalent for novels," argued Thomas Jefferson in 1818. "When this poison infects the mind, it destroys its tone, and revolts it against wholesome reading." One female cultural authority worried that "miscellaneous reading" made "profound thought . . . somewhat obsolete." This "mass of texts," contested a male colleague in 1848, has "leaped from the press like the frogs of Egypt," most of it "unmitigated trash, the froth of superficial thinking, the scum of diseased sentiment."[26]

Authorities addressed this "problem" in different ways. Many compiled manuals on reading—for example, John Pierpont's *The American First Class Book: Exercises in Reading and Recitation* (1831), Lydia H. Sigourney's *The Book for Girls* (1844), and Edwin Hubbell Chapin's *Duties of Young Men* (1840) and *Duties of Young Women* (1848). In the latter, Chapin argued that books should "inform the mind, refine the taste and improve the heart." Sigourney agreed. Books should "cultivate the intellect, . . . strengthen the moral principles and regulate the affections." Both were convinced of reading's ability to inculcate character and create a better-informed citizenry.[27]

Despite pressure to regulate their reading behaviors, however, most reading adults insisted on novels for reasons that had less to do with "escape" as traditionally defined, and more to do with empowerment and validation.

By empowering white women, people of color, and the lower classes to rethink societal roles others assigned them, the implicit democratic messages carried by the early-nineteenth-century novel threatened traditional authorities, including white male church and state leaders.[28] When debates occurred about what social libraries should collect, seldom did they focus on useful knowledge. Almost always debates centered on fiction.

In order to survive, social library board members had to find a balance between works containing "serious & erudite subjects," a Charleston Library Society official noted, and member desire for "light & trivial reading." "We must, at least for some time, think of popularity," one Boston Athenaeum member wrote in 1807. In public, founders continued to quote their charters when pressed to explain their library's raison d'etre.[29] This mattered little to their novel-reading members, however, who used the stories the libraries contained to identify socially acceptable norms of gentility and sociability, thus generating for themselves a very "useful knowledge" that "improv'd" their "general conversation."

When historians refer to the years 1790 to 1840 as the "golden age of social libraries," they speak mostly of numbers established, not libraries that survived. More than half did not last beyond mid-century. In St. Louis, for example, some citizens started a subscription library in 1811, others a Library Society in 1819, still others a Library Association in 1824. By that time St. Louis also hosted reading rooms in a newspaper office, a hotel, and a "Reading Room and Punch House." In 1839 the Library Society dissolved and sold its collections to the St. Louis Lyceum, which in turn passed them on to the St. Louis Mercantile Library Association at mid-century.

Unless membership libraries also provided space for social gatherings such as art exhibit openings, conversations, and lectures; unless they supplied the kinds of stories enough people wanted; and unless they enabled connections beyond reading "useful knowledge" they were likely to fail. Again, St. Louis provides an example. In 1850, the successful Mercantile Library Association reported a membership of 589. Its building—located within walking distance of the business district—boasted a large reading room and two lecture halls seating 600 in one and 1,500 in the other, the latter the city's largest auditorium. Men of commerce found it an ideal gathering place. Where social libraries were housed in separate buildings, they almost always included space for public lectures, at which listeners could demonstrate how "literate" they were by questions they asked and behaviors they modeled.[30]

St. Louis Mercantile
Library Hall, 1854. Its
2,000-seat Grand Hall
was the city's largest
auditorium. *Photography
Collection, The Miriam
and Ira D. Wallach
Division of Art, Prints
and Photographs, New
York Public Library*

Harnessing social library space to accommodate the nation's growing
lyceum movement would revitalize neglected libraries, many argued,
and help establish new ones. "There is scarcely a village of any size in
the country but what has a Lyceum," noted the *New York Evangelist*
in 1856, "or an association of men who, following in the wake of our
large cities, have sought to increase their public libraries by means of
lectures given by literary men of reputation." In antebellum America,
lyceums were scattered from New England (Massachusetts had 137
in 1839) to the Middle Atlantic, offering lecture courses on science,
agriculture, politics, morals, literature, and philosophy. Itinerants
like Ralph Waldo Emerson, Henry Ward Beecher, Oliver Wendell
Holmes, and Horace Mann regularly lectured in social library auditoriums hosting lyceum series. In 1841, Frederick Douglass gave his
first public lecture to white people at the Nantucket Island Atheneum
Library.[31]

Although all these libraries nurtured the democratizing tendencies that
reading cultivated, none were democratic; most were controlled by white
Anglo-Saxon Protestant, and generally middle-class, adult males who
preferred the society of their own kind. At the Boston Athenaeum, for
example, men of means controlled access to services and collections. Not
until the 1830s were the first women admitted to membership (one was

later ousted for her abolitionist views). Some protested the Athenaeum's class restrictions. "What literary advantages have the mass of our citizens derived from the Athenaeum?" the *Boston News-Letter and City Record* asked in 1826. "Things are becoming quite royal in our venerable old city; money buys a ticket for the wealthy to read the Hebrew language, while the industrious, worthy portion of the community may intellectually starve upon a six-penny almanack."[32]

But Brahmins nonetheless saw a bright future for the Athenaeum. "To this great establishment," Harvard professor George Ticknor wrote Daniel Webster in 1826, "I would attach all the lectures wanted, whether fashionable, popular, scientific . . . and have the whole made a Capitol of the knowledge of the town." Ticknor recognized the value of the social library as a place and saw ways the Athenaeum fit into Boston's evolving and dynamic public culture. The Athenaeum's Art Gallery proved especially popular. "All the world . . . was at the gallery yesterday," reported one newspaper in 1828, "and good judges pronounce the exhibition *superior* to that of last year." In 1839 the Athenaeum staged its first sculpture exhibition and years later moved it to the first floor, placed its library on the second, and its gallery on the third, thus dedicating two-thirds of its floor space to viewing rather than reading.[33]

Others mirrored the Athenaeum's experience. The new building Philadelphia's Athenaeum occupied in 1847 contained a lecture room, a "Chess Room," and two reading rooms. When the New York Society Library opened a new building in 1840, a reporter noticed not only a well-decorated building with a book room and a periodical room "brilliantly lighted at night," but also "two smaller apartments, used as conversation parlors, to avoid disturbing readers," and a lecture room that hosted entertainments, discussions, and assemblies. Edgar Allan Poe "entranced" an audience there in 1848 with a "brilliant lecture on 'The Cosmogony of the Universe.'" Shortly after organizing San Francisco's Mechanics Institute in 1854, the Chess and Checkers Club met regularly in its game room. At this writing, it still does.[34]

Use of space was important, but so were collections. If social libraries did not stock reading that people wanted, they often stagnated. "Give our members what they want," an 1870 New York Mercantile Library report announced. Some protested this trend. In 1851 Francis Wayland objected to the Providence (Rhode Island) Athenaeum's practice of buying books "of doubtful character, frivolous, and not innocent . . . because the young people desired them." He would "as soon give a child arsenic," he wrote. Other social libraries tried to stem the loss by admitting new groups—like women—but controlling novels they could access. To meet demand, the Boston Mercantile Library reported in 1851, "we have procured duplicate volumes of [fiction] works already in the catalogue." However, it was "undesirable," the librarian said, "that a modest young woman should have anything to do with the corrupter portions of the polite literature. A considerable portion of the general library should be to her a sealed book."[35]

At mid-century, American readers (90 percent of adult white males could read and write by then) were in an age of "cheap books" that included more novels—many serialized in penny press weeklies. Generally, male reviewers evaluated them, and out of their evaluations the word "serious" emerged to distinguish learned reading from commonplace fiction. In the mid–nineteenth century, however, "serious" had a coded meaning largely driven by male concern for the perceived vulnerabilities of the female reader. Cultural authorities worried about an intimacy females experienced in their reading. Frustrations with the popularity of "mere" novels by "serious" authors were obvious. "America is now wholly given over to a d——d mob of scribbling women," Nathaniel Hawthorne wrote George Ticknor in 1855, "and I should have no chance of success while the public taste is occupied with their trash." Herman Melville disparaged the "mere mob" of readers—"superficial skimmers of pages," he called them—"egregiously deceived" to miss deep meaning in his work.[36]

Yet a pattern of reading had already been set: women and girls read more fiction than men and boys. Although most of what they read reinforced the domestic world into which they were born, women subverted the restrictive norms of Victorian culture by mining commonplace fiction for self-empowerment. The act of reading books written primarily for a market of middle-class white women gave their readers spaces in which they could imagine different social environments and situations, and then either reject what those novels offered or select, modify, adjust, and adopt what seemed most appropriate to their personal daily lives. If looked at through the eyes of its readers, the nineteenth-century domestic novel rearranged culture to critique American society from a female perspective.[37] "Take some book, . . . read it and form your own opinion as to its character, its influence, its beauties, and its faults," one female told another in 1839. "Have an opinion about it, and then, if you like, you can find out what others think and compare your decisions with theirs."[38]

Commonplace reading was also instructive. The twenty-eight young adult books Jacob Abbott penned in mid-century taught children morals and facts about travel, history, and science. Biographies were often written as behavior manuals emphasizing the virtues of honesty, temperance, duty, thriftiness, and industry. They not only aimed to build a national culture that showed the world America's character but also to advance Christianity and Franklin's ideology of the self-made man. By that time Parson Weems's *Life of Washington* had gone through seventy editions and helped knit post-Revolutionary generations into a nation of "Americans." Abraham Lincoln read it as a child.[39]

Establishing social libraries was not entirely a white project. In the early nineteenth century enslaved black Americans had little chance for literacy. "If you teach that nigger . . . how to read," a Baltimore slave owner told his wife in 1827 when he learned she was working with nine-year-old Frederick Douglass, "it would forever unfit him to be a slave." In the North, however, free blacks organized literary societies that sponsored reading rooms and debates and used them to challenge slavery and racism. When members published their poetry and prose and read both at literary society meetings, they brought focus to their quest for freedom and equality. By joining the New York Ladies Literary Society in the 1830s, one organizer noted, black women could "challenge our enemies" who "say we do not . . . have any minds" and "are unsusceptible of improvement." By joining the Philadelphia Female Literary Society, black women "may break down the strong barrier of prejudice." Before she joined, one member testified, she had "formed a little world of my own." Thereafter, however, "the cause of the slave [has become] my own. . . . Has this not been your experience, my sisters?" she asked.[40]

The black Phoenix Society of New York deliberately crafted programs in the 1830s to build community and provide sociability. More important than locations to house books and other printed materials, black libraries were places where reading promoted conversation and where all kinds of printed texts were discussed and debated in a social setting. Because members were less interested in fostering literacy than cultivating character, readers often read aloud to extend appreciation of texts to the semi- and illiterate. The Society also sought to establish "lyceums for speaking and for lectures on science." Thus, they wanted their library to be a combination of reading and place. "Subjects of discussion generally relate to their own rights and interests," reported an observer at an 1830s meeting of the Philadelphia Library Company of Colored Persons, "and frequently result in decisions from which the prejudiced mind of the white man would startle and shrink with apprehension." Such societies, he noted, were "numerous, united and bitterly conscious of their degradation and their power."[41]

In 1859, New York's *Weekly Anglo-African* opened a reading room that hosted "a course of popular lectures" in hopes it would become a space "where the barriers of complexion, sect, or party shall have no existence whatever." The communal reading made possible by the printed texts in their collections enabled free black people to engage in public debates about their future and protest the lot white society forced upon them. By that time, nearly fifty black American literary societies had been established. Many were run by women.[42]

The nineteenth century witnessed numerous offspring from the eighteenth-century social library model. Mercantile libraries were sometimes supported by capitalists who saw them as self-help institutions to improve the skills of clerical workers and middle-level managers, but more often these were voluntary organizations of skilled laborers who pooled resources to acquire books for "useful knowledge" and "leisure" reading. Because upwardly mobile young men were expected to be conversant in the language of culture and finance, these new institutions recognized the value of combining oral and printed communications. In 1820, for example, young men established mercantile libraries in New York and Boston. In addition to reading rooms and an occasional chess room, these libraries often held classes, formed societies for debate and for exercises in declamation and composition, and hosted lyceum lectures. At its 1827 opening ceremonies, the Boston Mechanics' Institution announced a lecture series, then added: "To derive the greatest advantage" from a lecture, any listener "must also read."[43]

In 1851 another social library offspring appeared when the Boston Young Men's Christian Association (YMCA) opened reading rooms with books containing moral lessons for young men who, the YMCA believed, badly needed exposure to Christianity instead of urban "haunts of vice and dissipation." Membership fees were small, and reading rooms were generally open twelve to fourteen hours a day (including Sundays). Like most other social libraries, the need to survive eventually influenced collections, which a generation later included more general reading materials. By 1859, the United States had 145 YMCA libraries, twelve with collections exceeding 1,000 volumes. In 1875, New York's YMCA Library collection reached 10,000 volumes, including "acceptable" fiction by authors like Charles Dickens and Sir Walter Scott. In 1892, YMCA libraries reached their peak; 54 percent of the 1,400 reporting YMCAs housed libraries of 50 volumes or more.

Although they shared many YMCA library goals, Protestant denominations preferred more direct control of parishioner reading interests, including Sunday school libraries, which at mid-century benefited from a sophisticated publishing and distribution system called the American Tract Society that disseminated its products through the American Sunday School Union. By 1832, the Union employed seventy-eight itinerant missionaries to deliver free printed materials to America's Sunday school children. Not "books abounding with foolishness, vulgarity, and falsehood," but works that privileged virtue over vice and were wrapped in the "most attractive garb of blended instruction and amusement." Often these collections functioned as literacy texts. In 1843 the Methodist Episcopal Church reported that "no more powerful auxiliary to our enterprise exists than a good library." In 1870, the US Census reported 33,580 Sunday school libraries containing 8,000,000 volumes.[44]

As more educators pressed for compulsory primary education in the early nineteenth century, as more male cultural authorities worried over the reading tastes of women, youth, and the lower classes whose numbers increased with new waves of immigration, some leaders saw libraries as a solution to particular problems. In 1839, Horace Mann, the secretary to the Massachusetts Board of Education, surveyed the state "to learn what number of public libraries exist" and "how many persons do *not* have access to them." He found 299 Massachusetts social libraries containing 180,000 volumes, but costs required to access collections constituted "the strongest grounds of exclusion to the poorest people, who have most need of their benefits." Only lack of public funding, he concluded, denied "the blessings that would flow from establishing libraries."

Compulsory education supplied that imperative and for some states encouraged the establishment of another kind of library. In 1833 a New York legislator worried that unless young people had knowledge, it was impossible "to make competent citizens of our 500,000 youths." A year later the secretary of state told the legislature: "If the inhabitants of school districts were authorized to lay a tax upon their property for the purpose of purchasing libraries for the use of the district, such a power might . . . become a most efficient instrument in diffusing useful knowledge, and in elevating the intellectual character of the people." In 1835, New York passed legislation to establish school district libraries local citizens could access. By 1850 these libraries contained 1,500,000 books. Massachusetts followed New York's lead and in 1837 established a system that by mid-century housed 100,000 volumes in over 2,000 libraries. Connecticut, Rhode Island, Michigan, Indiana, and Ohio also established school district libraries, but with mixed results. Because state funds purchased only materials and did not fund staff necessary to manage them, collections deteriorated. In 1851, the secretary to Maine's Board of Education concluded that his state's nine school district libraries failed because of "insurmountable difficulties. . . . The only feasible way of establishing a general system of public libraries . . . is to apply the system to towns instead of school districts."[45]

In his *Report on the Public Libraries of the United States* (1850), Smithsonian Institution Librarian Charles Coffin Jewett identified 10,015 libraries in thirty-one states and the District of Columbia containing 3,701,828 volumes. But Jewett's definition of "public" was broad—"all libraries in this country . . . not private property (and indeed many which are private property) are public libraries," he said.[46] Jewett's use of the word "public" may seem strange to twenty-first-century librarians who define a "public library" as one supported by local taxes, but for their mid-nineteenth-century predecessors it constituted a definition most librarians held in common.

On April 24, 1841, the Boston Mercantile Library hosted a meeting at which visiting French ventriloquist Alexandre Vattemare discussed his plans for an international exchange of documents that he was convinced would foster goodwill between nations and minimize war. To accept, preserve, and circulate these documents he proposed that Boston consolidate its many libraries into one institution supported by public dollars—a "free" public library. Those attending unanimously passed a resolution supporting "the great project." For a while the idea languished. Outside the public eye, however, Harvard professors George Ticknor and Edward Everett agitated for an institution to supply "wholesome" reading materials to Boston's public, and especially to its lower classes that had been greatly expanded by uneducated, often illiterate, Irish immigrants. In 1847 Mayor Josiah Quincy anonymously offered the city $5,000 for a library if the city council would authorize a tax "to establish and maintain a public library for the use of the inhabitants." When the council approved Quincy's request the following year, Boston began planning its public library.

In justifying enabling legislation, Massachusetts legislator John Wight outlined four advantages "free" public libraries would bring—they would become "needful and valuable" extensions to public schools; "supply the whole people with ample sources of important practical information"; serve as depositories for government documents; and help their community's "intellectual and moral advancement" because they "will be favorable to all the moral reforms of the day, by leading to more domestic habits of life, by diminishing the circulation of low and immoral publications, and by producing higher and more worthy views of the capabilities of human nature." Wight's emphasis was clear: "useful knowledge," as he mentioned "stories" only pejoratively. In 1849 New Hampshire beat Massachusetts by passing the nation's first legislation authorizing cities and towns to maintain free libraries by taxation; Massachusetts followed in 1851.

New York had a chance to preempt Boston. In 1838 John Jacob Astor announced his intention to establish a "public library," and on his death ten years later left $400,000 for a public library "accessible at all reasonable hours and times, for general use, free of expense to persons resorting thereto." But the concept got lost in practice. After the Astor Library was incorporated in 1849, its trustees allowed director Joseph Cogswell to craft a library "suited to the wants of scholars, investigators, and scientists, and to the pursuit of exact knowledge in all the arts." Cogswell and the trustees then made it a non-circulating library open to no one under sixteen. Young people, Cogswell said, preferred "reading the trashy" like "Scott, Cooper, Dickens, *Punch*, and the *Illustrated News*," which the Astor would not collect. The day it opened (January 9, 1854), Cogswell kept most visitors away from the library's 90,000 volumes. "It would have crazed me to have seen a crowd ranging lawlessly among the books," he said, "and throw everything into confusion."[47]

Boston took a different approach. On July 14, 1851, Ticknor detailed to Everett his ideas for a "Boston Public Library." Not only should it have on its shelves information resources "accessible for reference as many hours in the day as possible," he reasoned, but its "*main* department and purpose [emphasis his] should differ from all free libraries yet attempted: I mean one in which any popular books, tending to moral and intellectual improvement, should be furnished in such numbers of copies that many persons, if they desired it, could be reading the same work at the same time." Such a practice would "create a real appetite for healthy general reading." As he helped plan the library, Ticknor consistently pressed this point—the library had to focus primarily on the lower classes who required assimilation into "our national character" through popular books.[48]

On July 6, 1852, a subcommittee of the board of trustees chaired by Everett issued its report: *City Document No. 37—Report of the Trustees of the Public Library of the City of Boston, July, 1852.* Part of it constituted the draft of an ordinance outlining a governance structure that later became the model that communities across the country adopted when they opened public libraries. This model kept American public libraries close to the people who were taxed for their support, and it worked against making public libraries extensions of big government. On October 14, Boston's Common Council adopted an ordinance that empowered the trustees to select a president and make rules and regulations to govern themselves, raise money, and care for and control the library.

The second part of *City Document No. 37,* authored by Everett, justified the library's existence and is often referred to as the charter of the American public library movement. The document argued for free admission to all, circulation of books for home use, and the acquisition of reading materials ranging from scholarly to popular. "It is of paramount importance that the means of general information should be so diffused that the largest possible number of persons should be induced to read and understand questions going down to the very foundations of social order . . . which we, as a people, are constantly required to decide, and do decide, either ignorantly or wisely."[49] This was lofty rhetoric, but Irish immigrants watching these activities from the streets undoubtedly recognized that the founders of the Boston Public Library were members of the local elites. They represented old-money residents who were worried about the potential for moral decline their community was exposed to by pressures of industrialization, urbanization, and especially immigration.

But the report also made it obvious that Ticknor had prevailed. On listing the four classes of books the library would acquire, the third—"Books that will be asked for"—got lengthiest treatment. Copies of "the more respectable of the popular works of the time . . . should be provided in such numbers that *many* persons . . . can be reading the same work at the same moment, and so render the pleasant and healthy literature of the day accessible to the whole people at the only time they care for it,—that is, when it is living, fresh and new." Because of this precedent, American public libraries owe George Ticknor a huge debt. If public libraries had not supplied popular books, Americans would probably not have supported them, and the Boston Public Library experiment would probably not have led to an American public library movement that Andrew Carnegie greatly accelerated half a century later. Because Ticknor also charged the library to "follow the popular taste" in its acquisitions, he automatically made it a mediator of local cultural and literary values.

On October 1, Joshua Bates of the London banking house of Baring Brothers, who by coincidence had read a copy of *City Document No. 37*—which Boston sent that summer as part of an informational packet to justify the city's quest for a loan (Bates was perhaps himself inspired by Great Britain's recently passed Public Libraries Act of 1850)— offered $50,000 for the new library, provided the building "shall be an ornament to the city" and have room for up to 150 "to sit at reading tables. . . . It will not do to have the rooms in the proposed library much inferior to the rooms occupied for the same object by the upper classes. Let the virtuous and industrious of the middle and mechanic class feel that there is not so much difference between them." A month later he was even more specific. "The architecture should be such that a student on entering it will be impressed and elevated, and feel a pride that such a place is free to him. . . . There should be an entrance hall, a room for cloaks and umbrellas, and a room for washing hands, with soap, hot water and towels provided. The rooms should be well-warmed in winter, and well lighted."[50]

Ten other New England towns followed Boston's lead between 1851 and 1854. Like New Hampshire in 1849, Maine authorized a library tax in 1854, Vermont in 1865, and Wisconsin in 1868. Several factors that characterized Boston's efforts to open a public library were evident in other communities that followed Boston's lead. All required relatively healthy economies—towns and cities had to be able to support public libraries once philanthropy diminished. They also needed a critical mass of materials community leaders considered worth acquiring, circulating, and preserving. In addition, local pride was essential in order to stimulate interest. "That Boston must have a great public library or yield to New York in letters as well as in commerce," wrote Everett to Ticknor as the Astor prepared to open, "will, I think, be made quite apparent in a few years."[51] Finally, community leaders had to believe that universal literacy would promote morality and self-improvement through reading. Within several years of the Boston Public Library's opening, many community leaders across the nation believed that the public library—as a self-education agency—was an essential supplement to formal education.

CHAPTER TWO

For "Plain People"

The American Public Library, 1854–1876

On March 20, 1854, in temporary quarters at a Mason Street school-house, the Boston Public Library (BPL) opened a reading room furnished with several hundred reference works and 180 US and foreign periodicals "said by eminent literary gentlemen to be the largest and best assort-ment . . . on the continent." As the nation's fourth-largest city (140,000), Boston already had a tradition of providing municipal services, including fire protection, primary education, public health, city water, and a brand-new police department. Bostonians saw the BPL as a natural addition to their city. That first day eighty people visited the reading room, open daily from 9:00 A.M. to 9:30 P.M.

On May 2, the BPL opened a second, larger room containing 12,000 volumes that the public could borrow to take home. To obtain a reader's card, applicants had to give their name, occupation, address, and the name of a guarantor. If applicants could not supply the latter, the library turned their names over to police for verification. Any Bostonian sixteen or older could check out books; so could children over twelve enrolled in school. More than 800 people registered that day. Patrons could check out one book at a time. To obtain a book, readers consulted short-title catalogs laid out on tables, filled out a call slip, and handed it to a librarian, who gave it to a "runner" who would retrieve the book. Catalogs offered lim-ited help; because they lacked recent acquisitions, they were out of date before they were printed. To keep track of circulation, librarians recorded borrowers' names in large ledgers, with each borrower assigned one page on which librarians listed the book's call number and date of issue. When borrowers returned a book, librarians crossed off the transaction.[1]

Daily applications for readers' cards averaged 300, the majority from women. Among registrants, *Gleason's Companion* noticed, "we find the names of many of our wealthiest people, intermingled with those of the poorest," including "traders, mechanics, laborers, quite a number of Irish, and a few colored men." Despite all the useful knowledge its collections contained, however, "a very large proportion of the books taken out have been works of fiction chiefly of the modern and popular tales," albeit "for the most part of good moral tendency," the *Independent* reported. *Gleason's* observed that "demand at present is very largely in favor of light fiction" but predicted that "as our population become readers they will become sober, industrious, frugal" and "will spend their time at home instead of at more injurious places." By year's end the collection had grown to 16,000 volumes, and 6,590 registered borrowers had withdrawn 35,389 books.[2]

Plans for a permanent structure began immediately. On September 17, 1855, BPL officials laid the cornerstone for a permanent building on Boylston Street. "Let this library . . . be the place where you will come not merely to study and store your minds with so-called 'useful' knowledge," the building commissioner told the crowd assembled, "but also often to have a good time." George Ticknor's attitudes toward commonplace reading echoed in the commissioner's words. "Let the boys find here wholesome books of adventure; . . . let the girls find stories which delight them and give their fancy and imagination exercise; . . . let the tired housewife find the novels which will transport her to an ideal realm of love and happiness." Like the Boston Common, he said, the library should be a place for play and pleasure, albeit monitored to prevent debasing tendencies.

To manage this new facility the trustees hired Charles Coffin Jewett, who from 1847 to 1855 had been librarian of the Smithsonian Institution in Washington, DC. After he arrived, Jewett supervised the BPL's move to the new building, which opened on January 1, 1858. At a dedication ceremony attended by 2,000, Everett challenged everyone there—including "the array of beautiful ladies" the *Boston Post* noticed "in the alcoves" ("women's rights shall be respected in this hall," Everett teased)—to donate at least one book. Crowd applause indicated consent; within weeks the library added more than

For being the only member of the Board of Trustees to advocate successfully that the Boston Public Library carry popular fiction, all subsequently established public libraries owe George Ticknor (third from left) a huge debt of gratitude. *Photo courtesy of the Trustees of the Boston Public Library*

a thousand donated books. The *Boston Evening Transcript* deemed the BPL "one of the most significant schemes for the culture of the public ever projected in our city."[3]

The first-floor "Lower Hall"—intended "to meet the ordinary demands of the people"—contained a 100-seat "Special Reading Room" for women. It also sported a general reading room (which women could also use) for 200. There periodicals sat on open shelves, where readers marveled at their accessibility. Patrons retrieved books in a Delivery Room, where they requested titles from closed stacks, and from which attendants often climbed stairs to a second-floor section housing additional books. The upper story (later named Bates Hall)—perceived by library officials as "the library proper" because it was stocked with "books of permanent and solid value"—was designed as a reference library of useful knowledge intended "to serve the higher requirements of the studious classes."[4] The physical plant accommodated demands readers made of early-nineteenth-century circulating and social libraries, but unlike many of the latter, the BPL had no auditorium, no dedicated community meeting rooms, no "chess and checkers" room.

Interior of the Boston Public Library, 1858, one public place in the city of Boston where men and women demonstrated the sociability of reading. *Courtesy Boston Public Library, Print Department*

By 1861, the library held nearly 100,000 volumes, averaged 1,000 daily visits, and boasted a circulation of 160,000. A year earlier, trustees quietly tried to shift away from commonplace reading by buying "only the best of the lighter class of literature." But circulation in Lower Hall fell precipitously. When trustees reversed their decision a year later, circulation climbed. By that time a pattern had emerged—fiction for adults and juveniles accounted for nearly 70 percent of BPL circulation. An 1866 examining committee noted "that although they might wish a different record, they must accept the condition as arising from the mental tendency of the masses of the community." Thus, a tradition took root; patrons clearly voted their preferences in this civic institution they did not have to use. Trustees had to meet these preferences, or lose them as patrons. When Jewett died in 1868, the trustees replaced him with Justin Winsor, a prominent Boston Brahmin who as chair of the 1866 examining committee had carefully analyzed the library's management. As the first in a large city, the BPL became a model replicated by a mushrooming number of small and large public libraries established in the late nineteenth century.

Within a decade, the public developed familiar public library behaviors. Saturdays were especially busy, one periodical noticed in 1866, when the reading room was "literally packed with applicants for books, a very large portion being young people."[5] When an *Appletons' Journal* reporter visited in 1871, he thought the reading room "one of the sights of the city" at 6:00 P.M.

> It fills to repletion. Children throng its floors, and are wonderfully sharp to the little tricks of competition for early attention. It is amusing to see with what rapidity an old stager of twelve years . . . will put his errand through. He will monopolize a wide section of desk-room with extended elbows, pounce in a single flourish upon the exact catalogue out of the many, get his number out of the multitude of other numbers, pencil it and his name with precise care upon his paper. . . . This well done, the boy must await developments; and, American-like, he improves the interval. He goes to the adjacent reading-room, and, securing an illustrated paper, sits himself down within sound of the attendant's voice, to wait and read until his book or disappointment turns up.[6]

At 8:00 P.M. all reading room seats were "occupied by a silent, mummy-like collection of people, who read with an avidity which resembles the satisfying of hunger. . . . Now and then one of the number rises and, going to the desk, silently exchanges his periodical for another. Every person is exceptionally neat, and this is very rare when such apartments open on the street. Nearly all come out of their lodgings and homes free of the dust of the day's labor, and come hither with the idea of having a 'read.'" In Bates Hall, the reporter noted, "Twenty or thirty people are usually to be found here, some writing, most of them reading hard, and a few gazing about them. All are quiet. Few sounds break the silence, except, now and then, the tap of the cancelling-stamp at the desk, a footfall in the corridors, or the faint rustle of book-leaves." Books housed in Bates Hall could not be taken home but could be used "within the rail," as contemporary parlance described it.[7]

Between 1866 and 1870, use of Bates Hall increased 400 percent, use of the reading room and Lower Hall 300 percent. In 1871, the library opened a branch in East Boston. That year it circulated 74,804 volumes. Within a decade the library added five more branches, yet circulation still increased at the central library. An 1869 annual report analyzed patron demographics. Of 5,432 men and 1,542 women who identified their occupations, 1,100 men and 542 women were in "trades and manufacturing," 243 men and 6 women were "shopkeepers," 2,006 men and 116 women were in "mercantile callings," 746 men and 360 women were "professionals," 165 men and three women were "officials," and 1,632 men and 434 women were in "miscellaneous classes of occupation," the latter including "oyster operators, cooks, errand girls, washerwomen, nurses, waiters, shopgirls, seamstresses, sewing machine operators, and servants." Clearly the library was serving the laboring classes, albeit not with the useful knowledge cultural authorities and many library officials thought they needed most. In 1871, the *Literary World* reported, "more of [youth series-fiction writer] Oliver Optic's books are taken" from the BPL than those of "any other authors."[8]

To protect ladies' delicate sensibilities, the institution had rules to ensure that none got questionable materials. "H." reported to the *Boston Daily Advertiser* in 1869 that a lady "who had often visited the library" wanted a medical book for her son. Although the book was on the shelves, librarians would not give it to her until she obtained a doctor's certificate to prove her son intended to study medicine. Insulted, "this lady offered me her family library cards," H. noted, "as she should use them no more." Increased circulation and visitation brought other problems. In the public sphere, people often felt entitled to express their opinions, and from its beginnings, the public library offered unintended yet tempting opportunities for patrons to converse with authors they were reading. "An offensive class of writers," the *Transcript* wrote in 1858, was leaving opinions on book pages. "Sometimes a passage of poetry will have 'How beautiful!' written in a feminine hand in the margin, or a proposition be flanked by 'True,' 'Right,' or 'Doubtful.'"[9]

Open access to periodicals also caused problems. Because "a *few* unscrupulous people" stole or mutilated them, "it became quite impossible to make up complete sets of popular journals for binding," the *Advertiser* reported in 1866. In response, trustees adopted "restrictive measures" that delayed service. Complaints poured in. Trustees "are in danger of losing sight of the *great public*, of which the scholarly *few* form only a part," protested one reader. "We hope that in selecting their remedy for such an evil," said *Advertiser* editors, trustees "do not forget that use of its great attractions has been its freedom from harassing rules and regulations" that made New York's Astor Library "practically inaccessible to the great mass of people." The Boston Public Library was not alone; the Detroit Public Library detailed fines for particular transgressions. "For each grease spot, 5 cents; for each ink spot, 5 cents; for each leaf torn, 10 cents; for each leaf turned down, 5 cents; for writing in a book, from 5 to 10 cents; and for other damage, including soiling the book or injuring the binding, proportionate fines up to the full value of the book."[10]

Although mutilation increased, theft did not. After reviewing BPL's 1871 annual report, *Appletons' Journal* marveled at the civic responsibility readers displayed. "How many volumes, out of the 180,000 possessed, are lost beyond redemption in a full working year? How many persons, out of the 300,000 who apply for favors, prove faithless and incapable of trust?" *Appletons'* asked. "Twenty! Twenty books, having the value of perhaps $50. In other words, one book in 9,000; or one issue in 15,000; or $1 in $10,000." By that time one in eight eligible Bostonians had borrowers' cards. Still, numbers were suspect. Some particularly voracious readers bent the rules by registering under false names to withdraw more titles. Others "have taken two cards on one name at different times."[11]

Censorship was never far from public library practices. In 1873, Congress passed the Comstock Act; it was named for Anthony Comstock, who led a movement for the New York City YMCA Committee for the Suppression of Vice to have any "obscene, lewd, or lascivious" book or other materials of "indecent" character (including information on contraception or abortion) banned from the mails. Thirty years later, George Bernard Shaw labeled overzealous efforts to purify culture "Comstockery," a term still widely used to describe acts of censorship. Libraries took note; federal and state laws had imposed parameters on what they could collect. Public libraries did not complain, however. But library censorship worked in other ways. In 1872 a San Francisco public librarian asked the editor of *Pomeroy's Democrat* to "stop sending your dirty sheet to this institution, as its politics is not tolerable." The paper responded that it would not act until a majority of trustees "shall make the request civilly."[12]

By 1876, American cultural authorities were endorsing four modes of reading. Among public sphere institutions, the church was the strongest advocate for the evangelical mode, the school for the civic mode, while social and public libraries established to disseminate useful knowledge advocated the self-improvement mode, illustrated nicely by the experiences of Thomas Edison. As a Detroit teenager in the 1860s, Edison decided to read through the entire public library. "He began with the solid treatises of a dusty lower shelf and actually read . . . fifteen feet in a line," an interviewer noted. "He omitted no book and skipped nothing in the book." Many were scientific treatises. A few years later in the Cincinnati Public Library, a colleague recalled: "Many times Edison would get excused from duty under pretense of being too sick to work, . . . and invariably strike a beeline for the Library, where he would spend the entire day and evening reading . . . such works on electricity as were to be had."[13]

Proof that the public library's self-improvement reading mode also included efforts to grow an informed citizenry was evident in newspaper reading rooms. When the Chicago Public Library opened in 1872, it had daily editions of all Chicago's newspapers, plus 23 US newspapers and more than 200 newspapers and periodicals from seventeen countries, all to meet the information needs of Chicago's growing immigrant population and all its "classes." In 1873, Cincinnati's reading room subscribed to 310 periodicals (138 US periodicals, 96 from English-speaking foreign countries, 60 German, 12 French, 3 Dutch, and 1 Welsh), all the city newspapers as well as one from New York and one from Boston.[14]

But the fourth mode of reading—cultural reading—describes the experiences of most late-nineteenth-century public library users. Although libraries claimed to be civic institutions primarily concerned with useful knowledge, the vast majority of readers wanted stories that satisfied their social and cultural needs.[15] And the interpretive conventions and social practices readers brought to these texts show that readers used these stories to locate themselves in the public sphere as particular kinds of actors. Because of print's ability to create mass culture, voluntary reading—the kind public libraries best facilitated—became a way to build and maintain social networks. Reading also functioned as a cultural project where individual readers read themselves into texts, and it facilitated a kind of character building and cultural refinement that was concerned with aesthetic as well as intellectual satisfactions.

Through their selections, public library readers displayed literary tastes that not only taught them social roles but also provided them scripts for everyday living. For mass audiences, novels connected readers to the personal histories and emotional roller-coasters others experienced. Because public libraries could not force "serious" reading on their patrons, for the

most part they instead unknowingly helped build a social life of reading in which readers met in real and virtual places and absorbed common messages defining a past and present. By popularizing reading and
enabling choice, public libraries also allowed patrons to determine the
most popular books, an essential component in the mass market of print
culture. And for patrons, that reinforced a democratic ethos they identified with use of their library, which made it hard not to love.[16]

Yet because generations of cultural authorities failed to understand
how "plain people" used literary practices and fictional stories in their
everyday lives, they continued to disparage the reading selections most
patrons made. Public libraries encouraged self-improvement reading but
acquiesced to cultural reading in large part because patrons demanded
it. If public libraries failed to provide the stories readers valued highly
(even if librarians and other cultural authorities did not), circulation
decreased. Boston found that out in 1859. In 1873, the St. Louis Public
School Library—a social library used mostly by St. Louis teachers and
students—tried an "anti-novel-reading experiment." Except for works by
Dickens and Scott, the library refused to buy novels. "The result was the
old and inevitable one," the librarian reported. "The income; the registry
of members; the issue of books—that had before steadily increased from
year to year, fell off seriously." So angry were the patrons that they voted
in a new library board pledged to revamp the policy. In 1875, the library
added "unobjectionable new popular books" (including Oliver Optic and
Horatio Alger) "in liberal quantities. . . . As a natural consequence," the
librarian noted, "the Library has about regained the popularity and pros-
perity it had begun to lose through the anti-novel experiment."[17]

Although late-nineteenth-century American public libraries supplied
popular fiction, attacks on it did not diminish. Much worry stemmed
from social class differences, as mostly middle-class authorities worried
about perceived lower-class vulnerabilities. When reading popular fiction, *Godey's Lady's Book* noted in 1860, "the mind is frittered away, and all
strength of reasoning and seriousness of reflection gradually deserts the
unfortunate." "Common sewers of society," the Reverend Henry Ward
Beecher called novels, "into which drain the concentrated filth of the
worst passions, of the worst creatures, of the worst crimes." Many critics worried particularly about women. "Novels, romances, plays," warned
the author of *On Diseases Peculiar to Women* (1868), could cause women
"undue excitation" that could "give rise to the whole tribe of dyspeptic and
irritable disorders," particularly in the "irritable uterus."[18]

Library officials tried to figure out ways to address what many regarded as a problem. In 1867, for example, the Boston Public Library began a quarterly *Bulletin* listing new acquisitions. "Such a publication would . . . not only promote the use of books that would otherwise be neglected," trustees noted, but also it would "tend to the advancement of knowledge among us."[19] Librarians were also defensive. "The question of the large amount of fiction read in popular libraries," Winsor noted philosophically in 1871, "is an inevitable experience, and the dreams of those hopeful for a change are in vain. The multitude not only crave fiction,—something imaginative as a counterpoise to the realities, often stern, of life,—but, in consequence of there being comparatively few trained imaginations, the style of fiction that is craved is oftenest of a low order." To counter this craving, Winsor posted bibliographies of "best books" around the library, hoping patrons would take the hint. They did not; in 1872 fiction still accounted for two-thirds of circulation.[20]

As public libraries across the country variously adjusted their acquisitions to accommodate demand for commonplace reading, their role in trying to find a balance between most of their readers and the cultural authorities (distant and local) who criticized popular fiction became obvious. Each public library had to find an acceptable center for its community's literary values in order to operate comfortably. But as literary history shows, that center shifted over time. For public libraries, these shifts created a set of dynamics requiring constant attention, frequent debate, and regular adjustment. For example, in 1863 the *Springfield* (Massachusetts) *Weekly Republican* contended: "A complete public library should meet two ends. It should contain every standard work of reference in every field of science and art, and it should contain besides only live, readable books, in which the masses for whom the library is designed, are interested." But not all were "live, readable books"—standards had to be set. "If we exclude the positively vicious books," Winsor noted in 1877, "we have gone as far as we can without thwarting the desires of the great masses of readers."[21] Because different people in different places differently defined "vicious," debates sparked by these differences turned the public library into a local platform for mediating the question.

For example, in 1872 the *Nation* noted that the Boston Public Library's three most popular authors were E. D. E. N. Southworth, Lee Hentz, and Mary J. Holmes. At this news one Cincinnati newspaper took great delight. Because all these authors were less popular at its public library than Sir Walter Scott, Charles Dickens, William Makepeace Thackeray, and James Fenimore Cooper, Queen City patrons showed "a higher stand-ing of popular taste," the newspaper concluded.[22] Left unstated was the fact that 76 percent of Cincinnati Public Library circulation consisted of "prose fiction and juveniles. . . . I am not disposed to mourn over or to apologize for these facts," director William Frederick Poole stated in 1873. "In the personal experience of all who attain to literary culture there is a time when they read novels." Because his board president regarded the library's top priority "to create and cultivate a popular taste for reading," in 1867 he "impaneled a jury of young ladies" from a boardinghouse to identify important novels women might want. In less than ninety minutes, they listed 300. After the library acquired them "they were so popular that they are now nearly worn out." At the same time, however, Cincinnati's Roman Catholic archbishop forbade Catholic children to use the public library "on account of the immoral works that are distributed from it." The *Cincinnati Daily Gazette* protested: "No book that is known to be immoral is purchased for the library." Catholics were not persuaded. "The Catholics of this city are not, as a body, interested in . . . the Public Library," the *Catholic Telegraph* responded. "They know that it is both an illegal and dangerous institution. They can not but believe that it will be the prolific source of immense evil to a large portion of those who frequent it."[23]

In 1874 *The Literary World* reviewed the Wakefield and Lawrence, Massachusetts, public library annual reports. Wakefield reported 67 per-cent of its circulation was fiction, and for Lawrence, 75 percent. In the lat-ter, the highest-circulating authors were the "sensationalists" Southworth, Holmes, Mrs. Henry Ward, Mrs. A. S. Stephens, and Mrs. Dinah Maria Mulock (also known as "Pansy"). "If we as fully met the demand for sen-sational literature as we do that for a better class," the librarian lamented, "the figures would be far different." The *World* was not sympathetic. "The standard of literary taste by which a city or town is known to the world will always remain in the hands of a few; the masses will always move below it." Bay State librarians had an obligation to encourage a "purer and higher taste . . . to fit the rising generation for nobler work" than "striv-ing to scatter the greatest number of scrofulous novels among the young of both sexes." And how were Bay State librarians doing? Although one Massachusetts public library had removed Southworth's novels, the *World* noticed, the Boston Public Library still owned 409, of which 357 were checked out at the time.[24]

A year later the *World* reported that fiction comprised 79 percent of East Boston branch circulation, 78 percent in South Boston, and 81 percent in Roxbury. By circulating this "perilous stuff," the *World* insisted, the "cause of evil is evident; why should it not be removed?" Yet the BPL did discriminate. When it refused to buy a copy of Marie Howland's *Papa's Own Girl* because it was "coarse," its author protested. "In so far as my abilities have enabled me," she wrote the *Boston Globe*, "I have sought to give expression to the legal and social disabilities of women and, further, to the outrageous injustice of our industrial system, by which the producers of wealth are so robbed of it that the army of paupers is yearly increasing." The BPL excluded her book, Howland believed, because "it may tend to teach the industry of the country how incompetent is the management which controls the distribution of the results of labor."[25]

When *Appletons' Journal* perused the BPL's 1874 circulation statistics, it was not alarmed. "If one attributes the fact solely to low critical taste, he very imperfectly comprehends the situation." The "average reader" did not have a critical attitude; instead, "the books that he reads . . . must be food for his sentimental and sympathetic being." Although this characteristic might show "inferior intellectual acumen," *Appletons'* reasoned, "it is not evidence of an inferior nature." The best intellectual books tended to be "juiceless" on purpose, because they were aimed at the "head"; the best popular books, on the other hand, were aimed at the "heart," and "this is why they possess a popularity so puzzling to the merely critical mind."[26]

Across the country, reaction to these pressures varied. In Germantown, Pennsylvania, the public library refused to stock any fiction. "This furnishing of unwholesome mental food or poison is gradually pervading our literature to an alarming extent," explained the librarian. "Could the directors of our public libraries but see the evil, and aid in checking its spread, they would be conferring a great benefit on the young people." When the Groton (Connecticut) Public Library moved into new quarters in 1867, the librarian declared "there would be no fiction at all in the Library." Upon hearing this, local youth called a town meeting and circulated a petition that gathered 160 signatures. They prevailed; the library stocked fiction. Initially the Chicago Public Library addressed the issue by refusing to acquire more than three copies of any book—to no avail, however. Southworth, Holmes, and Stephens remained patron favorites. In 1874, the *Chicago Tribune* reported, the library held 390 copies of 38 Southworth titles, 240 copies of 16 Holmes titles, and 176 copies of 22 Stephens titles. All were checked out. The *Tribune* later lamented that high rates of fiction circulation came "mainly, almost exclusively" from "the poor, ignorant classes." To this characterization one library regular objected. "The Library is certainly a popular one," he wrote the *Tribune*. "In this view it must be praised rather than blamed. Personally I have not felt that I was lowering myself by taking my turn democratically with those whom I found there, and I doubt if anyone else has, unless he be of a sort to object to mingling with foot-passengers because he belonged to 'carriage-folks.'"[27]

In 1874, the Indianapolis Public Library director explained: "Let it be understood, that by immoral and vicious books is not meant the class of books of which Mrs. Southworth and Mrs. Holmes are the exponents." These books "are merely feeble." To eliminate them would "discriminate unfairly against a class in the community who crave, and are only satisfied by them. . . . The loud outcry against this class of reading does not come from those who by experience have learned the needs of the poorer classes." Since his library opened in 1873, the director noticed an "increased literary activity of the city; never before have the number of 'reading clubs' and social meetings for the discussion of literary topics been so numerous."[28]

Finding an acceptable middle ground in this array of opinions was difficult; consensus was hard to find. For example, in 1867 "an indignant parent" complained to the San Francisco *Daily Evening Bulletin* when his daughter checked Dinah Maria Mulock's *Fairy Tales* out of the public library. "I promise you if it comes to my house a gain [*sic*] it will be burnt," he wrote; "I donte' [*sic*] allow my children to read sutch [*sic*] books." In 1874 a *Christian Union* letter-writer not only complimented an unnamed Massachusetts public library that weeded out "the Oliver Optic style" of books while retaining the "stirring, bold, adventurous, pleasing to the boy-heart, and *pure*" books, but he also praised its librarian who every Saturday, "when wide-awake boys throng there," would "very shrewdly . . . put [these books] before them." Yet in 1873, when a donor set up an endowment to create the Haverhill (Massachusetts) Public Library, he insisted it "be devoted largely to buying popular literature of the day." As a result, Haverhill stocked authors like E. P. Roe and Rosa Carey.[29]

Popular fiction readers saw things much differently from the critics. In letters to bestselling "sensational" novelists Susan B. Warner and Maria Cummins during the 1850s, fans emphasized their strong emotional connections to their novels' main characters. Through them, one wrote Warner, "I feel as if . . . you were my personal friend." Another wrote Cummins, "I have smiled and wept over our story." In 1875, William T. Adams—better known to the world as Oliver Optic—spoke at the dedication of the BPL's Dorchester branch, housed in a remodeled church. He recalled how he had worshiped and taught Sunday school classes to young boys there twenty-five years earlier. At the time, he said, he resolved to tell stories that would "influence and benefit" them. "I have never written a story which could excite the love, admiration, and sympathy of the reader for an evil person, a bad character," he said. "I have never made a hero whose moral character, or whose lack of high aims and purposes, could mislead the young reader."[30]

Just as parents do today, many late-nineteenth-century parents carefully monitored their children's reading; like today, many children protested—in their own ways. The mother of future president of Bryn Mawr College, M. Carey Thomas, tried to steer her daughter toward religious books and away from the novels she preferred when they visited the Baltimore Mercantile Library. Not until she was fifteen could Thomas read *Jane Eyre*. As a fourteen-year-old, Alice Stone Blackwell visited the Boston Public Library weekly. But when her mother, the suffragist Lucy Stone, threatened not to allow the *New York Ledger* (her favorite newspaper) into the house because it contained "trashy" serial stories, Alice protested. "To stop me off right in the midst of 'Mark Heber's Luck'! I straightway went off to bed mad, with tears in my eyes."[31]

While a child in the 1820s, Harriet Beecher Stowe and her sisters were forbidden by their father to read any fiction except Sir Walter Scott. Ironically, one cultural authority later contended, it was the wild popularity of Stowe's *Uncle Tom's Cabin* that fostered a desire for fiction three decades later in "hundreds of families where novels had hitherto been prohibited." As a child, Caroline Hewins, who in subsequent generations carefully monitored public library collections as a way to regulate youthful reading, read *Uncle Tom's Cabin* so many times she could recall minute details from the plot later in life. For her, reading the novel was a transformative experience. Not so in the South, however, where one reviewer dismissed the book as "the loathsome rakings of a foul fancy." Another sneered: "The Petticoat lifts of itself and we see the hoof of the beast under the table."[32]

Public libraries, however, were much more than repositories for reading material for individual users. Libraries had broader communal functions, including providing space for the emotional experience of community, enabling discussion groups, and at the same time cultivating a sense of freedom, status, and social privilege. And as public institutions, libraries across the country modeled and regulated socially acceptable conduct in multiple ways. Sometimes they were unsuccessful. "There is a need of four spittoons in the reading room," a Cleveland Public Library committee noted in 1875. At the Cincinnati Public Library patrons were not allowed to spit on the floor, put their feet on the furniture, or disturb their neighbors by loud talk. More confusing, however, were rules designed to separate the sexes. Some tables were set aside for women's use; at others men took one side, women the other. Sometimes, however, husband and wife chose to sit next to each other, thus confusing librarians unaware of the union. Some conduct was not only unacceptable; it was punished. In 1872 one Cincinnati patron was arrested for "indecently exposing his person" at the public library. He would not be the last.[33]

By 1876, many public libraries emulated the successes of social libraries by making space available for exhibits and lectures. Although the new Boston Public Library did not have an auditorium, patrons remade its Delivery Room into a "conversation room," and several years later the BPL responded to public pressure by converting the women's reading room into an art gallery. As Chicago debated whether to establish a public library in 1870, one citizen suggested that it ought to circulate more than books. "Their sphere of usefulness might be largely increased" if they would add "a series of familiar lectures, illustrated by objects." Four years later the library established an art gallery. But not all public requests were successful. In 1874, library trustees rejected a proposal to use the building for a benefit dance.[34]

And as civic institutions, public libraries were frequently objects of local philanthropy. For example, Providence Athenaeum members routinely donated personal book collections to the public library. Some communities took extraordinary, sometimes ingenious, methods to raise money for a public library. In Kentucky, for example, state legislators authorized a series of lotteries, each to sell 100,000 tickets at $10 each, and from the $1,000,000 produced give away $500,000 with gifts ranging from $3,000 to a "grand gift" of $100,000. The remaining $500,000 would endow the Public Library of Kentucky in Louisville. Ultimately, the effort failed and the library was never endowed.[35]

The public did not hesitate to complain about inadequate service at local public libraries—another way they participated in the public sphere. "There are new books on the Librarian's table that have been there over two months because he has not assistance enough to put them in shape for drawing out," complained "Patience" to the *Cleveland Herald* in 1869, a patron who had been waiting more than six weeks for a particular book. Chicago Public Library patrons protested long waits at the circulation desk. "Last Saturday evening I stood one whole hour in the mob of waiting book-seekers before I could get attention, and then had my list of fourteen books handed back with only one found," one patron wrote the *Tribune*. "'Hog pen' is none too bad a term for that place last Saturday evening," wrote another. "The stench of bad ventilation and the scramble at the troughs was suggestive of all that."[36]

Public libraries also functioned as sites that reflected class tensions. In 1875 "S.L.B." complained to the *Chicago Tribune* about exchanges she witnessed at the library. As female adolescents were "butting their heads together in their eagerness to compare the wonderful pictures in each other's books of hobgoblins and monsters," a "shrill speaker" yelled to a library attendant: "Say there, have you got [M. J. Holmes's] *Lena Rivers*?" "Anything of Miss Braddon's?" another shout came from the mob. "All out; more ordered," the attendant yelled back. "S.L.B." also noticed a "shrill voiced girl" clutching a Holmes novel "with her bare dirty hand and tucked it away as a treasure under her soiled and scanty shawl. Poor soul! It is all that will make her life tolerable for the next twenty-four hours." She fretted about the social effects these "unwholesome" activities would have on the girl. "Senex" castigated "S.L.B." for criticizing "a class of people going to the public library whose presence is not agreeable to her set. . . . To me, there is something in this allusion to . . . that soiled and scanty shawl which brings a tear into these old eyes of mine and makes me love the Public Library more than ever for the good it is doing for a class of our people who have no books of their own." Senex concluded: "To say . . . Mrs. Holmes' books should not be in the Library because the objector thinks they are trash is nonsense. They are simply trash to some people, and not to others."[37]

Class tension showed itself in other ways. As the Chicago Public Library prepared to open in new quarters in 1875, trustees decided to close it at 6 P.M. Reaction was immediate. One councilman insisted it would prevent "the working classes from enjoying its benefits." In a letter to the *Tribune*, "Vixen" was even more forceful. "I was much disappointed to find the Library closed tonight after a journey of nearly 3 miles, but as I am one of the working class [I] expect to be trodden on. . . . Will the working man submit to this outrage? I hope not."[38]

The act of building public library collections sometimes functioned as a democratic way to address ethnic tensions. After Chicago's mayor appointed a committee to explore the possibility of establishing a public library in 1872, a "Scandinavian" complained to the *Tribune* that none of his kind was on the committee. If Scandinavians should "not be counted among the illiterate classes of immigrants," they deserved "steady nourishment from the rich literature of their native countries, which want would best be satisfied by . . . the Public Library."[39] The issue of representation on the board exploded into open conflagration two years later when a Jewish trustee protested the acquisition of Roman Catholic authors on a booklist order he had recently screened. "Why should not Hebrew and Jewish works also be purchased?" he queried. To this the librarian responded—"quite red in the face," one Chicago newspaper reported—that the order had been cleared with two Catholic board members. Immediately a Protestant trustee jumped to his feet. "His eyes flashed, the tones of his voice indicated rage, and his portly frame fairly shook as he poured out sentence after sentence of odium on the minute head" of a Catholic trustee for "having books purchased because they were Catholic in tendency." To this the Catholic trustee responded that the absence of these authors was not only significant, it was also an injustice to the city's Irish-Americans. Besides, he explained, the books were not sectarian, just by Catholic authors.

Would the board "permit the Catholic and popish church to run in surreptitiously a large lot of their trash called 'literature' in direct conflict with the rules of the board?" demanded the Protestant. The Jewish trustee agreed, and "strenuously objected to their being purchased, because they belonged to Catholics." As the board erupted into cacophony, the chair shouted for order. "It happens to be a list of books that are written by men who had the misfortune of being born Catholics," he said injudiciously, "although their productions are classed among the standards of modern literature." It was only the subject heading for these authors as "Catholic" that drew objections, he insisted. A Catholic trustee pointed out it was "because he wanted a library acceptable to the Catholic people that he wanted these books on the shelves." Finally everyone calmed down and accepted a motion to submit the list to the selection committee, granting it "full power to . . . make any selection from the list they might deem proper." All this occurred, one reporter concluded, because the nine board members selected "were parceled out among the nationalities and creeds for the seeming purpose of securing to each what decent men consider a 'fair show' upon the shelves." The *Chicago Tribune* saw the meeting differently—as a fight between Chicago's German (largely Protestant but some Jewish) and Irish (largely Catholic) populations.[40]

Rhetoric justifying the need for public libraries continued. For example, in an 1862 report, Worcester (Massachusetts) Public Library directors identified their civic institution as the "one public place consecrated to the diffusion of knowledge, free and universal, within whose walls the jar of political and religious discord may never come." Other unsubstantiated maxims also invaded the rhetoric, such as this one: "Building a library means tearing down a jail." "I unhesitatingly affirm that if we had a good library crime within one year would be diminished at least ten percent," said a Chicagoan in 1868. In 1867, a businessman stranded in an industrial city one weekend lamented its lack of a public library, which he then carefully defined. "There should be good books in variety, reading rooms, a hall for debating and lectures, a place where young men can amuse themselves," he wrote the *New York Observer and Chronicle*. (That he specifically mentioned "hall" and "place" suggests he had previous social library experience.) "One such edifice would change the character of the town, and raise the whole people."[41]

Opening public libraries on Sundays also brought controversy, and the institution often became a platform for arbitrating the issue between sacred and secular communities. On the one hand, sacred communities maintained, Sunday was "the Lord's Day." On the other, secular communities saw moral and civic benefit to Sunday opening. "Should we not throw open doors wide to the young apprentice boy who is thirsting for knowledge?" a Boston alderman asked colleagues who were debating Sunday closing of the Boston Public Library in 1864. The alderman made no secret of his objective—to "draw them from the tempting haunts of vice—yes, from the two-thousand barrooms of this city whose doors are wide open . . . three hundred and sixty-five days a year." The city "aristocracy . . . have elegant and expensive clubrooms," he reasoned, bedecked with books they could access on Sundays; why not Boston's "plain people"? The *Boston Investigator* complimented the alderman for his "desire to benefit the working people who had no time on other days to visit that social institution," and castigated his colleagues for "abeyance" to Boston's religious leaders who believe only in "stiff-dickies and weak tea."[42]

Similar negotiations took place in other cities. When Worcester's Public Library considered the issue in 1871, a clergyman alleged that Sunday opening would establish "a precedent fraught with peril to the interests of that very class in the community in whose behalf the change is more especially urged, namely, the overworked and overburdened class." But clergy could be found on both sides of the question; the Reverend Henry Ward Beecher—who several years earlier called popular fiction "common sewers of society"—issued a pamphlet titled *Should the Public Libraries Be Opened on Sunday?* "Yes," was his firm conclusion. They were better than the billiard parlors and bars frequented by men on the Sabbath. After the library initiated Sunday opening in 1872, that first year it counted 5,706 Sunday readers; the second year there were 7,179, and the third saw 10,142. Sunday openings at the Indianapolis Public Library, the director reported in 1874, "has met with general favor. . . . The largest use of the rooms on this day is made by young men; and I cannot but look upon this fact as one of the best evidences of the good the library is doing."[43]

As the United States prepared for its centennial celebration in Philadelphia in 1876, the Bureau of Education—a new office established by the Department of the Interior in 1870—commissioned a centennial report on the state of the nation's public libraries, for which it engaged thirty-five people to write thirty-nine chapters and an introduction. The definition of "public" was deliberately broad and embraced any library to which any members of the public had access. As publication of *Public Libraries in the United States of America—Their History, Condition, and Management: Special Report* neared, the Bureau commissioner suggested to several prominent librarians they might use the *Special Report* as impetus to organize a national conference during the centennial. Leading librarians were unenthusiastic. Into the vacuum stepped the hyperactive Melvil Dewey, most recently associate director of the Amherst College Library, who at the time was putting the finishing touches on a classification scheme. He had just moved to Boston to begin work as an entrepreneur for educational reform, a large part of which (as he saw it) fit the future of the American public library. In May, Dewey visited the *Publishers Weekly* editors. Out of their conversations came a commitment to start a library periodical and to simultaneously introduce it at a national conference in Philadelphia with the *Special Report*'s publication.

All summer Dewey worked to organize the conference, sometimes against the wishes of prominent librarians. Once Dewey got Winsor to commit, however, other library luminaries followed. The time was ripe for a conference. The *Special Report* noted that in 1776 the thirteen original colonies had 29 "public" libraries containing 45,000 volumes. A century later the United States had 3,682 libraries containing 12,276,964 volumes; of those 3,682, the *Report* stated, 1,101 were "free to all the citizens of the municipality." Chicago Public Library Director William Frederick Poole disagreed. If one defined "public libraries" as "free municipal libraries organized under state laws and supported by general taxation," he counted only 188, and Massachusetts had 127.[44]

No matter the numbers, however, the implication was clear: much of the country would be settled by a rapidly increasing number of restless Americans who would form new communities, each in need of a public library. But all the useful knowledge these new institutions would acquire would need professional librarians capable of managing, organizing, and making it available to the public. These library leaders agreed with Benjamin Franklin that libraries should nurture the Self-Made Man; like Thomas Jefferson, they also believed these civic institutions would enable patrons to become informed citizens. In contrast to these beliefs, however, the Bureau of Education reported that in 1874, 75 percent of circulation in public libraries was popular fiction, largely led by authors like Southworth, Holmes, and Optic.[45]

On October 4, 1876, 103 delegates met in Philadelphia. Winsor, who had ghost-chaired an arrangements committee (Dewey did most of the work), called the meeting to order. Much of the conference's attention focused on the *Special Report*'s page proofs (which included as "Part II" Charles Ammi Cutter's *Rules for a Printed Dictionary Catalogue*), the first issue of the monthly *American Library Journal* that *Publishers Weekly* had just started, and Dewey's *Classification and Subject Index for Cataloging and Arranging the Books and Pamphlets of a Library*, a recently copyrighted decimal system that hammered the printed works of useful knowledge into ten broad categories.

On October 5, a Committee on Permanent Organization reported a constitution for a professional association. "For the purpose of promoting the library interests of the country, and of increasing reciprocity of intelligence and good-will among librarians and all interested in library economy and bibliographical studies," the constitution's preamble read, "the undersigned form themselves into a body to be known as the AMERICAN LIBRARY ASSOCIATION." The imperious Dewey signed his name "No. 1," and before delegates left Philadelphia the next day they elected Winsor president, four others vice presidents, and Dewey secretary. For the first time in their history, American librarians had a professional organization to help them network, to trumpet their accomplishments, and to voice their concerns. The first issue of *American Library Journal* (later retitled *Library Journal*) carried an article by Dewey that boldly stated: "The time has at last come when a librarian may, without assumption, speak of his occupation as a profession."[46] Three years later, the American Library Association (ALA) adopted a motto (another Dewey creation)— "The Best Reading for the Greatest Number at the Least Cost"—a phrase that neatly captured librarianship's professional agenda.

Dewey's 1876 article—still much referenced today—spoke for hundreds of librarians who wanted to become part of a late-nineteenth-century professional organization that was convinced humankind could be much improved—if not perfected. To improve social stability in a country challenged by immigration, industrialization, and urbanization, librarians sought to do their part by bringing structure and order to the useful knowledge fixed in print, then make it all accessible to the public in well-managed institutions open to all. Classification was a case in point. The nearly simultaneous publication of Cutter's rules and the Dewey Decimal Classification (DDC) scheme occurred at a unique moment in American library history.

First, both systems were imbued with a set of beliefs about classification inherited from previous generations. In order to educate people and facilitate the discovery of new knowledge, classificatory relationships had to give order to the universe of knowledge. Classifiers held it was possible to perceive the universe of knowledge as a single, cohesive whole in which elements had been revealed through intellectual discovery. These elements existed in a hierarchical relationship, and listing them in their "natural" order would help define the essential characteristics of subject classes that required a structure locating the broadest subject classes at the top.

Both systems also rested on a conviction that applying a universal classification scheme and set of common cataloging rules to library collections would locate the public library at the center of citizen self-education by providing a reliable way for patrons to retrieve the useful knowledge that would inform them about their culture, economy, and government. With notations placed directly on their spines, books could now be arranged in subject categories relative to each other and then quickly found by referencing the notation rather than the location. Librarians believed the arrangement was simple and efficient, and from their perspective a huge improvement over what they had inherited. Although librarians had used a number of classification systems before 1876, in the last quarter of the century most public libraries adopted the DDC.

What library classifiers failed to realize, however, was that these systems cemented cultural biases into library cataloging and classification practices, including its bias toward fiction. In the DDC, for example, fiction (which Dewey once referred to as the "deadly enemy of mental power") merited no attention. "Dealing as it does with the emotions and feelings of people," librarian Margaret Edwards complained a century later, fiction "is a kind of literary bastard since it does not fit into the library's philosophy of educating oneself by 'serious' reading." Instead, libraries adopting the DDC arranged fiction alphabetically by author surname.[47] Although patrons often groused about library classification systems that organized works of useful knowledge, they seldom complained about novels arranged alphabetically by author that quickly led them to the fiction they wanted. And want it they did.

In 1877, the *Boston Traveller* published a whimsical (likely fictionalized) circulation desk interaction that neatly captures social class tensions between library organizations favoring useful knowledge and the popular fiction most people demanded from their public libraries.

> "Say mister," said a small boy to one of the assistants at the public library. "I can't find the books I want to git in these here catalogs. I wish yer'd find 'em for me." "What work do you wish to draw?" paternally inquired the official. "Well, hev yer got 'Mulligan the Masher, or the Gory Galoot of the Galtees'?" The man shook his head. "Well, I'd like 'Red-Headed Ralph, the Ranger of the Roaring Rialto.'" "We don't keep any of that kind of trash, my boy." "Wot sort of a libery is this, anyway," retorted the gamin; "why, it's jus like everythin' else in this country—run for the rich, an' the poor workingman gits no show at all."[48]

At the time, the *1876 Report* noted, 67.4 percent of circulation in twenty-four public libraries surveyed consisted of "prose fiction for adults and juveniles."[49]

As members of an emerging profession, most library leaders perceived this as a problem to be addressed, but solutions varied. "There is in the mental development of every person . . . a limited period when he craves novel-reading," William Frederick Poole explained at the 1876 conference, "but from which . . . he passes safely out into broader fields of study, and this craving never returns to him in its original form." Others objected more forcefully. To combat the desire for fiction, librarians should become "professors of books and reading," insisted San Francisco Public Library director F. B. Perkins. By teaching the "method for investigating any subject in the printed records of human thought," Perkins said, librarians would encourage "the science and art of reading for a purpose." This was especially important for ordinary readers, he said, for whom "the printed records of past and present human knowledge and mental activity are . . . a trackless, if not a howling wilderness." Reading had three purposes, he contended—"entertainment, acquisition of knowledge, and literary production." Beyond efforts to "train to good taste in selection and good sense in indulgence," the first "is hardly worth teaching." While Perkins would not deny patrons all fiction, he was selective. Because it was "demanded by all considerations of Christian civilizations," he argued, literature by authors like Rabelais and Balzac, "such rascally French novels as Fanny and the Woman of Fire," and popular fiction about love and crime should all be "inexorably excluded from the public library as arsenic and laudanum and rum should be refused to children."[50]

CHAPTER THREE

"The Best Reading for the Greatest Number at the Least Cost": 1876–1893

The nation's centennial marked a turning point in American history when the efforts of its enterprising industrialists, salesmen, entrepreneurs, and inventors ushered in a period of abundance obvious not only to rural and urban dwellers born in the United States but also to the millions of late-nineteenth-century immigrants who sought to become naturalized citizens. Together, they formed a consumer society in the late nineteenth century that happily benefited from rapid improvements in the increased production of better food and housing and the introduction of refrigeration and electric power and light. Those born after 1870 recognized that life was better for them than their parents, and in remaking their nation they took great satisfaction in this shift to abundance.[1]

For ordinary citizens, American public libraries were part of this shift. Worcester (Massachusetts) Public Library director Samuel Green called the last quarter of the nineteenth century "the accelerated library movement." In his 1901 message to Congress, President Theodore Roosevelt called the growth of public libraries "the most characteristic educational movement of the past fifty years." By 1876 American public libraries had become vibrant examples of cultural democracy in action, persistently resisting the formation of a unified national culture by some distant group of cultural authorities. Still, in the late nineteenth century, many authorities worried that rapid industrialization, increased immigration, and accelerated urbanization threatened the social order. In their "search

for order," knowledge workers professionalized their labor into new organizations of lawyers, doctors, teachers—and librarians—all dedicated to
bringing stability to a seemingly unstable society through standardized
practices and conventions.[2] Although many librarians wanted to shape
readers' choices and mold literary tastes, public library patrons had the
power to push back—and they did, again, and again, and again.

Although librarians had established a professional organization, Melvil
Dewey was convinced that librarianship needed another footing to solid-
ify its foundation. Shortly after becoming chief librarian at Columbia
College (later, University) in 1883 he began working toward establishing a formal library education program. In 1886, he announced that the
school would open the following year. As preparations continued, however, the trustees learned that Dewey planned to admit women, a move
contrary to college conventions. They protested to the president, who suggested that Dewey postpone opening the school. Dewey refused. Because
no rule specifically prevented women from attending Columbia classes,
the trustees then denied him use of the college classrooms. Undaunted,
Dewey crossed the street from campus and fitted up a storeroom above
a chapel where, "without giving a hint of the volcano on which we all
stood, I welcomed the first class and launched the first library school."
Out of a class of twenty, seventeen were women.[3]

The curriculum Dewey established reflected his perception of librarianship's professional boundaries. Students were admitted if they had the
right "character," a word educated classes used to identify people with
social standing and knowledge of Western civilization's canonical works.
Once admitted, however, students saw three different "faculties." For
practical experience, Dewey and his staff taught courses designed to
develop skills in cataloging, classification, book selection, reference service, and the management of the institution in which it took place. For
inspiration (his generation called it "the library faith"—a belief that for a
democracy to survive it needed public libraries to help create an informed
citizenry) he brought in numerous practitioners as guest lecturers. For
theoretical grounding, however, Dewey relied on a Saturday-morning
public lecture series by Columbia faculty. In 1887, for example, Dewey
asked faculty members like classics professor Harry Thurston Peck and
philosophy professor Nicholas Murray Butler to discuss the best books in
their subject areas, then mandated that his students attend.

For Dewey, this structure reflected librarianship's appropriate "domain."
Experts from the sciences, social sciences, and humanities would identify

useful knowledge and "best reading" in research they produced in the modern university. Specifically for fiction, literary authorities (inside and outside academe) would identify disciplinary canons against which to evaluate new contributions. To make the best reading accessible, librarianship would then expand library services to "the greatest number at the least cost." After they got to library school, students learned a series of practices—how to acquire these new literatures (book selection), how to organize them (cataloging and classification), where to look in collections they had already amassed for answers to questions asked them by patrons (reference), and finally, how to govern the library (management). Thus, librarianship's structure and systems stressed useful knowledge, and the librarians functioned as cultural caretakers.

The domain interfered with no other profession, efficiently divided librarianship's workforce, and at the same time gave women (conveniently, they would work for less than men) opportunities to participate in a new profession. One golden opportunity for female librarians involved children. In the late nineteenth century, child welfare advocates began supervising children's physical and moral development in new public institutions such as settlement houses, juvenile courts, playgrounds, and public health programs. Children's librarians fit into this milieu nicely. The model of children's librarianship they pioneered included the creation of separate areas in public libraries, specially trained personnel, and services designed to bring children to carefully selected collections librarians believed suitable for children's moral and social improvement.

Dewey and his colleagues assumed that patrons would gravitate to the best reading identified by professional authorities if those texts were made accessible in a common classification scheme that organized the useful knowledge their collections contained. Because they were members of the same classes, librarians generally did not question what other expert communities decided was good and bad reading, and as librarianship's literature developed—both professional articles and bibliographic guides—it profiled and celebrated these external decisions. The fact that very little in the structure of librarianship addressed the commonplace reading patrons most wanted was intentional.

By today's standards, late-nineteenth-century public libraries forced patrons to negotiate an elaborate process in order to borrow books. In 1886, for example, San Francisco Public Library patrons could not touch any books in the collections, which were located on wooden bookstacks that rose to the ceiling behind a wire screen. Patrons consulted printed

A guarantor form for a Minneapolis Public Library card applicant, which all applicants had to complete and have approved to check out materials. The left side of the card cautions: "Women will not be accepted as Guarantor unless of Age and Independently Responsible." *Annual Report, Minneapolis Public Library, 1949*

catalogs (a large one for nonfiction, a smaller one for fiction, and both out of date), wrote shelf numbers on oblong slips (pink for fiction, white for nonfiction), then handed the slips through openings in the screen to attendants, who used sliding ladders to retrieve the items patrons requested. Because library attendants "were not bookish," a librarian later recalled, "it was a sort of hit and miss proposition for a member of the public to procure a desired book."[4]

Understandably, patrons grumbled. One Cincinnati reader complained that on three visits he had to wait forty minutes. "I have passed through the room when there were as many as twenty-five persons waiting. Lord pity the twenty-fifth on such an occasion." In Chicago "a disgusted lady" wrote to a local newspaper to ask "Why it is that the whole force [of library attendants] are placed at the gentlemen's counter, while on the ladies' side there is only one to wait on some twelve or fourteen ladies at a time. After climbing up the three flights of stairs to get to the library, and then to be compelled to stand there one-half hour to get a book, is an ordeal which not many ladies are willing, much less able, to pass through." Not only were gender issues obvious but so were social class distinctions. In St. Paul, Minnesota, one patron noticed uneven levels of service. "If one is poorly clothed he may see several later arrivals served first."[5]

During this period, the public card catalog appeared—a "new idea originated in the brain of some librarian," said one patron in 1881, which like "an epidemic disease . . . invaded" libraries across the country.

Generally, each book in the collection was represented on three to five cards that bibliographically described titles the library owned. Patrons could access any book via the main entry, which led with the author's surname but included a classification number that patrons usually wrote down on call slips. Added entries included title cards, and for nonfiction books (another not-so-subtle reminder of how the library profession undervalued fiction) also subject cards, whose vocabulary the library profession carefully guarded. Cards were 7.5×12.5 centimeters, not the 3×5 inches by which they became known in subsequent decades. That choice is testimony to Melvil Dewey's passion for the metric system, which all his life he tried to get the country to adopt.

Librarians loved the cards because they kept catalogs current. All they had to do was compose the cards—sometimes in "library hand" (a unique penmanship), sometimes typewritten—on stock thick enough to withstand heavy use from thumbing patrons, then file them in appropriate drawers that slid into and out of a large cabinet. Beginning in 1894, after scores of patrons dropped the drawers and spilled the contents across the floor, manufacturers inserted rods through holes punched in the lower middle part of the card to hold them in place. Thereafter came the familiar public library "slrrr-thwack, slrrr-clack" sounds of readers pulling drawers, placing them on tables, then replacing them in the cabinet. So did the command "Look it up in the card catalog!" ("probably the most hated six words in these United States of America," one twentieth-century librarian lamented), which was regularly issued by short-tempered librarians irritated with annoying patrons. Some readers loved the card catalog. "Innumerable little drawers with cards which I could push back and forth on rods in a delightful, diverting way, until an intriguing name popped up," recalled one a half-century later. "Standing on tip-toe, I would grasp a pencil on a huge chain and write the numbers on a slip to be handed to a lady with a green shade over her eyes." Other readers hated it. Said an irate patron in 1881: "It has wasted more" readers give "to the books consulted through its use."[6]

Central to many of these improvements was the Library Bureau, a library supplies company Dewey started in 1881 that marketed library furniture—including the ubiquitous circulation desk—which gave library interiors a consistent look and feel that library patrons came to expect. In 1876, patrons normally found their reading illuminated by gaslight; by 1893, electric lights replaced gaslights in most public libraries, thus making longer hours possible and enabling more working-class members to use them. Improved ventilation systems also rendered contact between middle-class patrons and what one librarian called "the dirtier type of reader" less objectionable. All these developments added to that sense of abundance patrons experienced in their everyday lives. And when libraries began using a "Vegetable Glue" called Higgins' Drawing-Board Mucilage to paste pockets into book covers, it created a common smell that mixed with the musty fragrance of old books patrons remembered fondly as part of their public library experience.[7]

During this period politicians also began sending government documents free of charge to libraries in their districts. The practice had several benefits. It fit librarianship's imperative to nurture an informed citizenry. In 1891, for example, when a congressman sent the Duluth (Minnesota) Public Library 1,100 volumes of documents, the library predicted the "additions . . . will prove invaluable to students of American politics." The practice also got politicians' "generosity" recognized in local newspapers.[8] Despite the anticipation, however, use of government documents in public libraries remained slight. Most patrons wanted fiction, not information their government generated and distributed free.

In the late nineteenth century, "best reading" gradually replaced "useful knowledge" in the profession's lexicon, and many patrons continued to use the public library for the best reading it held. In 1884, for example, twenty-four-year-old Hamlin Garland moved from Iowa to Boston to become a writer. Almost immediately he went to the Boston Public Library. There he "read both day and night, grappling with . . . all the mighty masters of evolution." Bates Hall "was deliciously comfortable," he remembered. "I had moments of tremendous expansion, hours where my mind went out over the earth like a freed eagle." Garland was not unlike other "serious" Boston Public Library readers, including Henry Wadsworth Longfellow, Oliver Wendell Holmes, and Mark Twain, who used the library regularly. On the West Coast a teenage wharf rat named Jack London started visiting the Oakland (California) Public Library, where he discovered a world beyond the wharves. For him the library became a refuge, and the librarian—poet Ina Coolbrith—a mentor who took an interest in the waif and became the first person to praise his reading choices.[9]

Disagreements among expert communities about serious reading and useful knowledge sometimes made public libraries a target; in the late nineteenth century, religion was often the cause. Cincinnati's *Catholic Telegraph* argued in 1881 that "the number of Catholic books in our Public Library is altogether out of proportion to the number of Catholics paying taxes in this city." When colleagues refused to subscribe to three Catholic periodicals he recommended in 1879, one Chicago Public Library trustee claimed Catholic information needs were not being fairly addressed. That initiated a flurry of counterclaims. A *Tribune* editorial asked: "When was [this trustee] appointed . . . as a representative of the 'Catholic thought' of this city?" A journalist surveyed newspaper and periodical subscriptions and found that while Catholics comprised 10 percent of Chicago's population, CPL subscribed to twenty-two Catholic serials compared to six representing other denominations. Although Baptists and Methodists were the city's two largest denominations, none of their major magazines were represented in the periodical collection. Irish Protestants also complained that the library subscribed to no newspaper representing their interests. These disputes had impact, as was evident at the next board meeting, when the trustees approved subscriptions to the *Illustrated Catholic American*, the *Irishman*, and the *Celtic Monthly*.[10]

While librarians loved to cite successful library patrons who engaged in serious reading, they still had to deal with popular fiction, which nationwide continued to account for 65 to 75 percent of public library circulation. Periodical and newspaper editors often wrote hyperbolic monologues proclaiming that novel reading was evil and that public libraries had no business supplying novels at taxpayer expense. "Think of the condition of these children's minds at the end of such a carnival of sensations!" marveled the *New Hampshire Sentinel* when it reported in 1879 that one boy withdrew 102 novels from the Hartford (Connecticut) Public Library in six months, one girl 112 during that same period. Without supplying any evidence, the editor then declared: "It is clear that the provision of so much mental excitement for our young people is doing them great damage."[11]

Some librarians echoed these concerns. The mind of the novel-reading factory girl, a Germantown (Pennsylvania) librarian said in 1877, "is filled with false ideas of life, and she is prepared easily to be beguiled into an improper marriage, or become the victim of some pretentious scoundrel." For the boy, he "reads of equally false deeds of daring. . . . A dashing life on the frontier, or one of adventure in distant countries is, to his mind, rather to be sought than patient industry in the lot in which Providence has placed him." Because small-town public libraries seemed less concerned about series fiction than larger urban public libraries, one urban library trustee fussed: "it is to be hoped that the directors of our smaller libraries will gradually attain conceptions of public duty which will prevent them from courting a temporary popularity by hastening to supply immature and unregulated minds with the feverish excitements they have learned to crave."[12]

Despite librarians' opposition, however, demand for commonplace reading persisted. In 1879, Boston public librarians counted call slips for books checked out one Saturday; 90 percent were for fiction—the vast majority by authors like Alger, Southworth, and Optic. A year later the trustees reduced the supply of popular fiction by replicating the experiment tried twenty years earlier, with the same results. Circulation rates dropped precipitously. In Milwaukee, fiction accounted for 70 percent of circulation. Titles like *The Bridal Eve*, *The Discarded Husband*, and *My Little Love*, the *Milwaukee Sentinel* reported, were read over and over, mostly by young and middle-aged women.[13]

Late-nineteenth-century competition in the world of print was keen. One expert estimated that circulation of true crime tabloids in the nation's barbershops and saloons exceeded 200,000 weekly. In San Francisco, a *Californian and Overland Monthly* reporter wrote in 1882 that this "pen-poison" literature "makes boys hate work and despise truth and dishonor purity." Readers, he said, fell into four categories—schoolchildren; factory and shop girls; men who tended bar, drove carriages, and worked on farms and boats; and finally, "fallen women, and, in general, the denizens of the midnight world, night-owls, prowlers, and those who live upon sin and its wages."[14] That same year a *Cincinnati Daily Gazette* reporter noted that the Queen City had 175 newsstands that weekly sold 10,000 story papers. The city's school superintendent had decided opinions about (but offered no evidence for) what happened to children who read this stuff: "Generally, they are poisoned intellectually." Unfortunately, the public library was well stocked with series fiction, he told the reporter. "A father once remarked to me that he would like to see the Public Library burnt to the ground, as it was ruining his son." When the Cincinnati Public Library curtailed popular fiction in 1876 and the librarian boasted "a change in the character of the people who use the library," the *Gazette* shot back: "Shall the Librarian pronounce it gratifying progress that the poor have ceased to use the library . . . even if they are unattractive in dress and unrefined in manners?"[15]

To those who objected to Alger, Optic, Southworth, and Holmes, the *Boston Daily Advertiser* responded that library trustees were "justified in providing the kind of reading which is sought for by a large class; gives them pleasure; does them at least no harm; and, being suited to them, brings them a certain amount of intellectual profit and a kind of moral instruction; and, finally, attracts them to the library, where there is a chance that something better may get hold of them." Social activist Thomas Wentworth Higginson agreed, albeit within the context of white racial pride that series fiction reinforced. What sends a boy to Optic, he contended, "is just that love of adventure which has made the Anglo-American race spread itself across the continent."[16]

In 1881 the nation witnessed a national debate on public library circulation of fiction. The spark igniting the firestorm was a series of late-1880 Boston *Sunday Herald* articles written by longtime BPL cataloger James M. Hubbard, which castigated the Boston Public Library for circulating series fiction to children. Hubbard followed these articles with another in *the International Review*, published a month after he sent the BPL board a list of 100 offending titles. He also petitioned the city council to make BPL collecting practices once again reflect the intentions of the library's founders. In the *Review* article Hubbard wrote: "I do not believe it is the proper business for the city to furnish amusing literature to the people free of expense." Public libraries across the country, he lamented, furnish "this literature in quantities almost unlimited; and they furnish it mainly . . . to the school-children" who ought not be exposed to stories that "instill pernicious doctrines . . . subversive of sound morals." He called for "a rigid censorship over all works of this class." The Boston Public Library could easily practice this censorship, he argued, and by example influence other libraries to acquire only the best books.[17]

The Boston Common Council held hearings on Hubbard's petition in early 1881. Using words like "vulgar," "immoral," "nauseous," and "reeking with sin," Hubbard castigated sensationalist authors at the hearings and demanded that the fiction and juvenile departments of the library that circulated these authors be closed. Library trustees countered that it would be impossible and improper to exclude authors read by millions of Americans and demanded by BPL readers. However, when Hubbard issued a pamphlet in late 1881 that listed offending titles (including several authored by what he called a "base herd of female novelists"), trustees caved. In January 1882, they removed the books Hubbard listed from circulation, promised to examine them all, to condemn those judged unsuitable, and to return those deemed unobjectionable to BPL shelves.[18]

Elsewhere, newspapers and periodicals joined the debate. A "theory has gained currency among librarians that constant reading of any kind will develop an improvement of taste," the *Cincinnati Daily Gazette* noted. "We doubt its truth." The Boston Public Library had become an institution, *The Friend* contended, "which was multiplying enormously the very evil which its projector had designed to lessen." With all the "trash that vitiates the taste and degrades the feelings" that public libraries circulated, an *Overland*

Monthly and Out West Magazine author noted, "it is certainly time that the influential men of every community . . . should insist on a strict and intelligent censorship." It might be "wiser to spend the public money on free beer than on wretched fiction," she quipped. The *Worcester Daily Spy* disagreed. Hubbard's assumption that public money should not be spent on "pleasure" novels "is not sound," the *Spy* said. "Pleasure in itself is not only not ignoble, but it is certainly one, and not the least among the objects of existence." The *Northern Christian Advocate* thought some kind of censorship was required, but said it had to come from parents. The *Critic* simply decried Hubbard's attempts to craft "an Index Expurgatorius."[19]

In Chicago, an *Inter Ocean* reporter used Hubbard's petition to query library officials. Chicago Public Library Director William Frederick Poole defended the acquisition of authors like Ouida, Holmes, and Southworth. "If every class is taxed for their support, every class should have its choice of books to read." To the question of whether these novels give "false ideas of life" he responded: "Any of these books are better teachers than the general conversation of the people they meet with in their daily life." The reporter also interviewed library trustees. One said public libraries should not acquire novels by authors like Southworth. Another agreed, but complained that he was consistently overruled by his colleagues. On the other hand, another trustee said he had met Southworth, and from her conversation he judged her incapable of writing anything damaging to the morals of a sensitive person. The board president noted that because the library could not compel attendance it had to furnish patrons with books they wanted. The city's school superintendent, an ex-officio board member, agreed. If people could not get series fiction at the library, he insisted, they would obtain worse reading material at local newsstands.[20]

In the midst of this controversy, the American Library Association's Cooperation Committee surveyed seventy public libraries to see whether their collections included the works of Southworth, Holmes, Alger, Optic, and Ouida. Among the thirty respondents, eleven refused to buy Southworth novels, three had removed Alger and Holmes from their shelves, and two had removed Optic. On the other hand, twenty-four had Alger, twenty-three Holmes, twenty-two Optic, and thirteen Southworth.[21] Except for some agreement on female authors, the survey showed little consensus. Each library, it appears, found an acceptable center of literary values for its community. Whatever their personal objections, librarians, within limits, collected what people wanted and demanded.

In early 1882, a BPL Board Examining Committee issued a report that recommended removal of most of the authors Hubbard had cited in his 1881 pamphlet to what became known as the "Inferno," a designated place librarians used to sequester certain books. To check out a book in the Inferno—identified with three stars in the card catalog—a patron had to fill out a slip giving age and occupation, a character reference, and reason for requesting the book. "This slip must receive the endorsement of the librarian before the request is complied with," the rule stated. About the Inferno one Bostonian wondered: "Is there a microscope of sufficient power to detect this grand inquisitorial expurgatorious [*sic*] of the library?"[22] The Inferno met with mixed reactions across the country. The *Congregationalist* called it indefensible, because even with this procedure "the library would be bound to furnish free-love publications if enough people called for them!" "The committee's task is a delicate and difficult one," the *Cincinnati Daily Gazette* noted, but "the community cannot be treated as if it were composed wholly of children."[23]

Although the Boston Public Library's definition of "immoral" and "objectionable" books shifted because of public pressure brought by Hubbard's attack, the Inferno provided a solution to a perpetual problem—what to do with titles some thought their community should have in its public library, while others did not. The Inferno helped librarians mediate these disputes in ways ultimately acceptable to both sides, and over the years not only did the Inferno become a place for series fiction that authorities questioned, but it also became a convenient place to park high culture titles whose value was still being debated by literary experts. For example, by 1882 the library relegated to the Inferno not only Ouida, Southworth, and Horatio Alger, but also Walt Whitman's *Leaves of Grass*, Boccacio's *Decameron,* and all of Emile Zola's works.[24]

Sticky late-nineteenth-century public debates on works that split the literary establishment were numerous. Hamlin Garland describes reading Whitman's *Leaves of Grass* at the Boston Public Library as a transformative experience. "I rose from that first reading with a sense of having been taken up into high places."[25] But others saw Whitman as a threat to society's morals and rejected all his works. Garland got *Leaves of Grass* out of the Boston Public Library Inferno, but the Chicago Public Library refused to stock it. One Chicagoan wrote the *Tribune* in 1884 that the library director "would not have any book in the library for the possession of which he might be prosecuted." *Leaves of Grass*, Director Poole said, was an obscene book "which ought not to be tolerated in any respectable library." Absurd, a *Tribune* reader responded; *Leaves of Grass* "is the only purely aboriginal, autochthonic piece of American literature we have." "Chaotic nonsense," another *Tribune* reader countered.

The "crude immodesty" of *Leaves of Grass* disqualified it from a place on library shelves, where it would be available to every child in Chicago.[26]

Other titles also occasioned disputes. For example, the Concord (Massachusetts) Public Library made *Huckleberry Finn* national news when it banned the book in 1885. "The veriest trash," noted one trustee; "more profitable for the slums than it is for respectable people," claimed another. "If Mr. Clemens cannot think of something better to tell our pure-minded lads and lasses," Louisa May Alcott wrote, "he had best stop writing for them." As a child, librarian Caroline Hewins loved Harriet Beecher Stowe's *Uncle Tom's Cabin* and in the 1880s had multiple copies in her Hartford (Connecticut) Public Library. So did most other public libraries north of the Mason-Dixon line. But for white readers in the South, *Uncle Tom's Cabin* was evil incarnate, and few southern libraries acquired copies.[27]

Hewins may have loved *Uncle Tom,* but she detested what she called "the Immortal Four"—Alger, Optic, Castlemon, and Finley. A year after Hubbard's attack she published *Books for the Young: A Guide for Parents and Children* (1882). In the same year she started a children's read-aloud program that became a model for the ubiquitous weekly children's story hour still with us today. As more women joined the library profession, males who assumed responsibility for defining the canons of serious literature willingly allowed female librarians to harness their "natural instincts" to identify good books for children. Pioneering females who advocated library services to children (and thereby increased the number of patrons those libraries served) seized the opportunity, and together they formed a professional group that fought the kind of series fiction newsstands routinely peddled. Books were rejected, Hewins said in her bibliography's preface, "when they make 'smartness' a virtue, encourage children in cruelty, rudeness, or disrespect to their elders, contain much bad English, or make their little every-day heroes leap suddenly from abject poverty to boundless wealth." In 1883, Hewins also began a *Library Journal* column entitled "Literature for the Young," in which she listed books and provided annotations addressing their character and appropriateness for reading.[28]

Hewins's bibliography fixed in print what some libraries already practiced. In 1877, for example, the Pawtucket (Rhode Island) Public Library director assembled a scrapbook of news clippings reporting on boys who were led to crime by reading too many dime novels. Included was a story about an infamous murderer who said "blood and thunder" dime novels he read as an adolescent turned him into a criminal. Routinely the librarian handed the scrapbook to lads she caught with dime novels they brought into the library. The Providence (Rhode Island) Public Library

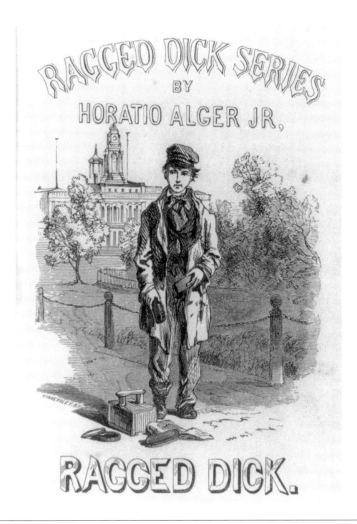

Horatio Alger's *Ragged Dick Series* and Oliver Optic's *Lake Shore Series* (see illustration on p. 66) were typical of the late nineteenth-century series fiction read by millions of young people that was heavily criticized and often banned by the nation's public library leaders as "bad reading." (*above*) Horatio Alger, Jr., *Ragged Dick* (Boston: Loring, 1868), Library of Congress, LC-USZ62-49663; (*next page*) Oliver Optic, *Lightning Express; or The Rival Academies* (Boston: Lee and Shepard, 1871), from archive.org.

did the same in 1885. "It is said," the *Boston Herald* reported, "that the dime novel boy usually reads the scrap-book, which is rapidly increasing in size as the fresh exploits of the dime novel adventurers are added to it. He then lays it down in disgust, and nothing can induce him to return to those stories again." The *Herald* encouraged other libraries to create similar scrapbooks; and newspapers across the country reprinted the story.[29]

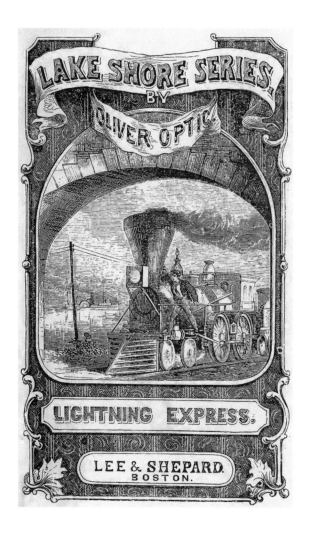

But some patrons resisted. When in 1889 the Los Angeles Public librarian instructed her staff to deny youth books thought harmful (the library had Hewins's bibliography), several parents protested. One insisted that the practice cease. Only then, she argued, "may we see what ought always to be as much a matter of pride as a 'well-kept library'—a well-used library." In a contrary move, one librarian became so frustrated with girls' endless requests for series fiction that he tore up request slips they handed him and instead handed them slips for biographies already filled out. One girl responded "with a scowl," a *Christian Union* reporter noted: "I don't want any *Lifes*." Not all librarians were so rigid, however. At his public library, a Portland, Oregon, reporter noticed in 1891 "the boy who revels in the border tragedies, the miss who reads 'The Wife's Secret' in a night, the fashionable mater-familias who exchanges one French novel for one more spicy, and the retiring student who keeps the 'Decameron' over time." None, he noted, "gain reverence in the eyes of the obliging librarian, who has the same deferential bow for all."[30]

Caught between millions of young readers of series fiction many expert communities thought damaging to the social order, and the need to attract these same millions into a civic institution people did not have to use, public libraries were forced to forge compromises acceptable to host communities. In 1891, even the Hartford (Connecticut) Public Library—run by the woman whose bibliography castigated the Immortal Four—bowed to public demand. "The boys have not left off their Optic, Alger and Castlemon or the girls their Elsie and Miss Holmes," Caroline Hewins lamented. "I wish that I could tell you that the children of Hartford had marched in procession to the park and there, Savanarola-like, burned their idols, but unfortunately my regard for the truth prevents any such statement." Her board president added: "It is no longer a question of whether a large supply of novels prevents readers from becoming familiar with English classics. It is whether they shall find at the library pleasant, wholesome stories, or go away without them to buy at news-stands and railway counters such stuff."[31]

And despite the rhetoric decrying the influences of bad books, reality for readers showed otherwise. "I took an exquisite delight in *Old Sleuth* and *Jack Harkaway*," Hamlin Garland remembered of his Iowa adolescence, when he regularly traded dime novels and weekly tabloids with his friends. It was impossible, he later recalled, "for any print to be as magical to any boy these days as those weeklies were to me. . . . The pleasure I took in these tales should fill me with shame, but it doesn't—I rejoice in the memory of it." In Ohio during the 1880s, teenager Sherwood Anderson "read greedily everything that came into my hands," including Laura Jean Libbey, dime novels, Cooper, Stevenson, and Mark Twain. Most he got from his public library—"I went every day. . . . The books . . . have always fed my dreams." About the same time Theodore Dreiser visited his Warsaw, Indiana, public library. At first he selected only recommended books, but then "turned again to romance, seeking in Ouida, Mrs. Harrison and even Laura Jean Libbey some phase of impossible sentimentalism which my nature appeared to crave."[32]

In their plots, dime novel authors almost always celebrated human dignity and routinely trumpeted the virtues of the self-made man pursuing success in what they represented as an American world of democratic equality. More recent research on dime novels read by urban working classes, however, shows that they became imaginative spaces in which readers experienced happy endings that evolved from successful class struggles. Strikes were always won; heroines always triumphed. For their readers, these stories were as powerful as any in the serious novels praised by literary professionals, yet critics so eager to impress the canons of serious reading on dime novel readers regularly missed these points. If the subsequent lives of youthful readers like Garland, Anderson, and Dreiser are any indication, however, none had been damaged by series fiction Caroline Hewins and others found so objectionable.[33]

Early forms of comics also sparked public debates. When the Boston Public Library allowed twelve-year-olds into the reading room in 1892, they quickly beleaguered librarians by requesting serials with colored cartoons like *Puck* and *Judge*, then laughing out loud at them. In response, the trustees let the library's subscriptions expire. In a counterresponse, many newspapers across the country commented. Any kindergartner could tell librarians that pictures educated, quipped the *Philadelphia Inquirer*. A majority of people, the *Toledo Bee* insisted, understood that satire and humor were "sharp teachers, while one pointed caricature can expose a humbug as dozens of discourses by Boston wiseneres [*sic*] can not." Sacramento's *Themis* teased: "The culchawed people whose ancestors roasted witches are welcome to live in the sixteenth century if they please. Other people prefer the nineteenth." Back home, the *Boston Daily Globe* joined the fun when a patron agreed to donate a subscription to *Puck* to the library. "Pall of Gloom Lifted from the Public Library," read an article subheading, located right beside a reprint of a recently published *Puck* cartoon lampooning BPL's decision.[34]

As public libraries were important civic places, the act of opening new ones in late-nineteenth-century America occasioned much community celebration. When Petersham, Massachusetts, dedicated its public library on the Town Common in 1889, for example, a local Civil War hero led a street parade of "12 virgins [records do not indicate how he knew this] bearing flags, old soldiers in numbers sufficient to form two corporals' guards, the Brass Band, followed by the scholars, while citizens generally brought up the rear."[35] Choosing a site for a public library occasionally brought public comment. As the Boston Public Library laid foundations for its new Copley Square building in 1887, some citizens complained. "Do you not see that it robs me of my chief delight, if they remove all of our cherished books to the Back Bay?" complained one. "Won't you please beg them to leave us our Reading Room?" asked a young girl. "I have spent my noon hours there for years; I eat my dinner as soon as I can, and go there to enjoy the papers," a "workingman" wrote, "and when I go home at night I share all I have read with my wife. Now all this will end if the reading-room and library are taken from us." With similar social class subtexts, others complained about the new building's exterior ornamentation. In place of Latin inscriptions, one patron urged, "The legends . . . should be in good, plain, English."[36]

Still, use of the library as community space was evident. When the Buffalo Public Library opened a new building in 1887, its first floor housed stacks behind a delivery room, a librarian's office, catalog room, study room, and reading room for periodicals ("SILENCE is the LAW of THIS ROOM," a sign said). Just off the lobby, however, was a porch described as "comfortable for summer reading." On the second floor, the building housed a ladies' reading room, lecture room, a classroom, committee room, chess and conversation room, and a three-room art gallery. On the third floor, the Buffalo Historical Society managed a museum, lecture room, library, and portrait gallery. The Buffalo Society of Natural Sciences managed the basement that included a geology and mineralogy room, a zoology room, two science library rooms, a herbarium and botanical laboratory, and a lecture hall.[37] The library building provided space for many activities that helped this ethnically diverse city evolve a sense of community.

Some middle-class Americans so valued the mid-nineteenth-century social library public lecture programs that they expected their new public libraries to replicate them. "This portion of the building in which we are assembled tells its own story," said a speaker at the dedication of the South Kingstown (Rhode Island) public library. "Here lectures will be delivered and here concerts will be given. Here the flourishing Choral Society, of which we are already so justly proud, will have its home and here music will lend its charm to elevate our social life." When listing reasons a public library was an investment "which returns the largest dividends" to host communities, the

St. Louis Public library director noted that its reading room regularly hosted lectures (in 1889, for example, one professor delivered four-teen "social and political science" lectures on Friday evenings), and its meeting rooms hosted many community groups, including a women's club (which in 1891–1892 discussed Schiller's dramas, Balzac's place in fiction, and the rise and fall of Romanticism) and an Eliot Society studying Shakespeare. By such means the library contributed to the intellectual life of the city.[38]

By this time the public library had evolved familiar patron types, many still recognizable in the twenty-first century. On an 1889 Saturday afternoon at the Detroit Public Library, main reading room librarians recognized "Ye Bibliophile," "The Everyday Visitor," "The Afflicted One, Reading with His Nose," and the "Chronic Newspaper Reader" who "regularly goes to sleep over his paper, and as someone else is waiting his turn the attendant slips up and takes it away while he sleeps." Boys in search of comic papers were also regulars. "They are full of life and spirit and usually have to be warned . . . not to disturb others by their innocent sport over the gay cartoons." A "demented woman" came in regularly, sat by the front door, "and watches every man who comes in. Her husband ran away . . . a year ago, but she is always looking for him." Then there were the "lovers, who sit by the pedestal with the bust of Lincoln. They have been there all the morn-ing reading in each other's eyes the old, old story." When queried by a *Boston Herald* reporter in 1887, library attendants quickly named three "literary cranks" who daily sat in the same place: "encyclopedia crank" read *Britannica*; "coffee and cake crank" read only books about raising children, and every hour on the hour handed his book to attendants to hold while he went out for coffee and cake; "Heavenly Arcana" read a book by Emmanuel Swedenborg so often he wore out the binding. When librarians sent it out for rebinding, "Heavenly Arcana" threat-ened to report them to the mayor.[39]

Public library rules—enforced variously by librarians—frequently attempted not only to govern social behavior, but also to enforce commu-nity hygiene. Some efforts were more successful than others. In 1879 one Chicago patron complained: "The absence of spittoons is a crying shame, and the nooks and crannies reek with filthy expectorations as a consequence." Another patron fussed about "the actual risk of life and limb . . . from slipping on the 'gobs' (spitters will understand the expression) of different varieties of saliva, unreservedly squirted over the steep stairways." When the library opened reading room windows in November to drain foul air, someone complained the cross-ventilation exposed "visitors to the numerous illnesses prevalent at this season," thus making the library "a death-trap instead of a useful institution." But another maintained that because reading rooms were regularly filled with "the great unwashed," the library had to open the windows. "If a brisk ventilation were not kept up . . . people of delicate olfactories could not endure the atmosphere." In 1886 the library closed its newspaper reading room to eliminate "an army of ill-smelling vagrants and tramps who come in mainly . . . to keep warm."[40]

Branches of urban public library systems that opened in new immigrant neighborhoods quickly became gathering places. By 1891 the Chicago Public Library supported twenty-four delivery stations and five reading rooms across the city, all deliberately located near newsstands and bars. At one reading room, scores of boys came after school closed at 3:30, "followed by a big policeman who sat in a conspicuous position and swung his cane and twisted his buttons until 6:00 p.m.," wrote a reporter. "By this time the pangs of hunger had overcome the passion for pictures which had kept two dozen young Americans quite aloof from the attraction of the outside world, and a general exit was observed." A half hour later came workingmen who, until 10 P.M., occupied every chair. At a Czech neighborhood reading room, another reporter noticed, patrons "read and reread the Bohemian literature furnished by the library until they have absolutely worn out its books, and now are left, hungering and thirsting as it were, for something to read. . . . The younger generation, of course, takes up the English books, so that the circulation is gradually changing its national character."[41]

During this period American public libraries began cooperative efforts with public schools. Every Saturday morning in 1883, a Chicago public school teacher brought his class to the library for a presentation. "Standard books and illustrated works . . . are laid out on the table in the director's room, the teacher supervising the selection and preparing himself to speak upon it, and especially with reference to the books before him indicating such as are of the best authority, and describing the best methods of using them." The librarian then welcomed the students, invited them to use all these resources, and toured them through the building while explaining its organization and catalogs. Public libraries also provided collections to schools, oftentimes to wean children from series fiction.

In Cincinnati, the public library exhibited local student artwork in its third-floor gallery in 1878. An "opportunity," the *Daily Gazette* said, "to inspect and investigate the systematic and continuous training in matters of taste and aesthetic culture pursued in our Cincinnati public schools." In Los Angeles, patrons complained in 1882 when officials prevented them from playing chess and checkers in the building, a practice carried over from the old Los Angeles Library Association "Conversation Room." "Public sentiment seems to be, re-establish the games, but enforce order," the *Los Angeles Times* noted. In 1877 the Macon (Georgia) Public Library exhibited hand-carved scrolls made by local woodworkers in rooms "which are now assuming the appearance of a gallery." In 1886 the library hosted a lecture attended by "an audience composed of many of the cultured people of Macon on 'The Dissection of a Joke.'" Four years later the *Macon Weekly Telegraph* reported a community floral display: "Geraniums, chrysanthemums, and other brilliant hued blossoms made the Public Library gay yesterday and filled it with a delicious fragrance."[42]

But public libraries were also places to make political statements. In 1880 the Macon Public Library exhibited its collection of Confederate regimental battle flags, Confederate currency, and a Confederate army biscuit baked in 1864. Two years later the library hosted an exhibit of works by local artists, coin collections, fans, dolls, china, and especially Confederate mementos. In 1890 a women's club met in the Library's Chess Room to plan the annual Confederate Veterans Fair. On the other hand, in 1892 the Worcester (Massachusetts) Public Library placed in its new lecture room an exhibit of illustrations of uniforms worn by soldiers and sailors from the Revolutionary to the Civil War. Months later it exhibited photographs of Civil War scenes, including battlefields strewn with fallen soldiers. In some places, however, public libraries tried to bring North and South together. In Washington, DC, the United American Veterans, an organization of former Union and Confederate soldiers, met in 1891 to discuss the possibility of establishing a public library in the District of Columbia.[43]

Many believed that public libraries should address social problems. In 1884 the Bridgeport (Connecticut) public librarian enumerated the benefits her institution brought its community. It reached "as low a class as any library reaches, since many members belong to the poorest orders of the population," she said, "and many of our regular Sunday attendants have told us voluntarily that they used formerly to spend their Sundays in low saloons because they had no home but a boarding house." But the library also fostered informal educational activities within the community.

"Before it opened, there was not a single debating or mutual improvement society here," she noted. "Now, there are several which are very sensibly managed and well attended. Chautauqua circles, scientific classes, and clubs for study of art and literature also flourish; all of which are more or less dependent upon the library for help."[44]

Across the country urban immigrants used public libraries for many purposes. In the Boston Public Library reading room, a reporter noted one evening in 1888, "Here may be seen, side by side, the representative of a proud English family and the evicted Irishman, the Polish refugee and the Russian Nihilist, the German student fresh from Göttingen or Heidelburg, the natty Frenchman and the brawny Scot, merchants and mechanics, clerks and workmen, the laughing schoolgirl and the bright high school boy who are reading up the subject of tomorrow's lesson." When the reporter asked an attendant about immigrants, the latter noted: "It is pleasant to see men, mostly foreigners, who have reaped benefits from the reading room bring their newly arrived friends to share in them. . . . I notice how soon these men gradually call for American papers and plod through them to acquire a knowledge of the language." When Olga Tuvin arrived in the United States as a fifteen-year-old from Ploksch, Russia, she tried night schools to learn English, but abandoned these "stifling" classrooms that taught from children's primers and assumed immigrants were ignorant. "I knew then that the Public Library must become my school room. . . . I had an overwhelming desire to become a good useful American."[45]

Sometimes accommodating children as new patrons in late-nineteenth-century library spaces met resistance. Before 1900 a common public library sign read: "Children and dogs not admitted." "You can't bring her in here, sir," a library guard told a father with daughter in hand in 1891. But the father protested; he did not want his daughter standing in the rain while he checked out a book. The two men compromised "by checking her with the umbrellas." The Brookline (Massachusetts) Public Library opened a children's room in 1890 to address a different problem; "The librarian could not bear to have them [children] around," a colleague recalled. To appease her, the trustees set up a basement room for children and put the janitor in charge.[46]

As public space, public libraries also attracted undesirables. In Wheeling, West Virginia, young boys loafing in front of the public library in 1877 persistently swore at pedestrians. "Ladies cannot pass without being insulted by these young scapegraces," the local newspaper reported. The *Milwaukee Journal* complained in 1885 about gangs of young men walking in front of the library, "and by word or deed insult every lady that is so unfortunate as to meet them." As always, libraries also attracted the homeless and unemployed. In 1877, derelicts in the Indianapolis Public Library reading room were bounced by a police officer and told not to return. In the 1890s, Boston Public Library patrons dubbed the lower hall the "Tramps' Retreat," a place where in the winter homeless who abandoned benches on the Common "sat with their damp stockinged feet toasting at the warm radiators—their boots slyly removed when the attendant's back is turned." Not everyone objected to their presence, however. For the homeless, a reporter noted, the Chicago Public Library reading room "is an oasis in the desert of a hard, struggling world, and the few hours they spread daily in its dreamy quiet are the only glimpse of happiness their barren lives know." Because society does not provide work for all, the Los Angeles public librarian wrote in 1893, "a whole community is physically safer when the loafer, be he chronic or otherwise, is sitting with a book before him in an atmosphere and surroundings of wholesomeness. When the extent of this usefulness is better realized, every employment office and corner loafing-place will contain an invitation to the library; loaf at the library if need be."[47]

By 1876 the American public library had become so much a part of many people's lives they rushed to its defense when it was attacked. For example, when one councilman recommended closing the Chicago Public Library in 1876 to save taxpayer money, reaction was immediate. The *Tribune* editorialized: "The Library affords no picking for anybody, and it does disseminate useful knowledge—two very potent reasons in the eyes of a certain class for abolishing it entirely." Others saw the move as a class issue. "The big tax-payers take care of their interests; we, who by our labor and industry don't amass such great fortunes, but, nevertheless, enrich the community at large," deserved a well-supported public library. Another taxpayer disagreed. The library "is only one of the many institutions foisted upon us by those who possess nothing, and I propose that the right to vote concerning municipal affairs involving taxation be restricted to those who own the city." That comment also won immediate response. "I don't ask as a favor from the Council—a liberal appropriation for the Public Library—but with the law in hand I demand it as a right."[48]

CHAPTER FOUR

"The Liberty to Read What They Will and When"

The Carnegie Era, 1893–1917

Between May 1 and October 31, 1893, nearly 27 million visitors walked through the gates of the Chicago World's Fair on 600 acres bordering Lake Michigan's shoreline. There visitors viewed tens of thousands of exhibits from all over the world on display in more than 200 buildings. A central Court of Honor—dubbed by locals the "White City" for its stucco-covered classically designed architecture—drew most attention. Windy City officials had determined to use this World's Columbian Exposition celebrating the 400th anniversary of Christopher Columbus's arrival in the New World to show all who gathered that Chicago was a dynamic American city of great culture.

It was there that the American Library Association (ALA) gathered for its annual conference in July 1893. Fourteen years earlier it had adopted the motto "The best reading for the greatest number at the least cost." To identify best reading, librarians looked to expert communities with pedigrees considered essential for sound evaluations of printed books and articles. Most shared an ideology of reading. "Good" reading, this ideology dictated, led to good social behavior, "bad" reading to bad social behavior. Sometimes these authorities disagreed (was *Huckleberry Finn* "good" or "bad"?), but mostly they were comfortable with the Western canons they inherited, and their recommendations for best reading were more alike than different. Combing through book reviews by these expert communities and compiling "best book" bibliographies had become a central task for librarians. At the conference, the ALA proudly exhibited a "Model Library" of 5,000 books recommended for any public library; only 15 percent were fiction. A year later the Bureau of Education of the Department of the Interior published a bibliography of the library's contents as *Catalog of the A.L.A. Library*, and printed 20,000 copies as government documents that congressmen then sent free to public libraries.[1] The *Catalog* immediately became a standard acquisitions tool.

But one session in this 1893 conference took place in the Woman's Building, which itself hosted a first-of-a-kind library of 8,000 titles written by women from around the world. Because this library included many authors disparaged by professional librarians, however, the collection confronted the Model Library's literary canons. In contrast to the exhibit the ALA put together sporting new technologies and professional appliances, Candace Wheeler—a nationally known interior designer—decorated the Woman's Library to evoke a "homelike" literary atmosphere. Between May and October thousands of women's club members viewed the room, and what they saw impressed them. Public libraries they subsequently established back home reflected not only their organizing skills and civic responsibility but also a desire to replicate the library's "homelike" atmosphere.[2]

In 1893, the ALA conference gave less attention to the quality of reading materials and more to "the largest number at the least cost." To address least cost, ALA president Melvil Dewey and his allies continued to push libraries to adopt centralized systems like common classification schemes and uniform subject headings. By these means librarians participated in the Progressive Era's efficiency movement. The standardization of library equipment and forms, centralization of bibliographic control made possible by widespread adoption of the Dewey decimal scheme, common cataloging practices that the ALA had refined, and compilation of bibliographies guiding librarians to best reading—all improved the American public library's efficiency and offered readers across the country a common set of library experiences.

Library leaders believed that by bringing the public to printed works that contained reliable information and useful knowledge, the public library would inevitably contribute to progress and social order. This belief was often referred to as the "library faith." Feeding it were successes many readers experienced. "By the time I was twelve or fourteen," Harry Truman recalled, "I had read every book in the [Independence, Missouri] library, including the encyclopedias. . . . Those books had a great influence on me." In 1899 Wilbur and Orville Wright came upon an ornithology book (probably a Smithsonian report) in the Dayton Public Library that sparked an interest in human flight. As a teenager, Ernest Hemingway frequented the Oak Park (Illinois) Public Library stacks. On its fiftieth anniversary in 1953 he wrote "how much it has meant to me all my life" and sent a $100 check. "If you find that I owe any fines or dues you can apply it against them," he teased.[3]

During this period, reference service became standard practice in public libraries. In 1909 the St. Joseph (Missouri) Public Library detailed everyday reference room activities that focused on the useful knowledge public libraries favored—"to aid the pension department in detecting a fraud or assisting a worthy woman in establishing her right to government aid; to assist in finding who was one's grandfather or great-grandmother, and something of their lives; to furnish the newspaper with a portrait or illustration on a rush order; to supply . . . the spelling of a word; a date in history, the name of a cabinet officer or other official; to provide statistics for the minister . . . for his sermon . . .; and, not the least of all, to get the earnest student in any branch of study, the energetic club woman, the teacher with heart and mind in her work, the help they need."[4]

The country was in the midst of a public library movement at the same time it experienced huge increases in numbers of books published in the United States, from 2,076 titles in 1880 to 13,470 in 1910. Other publications also increased. Circulation of monthly magazines went from 18 million in 1890 to 64 million in 1905; the number of daily newspapers reached 2,600 in 1909 (nearly half in non-English languages). To meet this rapid growth of print, librarianship developed efficient ways to identify best reading, a process that was the end product of a filtering system heavily dependent on expert communities. For example, in 1901 the H. W. Wilson Company began issuing *Readers' Guide to Periodical Literature*, which initially covered twenty periodicals (e.g., *Atlantic Monthly*, *Current Literature*, and *North American Review*), each edited by an authority dedicated to publishing material fitting the canons of his culture. Because *Readers' Guide* increased access to this literature, libraries favored publications that the *Guide* indexed. Modifications to the *Guide's* scope came slowly, thus placing periodicals issued by marginalized groups like African and Hispanic Americans at a distinct disadvantage—they could not get indexed in *Readers' Guide*, so public libraries tended not to subscribe to them. As a result, the books and articles indexed in the

Guide imposed limits on collections the library provided that tended to support an American way of life that dominant white Anglo-Saxon Protestant (WASP) cultures defined; there were few ways to challenge the status quo.

Similarly, within the decade the Wilson Company began issuing bibliographical aids such as its *Fiction Catalog* and *Children's Catalog*. Like the ALA *Catalog*, *Fiction Catalog* took its cues from experts whose reviews appeared in periodicals Wilson indexed. Librarians loved these guides. When the ALA *Catalog*'s second edition appeared in 1904, for example, the Louisville Public Library decided that all works of fiction listed there that were not already in its collection should be purchased. *Booklist* magazine, issued ten times a year when the ALA began it in 1905, met a similar response. Librarians in Sedalia, Missouri, regarded it as "our best guide in the purchase of books." In columns they wrote for local newspapers, many librarians simply copied *Booklist* annotations. In 1915, the Clinton (Iowa) Public Library reported that its readers regularly came to the circulation desk with columns containing *Booklist* annotations that they had cut out of the local newspaper. Sometimes, however, librarians met resistance. "Model libraries on the 'expert' plan possess a certain interest, but they are scarcely likely to 'fill a long-felt want' in this country of liberty and individualities," the *Boston Globe* said in 1894. "That public library is best for any community which grows up with it, and receives its accretions from the best public spirit around it."[5]

And a shortage of professional librarians inadvertently supported this *Boston Globe* sentiment. Because library schools could not supply enough professional librarians to staff all the new public libraries opening during this period, smaller communities generally hired untrained local women, usually from leading families who reflected community values. As a group, these untrained librarians operated largely outside the profession's influence, had little voice in the ALA, and showed little resistance to the popular fiction they and their families had enjoyed for years. For example, in 1910 the director of the Charles H. Moore Library in Lexington, Michigan (population 519), was not a member of the Michigan or American Library Association and did not subscribe to its periodicals. At the time, the Moore library had twenty-one Alger volumes, thirty-seven Martha Finleys, and forty *Bobbsey Twins*. The Wisconsin Library School graduate who ran the Rhinelander (Wisconsin) Public Library (population 5,637), however, was a member of the Wisconsin and American Library Associations, subscribed to *Readers' Guide* and *Booklist*, and had both ALA *Catalog* editions. Her library had two Algers, one Finley, and no *Bobbsey Twins*.[6]

Who frequented these new public libraries? Of the St. Joseph (Missouri) Public Library's 468 borrowers in 1902, there were 125 schoolgirls, 78 schoolboys, 62 housewives, 38 laborers, 27 clerks, and 14 butchers. The latter demonstrated the community's industrial base; 20 percent worked in local meatpacking plants. Similarly, of the Bradford (Pennsylvania) Public Library's 3,239 registered readers in 1907, 1,637 were women, 779 men, and 822 children. Of 976 who identified an occupation, 159 were stenographers and bookkeepers, 139 clerks, 93 teachers, 76 laborers, 69 machinists, and 61 dressmakers.[7] Patrons of these two libraries were clearly working and middle class more than town leaders, and women and children more than men. Yet for both, fiction accounted for two-thirds of circulation.

Some saw a problem in these gender and age demographics. The nationally circulated magazine *Independent* found public libraries "useful to the women and children, but not so much to the men. . . . Women use books as playthings; men as tools. . . . A reference library rather than a reading library is best suited to masculine minds." And the library profession itself was part of the problem, the *Independent* argued. "The large predominance of women in library work and management has tended to increase the feminization of the public libraries. . . . they are excellent catalogers and keep things neat and maintain order, . . . but they are somewhat out of touch with the life and work of the community in which they live."[8] By that time over 70 percent of librarians were women, most reconciled to being paid less than male librarians but at the same time so grateful to be a member of this fast-growing profession they seldom challenged the sexism evident in the *Independent*'s remarks.

After 1893 libraries began opening their stacks to readers. "How I enjoyed a half hour among those bookstacks," said a Bostonian in 1895 after visiting a Rhode Island library. What a contrast to Boston's "wait-for-your-book plan," at the end of which "you are made to feel that you are the recipient of a great privilege." Librarians regularly used open stacks to discourage patron preference for fiction. In 1897, for example, the Los Angeles Public Library opened stacks for nonfiction to make the useful knowledge organized by the Dewey Decimal Classification system more accessible, but they kept novels "behind the rail" to make fiction more difficult to obtain. On the other hand, some libraries opened stacks only for fiction, largely to reduce the labor necessary to retrieve the stories people wanted most.

To encourage patrons to read nonfiction, many librarians shifted from a one-book-per-visit rule to a "two-book" system that allowed patrons to withdraw one fiction and one nonfiction book. "The effect of this rule will be to increase the circulation of all kinds of books except fiction," the Minneapolis Public Library said in 1897, and "promote a taste for reading of other kinds than stories." An 1898 survey of two-book systems showed nonfiction circulated 15 to 20 percent more than in libraries with a one-book rule. Within a decade, most libraries adopted the two-book system. Many used one color card for fiction, another for nonfiction. When children visiting the Louisville Public Library in 1906 told attendants they wanted "a good story" for one of their parents, the librarian sometimes sent them home with a work of history or biography. Upon returning, however, one child specifically said his parents "don't want nothing on the blue [nonfiction] card." But readers still found ways to subvert librarians' intentions. At the Jackson (Mississippi) Public Library, for example, circulation rules permitted patrons to withdraw two books at a time (one fiction, one nonfiction), but they could not return either on the same day they borrowed them—another ploy turn-of-the-century librarians invented to discourage rapid reading of commonplace fiction. That did not stop Eudora Welty. "Two by two," she later recalled, "I read library books as fast as I could go, rushing them home in the basket of my bicycle," then frequently returning the fiction book a day later.[9]

To address reader demand for popular fiction yet mitigate the cost of buying duplicates that subsequently sat unused on their shelves once they lost popularity, some libraries devised rental systems, thus replicating the circulating library model inherited from the eighteenth century. To objections that it should not be charging for books on a duplicates rental shelf, the St. Louis Public Library replied: "The Library contains several free copies of every title in the collection of duplicates; . . . the latter exists only as a convenience for those who prefer not to wait for their new fiction." In the late 1890s the Kansas City (Missouri) Public Library canceled its rental service; it did not fit the "idea and spirit of a free library," trustees insisted. At the "earnest solicitation of our patrons," however, the library reinstituted it a year later.[10]

Liberalizing circulation rules sent more patrons into open stacks, but they also brought problems. Generations of patrons were now forced to read narrow vertical book spines by uncomfortably contorting their necks. In addition, "The books on the lower shelves are too near the floor," griped one New Jersey reader in 1912. Because of prevailing fashion, "it is difficult, almost impossible, for a woman to kneel to read the books' titles." Another lamented: "No woman is tall enough to reach the books on the top shelves, and if she wears a 'hobble skirt' she cannot climb the little ladders that lean against the bookcases. You seem to think a woman should not be both well dressed and well informed."[11]

As more libraries opened their stacks, many also installed improved circulation systems. The Newark (New Jersey) Public Library's two-card system became the model. Basic components included a book pocket inside the book's back cover, a book card inserted in the pocket, a date due slip, and a borrower's card. When readers brought books to the desk they removed the book card from the pocket, signed it, and handed it to an attendant, who stamped a date on the reader's card, the book pocket, and the book card, which she then filed. To early-twentieth-century readers checking out library books, the resulting "thump, thump, thump" patrons heard became a familiar sound that ended a transaction. One youth vividly remembered "that marvelous, violet-stained date stamp" clipped to the end of a pencil his librarian would pull from "a bun on top of her head."[12] When readers returned books, a librarian stamped the borrower's card again, and replaced the book card in the book pocket.

Circulation desk encounters continued to provide librarians with humorous experiences. At an NYPL branch in 1903, for example, a small girl handed one librarian a note: "Please give this girl 'East Lynne.'" "East Lynne isn't in," the librarian responded, "won't anything else do?" The girl took the note, ran outside, and came back minutes later with another that read: ". . . or any other sad novel." Several days later a "'grave-looking boy' asked for 'The Hunchback of Not a Dam.'" "His innocence of any intentional profanity," the *New York Times* reported, "was so obvious that the assistant ducked her head under the counter to laugh." At another branch a lad insisted: "My brother wants 'The Three Mosquitoes,' by Dummass."[13]

And like previous generations, turn-of-the-century readers felt compelled to respond to materials public libraries provided. Marginal comments found in Chicago Public Library books in 1904, for example, included "lovely book" and "I think Reginald is a splendid fellow." Criticisms were briefer, a reporter noted, and politics and religion occasioned the most "bitter, and even profane" comments. Besides marginalia, readers left many items as bookmarks—bills, photographs, "love letters galore (some of which make one blush," noted a Detroit librarian in 1899), locks of hair, dress samples, and a dried human ear found in a medical book, probably placed there by a medical student.[14] Newspapers loved these kinds of stories and ran them often.

Many public libraries expanded services. In 1912 the Cleveland Public Library opened a "municipal reference room" in city hall that housed charters, ordinances, reports and statistics, clippings from 200 newspapers, and 25 magazines—all covering municipal affairs. Now "no ordinance need be passed nor any new plan tried," the librarian told the city council, "without full knowledge of what other cities have done and with what success." Some public libraries developed special services for the handicapped. The New York Public Library pioneered several. In 1912 a "Work with the Blind" department circulated 23,325 volumes to 806 "active readers" in thirty-seven states. "There is something of tragic poetry in this room," noted a visitor. "We see a young man, with quenched pupils, lofty of brow, his head thrown back, his eyes to Heaven, as if he hoped for the light. He is passing his slender hands feverishly, as though wishing to search the very depths of the ideas, over raised letters that are telling him of the deep, bitter sorrows of King Lear."[15] Municipal reference and work-with-the-blind services were important, but numbers served were nowhere near the millions reached by other initiatives, like traveling libraries.

"Say ma, she's a-coming' here!" shouted an Iowa farm boy in 1914 as an Onawa Public Library employee approached on horseback with a bag of books. Through traveling libraries new state agencies expanded service to rural Americans. In 1890, Massachusetts created a Free Public Library Commission "to promote the establishment and efficiency of the public libraries." Others followed, and by 1899, 32 state library commissions hosted 2,500 traveling libraries containing 110,000 volumes read that year by a million people. Traveling libraries went many places—lighthouses, lumber camps, rural schoolhouses, and farmhouse parlors. At one Ohio library station a reporter watched patrons hover over a newly arrived book box in 1897. "One dear old lady whose hair was silvered, whose hands bore the marks of toil, . . . stood anxiously by as the key was turned in the lock." With "eager hands" she sifted through the books before settling on one—a popular novel. "Oh, God, I thank thee!" she murmured as her "eyes were uplifted in praise, while hot tears bathed her face." The novel she selected, however, was a tease librarians used to lead her to the more serious reading in the box. Traveling libraries full of "solid reading" sent to 10,000 rural readers were, the Michigan state librarian insisted, "surely . . . refining and purifying the intellectual appetite." In 1898, the Wisconsin Free Library Commission (WFLC) monitored 34 stations that circulated 10,000 volumes; 22 were in farmhouses, 9 in post offices, 2 in country stores, and 1 in a railway station.

Urban public libraries also reached out to working classes through delivery stations. One "Free Reading Room" was mostly stocked with "light reading and picture papers," a Chicago reporter noted in 1900, to attract stockyard workers who "wade home from their day's work in blood." By 1902, Chicago's delivery stations had become so popular that 20,000 people signed petitions when officials cut deliveries from daily to three times a week. In 1907 the Los Angeles Public Library established deposit stations in places like telephone exchanges and department stores frequented by thousands of women.[16]

Public libraries also increased their services for children. Minneapolis opened a children's room in 1893. In 1897 Brooklyn's Pratt Institute Library opened a children's department. "Such was the passion and the wildness to see and enjoy these beautiful books," the *Christian Advocate* noted, "that the boys jumped in and out the windows, slid down the stair rails, and made such an uproar that the Pratt people were alarmed." To control mayhem, Pratt hired Mary Wright Plummer, "endowed with such patience and discretion and knowledge of the temperament of the children that she has become a guide to them in their reading." To staff the room and tell stories Plummer hired Anne Carroll Moore, who in the early twentieth century pioneered the field of children's librarianship.

To justify their need for children's rooms, many cited benefits these segregated spaces made possible. The children's room should be airy and bright, said a Milwaukee librarian in 1896, contain a variety of plants, have open stacks, small yet comfortable chairs and tables, walls large enough for framed pictures, and bulletin boards to hang children's artwork. "No wonder the children are happy here," the *Boston Daily Advertiser* reported in 1897: "pictures on the wall to look at, chrysanthemums blooming in the windows," and two cats, one named Mark Anthony, "who sits like a statue on the librarian's desk," the other Moses, who "sits on the top shelf looking down at the children." In 1913 a San Jose, California, librarian recognized her distinct advantage over schools—children came "because they want to, not because they have to."[17]

In Pittsburgh, librarians organized a Carnegie Home Library League, which provided 15- to 20-volume collections on loan for 4 to 6 weeks to carefully selected homes of "the poorer classes," and organized 11 library clubs in districts where it was difficult to find a home large enough for library groups to meet. By 1909 the library supported 22 deposit stations, 12 summer playground libraries, 23 home library groups, and 56 reading clubs. In total, it managed 228 distribution agencies that year. By that time the Cleveland Public Library had a Library League whose motto was "Clean Hearts, Clean Hands, Clean Books." In 1910 Cleveland had 62 home libraries; 11 were German, 10 Hungarian, 5 Norwegian, 2 Syrian, 2 Polish, 14 Italian, 6 Slovenian, and 3 Jewish. Selecting the right apartment to house them was essential. "It must not be one of extreme poverty, else the better class of children will not come," a librarian noted. "Nor must it be a whit too high above the average, else the poor children feel out of place." Once the St. Louis Public set up a home library in a three-room house in the city's Italian-American neighborhood, the librarian was regularly escorted on her weekly visits "over the muddy half-mile from the [street]car by a large delegation, . . . including eleven children, four dogs, and two goats." Other urban public library systems established similar home libraries.[18]

American public libraries also reached out to schools. In 1891 the Milwaukee Public Library invited every public school teacher to come to the library and pick out one book per student. If librarians thought the teacher included anything "unsuitable," she was helped to find better books. Librarians then sent the collections to the teacher's classroom. The first year 2,235 books circulated 6,728 times, the second year 4,351 books circulated 14,275 times, and the third 14,980 books circulated 42,863 times in 45 schools.[19]

While many librarians pushed to extend "for the greatest number" by age and ethnicity, few pushed to extend it by race. When the Atlanta Public Library opened in 1902, W. E. B. Du Bois asked the trustees why "black folk" could not use a free public library serving a city of 90,000, 40 percent of whom were black. "The spirit of this great gift to the city was not the spirit of caste or exclusion," he explained. "Do you not think that allowing whites and negroes to use this library," the board chairman responded, "would be fatal to its usefulness?" To Du Bois, the answer seemed "so distressingly obvious that I said simply, 'I will express no opinion on that point.'" Du Bois later noted the irony: "I am taxed for the Carnegie Public Library of Atlanta, where I cannot enter to draw my own books."[20]

In 1905 the Louisville Public Library opened a Colored Branch for the city's 40,000 blacks. "When we first opened, there were some of our race seriously opposed to the project," recalled a black assistant librarian. "The segregation idea was repulsive." At the same time, however, she recognized that "those of another race cannot know our wants, our habits, our likes and dislikes as we do. . . . It would be impossible for them to give us the service that one of our race can give in an atmosphere where welcome and freedom are the predominant elements." A Carnegie-funded building opened in 1908. From day one the branch had open stacks and intentionally collected black American literature. *Colored American* (not indexed in *Readers' Guide*) was the most popular periodical, *Up From Slavery* was the first book withdrawn. Other popular authors included black authors Charles Chesnutt, Frederick Douglass, Paul Lawrence Dunbar, and W. E. B. Du Bois. In 1913 the Houston Public Library also opened a Carnegie-funded Colored Branch. Local blacks raised funds to buy the lot and furniture. A year later the Gainesville (Texas) Public Library opened, allocating to blacks a reading room "on the lower level . . . with separate entrance." At the Fort Worth (Texas) Public Library, blacks could check out books but not sit at tables in the reading room.[21]

The public library's capacity for resolving turn-of-the-century disputes about what were acceptable reading materials in its collections was especially evident in interactions with Roman Catholics. In 1895 Portland, Oregon, Catholics complained that the library subscribed to no Catholic magazines, and of the 1,400 books the Dewey Decimal system classified as religion, none was by a Catholic author. A Fort Wayne, Indiana, priest was more forceful. Because Catholics were taxed to support the library, they should be represented on the board, he said, and any books attacking the church should be removed. A Denver bishop called public libraries "sinks of corruption" that "place within the reach of all classes the infidel teachings of Voltaire and the sensational dime novel." "All we want is fair play," an Atlanta archbishop argued; it would be "very sad if we, one-half the people of the city, paying our taxes, were made to suffer."[22] The archbishop said nothing about Atlanta's black people.

Catholics had a point; most public library founders were Protestant, and their cultural biases showed in the religious literature libraries acquired. But gradually, public libraries yielded. In 1898, the Providence (Rhode Island) Public Library issued a list of Catholic literature in the library in its monthly bulletin. "Attention is called to it as meeting the objection which was very properly raised." In 1904, the Milwaukee Knights of

Columbus (KC) authorized a *Catalogue of Catholic Books in the Milwaukee Public Library.* A Cedar Rapids, Iowa, KC chapter did the same. With the archbishop's approval, the St. Louis Public Library noted in 1910 that a list of Catholic works in the library would be published shortly.[23] Public libraries in the District of Columbia, Louisville, and Grand Rapids, Michigan, soon published similar lists of Catholic books in each library.

Libraries also continued to function as sites for resolving literary disputes, albeit seldom to anyone's complete satisfaction. Because one trustee objected, the Butte (Montana) Public Library banned Mark Twain's *Huckleberry Finn* in 1894. Although a 1905 survey of 3,000 Chicago children put *Huck* in their top twenty, the Brooklyn Public Library put *Huck* and *Tom Sawyer* on a restricted shelf because they were "unfit for youth." Public protest forced Denver and Omaha to do the same in 1902, and the Des Moines Public Library also "sequestered" the two. "Namby pamby public library boards," protested the *Omaha World Herald.* In response, Twain wrote the *World Herald:* "I am tearfully afraid this noise is doing much harm. It has started a number of hitherto spotless people to reading Huck Finn . . .—people whose morals will go to wreck and ruin now." Another letter to the *Denver Post* generated public pressure to get *Huck* back on library shelves. Once literary authorities agreed *Huck* deserved canonical status, however, librarians embraced him. Although not cited in the 1893 ALA *Catalog, Huck* did make the 1904 edition.[24]

At the turn of the century the Boston Public Library's Inferno contained 200 works the card catalog identified with one star ("the book cannot be taken away for use at home except by special permission of a trustee or the librarian") or two ("cannot be taken away under any circumstances"). There rested the works of Zola, Ouida, Balzac, Boccaccio, "and quite a collection of medical works," noted a *New York Times* reporter. Books dealing "too literally with tramps, detectives, police and the criminal classes" did not even make it into the Inferno, he noted; they were simply "rejected by the library." When the Watch and Ward Society took Boston booksellers to court in 1903 for selling Boccaccio's *Decameron* and Rabelais's *Heroic Deeds of Pantagruel*, the BPL had no worries. Both were in the Inferno, thus allowing the library to mollify two constituencies on either side of the debate.[25]

When Charles Lummis became Los Angeles Public Library director in 1905, he discovered an "Index Expurgatorious" his predecessors had established where they placed sensationalist novels. Other books in "purgatory" were works on Mormonism, Christian Science, socialism, anarchism, and Communism. "I have restored them all," Lummis bragged. A librarian's "personal creed, politics or literary taste . . . should not be allowed to play Czar to the users of books." Lummis also restored magazines his predecessors had pulled "solely because *too many people used them*" (emphasis his) and "were alleged to interfere with the readers of books." Authors in other libraries were not so lucky. In 1906 the Topeka Public Library pulled Upton Sinclair's *The Jungle*. The St. Paul (Minnesota) Public Library also withdrew the book, calling it "immoral." The *Duluth News-Tribune* noted the big meatpacking plant there: "St. Paul is known as a highly moral town when it comes to protecting its people from too intimate a knowledge of the inner workings of its great corporation." In 1910 the Minneapolis Public Library placed Robert Herrick's *Together* and H. G. Wells's *History of Mr. Polly* in its Inferno. "Books . . . questionable and lacking in qualifications of permanent literature are not even considered," the librarian explained.[26]

Some nonfiction printed works also troubled libraries. Unless one considers local community priorities, consistency is hard to find. In 1897, for example, the Newark (NJ) Public Library banned the New York *World* and *Journal* (Pulitzer and Hearst papers) because the "mass of filth" in its pages daily exerted a "demoralizing influence" on the library's readers. Within months, libraries in fifteen other cities across the country did the same. In 1913 Oregon socialists complained when the Bandon Public Library removed *Prison Memoirs of an Anarchist*, and a year later Oregon City librarians destroyed donated copies of another socialist publication as soon as they arrived. A trustee protested. "So long as it is carried (New Jersey) and delivered by . . . postal authorities and is demanded by the patrons," he insisted mayor of Two Harbors, Minnesota, complained in 1911 of a shortage of books on sociology and political economy in the public library, the librarian responded that 60 of 488 nonfiction books the Dewey Decimal system classified as sociology included Marx, Jack London, and Upton Sinclair, and works of opposition like *Critical Examination of Socialism*.[27]

Regional biases also brought protests. In 1899, the *Columbus* (Georgia) *Daily Enquirer* complained that in Civil War history books on public library shelves southerners were "invariably referred to as 'rebels,' invariably classed as ignorant, vicious, and cruel" people who wanted to destroy the Union and make slavery the foundation of an empire. The *Enquirer* called for inspection of the library and cited a "need for good, live juvenile works" by southern authors portraying southern realities—at least as the *Enquirer* perceived them. Similar protests occurred in the North. In 1905 a Somerville, Massachusetts, Union Army veteran found at his public library Charles L. C. Minor's *The Real Lincoln* (1901)—a "scourging of his beloved President by embittered southrons . . . blinded by prejudice," the *Boston Globe* noted. Other veterans also protested, and librarians quickly took it off the open shelf. When the *Boston Journal* discovered the same book at the Cambridge Public Library, one veteran immediately phoned the library. How could such a book be in a public library, he asked a librarian, who suggested a solution might be to place it in the library's Inferno. The veteran was not mollified, however. Days later, the title was withdrawn.[28]

But novels still perplexed librarians most. In 1890 the *Library Journal* published an anonymously authored "Fiction Song."

> At a library desk stood some readers one day,
> Crying "Novels, oh, novels, oh, novels!"
> And I said to them, "People, oh, why do you say
> "Give us novels, oh, novels, oh, novels?"
> Is it weakness of intellect, people, I cried,
> Or simply a space where the brains should abide?"
> They answered me not, or they only replied,
> "Give us novels, oh, novels, oh, novels!"
> Here are thousands of books that will do you more good
> Than the novels, oh, novels, oh, novels!
> You will weaken your brain with such poor mental food
> As the novels, oh, novels, oh, novels!
> Pray take history, music, or travels or plays,
> Biography, poetry, science, essays
> Or anything else that more wisdom displays
> Than the novels, oh, novels, oh, novels!
> A librarian may talk till he's black in the face
> About novels, oh, novels, oh, novels!
> And may think that with patience he may raise the taste
> Above novels, oh, novels, oh, novels!
> He may talk till with age his round shoulders are bent
> And the white hairs of time 'mid the black ones are sent,
> When he hands his report in, still seventy per cent
> Will be novels, oh, novels, oh, novels![29]

Indeed, fiction continued to make up 65 to 75 percent of books circulated at the turn of the century. The public library is a place, teased the *Idaho Statesman*, "where solid reading collects cobwebs and the light fiction stalls are congested with people who gallop through a book in search of the love scene." In 1915 one New York City official recommended that the public library purchase no more fiction. The *Tribune* agreed. It was difficult to justify spending money on *"trashy fiction"* (the newspaper's emphasis). Adopting the term "shiftless reader" to describe popular fiction loyalists, a Cedar Rapids library trustee reassured his community: "To this class we have never catered, because we believe the butterfly reader who flits from book to book . . . will in the end be unable to read anything seriously." Librarians added to the rhetoric. "The silly, the weak, the sloppy, the wishy-washy novel, the sickly love story, the belated tracts, the crude hodge-podge of stilted conversation, impossible incident, and moral platitude or moral bosh for children—these are not needed," John Cotton Dana said in his widely read *Library Primer* (1906).[30]

Some librarians saw things differently, however. *Library Journal*'s Helen Haines objected when librarians "who as a class sternly reprobate the reading of novels and yearn to see mankind . . . following the straight and narrow path." Another librarian claimed that failure to understand why readers of any age regarded books of imagination as so important constituted a failure to understand what culture really meant. He particularly bristled at the Progressive Era emphasis on efficiency that marked his times. "Figures are cold, the human element alone is really significant," insisted a Boston librarian in 1916.[31] In 1903 Dana surveyed thirty-four public libraries that he considered typical. Each identified fiction that circulated most in a three-day period. After reviewing the results Dana concluded the obvious. People wanted stories—particular stories for particular readers. Women "whose literary life is not unduly strenuous, who like a story of true love dealing with a manner of life not conspicuously different from their own," favored romance novels—all written by "proper, conventional . . . clean, even wholesome" authors. Men showed similar characteristics. Public libraries circulated 100 million novels a year, Dana noted.[32]

Commonplace readers frequently discussed the influence of commonplace fiction on their lives, albeit not in the library press. In 1911, for example, novelist Gene Stratton-Porter shared her fan mail. One recalled reading *The Harvester* (1911): "For five hours it held my thought, gripped my heart, and set my blood a-tingling, . . . till it seemed that I was in a fair way to choke with the emotions it evoked." A retired Princeton literature professor wrote: "My ten years of University teaching might have made me feel as snobbish as some professors about the best seller, but . . . since leaving, I have been learning to become a human being. There is something large and clean and stimulating in all you do that makes me prefer your work greatly to . . . our so-called 'modern' writers." Stratton-Porter chimed in: "I am desperately tired of having the high grade literary critics of the country give a second and at times third class rating to my literary work because I would not write of complexes and rank materialism."[33] Although it was the "high grade literary critics" librarians listened to as they compiled their prescriptive bibliographies, they still had to supply Stratton-Porter novels to the thousands who demanded—and so obviously loved—them.

Sometimes, readers described how their own public library addressed its community's different literary tastes. "Our town library belongs to the public in fact, as well as in name," wrote an Ohio resident in 1894. Her librarian hated French novels but was a "great reader of Pansy." Children were "the chief patrons" and could find there plenty of Horatio Alger and Oliver Optic. Evans was particularly popular with adult readers, who read her books "until their pages, redolent with tobacco and that indescribable combination of odors noticeable about old paper money, fairly drop to pieces." Among library users, she said, were "as many grades of literary taste as there are social circles, and each feels its superiority to some other." This small-town patron was also grateful for library services to the old and poor.[34]

But series fiction for youth continued to trouble librarians most. Solutions to this perceived problem varied. In 1896, for example, the Boston Public Library director appointed a volunteer "Fiction Committee" of twenty women. The committee did not select books, he said, "but gives such information in regard to them as will help the Library authorities to make a wise selection." Two members read every title considered, and if they did not agree passed it to a third. Recommendations then went to librarians, who made final decisions. In 1899 the committee read 467 books, and from the ones approved BPL bought multiple copies for the main library and branches. But the committee also bolstered the preferences of library officials, who in 1897 pulled books by Ellis, Fosdick, Holmes, Optic, and Stephens. Thereafter, the Children's Room had on open shelves books that "are mainly, of course, the better class of 'juveniles.'" "Better class" became a coded phrase all children's librarians recognized to exclude most series fiction. Boston's efforts encouraged others. The Milwaukee and Kansas City (Missouri) public libraries withdrew Bertha M. Clay and Laura Jean Libbey in 1897, same year the Enoch Pratt pulled Mrs. E. D. E. N. Southworth, Clay, Mrs. A. S. Stephens, and Dora Russell. Public libraries in Allegheny, Pennsylvania, and St. Joseph, Missouri, refused to replace worn-out titles by thirteen series fiction authors. "They are not immoral, but they are not literature," justified the Allegheny librarian, who called their readers "fiction fiends."[35]

Yanking series fiction was one ploy; pressure to "try this" was another. Some did this diplomatically. One reader recalled his village librarian "Fanny Crittenden":

> We revered her and we feared her, but where she counted most was at that circulation desk. She never insisted on anything; we just found ourselves choosing the books Miss Crittenden might enjoy date-stamping for us. At say fourteen, I'd approach her with a newly accessioned *Tom Swift*. . . . "My, my, I can't help noticing how grown up you've become lately,' she'd say. 'Yes, Miss Crittenden," I'd murmer. "And you're taking out a *Tom Swift* for your brother Ed, of course. Let's see now, are you two or three years older than Ed?" At that point I'd feel two or three years younger than my young brother, but there would be no more *Tom Swift* for a while. Time to move up a step, but not too many steps at a time. At say sixteen, I'd emerge daringly with an Elinor Glynn, then thought naughty. . . . "*Three Weeks* is a book you must of course read, but Elinor Glynn is a knowing woman and she would want you to come to her only after you had finished all of Walter Scott."[36]

Not all were as diplomatic as Fanny Crittenden, however. The "management reserves the right to refuse these books to borrowers who, in its judgment, are not proper persons to have them," noted the Atlanta Public Library in 1904. In 1911 the NYPL children's department banned Horatio Alger, Oliver Optic, and John Townsend Trowbridge—"scarlet poppies of reading," one librarian called them. Still, children learned to work the system for inconsistencies. In 1914 one twelve-year-old knew the "Tompkins Park Branch had all the Gypsy Breynton series; the Bond Street Branch the Hildegarde books; and the Ottendorfer Branch all the Patty series." When alerted to a new series title, she and a friend would watch the branch circulation desk most likely to stock it, and when some other girl returned it she would ask: "Please could we have that book?"[37]

To justify their position on series fiction, librarians' rhetoric soared. With much conviction but no evidence the Chicago Public Library director wrote in 1912: "The small boy who reads these thrillers . . . loses faith in himself and the world." Said the chief librarian of the Boy Scouts, "I wish I could label each one of these books: 'Explosives! Guaranteed to Blow Your Boy's Brains Out.'" Many members of the public agreed. "Sloughs of despond," one Ellenville (New York) citizen labeled series fiction. "An evil . . . affecting the children," said a *New York Times* book reviewer who despaired the practice among small public libraries that supplied generous amounts of Alger and Optic. *The Literary World* could not understand why every public library should not have an advisory committee like the one at the Boston Public Library.[38]

Some newspapers disagreed. The *New York Evening Sun* chuckled that a Boston "old ladies" committee condemned novels most readers wanted. The *Chicago Times-Herald* noted that books these "fiction fumigators" cited were available in many small-town public libraries. The *Omaha World Herald* wrote: "The gray-haired men of today" who read Harry Castlemon and Horatio Alger "years ago will readily testify that they had not only derived pleasure from reading them, but that they were helped to better living." In 1907 a *Detroit Free Press* editor insisted he knew many men who read Alger in their youth, and not one "met with any serious injury thereby. . . . Our libraries are in the control of too many foolish old ladies belonging to both sexes."[39]

Series fiction writers sometimes fought back. When the Boston committee called Edward Stratemeyer's highly successful *Rover Boys* series "clean rubbish—very cheap and melodramatic," Stratemeyer wrote his publisher: "I think I know more about what such books ought to be than does some person who has probably never written a juvenile in her life." Although his books were banned in Boston, Newark, and other big cities, Stratemeyer fared better in small-town libraries, where librarians ignored the canons that *Booklist* and the *Children's Catalog* replicated. "The public is the sole judge of what it wishes to read," the much-condemned Ouida wrote. Librarians "are not popes or police officers." William Heyliger, frequent essayist for the *American Boy* magazine and author of the popular young adult novel *Off Side* (1914), insisted that his books were good for adolescents and cited three librarians who applauded them. Yet *Booklist* would not review them. "So there we are," Heyliger concluded. "Men who ought to know say that my books are worth while. Librarians of the A.L.A. who ought to know say, by the inference of not recommending them, that they are not worthwhile. Which camp is right?"[40]

Although many librarians worried about the fate of "fiction fiends," real readers did not appear to lose faith in themselves or the world. In the century's first decade a young Dashiell Hammett devoured swash-bucklers and mysteries he could not get at his Enoch Pratt Free Library branch. Similarly, Baltimore teenager Zora Neale Hurston read through Horatio Alger, Bertha M. Clay and scores of other dime novels the Pratt refused to stock. "I do not regret the trash," she wrote later. "It was a help, because acquiring the reading habit early is the important thing." As an eight-year-old Kansas City boy in 1909, Walt Disney disliked classroom reading assignments but made good use of his public library. He loved Twain, but also devoured Alger and Tom Swift. When librarians at the Worcester Public tossed its Alger books in 1907, twelve-year-old Jimmie Maroney was incensed. "I've gotta pinch myself ter see am I awake," he told a reporter who mimicked his Irish accent. "I goes inner de children's library and shoves in me card for one o' Mr. Alger's books. Den I'm handed de frosty stare with one o' does 'Oh-yer-wicked-youth' glares, and gets me card back. . . . Cause why? His books is all tooken out cause dey ain't truthful an' is too sensational." In the wake of public protest, Worcester trustees discovered librarians had also tossed Oliver Optic. One trustee objected: "They were good enough for me to read, and they are good enough for the present generation to read."[41]

In the nineteenth century's last decade, Boston and Chicago opened impressive new libraries. Approaching Boston's new Copley Square building, said a writer for the *Christian Science Monitor*, was symbolic "of human ascent from ignorance to knowledge, from darkness to light." The Chicago Public Library crowned the best authors—all icons of Western literary canons—by chiseling their names on outside cornices. On the other hand, the New York Public Library evolved a unique profile. Established in 1895 as a free public reference library, it emerged from combining three corporations—the Astor Library, the Lenox Library, and the Samuel Tilden Trust—into a bifurcated institution: one part consisting of a circulation department supervising scores of local branches, the other part dedicated to research and housed in a Beaux-Arts building on Forty-second Street and Fifth Avenue. On the steps, two large sculpted lions named Patience and Fortitude took their place in 1915, and over the next century they sported holiday wreaths, found their way into product ads and onto a postage stamp, became subjects—and titles—of books, and wore baseball caps (one a Yankee, the other a Met) during the 2000 Subway World Series. By the turn of the twenty-first century they had become national symbols for public libraries and reading.[42]

Although the Boston, Chicago, and New York public libraries were impressive, it was Andrew Carnegie who had the largest impact on public library architecture before 1920. Between 1889 and his death in 1919, he gave $41 million to construct 1,679 public library buildings in 1,412 US communities. Carnegie's benefactions encouraged others to give. Between 1890 and 1906, philanthropists donated $34 million to fund library buildings. The generosity of corporate robber barons greatly accelerated the American public library movement, and public libraries strengthened community in myriad ways. In this they had Carnegie's blessing. "I trust you will not forget the importance of amusements," he said at the Braddock (Pennsylvania) Public Library dedication in 1889. The building contained two bowling alleys, eight billiard tables, a gymnasium and swimming pool, twenty-one bathtubs and twelve showers, a game room for checkers and chess, but no cardplaying—thus marking the limits of this library's morality. Its auditorium seated 1,000 and had

The public library in Hayward, California, is a typical small-town Carnegie Library building, but in Spanish adobe style. *American Library Association Archives*

cushioned opera chairs and an organ. In 1916, librarians estimated that half a million people had used the library since its opening—an average of 1,600 for every day it was in operation.[43]

This commitment to providing community space carried over to most other Carnegie library buildings. Because so many communities receiving grants asked for architectural advice, in 1910 Carnegie's secretary issued a pamphlet containing six recommended designs. Each included a lecture or community room that many then used as an auditorium, thus replicating the programming capabilities of successful mid-nineteenth-century social libraries. But Carnegie libraries differed from their social library predecessors, all put together by men. In the late nineteenth and early twentieth centuries thousands of women's club members—many had witnessed the "homelike" character of the 1893 Woman's Library—took responsibility for decorating the buildings. Readers noticed. In 1901 a "book lover" wrote the *Brooklyn Eagle*, "I wish to commend the atmosphere of culture and refinement which pervades" the Brooklyn Public Library. He noted the flowers on the circulation desk signifying "the good, the true and the beautiful," the "beautiful grouping of summer scenes" in the reading room (one aroused his "spirit of patriotism"), and in the children's room displays of butterflies, animals, and flowers that call "to the eye of the little folks the beauty of nature's realms." Many librarians—usually women—agreed. The library "should be managed in the broadest spirit of hospitality," argued the Minneapolis Public Library director in 1905. "The atmosphere should be as gracious, kindly, and sympathetic as one's own home."[44]

Some communities rejected Carnegie grants, however, often using the occasion to make statements. Justifications varied. Sometimes it was a matter of pride. Louisville did not need "a monument to beggary," the *Evening Post* insisted. Sometimes it was race. Because in the South many believed a Carnegie Free Library would have to admit blacks, the *Jackson* [Mississippi] *Clarion Ledger* happily noted in 1901 that "as yet no town in Mississippi has been Carnegieized." Mostly, however, it was class. "There will be one place on this great green planet where Andrew Carnegie can't get a monument with his money," said a Wheeling (West Virginia) union delegate when voters rejected a grant in 1904.[45]

But disputes about accepting Carnegie grants also demonstrated that public libraries meant much more to people than just access to useful knowledge. "Do these thoughtless cavilers . . . appreciate the civilizing effect of beautiful architecture and its natural accompaniment of flowers, trees, grasses, etc.?" asked the *Duluth News-Tribune* in 1902 when some local citizens groused about their Carnegie building. "Constant passing of this building is bound to develop in the humblest citizen a certain sense of the artistic and an unconscious desire to assist, even in his small way, in the effort for general civic physical improvement." And, the *News-Tribune* reminded readers, all work on the Carnegie-funded library was performed by Duluth artists and artisans, "which fact also should give us a thrill of local pride."[46] The editorial focused on the library's homelike atmosphere; nowhere did it mention best reading.

Big buildings impressed, but branch libraries frequently won deepest community loyalties because they focused on neighborhood needs. Shortly after the five boroughs consolidated into the City of New York at century's turn, Carnegie money erected sixty-five NYPL branches; each had community rooms. In 1910, for example, ten branches hosted evening English classes for foreigners. Boy Scout "battalions" of 80 to 100 met in two branch library assembly rooms, and at another a boys' Aero Club exhibited six model airplanes. In 1912, girls practiced needlepoint at one branch while one read aloud from books. For many, these branches functioned as second homes. Nearly all branches had full reading rooms on cold days when they were one of the few comfortable public places in the city, a librarian reported in 1911—especially important for twelve- to fourteen-year-olds who had no place else "equally wholesome to go."[47] The St. Louis Public Library reported in 1911 that owing to the "neighborhood character" of libraries, efforts to make them social centers had gone furthest in its six branches, where 139 organizations ranging from socialists to immigrant English classes to regular gatherings of the Daughters of the American Revolution met 1,404 times in 1910. When librarians asked young dancing party organizers why they used the Cabanne branch rather than a dance hall, one responded: "We all grew up in this Library." At another branch, librarians organized folk dancing classes.[48]

Many public libraries installed outside benches to foster conversations during pleasant weather. In Fort Worth, the nine benches on the library lawn became downtown "breathing spots"—places where the public could enjoy the outdoors. In the summer of 1898, the Brooklyn Public Library opened a "reading room" in a public park—a "library in a garden," *Youth's Companion* called it. Readers took books and magazines to read under the trees, noted *Outlook*, and turned it into a neighborhood center. By 1910 NYPL branches had five open-air, roof top reading rooms, especially cherished by children. The reading and fresh air that poor children experienced there, the *New York Evening Post* noted, contrasted sharply with hot summer days and nights they endured in crowded tenements and on steamy streets.[49]

In large part because they were among the few welcoming places in segregated Louisville that blacks could gather, the library's role as a neighborhood social center was much in evidence in the Colored Branches of the Louisville Public Library. The first black branch opened in 1905 and moved into a new Carnegie building in 1908. In 1914 library officials gave another Carnegie to a second black neighborhood, this one with three classrooms and a 350-seat auditorium. During one month in 1914, ninety-three meetings were held in the two buildings, including baby clinics, Sunday school training classes, story hours, and meetings of the Ministers' Alliance, Boy Scouts, Inter-Racial Committee, Bannecker Reading Circle, Dunbar Literary Club, Douglass Debating Society, Parent Teachers Association, Girls' Library Club, and the Urban League. "There are more colored people reading in Louisville now than in any time since the days of freedom," said one patron. In 1905, librarians also established classes to train black female (mostly southern) library workers who could get their training no other way, and who then found employment mostly in southern cities that like Louisville established black branches.[50]

As neighborhoods changed ethnic and racial profile, the public library—main or branch—often became a place where newcomers assimilated. Between 1893 and 1917 7 million immigrants arrived from southern and eastern Europe. Shortly thereafter, many showed up at public libraries—such as Mary Antin, a first-generation Russian Jew and future immigrant rights activist who as a child quickly found the library. "It was my habit to go very slowly up the low, broad steps to the palace entrance, pleasing my eyes with the majestic lines of the building, and lingering to read again the carved inscriptions: *Public Library—Built by the People—Free to All*. . . . All these eager children, all these fine browed women, all these scholars going home to write learned books—I and they had this glorious thing in common. . . . It was wonderful to say, *This is mine*; it was thrilling to say, *This is ours*."[51]

Public library newspaper reading rooms also functioned as community crossroads. "This is an American room," a Kansas City (Missouri) Public Library reading room attendant said as he observed readers' many ethnicities in 1907. And in 1904 a reporter observed the Boston Public Library newspaper reading room one Sunday. "There is a Pole reading the *Warsaw Gazette*, a German with a copy of *Berliner Zeitung*, a typical Slav with a

Because African Americans had few public places to gather in early-twentieth-century Louisville, the two "colored" branches of the public library system managed by Thomas Fountain Blue became community centers for active self-improvement groups such as the Douglass Debating Society. *Photo courtesy Louisville Free Public Library Collection, Accession No. 92.18.005, Archives and Special Collections, University of Louisville*

copy of *Novojo Vreinja* before him, and a group of Russian Jews reading the *Russky Vjestnik, Odesskaj Gazeta,* and one or two French newspapers edited in St. Petersburg. The readers civilly exchange the copies of papers and this often serves as a means of introduction between strangers."[52]

Amid the rustle of newspaper pages these rooms often showed humanity's pain. "Before she was halfway through" an Atlanta paper, a Georgia woman wept "silently to herself," one Boston librarian noted in 1901. "She tried not to let anyone see her, but one motherly old lady, sitting near, discovered her in tears, and the fair southerner told her that the paper made her so lonesome that she simply could not help it." The librarian also observed homesick strangers, unknowingly from the same town, meeting at the delivery table because both had asked for the same newspaper. In 1896 a Chicago Public Library guard noticed a derelict daily frequenting the room to look only at San Francisco papers. One day "his gaunt face took on an extra shade of pallor and he beat his head on the high desk and wept audibly." "Don't make noise in here," cautioned the guard. The man pointed to an article. His five-year-old son had fallen from a building two months earlier, and the papers had been following his condition. "I wrote to his mother day after day after the accident," he said, "but she has always returned my letters unanswered after she married again." The boy died, the guard discovered.[53]

Turn-of-the-century reading rooms remained havens for the homeless—"the nightmare of every library," the Milwaukee Public Library noted in 1915. Urban libraries routinely located reading rooms near entrances to minimize contact with children and adult readers. In Cincinnati and St. Louis, librarians even removed chairs to minimize loitering. At the Boston Public Library the homeless used toilets just outside the room "for their morning ablutions." Cleveland's newspaper reading room was "repulsive to the better class of readers," a clerk remarked in 1908. A Detroit trustee called the homeless "scum of the earth" and suggested moving the reading room to the basement—"good enough for them."[54]

As places, public libraries also regulated social conduct. Growing up in Jackson, Mississippi, Eudora Welty was afraid of the librarian, "her dragon eye" on the front door. "If she could see through your skirt she sent you straight back home; you could just put on another petticoat if you wanted a book that badly." Although early-twentieth-century parents considered public libraries safe places, as they were public spaces they also had downsides. In 1914, for example, San Jose, California, police arrested a thirty-four-year-old man for molesting schoolgirls in the public library. Sometimes patrons self-policed these civic institutions. At the Los Angeles Public Library, one irritated patron followed a persistent cougher to the lobby, where he promptly gave the offender a "swift kick, delivered in the vicinity of his coattails."[55]

Besides best reading, children's librarians also advocated cleanliness. The Pasadena (California) Public Library located its juvenile department next to a lavatory. "Any youngster who appears with unclean digits will be requested to step to the washstand and clean up before drawing a book." But children still figured out ways to subvert library goals. When asked why they reappeared with clean hands so quickly after being told to wash, one child answered: "We just licked 'em." To an NYPL branch librarian, another lad with soiled hands protested: "I was born that way." Said yet another: "The wind blew the dirt on 'em between home and library."[56]

To capitalize on the public library's potential to foster community, many librarians stepped outside conventional practices to meet a community need. In 1917 the Virginia (Minnesota) Public Library installed a kitchenette in the basement to demonstrate efficient modern meal preparation to farm wives on their Saturday shopping trips to town. The Chisholm (Minnesota) Public Library purchased a sewing machine for local sewing circles. "We are conducting a social center library in a town of 5,000 people, more than half Mexicans," a Corona, California, public librarian noted in 1917. She needed "all the loose pictures and colored illustrations" she could gather. "Until they learn English, pictures talk to them better than books or people."[57]

Public libraries also frequently hosted art exhibits. In 1902 the Dallas Public Library opened its Art Room—the state's first free art gallery. In 1905 the Clinton (Iowa) Public Library hosted a week-long exhibit sent by a Chicago art gallery. Nearly 7,000 visited, many of whom had never before been in a library. In Cedar Rapids, the public library purposely organized a Library Art Association to bring in exhibits. For one 1908 traveling exhibit, the librarian reported, hundreds of children came daily. And shortly after the New York Public Library opened in 1911, officials were surprised at the thousands who weekly visited its galleries.[58] Some libraries also housed museum collections. In the Omaha Public Library, the Western Art Association managed the top floor. To it William Thompson donated his scalp, rescued from an Indian attack he survived near Omaha in 1867. The library still has the "piece" and on occasion brings it out for exhibit. In Perry, Oklahoma, one patron was especially generous to the museum the Carnegie housed. He donated several stuffed specimens: a badger caught near Perry, a pea fowl from a local farm, two pelicans from a visit to Orlando, an ostrich egg, a Louisiana baby alligator, and the head of a fifty-pound Arkansas River catfish he had caught. Other gifts from locals included a corn stalk with nine ears, a chair made from Texas longhorns, and a locally raised four-foot gourd. However, the library museum turned down a large cuspidor used around town in previous decades.[59]

Other public libraries were equally creative with use of space. In 1905, the St. Cloud (Minnesota) Public Library bought two checkers and chess tables for the smoking room in its new Carnegie building. Five years later the Marion (South Carolina) Public Library served as the site for the Civic League's May Day flower show, while Kearney (Nebraska) Civic Club used the public library basement to observe Baby Week. The State Board of Health provided information, an insurance company donated booklets on child care, and the library compiled a bibliography on baby care and feeding. A thousand families attended. In 1912 the Cleveland Public's West branch sponsored a neighborhood Health Campaign. The auditorium sported charts by the Anti-Tuberculosis, Visiting Nurses, and the Babies' Dispensary; a dental clinic met two mornings a week in a library club room.[60]

Libraries also became sites for political activities. On May 2, 1913, NYPL's Fifth Avenue steps became a reviewing stand for a suffragette parade of 20,000. That same year the Columbus (Georgia) Public Library hosted National Association Opposed to Women Suffrage chapter meetings, and a lecture by a National Equal Suffrage Association member. So did the Butte (Montana) Public Library. In 1916 the Portland, Oregon, public library hosted a mass meeting for twenty-three eastern suffragists touring the country. In one Texas town, however, a citizen complained that the female librarian routinely distributed suffrage literature to every adult patron who approached the circulation desk.[61]

The public library also reinforced regional politics. In the South, the Franklin (North Carolina) Public Library annually sponsored a lunch for Confederate veterans. Annually, the Columbus (Georgia) Public Library celebrated Robert E. Lee's birthday. The Anaconda (Montana) Public Library devoted story hour to Abraham Lincoln every second Saturday in February. About the same time, the Duluth Public Library hosted a Lincoln Day mass meeting for recent immigrants, and at the Pawtucket (Rhode Island) Public Library children hailed the flag on the Great Emancipator's birthday. There were not only celebrations, but also decorations. As visitors looked around the Greensboro (North Carolina) Public Library Children's Room in 1911, they experienced "lessons of patriotism and heroism." On one wall were portraits of George and

Martha Washington, a picture of Mount Vernon, and portraits of John J. Audubon, Frances E. Willard, and Robert E. Lee. Lincoln was not represented.[62]

"Use of the public library auditoriums for the spread of the SPOKEN word is quite as legitimate as . . . use of reading rooms for the dissemination of the WRITTEN word," wrote the Gary (Indiana) Public Library director upon moving into a new Carnegie in 1912. In 1914–1915, the District of Columbia Public Library reported auditorium meetings of the Woman's Single Tax League (six meetings, average attendance 164), the Housekeepers' Alliance (attendance 307), Washington Readers' Club (381), Intercollegiate Socialist Society (376), German Readers' Club (640), the "Wanderlusters" (413 attended a lecture on "Our Common Birds"), and the Washington Theosophical Federation (348).[63]

As community centers, public libraries sometimes functioned as sites for arbitrating disagreements about public art. Always people worried about the potentially prurient. When the Queens (New York) Public Library's Elmhurst branch put up photographs of Michelangelo's *David* in 1909, the Women's Christian Temperance Union complained; police promptly confiscated the pictures. "I'm not going to have any exhibitions of shady pictures around Elmhurst," said one officer. In the late nineteenth century, however, no American public library experienced as much controversy over its public art as Boston's. In 1894 the city council asked the library to remove a seal with nude male figures from the new building's exterior. The request occasioned much debate. For the next several months, the *Globe* noticed, thousands passed by to stare at the nude figures, which they "alternately admired and denounced." Months later the BPL rejected the council's request; the nudes stayed. A second controversy erupted in 1897 when many objected to Frederick MacMonnies's nude statue of Bacchante commissioned for the building's inner courtyard. For months the controversy played out on the front pages of local and national newspapers. The *Boston Daily Advertiser* approved the statue, but the *New York Evangelist* said it "typified an immoral existence." Ultimately, the library bowed to public pressure and shipped Bacchante to New York's Metropolitan Museum of Art—at least temporarily.[64]

Often citizens engaged controversial issues in American public libraries. In 1916 birth control activist Margaret Sanger planned a transcontinental lecture tour, including Minneapolis. "You won't get six people to come out to hear you" in America's "most conservative city," friends told her. Sanger went anyway and lectured at the public library. "To my surprise the audience was one of the largest on my schedule, . . . and hundreds of chairs had to be brought in to take care of the overflow." Although socialism frightened many Americans, in 1907 a Salt Lake City Public Library audience heard Daniel De Leon, editor of the Socialist *Daily People*. In 1908 the Duluth Public Library entertained the "Question Club," at which a socialist debated a "single tax" advocate. "The debate became so warm at times as to include personalities," reported the *Duluth* (Minnesota) *News-Tribune*, "and many members of the audience interposed questions and arguments that helped materially to increase the chaos in which the matter was left when the meeting was closed." At the St. Louis Public's Barr branch in 1915 and 1916 the Missouri Socialist Party held four-day conventions, while at the Crunden branch the Young People's Socialist League met monthly to study Marx.[65]

This period also witnessed the arrival of the moving picture. Some librarians resisted. Now the library also "had to counteract the lure of the nickelodeon with its moving pictures that often arouse a morbid curiosity," one Iowa librarian complained in 1911. Others, however, welcomed the new medium. The Cleveland Public Library noted in 1915 that it routinely followed local movie theater announcements because movies created "a remarkable demand for books." In 1915 the Madison (Wisconsin) Public Library operated a moving picture show in its auditorium; so did the Ithaca (New York) Public Library, although the librarian complained that peanut shells and popcorn littered the floor after each showing. The Cincinnati Public Library circulated hundreds of lantern slides a day in 1909 to churches, schools, and women's societies, and discovered the slides increased the circulation of history and travel books. That same year the Portland, Oregon, public library purchased stereoscopes and sets of "stereoscopic tours" of Egypt, European countries, Canada, China, and the United States. Both could be checked out like a book.[66]

Improved technology in musical recordings also influenced public libraries. In 1909 the Cedar Rapids librarian pushed her community to start a musical society, then begged library funds for a piano and a pianola. The library's auditorium would be a great meeting place, she said, where the society could "lead the young people's minds to a higher and higher plane of enjoyment." A year later a piano company donated 480 music rolls; within months the library circulated 1,837. In 1910 the Virginia (Minnesota) Public Library purchased a Victrola and fifty records, then turned the reading room into a Sunday afternoon concert hall. Seven thousand attended that first year. In 1916 public libraries in five other small public libraries with new Carnegie buildings housing community rooms did the same.[67]

American public libraries were a major beneficiary of Progressive Era activities. By 1917 few questioned their social and cultural value; most parroted the rhetoric that justified them. In "centuries to come, when historians of an enlightened world shall look backward to determine the chief factors which made for progress from a state of barbarism to the higher civilization," noted the *San Francisco Chronicle* in 1900, "the present epoch" would be known as "the age of the public library." No other influence "is so widely uplifting." The *Los Angeles Times* agreed. That "the standard of intelligence and culture was never higher among the mass of the people" was "largely due to the remarkable development of the public library system."[68]

Between 1893 and 1917, the United States shifted from an agrarian republic to a world industrial power. Cities grew, incomes rose, millions of immigrants diversified the population, but at the same time injustices moved many to protest their plights (sometimes violently) and seek redress of grievances. A belief in Manifest Destiny led private capital and government power to conquer the West, exploit its resources, and subjugate its peoples, while the South settled into a Jim Crow society that denied basic rights to millions of black Americans. Railroads and automobiles, telegraph and telephone—all helped people connect as never before; electricity transformed their lives. Also helping them connect in the midst of this dynamic environment was the American public library. Since the organization of the American Library Association in 1876, the number of public libraries increased from 1,101 to 2,849 in 1917. Per user they circulated twelve books per year.[69] And the vast majority of books both youth and adults checked out continued to be fiction.

By 1917 the growing numbers of American public libraries had taken their place with museums, concert halls, and parks as public spaces designed to construct and celebrate local community. Public library buildings became familiar spaces that organized reading and social experiences by a set of rules reflecting middle-class norms. In them individuals could pursue social mobility, immigrants could assimilate, and young people could publicly display the acceptable behaviors they had learned there—or suffer the consequences. For ordinary people, public libraries had become valued places that provided moral guidance people wanted and promised a set of variable rewards they came to expect, all within a shared environment where they felt privileged—in part because by force of numbers they had already put their stamp on the contents of this civic institution they did not have to use. In many respects, the services public libraries offered, the physical spaces they provided, and the stories they made accessible became essential equipment in many people's everyday lives.

When Arthur Bostwick described this evolving civic institution in his influential *American Public Library* (1910), he saw it as an active neighborhood center that brought books together with readers in cheerful and attractive buildings offering homelike decorations. Public libraries also managed well-organized and bibliographically controlled stationary and traveling collections, open shelves, children's rooms, long hours of opening, cooperative arrangements with local schools, and in its meeting rooms and auditoriums hosted community meetings, lectures and exhibits. With "the thousand and one activities that distinguish [it] from its more passive predecessor," he said, the "modern library" serves "the entire community, not merely . . . those who voluntarily entered its doors."[70]

CHAPTER FIVE

"Habitations on a Literary Map": 1917–1929

Between August 1914 and April 1917, the United States remained a neutral power in World War I, but as civic institutions, public libraries were inevitably affected. In late 1914 the Pawtucket (Rhode Island) British Relief Society met at the library to figure out ways to help the Allies. In Duluth, pacifists insisted that the library purchase books on peace to counter information the library had on war. After the *Lusitania* sank in 1915, the Oyster Bay (New York) Public Library discarded a portrait of Kaiser Wilhelm II donated by Theodore Roosevelt a decade earlier. When the Kansas City (Missouri) Public Library mounted a map of the war in Europe in the lobby in 1916, "war fans," as the *Kansas City Star* described them, crowded around it during lunch hour to discuss military movements. "The mighty international struggle . . . has generated a chronic craving for war literature," noted the annual report of the Detroit Public Library, and partisanship showed. "Numerous readers have vented their deep-rooted racial feelings in terse annotations discovered in books and journals."[1]

Once the United States entered the war, however, any pretense of neutrality disappeared. The public library became, one librarian said, "an active instrument for propaganda." To purify their collections, many librarians used the "Army Index"—a list of pro-German and pacifist materials the army did not want in training camp libraries. "There will be a better atmosphere about the Public Library," the *Oregonian* said in 1918, "now that books of German propaganda have been interned." At the Boston Public Library, patrons requesting books listed in the Army Index were told they were "missing." They received the same response at the New York Public Library and the Redlands (California) and Huntington Beach (California) public libraries. The Fort Wayne public library removed everything in German published after 1914. In Butte, Montana, local officials burned all public library books in German. The Cincinnati Public Library not only discontinued circulating German books but it also removed Hearst newspapers because they opposed the war. When the Fulton (Missouri) Public Library discontinued subscriptions to its local newspaper for showing "disloyalty to the present administration," the *Kansas City Star* protested. Three days later the library barred the *Star* too.[2]

Not all public libraries followed suit. The Dallas Public Library retained all 278 German-language books on central library shelves. "We can see no reason why those German works which have been on our shelves for years should be discarded at this time," the board argued. When an anonymous letter-writer accused the Belleville (Illinois) public librarian of "pro-Germanism" because the library subscribed to local German-language newspapers and periodicals, the *Belleville News Democrat* came to his defense—they were "silly and ridiculous charges," it said.[3]

During the war, American public libraries eagerly circulated federal government war information and opened their buildings to all types of war work, including Americanization programs to more quickly assimilate immigrants—especially German Americans. Because providing food to fighting forces overseas forced Americans to conserve at home, American public libraries adopted food conservation as a program priority. The Dallas Public Library, for example, hung posters made by public school children advocating food conservation. "They are attracting much attention and will be really educative to the public mind," noted the librarian. "Knowledge Wins" posters also went up in libraries across the country to advocate book collection campaigns for soldiers and sailors. Through participation in the war effort, the library solidified its niche among American public institutions. "The war put the public library on the map," Chicago Public Library director Carl Roden later declared.[4]

At the same time, however, the war modified the profession's ideology of reading. Because librarians eagerly participated in three national campaigns to collect millions of donated popular books—what one Minnesota volunteer labeled "decent but not too highbrow"—for servicemen at home and abroad, librarians had to temper their criticism of commonplace reading. They were reluctant to dispute an authority as powerful as the federal government. Besides, much of this fiction was being serialized in periodicals like the *Saturday Evening Post* and *Ladies' Home Journal*, to which libraries routinely subscribed, or in newspapers edited by community leaders who regularly rubbed elbows with library board members. Thus, by war's end, library leaders generally came to accept that at least for adults the "light" reading they had disparaged for a half-century fell somewhere between good and bad, and was at most harmless.

Between 1917 and 1929, librarians continued to focus on "the best reading for the greatest number at the least cost." Much involved improving services. Although familiar library equipment remained, new elements were introduced. In 1925 the New York Public Library began a photostat service. More significantly, the telephone transformed reference services. In major cities, public libraries set up separate telephone installations where staff consulted a revolving ready-reference bookcase to answer questions, first come, first served. More than half of all public libraries also had rental or "duplicate pay collections" of popular fiction. The Galesburg (Illinois) Public Library considered its rental collection "the solution of the fiction problem" because it minimized the need to purchase duplicate copies. Rather than waiting for a book in high demand to become available, noted the Cedar Rapids Public Library in 1922, many people preferred rentals.[5] Improving efficiency showed in other ways. In 1919 the American Library Association adopted an interlibrary loan code—a uniform communication system linking a requesting library with a library holding the item a patron requested.

Other activities further standardized professional practices. In 1923 Minnie Earl Sears published *A List of Subject Headings for Small Libraries*, which followed a common vocabulary the Library of Congress (LC) used for its subject headings. The list became staple fare in thousands of small public libraries. Some changes were evident. W. E. B. Du Bois's *Souls of Black Folk*, for example, had been reclassified from 325—"Colonies and Immigration" to 326—"Negroes."[6] Thus, twenty years after Du Bois's book was published the Decimal Classification recognized black Americans as a "class," so when members of the Banneker Reading Circle or Douglass Debating Society browsed the 326 shelves at Louisville's two "colored branches" in 1927 they also found, among many others, Benjamin Griffith Brawley's *Social History of the American Negro* (1921) and Alain Le Roy Locke's *The New Negro: An Interpretation* (1925). Nonetheless, racial biases persisted. Among its indexes, Wilson covered no black periodicals or newspapers—not the black branch favorite, the *Colored American*, Marcus Garvey's *Negro World* (weekly circulation

200,000), nor the *Chicago Defender* (circulation 280,000). Few non-black branch public libraries subscribed to any of these serials.

The bibliographic structure designed to filter "best reading" grew. Many libraries now ordered books through jobbers such as Baker & Taylor and A. C. McClurg, which enabled them to pay one invoice for many titles; at the same time, however, jobber inventory automatically constrained the universe from which they made choices. Most public libraries also followed an acquisitions routine the Brookline (Massachusetts) Public Library outlined in 1926—the librarian regularly screened *Booklist*, ALA *Catalogs*, and Wilson Company guides like *Book Review Digest* and *Fiction Catalog*; read reviews in periodicals such as the *Saturday Review of Literature*; and watched popular stock at a local bookstore for cues on his rental collection.[7] New guides also appeared. The *Horn Book* (started in 1924) focused on children's literature. In 1922 children's librarians began recognizing books they judged best with the Newbery Medal.

Despite librarians' efforts to identify best reading, readers often made selections based on a book's condition. "If the pages were worn and dog-eared," said one twelve-year-old NYPL branch patron in 1923, "I knew I had a winner." Her selection practices mirrored others. "How do you select a good book from the library?" a San Jose public library patron asked a friend in 1921. "I look at the slip of paper where they stamp the date," she responded. "If it is all stamped up," she knew "people couldn't put it down until they'd finished it."[8] Patrons also continued to talk to library books. In a Columbus (Georgia) Public Library book titled *The Riddle of the Universe* one reader inscribed: "There is no hereafter; I know it absolutely." In an encyclopedia article on marriage another wrote: "I wish I was married." At the Nantucket (Massachusetts) Public Library, a well-tailored man who covered the margins of book pages with comments "was seriously grieved when informed . . . that his decorations were unwelcome. . . . He really believed that he had added to the value of the work."[9]

Book theft also drew several responses. "Samuel Wardlaw, Special Investigator, Los Angeles Public Library," said the man approaching a reader he caught concealing a title as she walked out the door. "If you don't mind, will you please return it to its proper place on the shelf and we'll say no more about it." Embarrassed, the patron complied, then hurried away. In a *Los Angeles Times* interview, Wardlaw recounted his daily grind, including pursuit of delinquent borrowers, identifying thieves (including a clergyman and movie star), and monitoring "cranks and eccentrics." Some investigations "led to perpetrators with rooms full of other stolen goods; others led to mentally disturbed patrons who argued spirits were responsible for stealing books that somehow found their way into their possession."[10]

By 1920, the United States had nearly 6,000 public libraries, almost one-third built with Carnegie money. (When Andrew Carnegie died in 1919, libraries across the country closed for one hour during his funeral.) Although half the population across the country could access public libraries in 1920, in rural America only 17 percent had local library service. To address their reading needs, some librarians advocated county library services like California's, where books from centrally located libraries were delivered by bookmobile or parcel post. To get reading materials to cannery workers, the Juneau (Alaska) Public Library sent books and magazines by boat. In Hibbing, Minnesota, the public library ran a truck filled with books that even in thirty-below-zero weather visited every mine and work camp once a week, and all schools every two weeks. In western Montana, in 1921 the Anaconda Company built a 14 by 40 foot "library car" that the Missoula Public Library stocked to circulate among the company's lumber camps. In 1926 a reporter observed several young "giants of the forest" leave the car with six books tucked under their arms. The Greenville (South Carolina) Public Library offered bookmobile service to immigrant English and Scottish millworkers living on the city's outskirts. Many adults were illiterate, but their children who attended school loved bookmobile visits.[11]

At a roadside stop in rural Louisiana a mother of five at first refused bookmobile service. When asked why, she said she saw no value in reading books. Once told she could borrow them for free, she changed her mind. At another rural Louisiana location, a bookmobile librarian reported, a teenager "tore pell-mell from the field where he was at work" when he saw the vehicle. Because he was the only one in his family with enough literacy skills to write letters, he had determined to be the family scribe. Not all welcomed the service, however. When the Durham (North Carolina) Public Library bookmobile stopped at a farmhouse in 1926, several people "feared for their soul's welfare if a novel—anathema of Satan—be allowed to enter their homes."[12]

Urban public libraries also extended delivery services. In 1920 the Evanston (Illinois) Public Library started an "auto library, . . . which you can hail in the street to get the book you want." The bookmobile also made regular stops. "No longer are the people shy of the 'library lady,'" the *Independent* observed. "The tired eyes of the women have a new light in them as they crowd round her, while the children greet her vociferously. Even the men-folk, who at first kept out of sight, now regard the occasion as a red-letter day." In 1925 a lad pushing a cart loaded with Boston Public Library books rang a bell to announce its biweekly arrival. Depending on the neighborhood, the cart might contain books in Chinese, Greek, Yiddish, Italian, or English. In 1927, the New York Public Library began book wagon service in the Bronx. "To see the bright green wagon mounting over the brow of the hill," said one reader, caused "voices of children . . . to be lifted up joyfully with a corresponding raising of spirits" of adults. "It's like a kindergarten," a child observed as he watched a librarian set up a table loaded with picture books. "More like a picnic," said his brother.[13]

The war accelerated another library service—outreach to hospitals. When the Sioux City (Iowa) public librarian returned from the war he crafted a hospital service modeled on military recuperation facilities. "I'm

Messenger boys wait for the Cincinnati Public Library to open, about 1924. For a fee, boys delivered books to patrons' homes in Cincinnati. *From the collection of the Public Library of Cincinnati and Hamilton County*

not nearly so lonesome since I can have books to read," one patient told a librarian as she wheeled a book cart from ward to ward. One mother commented: "You have surely brought much sunshine to my son," a long-term patient. By 1925, the library also provided services to patients and inmates in thirteen other city and county health-care and social welfare agencies.[14]

But segregated public library services continued to limit the numbers served in the Jim Crow South. As long as *Uncle Tom's Cabin* remained popular in libraries north of the Mason-Dixon line, complained an *Atlanta Constitution* columnist in 1928, sectional animosity would endure. Public libraries that stock this "colossal libel upon the southern people," he wrote, nurtured a "serpent of sectionalism." These attitudes met no ALA resistance. After the war, the executive secretary reassured the ALA's southern members that the Carnegie Corporation had acquiesced to their position on race and required communities seeking grants to base their appropriations requests "only upon the white population of the towns." The secretary also reassured southern librarians that the idea that "negroes have the right to ask for the privileges" of a Carnegie library was a "misconception."[15]

When Thomas Fountain Blue, the director of Louisville's two black branches, delivered a paper at a meeting of an ALA Round Table on Work with Negroes in 1922, he became the first black American to address an ALA conference session—forty-six years after the association organized. The Round Table subsequently studied library services to black Americans and found that "demand for properly trained colored librarians is increasing." In 1925 the Carnegie Corporation announced it would follow an ALA recommendation to fund a library school at the Hampton Institute in Virginia, a leading college for blacks, to train librarians for the "colored branches of city library systems." Ernestine Rose of NYPL's Harlem branch and Howard University's E. C. Williams protested strongly, albeit privately, to the National Association for the Advancement of Colored People (NAACP), arguing that "before long colored librarians from all parts of the country would be debarred from the regular schools and shunted off to Hampton," which would "probably mean a lower standard at the school." The NAACP agreed, and protested to the ALA and the Carnegie Corporation against the establishment of a "segregated library school." Despite this opposition, the Hampton school opened in September, and for the next thirteen years its graduates found jobs in southern segregated and northern ghettoized public libraries serving black Americans.[16] In 1940 the school moved to Atlanta University, where it produced nearly 90 percent of black librarians working in late-twentieth-century American libraries.

Despite Jim Crow, quietly but persistently blacks continued to push for public library services. In response, the Birmingham (Alabama) Public Library opened a black branch in 1918. Three years later Atlanta used a $25,000 Carnegie grant, matched it with $10,000 in city funds, $10,000 in county funds, and $5,000 from white citizens of Atlanta to open a black branch on Auburn Avenue. It quickly became "a center for many activities" among local blacks, and "the building itself a thing of beauty in their community," noted the branch's black library director. The yard was "planted with shrubbery and flowers, and we want the whole appearance of the building and its surroundings to set a standard for their homes."[17]

Some blacks subverted Jim Crow public library practices, however. In 1927 nineteen-year-old Richard Wright puzzled over how to access the Memphis Public Library collections. As a sixth grader in Jackson, Mississippi, he marveled at a *Chicago Defender* article describing "Lake Michigan Negroes" who went to public libraries and took out any book they wanted. In Memphis, however, blacks could not patronize the central library except to get books for white people employing them. One morning he approached a white co-worker. "I want to ask you a favor," he whispered. "What is it?" "I can't get books from the library. I wonder if you'd let me use your card?" The white man balked. "You're not trying to get me in trouble, are you, boy?" Eventually, he agreed, and after pledging Wright not to mention to the other white men what he had done, he gave Wright his wife's card.

> That afternoon I addressed myself to forging a note. . . . *Dear Madam: Will you please let this nigger boy*—I used the word "nigger" to make the librarian feel that I could not possibly be the author of the note—*have some books by H. L. Mencken?* . . . I entered the library as I had always done when on errands for whites, but I felt that I would somehow slip up and betray myself. I doffed my hat, stood a respectful distance from the desk, looked as unbookish as possible, and waited for the white patrons to be taken care of. When the desk was clear of people, I still waited. The white librarian looked at me. "What do you want, boy?" As though I did not possess the power of speech, I stepped forward and simply handed her the forged note, not parting my lips. "What books by Mencken does she want?" she

asked. "I don't know, ma'am," I said, avoiding her eyes. . . . "You're not using these books, are you?" she asked pointedly. "Oh, no, ma'am. I can't read."

The ploy worked; the librarian delivered copies of Mencken's *Prejudices* and *A Book of Prefaces*.[18]

While southern blacks continued to experience resistance to obtaining public library services, other groups fared better. After the war some urban public libraries developed special services directly for teenagers, often coordinated with the public schools. The New York Public Library's Supervisor of Work with Schools stressed class visits (she made 250 in 1926), reading guidance, trained staff, and library sites specifically designated for youth, including the Nathan Straus branch for young adults. To run it NYPL hired Margaret C. Scoggin, who used the "lab" library for teenagers to pioneer youth services that urban public libraries replicated nationwide. In 1925 Jean Roos set up the Cleveland Public Library's Robert Louis Stevenson Room for young people. She worked with other community organizations to develop library services to youth, especially immigrants who no longer attended school. She also sponsored an art group and a poetry group.[19]

By 1922 people under eighteen accounted for most use of American public libraries, in part because libraries expanded services to elementary and secondary schools. In Milwaukee, for example, the public library provided 2,237 separate book collections to public and parochial schools—"essentially a proper function of the public library," a 1922 report emphatically stated. At mid-decade, all eighth-grade students visited the library during the year for a lecture on library service and a tour of the building. As a writing exercise, in 1921 District of Columbia schools asked children of recent immigrants to discuss public library books they checked out. "My mother and father liked the books so they read the books too," wrote one. "My father read nearly all of them," wrote another.[20]

At the Des Moines Public Library 2,400 sixth- and seventh-graders visited the children's room in 1925. In Davenport, the public library supplied 150 classroom libraries containing 8,000 books to the city's schools. "We are sure through these . . . schools library books went into homes not reached before," librarians said. In Cedar Rapids, librarians challenged schools to see which could bring in the most new patrons, and on a 1928 summer Saturday gave a book party at which 300 children dressed as their favorite book characters. The Los Angeles Public Library held a similar event in 1929. Photos in the *Los Angeles Times* showed many Asian American children among Anglos who took part in the celebration.[21]

In the 1920s librarianship introduced a new professional—the readers' advisor, or RA. Like mid-nineteenth-century reading conduct manuals, the reader's advisor promoted purposeful, productive reading through a systematic process that favored useful knowledge and high culture literature. The RA's job, said an NYPL reader's advisor, was to "prescribe" books. In 1924 William S. Learned published *The American Public Library and the Diffusion of Knowledge* (a Carnegie-funded report), which claimed that through readers' advisors public libraries could function as active agencies in adult education. As "community intelligence centers," public libraries would serve as antidotes to agitating "soap-box orators" plaguing urban street corners (in the early 1920s the country was in the midst of its first "Red Scare," and Learned was worried).[22]

In most metropolitan public library systems with the service, a full-time RA skilled in the use of bibliographic tools and reviewing sources interviewed readers to discover their goals, interests, and capabilities. After the interview she compiled a bibliography tailored to the reader's needs, then kept records for follow-up consultations. Sometimes RAs also worked with groups by designing prepackaged reading courses. To support this professional initiative, in 1925 the ALA began publishing ten-cent "Reading with a Purpose" bibliographies.

In 1922, the Milwaukee Public Library named a "Chief of Adult Educational Service" to work with city agencies to bring the Beer City's 30,000 workers (not coincidentally the socioeconomic group many authorities considered most vulnerable to soapbox orators) to the library. The chief developed an information index of the city's adult education opportunities, ensured that relevant books made it to branches hosting evening classes, and interviewed "every individual contemplating serious reading." Use of the code word "serious" told the profession that RAs would not create bibliographies of westerns, mysteries, or romances. At the Los Angeles Public Library, the Adult Education Department had five librarians staffing two desks located in the rotunda. One was general information (i.e., traditional reference), the other readers' advisor. At her elbow the RA had up-to-date lists of Los Angeles–area adult education courses, and a stack of "Reading with a Purpose" pamphlets for sale. By 1929 the library had sold 300,000 copies. Two years after the Buffalo Public Library's Readers' Bureau opened, patrons had requested

2,337 specific reader courses, 309 of which followed "Reading with a Purpose" bibliographies. By 1929 nearly fifty other urban public libraries adopted similar services. Only a small percentage of enrollees stayed the course, however. Of 417 patrons who approached the Boston Public Library readers' advisor in 1928, 81 started courses of recommended reading; 21 finished.[23]

Not everyone welcomed this new service. A "Fiction Reader" complained to the *New York Times* in 1926 that the new service was evidence that all libraries "are trying to decrease the proportion of fiction in circulation and to force the circulation of 'serious' books." In 1929 a Brooklyn Public branch librarian who was pressed by system administrators to fund RA services and reduce popular fiction acquisitions argued that these priorities were driving people away. "We have only to consider the rental libraries flourishing everywhere to realize that fiction-reading is not dying out, but that fiction-readers are going where they can get what they want, without any great delay."[24]

But public library leaders reasoned that facts helped create knowledge and ground prudent decisions to vote, to build, to invent, and to purchase, and the kinds of information disseminated in reference works and by readers' advisors was much more important than the needs of a female romance or male western reader. In the 1920s useful knowledge remained at the center of the library profession's agenda, governing its structure and practices. And librarians saw plenty of examples to justify these priorities. Millions of people continued to use America's public libraries to acquire knowledge highly useful in their lives.

When DeWitt Wallace moved to New York City in 1922, he spent many days in the NYPL periodical room copying out articles from magazines he later used to start *Reader's Digest*. In 1925 Willa Cather spent two weeks "incognito" at the Denver Public Library researching *Death Comes for the Archbishop*. In Tahlequah, Oklahoma, young Cherokee Woodrow Wilson Rawls, who later penned bestselling children's books *Where the Red Fern Grows* (1961) and *Summer of Monkeys* (1976), discovered his local public library just off the reservation. "I read everything I could get my hands on pertaining to creative writing," he later recalled. "I didn't just read those books, I practically memorized them."[25]

But patrons in quest of useful knowledge—at least as they defined it—sometimes pushed too hard. For example, a mid-1920s crossword puzzle craze placed unusual pressure on library dictionaries. More than 500 people daily sought to use NYPL's 150 English-language dictionaries, according to one librarian's tally. Los Angeles Public Library officials set a five-minute limit on their use. "We will go insane if this crossword puzzle craze doesn't stop," one librarian said. For some patrons, certain facts in public library books threatened the social order. "If the liquor traffic is to be abolished," complained an Akron citizen before passage of the Eighteenth Amendment, "our public libraries should . . . clean from their shelves all books that tend to harden, stupefy, demoralize, confuse and mislead the public." On the other hand, at the Duluth Public Library books on how to make beer and bathtub gin suddenly became popular once the amendment passed.[26]

After World War I hostilities ceased, public libraries continued many of the censorious practices they had begun during the war that the federal government had endorsed and accelerated. "Library censorship is a benign necessity," an "essential part of every librarian's work," wrote John Cotton Dana in 1919. Because of limited funds, all public libraries exercised two kinds of censorship, he said—one of "exclusion" (books not purchased) and one of "seclusion" (tomes sent to the Inferno). In postwar American librarianship few voices emerged to fight either kind—the profession was still largely blind to the vital role it played in mediating a constantly shifting center for local public culture. Helen Haines told a California Library Association audience in 1924: "The duty of the librarian is selection, not censorship"; Scott and Dickens were once considered "trashy" writers, she reminded her listeners. Many titles sent to public library Infernos in the Roaring Twenties—Sinclair Lewis's *Main Street* (1920), F. Scott Fitzgerald's *This Side of Paradise* (1920), John Dos Passos's *Three Soldiers* (1921), Theodore Dreiser's *An American Tragedy* (1925), Ernest Hemingway's *A Farewell to Arms* (1929)—were later judged part of a very rich literary decade.[27]

Yet few librarians acknowledged the Inferno's essential value. When US Customs seized a copy of the *Decameron* one bookseller had imported from London in 1929, the bookseller noted many public libraries had copies any adult patron could access. He neglected to say that most were in public library Infernos. By this time librarians had also begun dropping "Inferno" from their professional lexicon and replacing it with "permissions shelf." The purpose was the same, however. In 1927 NYPL's Jennie Flexner advised librarians that circulation of contested books had to be limited to adult readers who, in their judgment, would use them intelligently. "The book card for this type of book bears a signal for the staff which should be unobtrusive and not readily noticeable to the general public, since an indication of restriction may whet the appetite of the reader."[28] In other words, buy it, but hide it and be quiet about it so only a few people know the library has it.

Examples of these practices abound. When a Chicagoan went to the public library in 1927 to borrow Voltaire's *Candide,* a clerk whispered to him that this author's books were banned. Library rules did not allow "permission shelf" books out of the library, and only people over twenty-one were allowed to use them in the library. The Duluth Public Library established a "purgatory shelf" for any books "that have brought pious objection from one or more moral, upright, tax-paying citizens as contrary in sentiment to the moral principles that should be taught young people." In 1920, titles in "purgatory" included Elinor Glynn's *The Reflections of Abrozine,* three of five Dreiser titles the library owned, and Balzac's *The Harlot's Progress.*[29]

In 1921 several public libraries banned Henry Ford's anti-semitic weekly, The *Dearborn Independent,* which they received free from the publisher. "Propaganda," the Lynn (Massachusetts) Public Library director called it. The Boston Public Library never accepted the *Independent.* The *Christian Science Monitor* criticized all these libraries. Ford's magazine was not "propaganda," but a "point of view," and the fact that it circulated weekly to 300,000 people demonstrated that people wanted it. "Prejudice can never be a true guide to right action in the matter, if public libraries are really to be free." The Carnegie Library of Pittsburgh, where the *Independent* was used heavily, refused to ban it, despite protests from prominent Jews. "It seems to me essential and self-evident that a public library must not refuse entry to any printed materials of interest to the public which is not subversive of law and good government," the director noted, "or is not generally . . . injurious to our moral standards of living."[30]

In the postwar period the United States witnessed fewer Catholic protests against public library bias, but worries about sin lurking in the stacks continued. As always, controversy stimulated library book circulation. When the Scopes trial started in Tennessee, Darwin's *Origin of Species* became highly popular at the Lexington (Kentucky) Public Library. Darwin's works had gathered dust on the Atlanta Public Library's shelves before the trial, noted the *Constitution,* "but now the dust has gone and librarians are struggling to provide sufficient material to meet an excited public taste." At the Boston Public Library, however, evolution drew little interest. Boston readers, said one librarian, took evolution for granted.

The title's popularity, however, did not mean readers understood what the book contained. At an NYPL branch, one patron asked for Darwin's "Oranges and Peaches."[31]

In the 1920s a wave of anti-British sentiment spread across the country as pundits questioned US participation in World War I, some even suggesting the country had been duped by British propaganda. In 1922, a Boston city councilman called on library trustees to remove Webster's dictionary because it contained matter "as British as London Bridge." As evidence he cited the definition of "constitution," which did not reference the United States. More serious, however, was Chicago mayor William Thompson's 1927 threat to ban pro-British books from public library shelves, and a trustee's threat to burn them. Because Andrew Carnegie was a well-recognized Anglophile, Thompson saw Carnegie libraries as tools to evolve an "international mind" essentially British in nature. "Our national greatness was achieved, not by one, but by many nationalities," he wrote the library board.[32]

The situation was awkward for several reasons: Queen Victoria and many English organizations had donated books to the public library after Chicago's devastating 1871 fire, the American Library Association was headquartered in Chicago, and library director Carl Roden was ALA president that year. Newspapers and citizens writing letters to the editor complained frequently. "Ignorant was the mildest of the words used to describe the people of Tennessee for trying to dictate" in the Scopes trial what the public schools should teach, wrote one citizen. Now Chicago's mayor was trying to dictate "what we grown, free citizens shall read in the library."[33]

A moment of drama occurred on October 26, 1927, when Thompson sent an aide to the library with a list of four titles he considered Anglophilic. Roden met the aide, showed him the library's "permission shelf" ("here in a dark hidden closet," the *Tribune* reported, "are locked obscene volumes and others considered unfit for general circulation"), then suggested if the volumes he found were determined objectionable they could be sequestered there. After checking the card catalog the aide retrieved the four titles—Albert Bushnell Hart's *The American Nation—A History* (1907), Willis Mason West's *The Story of American Democracy* (1922), and C. H. Van Tyne's *Practice of American Ideals* (1905) and *The Cases of the War of Independence* (1922)—and withdrew them on his library card.[34] But there the controversy ended. Because of the public outcry his actions brought, the mayor chose not to pursue the matter further and eventually the brouhaha withered; no books were burned, and when returned, the four titles went back on open shelves.

The postwar "Red Scare" that concerned William Learned also affected American public libraries. In 1919, newspapers carried a story about an anarchist facing deportation who claimed his ideas came from books he read at the New York Public Library. "The youthful exponent of terrorism explained that many other boys and girls freely read similar literature," the *Pawtucket Times* reported. The next day a reporter visited the Free Library of Philadelphia and found the same works had been checked out. But the library stood firm; books would stay on open shelves. Books are like mirrors, explained the director; "the reader sees in it exactly what he wants to see." In 1920 the Long Beach (California) Public Library director deliberately ordered Soviet literature so the reading public would have information "on all sides of the subject." On the other hand, when two Industrial Workers of the World (IWW) members were arrested for posting literature on a Eureka (California) Public Library bulletin board in 1918, the library said nothing. In 1920 public libraries in Springfield, Massachusetts; New Haven, Connecticut; and Salt Lake City removed "Bolsheviki" books from circulation.[35]

The library profession had modified its attitude toward popular fiction after World War I ("harmless" was an adjective many used to describe it); this became obvious when the ALA openly solicited "fiction of the adventurous-romantic school" for soldiers in postwar hospitals and demobilization camps, even mentioning specific authors—Zane Grey, Edgar Rice Burroughs, Rex Beach, Mary Roberts Rinehart, Gene Stratton-Porter, and Harold Bell Wright—all banned or not collected by many public libraries before the war. *Bookman* magazine began publishing monthly lists of books demanded at public libraries across the nation. "The similarity of the lists is amazing," the San Jose *Evening News* noted. "Often they don't contain more than nine or ten different books in the whole lot." Compilers of the *Fiction Catalog*'s 1923 edition forewarned librarians that it "includes, for the sake of the average reader, some recent novels the permanent worth of which is open to question."[36]

Efforts to use circulation rules to limit fiction reading continued. Before the war the Los Angeles Public Library allowed patrons to withdraw three books at a time; all could be fiction. After the war, the library extended the limit to five, but only two could be fiction—with little effect, however. Although nonfiction circulation increased 7 percent, fiction still accounted for 74 percent of the total. The Grand Forks (North

Dakota) Public Library circulation rules were typical. "To stimulate the reading of better books," one said, anyone could "take out two books at a time, providing one . . . is not a story." At a New York Public Library branch circulation desk in 1922 one lad explained the two-book rule to a friend—"You may have one book you want and one book you don't want."[37]

Although fiction still accounted for 65 to 75 percent of circulation, in the Roaring Twenties readers wanted more mysteries and westerns. Many public libraries complied. "Sometimes we feel that all we need to do is to fill the shelves with mystery and western stories," a St. Louis Public branch librarian reported. At the Albuquerque Public Library, demand for westerns was so heated the library bought every volume it could. When LAPL shelved the mystery and western genres separately from other fiction, the practice not only "pleased the public" but it also increased demand.[38]

Other libraries, however, resisted. "We will not bow our heads in shame if unable to satisfy the butterfly mind that dips into the 'best seller,'" insisted the Detroit Public Library director in 1929. To "promote a better grade of reading," the Los Angeles Public Library created a fiction department headed by a "principal" (miming formal education's hierarchy in elementary school) who prepared annotated catalog cards (many annotations lifted directly from *Booklist*) and guided lists, and segregated certain titles as recommended. "No effort has been made to increase the quantity of fiction circulated," the fiction department principal reported in 1921, "but the purpose has been in many ways to direct readers to better books." Other urban public libraries followed LAPL's example.[39]

But some librarians showed empathy, if not understanding, for commonplace readers. Residents of Detroit's West Fort neighborhood, the branch librarian noted, were not highly educated. All day women tended family and home, "too completely engrossed in their own little kingdoms to be interested in many of the new movements of the day." Men were employed "in some monotonous, mechanical job, which so tires them physically that they are unable to satisfy their hunger for breezy, outdoor life and adventure except by an eager perusal of the pages of Rex Beach or Zane Grey. If we want them to read at all," she concluded, "we must give them what they want. . . . In a neighborhood where there are no playgrounds, no community centers, and no public parks, . . . we feel that a Branch Library would be justifiable if it existed purely as a Recreational agency and circulating NOTHING but fiction."[40]

Public librarians certainly acknowledged reader demand but seldom indicated that they comprehended reader motives beyond "entertainment." Instead, experts outside the profession had to explain. "Yes," the detective story constitutes "escape; but it is escape . . . from literature," Smith College literature professor and mystery reader Marjorie Nicolson wrote in 1929. "We have revolted from . . . long drawn-out dissections of emotion to straight forward appeal to intellect; from reiterated emphasis upon men and women as victims either of circumstances or of their glands to a suggestion that men and women may consciously plot and plan; from the 'stream of consciousness' which threatens to engulf us in Lethean monotony to analysis of purpose controlled and directed by a thinking mind," she claimed, but "most of all from a smart and easy pessimism which interprets men and the universe in terms of unmoral purposelessness to a rebelief in a universe governed by cause and effect. All this we find in the detective story." Too often "critics are mistaken," wrote Jeannette Meehan, Gene Stratton-Porter's daughter, in 1928. "They sit, smug and secure, barricaded by their own self-sufficiency, and write criticisms, bounded by their own scope of knowledge and their own experience."[41]

Meehan spoke for others. In 1927 a student at the Bryn Mawr Summer School for Women Workers maintained: "The highest use of books is their use as friends. . . . There arises within us a feeling of personal contact and fellowship with the characters of a book." Most of the 1,500 summer school alumnae who attended this school over a seventeen-year period obtained their books at a public library. One student described an occasion in 1927 when her priest saw her with a public library copy of Herbert Spencer's *Study in Sociology* and lectured her on socialism's threat to Catholicism. The student chafed. "I felt capable of judging for myself whether a thing was good or bad for me," she recalled. Another student focused on reading as escape, and like early-twentieth-century literary scholar Marjorie Nicolson, quickly complicated its definition. "Sometimes, in the land of Novels, I would see strange peoples, witness struggles between heart and mind. There I would hear things which my heart had often felt but could never have spoken. Always, after locking the door to these strange lands, I felt that something in me had been satisfied. My possessing this magic key somewhat made up for my dull world." For her and people of her class—if this group of readers is indicative—commonplace reading enhanced their lives, fed their aspirations, and provided comfort and companionship. They had little desire to mark cultural status with literary knowledge.[42]

Although public library leaders were much more comfortable with the kind of "middlebrow" reading profiled by the Book-of-the-Month Club that emerged after the war, they were not sure why. Nonetheless, what readers got from middlebrow fiction matched what Bryn Mawr readers got from popular fiction. "What you've done for us is to give us a habitation on the literary map," wrote one reader to middlebrow fiction author Dorothy Canfield Fisher. About Fisher's *Rough-Hewn* (1922) another reader wrote in 1922: "I judge you were writing for . . . the average person—and not for tired literary experts." Others found in Fisher's fiction a "friend" for lonely times. Because of domestic constraints, "I could not go out and find the friends I longed for," wrote one. "So I grew to love and count on those I found in books. And it happened that the best of all were the ones you gave me."[43] Literary authorities might label as escape the reading of Bryn Mawr students and Fisher's middlebrow fans, but that word cannot capture the multiple benefits these readers obtained from stories they chose.

And choose they did. By the mid-1920s a common phenomenon occurred at public libraries in factory towns. Every Saturday morning adolescent girls showed up with a market basket, which the *Christian Science Monitor* noted in 1924 was "becoming a badge of culture." Typically they would ask for a couple of love stories, a couple of western books and a "fairy book"—standard family reading fare on Sunday, a common laborer's one day of rest. Librarians knew Gene Stratton-Porter, Harold Bell Wright, and Grace Richmond qualified for the former, not Sherwood Anderson, Sinclair Lewis, and Willa Cather. They also knew Zane Grey was usually the desired western author, if the library had any of his books on the shelves. As for the fairy book, the little girl picked her own, regulated though she was by literary boundaries that children's librarians imposed on collections. Then off she went, satisfied she had fulfilled her responsibility to her parents at the same time she had exercised her own power to choose.[44]

But when a 1926 ALA poll of 36,000 children in thirty-four cities revealed that 98 percent named a book by the hugely popular series fiction author Edward Stratemeyer as their favorite, alarmed children's librarians countered. Some developed programs for Children's Book Week, an annual event established in 1919 by an alliance of librarians, publishers, and book dealers to promote "good" books. Mary Root took another approach. For *Maryland Library Notes* she compiled "Not Recommended for Circulation," a list of sixty-one separate series, including all books by Horatio Alger, Martha Finley (the *Elsie Dinsmore* series), Harry Castlemon, Oliver Optic (pen name of William Taylor Adams), Edward Ellis, and Edward Stratemeyer. The following year several state library association journals reprinted Root's list; Minnesota's *Library News & Notes* even called it "a warning" to librarians.[45]

Some booksellers objected. When the *Wilson Bulletin* reprinted Root's "Not Recommended for Circulation" bibliography in 1929, the proprietor of a Boise, Idaho, bookstore took exception. "Why worry about censorship, so long as we have librarians?" he asked. "True, these worthy arbiters of our literary pablum cannot haul an author into court for offenses against their esthetic preferences, but they can—and do—exercise a most rigid censorship over what the dear public shall—and shall not—read." Was it librarians' place "to tell men and women who enjoyed those books when they were young, that their children shall not be allowed to read the same titles?"[46]

And then there were youthful readers themselves. As a recent immigrant, six-year-old Isaac Asimov obtained a New York Public Library reader's card in 1926. He read "omnivorously and without guidance," but because he could not find everything he wanted there he also frequented newsstands where he discovered the science fiction stories NYPL refused to stock. In Dixon, Illinois, young Ronald Reagan visited his public library twice a week in the early 1920s, mostly to check out popular series fiction he often read on the library's front steps. Although these authors were not available for circulation to adolescents at the New York Public Library, when the library exhibited a donated collection of 1,300 dime novels in 1922 newspapers across the nation covered it. "An absorbingly interesting assemblage of a pioneer literature which has now wholly vanished, but which for a generation exercised a profound influence on the country's thought, character and habits of mind," the NYPL *Bulletin* noted. The *Bulletin* said nothing about how professional librarians had railed against these tomes for two generations.[47]

In postwar America people's desire to establish new public libraries did not abate, even if that meant finding unconventional spaces in which to house them. In Huntington, Utah, a jail was converted into a public library in 1921. In nearby Bingham, children circulated through the town requesting book donations to a library opening in a former police station. In 1929 the North Western Railroad donated a car to Adams, Wisconsin, for a public library. But traditional Carnegie libraries continued to own the stereotype. "In any middle western country town there are buildings impossible not to recognize," wrote novelist Helen Hooven Santmyer in *Ohio Town*. "All Carnegie libraries are so alike that one's memories hardly seem associated with an individual set of yellow-brick walls . . . and granite steps."[48]

When a Chicago reporter visited Atlanta, Illinois (population 1,100), in 1926, he noticed on the village green "an ivy-clad, pillared structure with the words 'Public Library' deeply carved into the massive pediment above the portico." It's "the bone and flesh . . . of the community," he wrote. "It functions in every fiber of the town's being." In 1924, when the Boston Public Library opened its interior courtyard for noontime readers, hundreds flocked to this quiet location in a noisy city. "They have brought with them the most diverse tastes," librarians noticed, "and they have been of the most diverse types themselves." A reporter noticed "a blue-overalled workman . . . sits placidly content in the peaceful surroundings. Equally serene is a colored man who sits at the end of a bench contemplating the fountain and the pigeons, to whom a more energetic occupant . . . is scattering peanuts."[49]

After reviewing annual reports of department and branch heads in 1925, the Detroit Public Library director declared his institution "a civic laboratory." One librarian recognized that laborers living in a single boardinghouse room came to the library evenings to "enjoy the impersonal association that comes from being with others who are enjoying the same thing at the same time." Another noticed that amid the city's dreary streets "the library stands out as the only example of good architecture, surrounded by a beautiful lawn." Los Angeles Public Library officials noted in 1920 that the use of the library by high school students seeking quiet spaces or old men reading newspapers might not count in circulation statistics, but they did recognize that as centers of "community activities and local organizations, branches serve a purpose almost as important to the public they reach as is their primary purpose of book distribution"— maybe even more important than book distribution. In 1920, Cleveland Public branch club rooms hosted 2,703 meetings attended by 43,017 people; in addition, 55,213 children attended 1,225 story hours.[50]

For no group was the library's role as community place more important than for black Americans in the segregated South. Speaking to a Hampton Institute audience in 1927, Thomas Fountain Blue, director of the Louisville Public Library black branches, said that as a community center, the black branch contributed "to the public peace by providing a public meeting place, free from political and partisan influences; . . . to the public welfare by providing for social workers, representing different denominations, a suitable meeting place free from sectarian bias"; and "to the welfare of the community by providing for our boys and girls a suitable place for amusement and recreation, without which many would be denied this privilege." It also contributed to "the educational, professional, business, and social uplift of the community in that it has provided for teachers, doctors, and businessmen and women an acceptable meeting place, where they can hold their conferences and discuss problems under pleasant and cultural surroundings," and "has been a means of reaching other groups and making new readers."[51] Although largely ignorant of this history, scores of unknowing white American librarians have reinvented Blue's concept of the "library as social center" for every generation since.

During and after World War I, many of the 6 million black Americans who emigrated from the South moved into urban northern neighborhoods. "There is no mistaking what is going on; it is a regular exodus," reported the *Cleveland Advocate* in 1917. For the most part, however, black Americans were not welcomed; as a result, what public library services they received tended to be ghettoized in neighborhoods where they lived. Still, public library branches serving them often provided an important means for black Americans who made the Great Migration to improve their lives. In 1920, for example, Cleveland librarians noticed the "migration of negroes brought many hundreds" to the Sterling neighborhood, where they "huddled together, victims of over-crowding, awful living conditions, and general profiteering." In 1921, branch librarians observed many were, "like the uneducated from abroad, slow-minded and present problems of various sorts." With increased contact, however, white attitudes changed, and librarians reached out. By 1925, librarians were working with the Health Council of the Negro Welfare Association to promote hygiene. Meetings held in public library club rooms were well attended.

In 1927 librarians started a "Negro Progress in Print" corner. Black patrons "are interested in knowing who their writers are and of what they write," librarians reported. "It gives them a renewed self-respect and tends to a greater self-understanding." Although "books of spirituals are always in circulation and collections of Negro poems are seldom seen on the shelves," Quincy branch librarians noted, circulation was not so important. Blacks made "broader use of the branch as a social center." "The Negro's development and increased sense of race pride," branch librarians observed, "is more and more manifest and the branches are working to keep step with this progress."[52] No longer were librarians using the term "slow minded" to describe black Americans. While black branches in the South had from their origins established themselves as social centers, in the North migrant blacks who frequented branches in their neighborhoods turned them into social centers that not only helped assimilate black readers into their new environments, but they also made it possible for white librarians to experience the richness of the black cultures these migrants brought with them.

Pittsburgh's Wylie Avenue branch had similar experiences. "This class had no ideas beyond the fact that they wanted a book and realized that they were not equipped for life in their new surroundings," a branch librarian reported in 1920. Four years later librarians noted that these new patrons—"but sixty-three years removed from slavery"—regarded the library as "their only education, cultural, even recreational opportunity. . . . Uneducated adults are pathetically anxious for spellers, grammars, American histories, and easy reading books. . . . Night school classes are almost entirely colored." At the branch, black women organized social clubs, many of which then studied race achievement. Reading groups also formed. One read Du Bois's *The Souls of Black Folk,* another Chestnut's *The House Behind the Cedars,* a third Dunbar's *Life and Works.* "The growth of Negro writers during the last few years is amazing," one librarian commented.[53]

Spaces in public libraries serving largely white populations also found new uses. To attract more men, for example, the Buhl (Minnesota) Public Library organized a "smoker." "All hunters who have stored up a crop of new deer stories are asked to be in attendance." In Chisholm, Minnesota, the American Legion fitted the library's auditorium with chairs and rockers, a billiard and two pool tables, reading and writing tables containing daily and weekly newspapers and magazines, a phonograph, and cigar and candy cases. In 1920, the Los Angeles Public Library opened a men's reading room and a backroom for mostly male checker players, where multiple games were usually in progress, all observed by an ever-shifting group of mostly male onlookers.[54]

Deportment rules for public library use continued to vary across the country. Although male Venice (California) Public Library users were allowed to go coatless in the reading room, not so at NYPL, where "no matter the temperature," the *Times* reported, the rule for wearing coats "can have no exception. If one coat is removed, a hundred coatless men will soon be seen and this," librarians felt, "makes for a distracting lack of dignity." On a hot 1926 summer day, however, one reader tested the rule by entering the building sporting a shirt, "undeniably clean but open at the throat." A guard stopped him. When the reader protested, the guard led him to the director's office, where he learned that the long-standing rule could not be changed.[55]

In some cases the library's public spaces allowed users to display acceptable public behaviors, including romantic behaviors. On the Fort Worth (Texas) Public Library grounds, for example, the local newspaper reported in 1922 that "spooners" found benches "a favorite place for intimate conversation at dusk." Few people realize, the *Chicago Tribune* wrote in 1926, "that this severe aloof building is the meeting place . . . of many pairs of lovers; that under its towering roof many romances blossom." In some cases, however, the library's public spaces became sites for unacceptable social behavior. To discourage "petting parties," in 1925 the New York Public Library illuminated the front terrace between Patience and Fortitude after 10 P.M. In 1920 female San Francisco Public Library staff members working in the stacks experienced a "startling grasp of the hands," reported the *San Francisco Examiner*. "Strange men have been disappearing in the corridors, simultaneously with the molestations."[56]

Rules governing patron behavior were sometimes unintentionally funny. "Only low talk is permitted here," one reading room sign said. "Please do not sneeze into the books," read another. In 1926 the St. Louis Public Library reading room posted its rules in a prominent place. One stated: "Periodicals would not be given into dirty hands," and to assist patrons the library provided soap, towels, and a washstand in the room. "A washstand and roller towel was easy to manage," a librarian reported, "but the soap was difficult, as nothing seemed too small to carry away. We finally made small bags of strong net in which we enclosed the soap, securing it with strong linen thread, attaching the whole to a chain which was firmly anchored to the washstand. This worked fairly well, though at intervals soap, chain and all disappeared, leaving only the stand."[57]

In 1924 Congress passed the National Origins Act, which reduced to 164,000 the number of aliens allowed to enter the country annually; three years later it banned all Asians, capped the total number at 150,000, and restricted immigrants from any one country to 2 percent. As a result, the number of immigrants fell from 4.1 million in the 1920s to 528,000 in the decade following. Despite that action, many public libraries still functioned as places to assimilate first-generation immigrants. "Upon the public libraries rested largely the responsibility of transforming the aliens into loyal and patriotic Americans," the *Christian Science Monitor* observed in 1922. "Among the numerous agencies at work for the foreign-born population in this country," the *New York Times* wrote six years later, "public libraries are one of the most effective though least conspicuous."[58]

In St. Louis, US naturalization officials regularly distributed cards to applicants that outlined public library services; the library also hosted Visitors' Nights, organized by nationality, for foreign-born residents. "Americanization classes are more and more a community activity," a Cleveland branch librarian noted in 1921. The Lorain branch hosted 56 Americanization classes for 1,465 people of 15 nationalities. To those who said the "America our fathers knew" was threatened by immigrants, a branch librarian insisted, the public library actually helped immigrants "adopt those moral and social principles which characterize what we vaguely glimpse when we say 'My country.'"[59]

In 1929 the Denver Public Library worked with the Denver Art Museum to sponsor a series of branch programs featuring the cultures of local immigrants. Their breadth of coverage and sensitivity to local immigrant cultures was impressive:

> In Globeville where the population is made of Polish, Russian, Austrian, Czecho-Slovakian and other nationalities, the exhibit was made up of gay scarves and jackets richly embroidered and some brasses. In the Dickinson Branch where the community is largely Jewish the exhibit was brass candlesticks, samovars and copper pans and kettles of most unusual shape. They also had hangings from the Balkan States, embroideries from Rumania and wrought iron candelabra from Spain. . . . Decker Branch had a Dutch settlement and the predominating note in the exhibit was old silver, china, and some carved wood besides rare caps and laces from Holland. Broadway Branch made a specialty of handwoven coverlets, quilts, and old bottles. . . . Park Hill had early American furniture and rare old samplers. Woodbury Branch had a chest bound in scarlet leather and studded with brass which came to this country from Siberia by way of Alaska. The exhibits had immediate effect—arousing a real community interest and bringing people to the branch libraries who had never been there before.[60]

In the 1920s, social issues and natural disasters also had an impact on public libraries. For example, prohibition—one of America's worst social engineering experiments—affected libraries in many ways, some positive, some not. In some towns vacated saloons became branch libraries. When saloons closed in Butte, Montana, however, men began visiting the library more frequently, mostly to relieve themselves. In 1920 the Galveston public library became a refuge for people affected by a devastating hurricane. When Vermillion, Louisiana, experienced a massive flood in 1927, water came up to the library's front porch. By removing the steps, librarians enabled readers to dock their boats at the door. Sectional bias continued to mark public library celebrations. While the Belleville, Illinois, and San Jose, California, public libraries closed in 1919 for Lincoln's birthday, the Columbus (Georgia) Public Library remained open to celebrate "Georgia Day." Months later the library celebrated Robert E. Lee's birthday, which Belleville and San Jose ignored.[61]

Contesting particular uses of library spaces could be as divisive as book selection. In 1919, the Women's Christian Temperance Union (WCTU) and Purity League members objected to reproductions of Renaissance paintings containing nudes on a Queens (New York) Public Library branch wall. To no avail, however. "They are all examples of acknowledged art," the director noted, and "until the library trustees order their removal, they will stay where they are." Although exhibiting a human scalp brought no objection at the Omaha Public Library, a painting of Cupid "fanning the spark of love in the breast of a woman" did. One patron destroyed it by slashing the painting.[62]

Public library story hours were by this time ubiquitous. "Why do you go to story-hour?" a librarian asked a Boston boy in 1920. "Same reason we go to the movies," he answered. "For fun." The librarian had additional motives, however. "Through this pleasure the better books are found and read with keen interest, the imagination is stimulated, a higher standard established, sympathies deepened, and the sense of humor directed." The boy cited emotions evoked by a particular library service; librarians used these emotions to work a professional agenda.[63]

Story hours certainly stimulated imagination, but not always in the direction the storyteller wanted. At a Chicago Public Library branch in 1926, a seven-year-old listened to a story of Lancelot and Elaine. "I saw myself as Lancelot and the librarian as Elaine," he later recalled. "I reversed the romantic situation and, my unrequited love knowing no bounds, I saw myself dying for love of the sublimated librarian"

Outdoor story hour at the Wylie Avenue branch Library, Carnegie Library of Pittsburgh, 1924. *Annual Report, Carnegie Library of Pittsburgh, 1924. Photo courtesy of the Carnegie Library of Pittsburgh, Pennsylvania Department, Pittsburgh Photographic Library*

who told the story. Generally, story hours satisfied. "Ain't she some storyteller," noted one boy leaving a Duluth Public Library story hour in 1919. "I wish Saturday came every day," said his companion. One summer day in 1923 a Pittsburgh librarian posted on a school fence a sign announcing an impromptu story hour. Shortly thereafter seventy eager children sat listening on the school steps, the librarian reported. "The mothers were as excited as the children, and one father . . . said, 'Very good thing.'" Next day the father came to the library asking for books to help him learn English. "These street stories were continued throughout the summer with marked success," the librarian reported. For the year, the library delivered nearly 3,000 story hours to 130,000 children.[64]

During Children's Book Week in 1927 the Sacramento Camp Fire Girls crafted a miniature scene from the "Sleeping Princess" for a library exhibit, and placed delicately dressed tiny dolls on a throne next to the fatal spinning wheel. The display drew more parents and children than anything the library had done before. One Portuguese boy whom teachers thought a troublemaker was inspired to make a model train engine. "He used odds and ends of wood-cigar boxes and spools—painting the finished product black with silver for the steel. . . . It was the first time he has shown any interest of any kind." To teach children more about nature, in

1928 the Milwaukee Public Library put feeders outside children's room windows so they could watch migrating birds.[65]

In 1921 the *DeLand* (Florida) *Daily News* described one particular public library story hour. "In the yard back of the library building is a tiny little park with a big tree and flowers growing in it." There post office officials erected a platform and placed benches, and DeLand's Boy Scouts decorated the grounds. On the platform children gave dramatizations of the "Three Bears," "Cinderella," and "Red Hen," all under the direction of a group of mothers. Children also played games, heard stories, and listened to records on a record player donated by a local drug store.[66] Things the reporter observed—homelike atmosphere, carefully selected stories, local philanthropy, community participation by people of both genders and different ages (albeit not races), the mixing of media—reflect some of the reasons people came to love their public libraries as special places over the years.

Across the country public libraries also incorporated into their services the new media of the day. All libraries experienced their impact; some adapted more quickly than others. Stereopticon slides continued to be children's favorites. "Can we have the spy glasses" or "scaroscopes?" were routine requests at the Des Moines Public's Waveland branch. By the mid-1920s, records had become staple public library fare. Collections generally included classical (seldom popular or ethnic) music, foreign-language instruction, and readings of plays, poetry and speeches. Two-thirds of American public libraries with 20,000 or more volumes had music collections in 1925.[67]

A 1919 film release of *Riders of the Purple Sage* brought revived interest in Zane Grey's books. The Crunden Branch holdings of the St. Louis Public Library were "inadequate to fill the call" for Gray's novels. Recently filmed O. Henry stories brought the same reaction. "Just as soon as a movie is advertised . . . adapted from some novel," observed a Boise librarian, "I immediately notice that everyone seems to want it." A Brooklyn branch librarian noticed more young people came after seeing a motion picture at the corner theater. "Mystery-stories are ever popular, and ofttimes outdoor stories teeming with adventure are cast aside for the detective 'movie-thrillers.'"[68]

The early-1920s radio rage caused some librarians concern. One LAPL librarian worried the radio was "weaning people away from the printed word" because thousands "now sit back in comfortable chairs, with their eyes closed listening to lectures, concerts and news broadcasts from general centers of entertainment." In Pomona, California, the public library discontinued weekly recorded music concerts because home radio use reduced their audiences. In Madison, Wisconsin, the public library ended its lecture series for the same reason. At the Salt Lake City Public Library, however, the Utah Radio Association met in 1921 to participate in a cross-continent wireless relay contest. Some public libraries started their own radio programs, in which they discussed library services and recent acquisitions. The Cincinnati Public Library broadcast a weekly half-hour book review program. "Comments regarding them have come from remote sections of the county," librarians said. Over three local stations the Cleveland Public Library broadcast nightly bedtime stories.[69]

Public libraries used newer media in other ways. In the Cincinnati Public Library's auditorium, 2,400 attended twenty lectures in 1919–1920 by local residents who had traveled to distant lands and brought back lantern slides, which they showed with their talks. In 1928 drama clubs rehearsing in Cleveland Public Library club rooms participated in an acting contest. Finalists included the East 79th Street Fairy Footlights, the Rice Twinkletoes, and the Superior Bright Lights. That same year at a branch of the District of Columbia Public Library, the Woodbine Circle of the Chevy Chase Methodist Episcopal Church hosted for 225 attendees a "fashion revue" of the "latest women's wear from sport costumes and afternoon dresses to hosiery and negligees." No report on whether men were allowed to attend.[70]

In 1923 the Milton (Massachusetts) Public Library hosted an exhibit of local artists that became an annual event. In 1925 several Fort Worth, Texas, art lovers bought Thomas Eakins's *The Swimming Hole*, a painting of six men skinny-dipping in a pond, for the public library. There "it influenced generations of artists and inspired pilgrimages from all over west Texas," the *Chicago Tribune* later reported. "Thousands of schoolchildren on field trips trooped into the small, hushed library alcove to behold 'fine art' for the first time." In 1929 the Society of Oregon Artists made it possible to borrow art prints just like books through the public library. "Pictures are lent . . . for one month and may be renewed for another." Within six months, 100 Portland families had checked them out. In the 1920s the Los Angeles Public Library amassed a collection of 25,000 mounted pictures and clippings, many framed for circulation. By 1929 most urban and over half of American public libraries with more than 20,000 volumes maintained picture collections.[71]

Statistics proved that librarians' postwar worries about new media were unfounded. "Recreational diversions such as the automobile, the movies, the radio, and the widely circulated popular magazines have not reduced the number of readers of books," the Denver Public Library director noted in 1926, "but on the contrary have created new readers by stimulating interest in things observed on tours, pictured on screen, or widely broadcasted." The claim that the book "has gone the way of the horse-drawn carriage and that motion pictures and motor cars are all that can 'hold' the average individual" was silly, the Kansas City (Missouri) Public Library director noted; circulation for 1922 increased 14 percent from the last year, up 300 percent from a decade earlier. "New interests, new inventions and movements do not detract from book reading," he noted, "but increase it."[72]

Public libraries are more than circulation statistics, the Bangor (Maine) Public Library director maintained in 1927. "It is the more intangible question of influence on the community and value to the individual. The library supplements the schools, extends their service though life, and takes their place. It serves as a center of recreation and inspiration, a storehouse of mental treasure available for the varied needs of our citizens. In arousing worthy interests and ambitions, satisfying mental longings, bringing practical advice, information, cheer and comfort to the average citizen, the library proves its value and worth." St. Louis Public Library director Arthur Bostwick called this phenomenon "the socialization of the library." He complained that of the fifty-seven items of statistical data the American Library Association requested annually, "only seven refer to persons, making a liberal interpretation of the word. There could, perhaps, be no more striking demonstration of the fact that our records are not keeping pace with our practice."[73]

On the occasion of the ALA's fiftieth anniversary in 1926, John Cotton Dana recounted the library profession's accomplishments in the past half-century: the card catalog ("tamed for daily use"); classification ("made helpful to a thousand ends and tractable to the humblest workers"); credos that a community owns its library's books, can use them as it sees fit, and that a book's worth is in its use; a public library building suited to community needs and easily reached; children as library readers ("discovered only thirty years ago, and now have their own rooms"); branch libraries ("a city's books are not useful to all a city's people if kept in one place only"); public library books in schools; and more recently, libraries in schools. While Dana saw progress in many ways, he never lost his concern about supplying readers with too much fiction. Given the reduced cost of novels in recent years, he contended in 1929 that perhaps public libraries should devote more of their budget to "those few hundred novels which are generally accepted as the best," and save the rest for more worthwhile nonfiction.[74]

CHAPTER SIX

"One Island of Refuge"

The Great Depression and World War II, 1929–1945

Times were hard for many Americans between 1929 and 1945, but at their public libraries, patrons could still experience familiar surroundings, emotions, and noises. In 1938, for example, a New York branch librarian described a typical day:

> The old lady with the ailing Pekinese in one arm and Dr. Little's dog book in the other, the two German refugees at the Registration Desk shepherded by a small boy who knows all the answers, the mob around the catalogue elbowing each other with the unseeing detachment of Macy bargain hunters, the look of expectation on the faces of those waiting for a truck of Closed Shelf books and its lightning shift to joy or woe as the gleaners gauge the crop; on the stairs the line of children gazing down into the promised land of "detectives and westerns," the magnificent gesture with which as young Sam exits, he throws wide his coat to proclaim, "No contraband." All these could be caught in snapshots, but it needs a movie with sound to reproduce the peculiar atmosphere which prevails at busy hours; the shuffle of feet on a city block of cement, the rumble of book trucks, the hum of voices, the occasional spontaneous guffaw, the blood-curdling crash of the catalogue drawers as they hit the concrete floor, the buzz of the telephone and the click of the cricket as we relay the calls. It is all part of a pattern of activity and would shock into coma the librarian conditioned to SILENCE signs.[1]

Perhaps this is indeed a typical day of public library experiences, but the effects of the Great Depression on public library services were historically untypical in many ways. In 1932, 28 percent of Americans—34 million men, women, and children—had no income at all. Many questioned the viability of the American way of life and lost their optimism for a better tomorrow. Feeding this shift were writers and intellectuals forming a "Cultural Front" that criticized the free market, capitalism, and a form of government that to many seemed incapable and unwilling to help. President Herbert Hoover caught the brunt of criticism, and across the nation in shantytowns for the homeless, dubbed "Hoovervilles," people used "Hoover blankets" (old newspapers) to keep warm at night and displayed "Hoover flags" (pants pockets turned inside-out) to show their economic status. The Depression's effects were profound, and widespread. Total book sales, for example, dropped abruptly. "When people are broke," said John Steinbeck, "first thing they give up is books."[2] To fill the vacuum many turned to their public library, where they found—albeit in diminished numbers—not only the bad news Cultural Front writers peddled but also uplifting messages like Dale Carnegie's *How to Win Friends and Influence People* (1936) and Norman Vincent Peale's *You Can Win* (1938).

For Pittsburgh's Carnegie Library, the Great Depression began in November 1931, when news reached the staff that book budgets were cut 26 percent. In 1932 the Detroit Public Library's book budget dropped from $175,000 to $40,000, the Cleveland Public Library's from $160,000 to $96,000. Because of a serious revenue reduction, the Chicago Public Library stopped purchasing new books in 1931. The city declared the Library "not an essential municipal activity" and thus ineligible for emergency public funding. To generate revenue, Cleveland sponsored "overdue weeks," encouraging patrons to keep books a week overdue and pay the twelve-cent fine. A Brooklyn librarian recommended that his library substitute for "fine" the phrase "appreciation fee"—a sum "paid for the privilege of keeping books beyond the stated period." Many parents refused to allow their children to borrow books, an NYPL branch librarian noticed. "They do not wish to be responsible." Some libraries forgave fines during amnesty weeks to get back desperately needed books. In 1932, the Boston Public Library cleared 12,139 people of fines this way.[3]

Demand for books was so high that discarding anything became "a luxury," the Los Angeles Public Library noted in 1935. Shelves in branches of the New York Public Library held volumes "unlike any books

I'd known before," one librarian recalled. "They had been read and circulated for so long that the pages felt thick, somehow, and pulpy, and they were almost gray in color, not from abuse but from the many, many hands that . . . turned the pages." At the East Orange (New Jersey) Public Library, a 1934 report noted that 4,000 books stood on reserve shelves waiting to be re-bound. In Santa Barbara, the public library repaired so many books so many times that workers typed in missing pages just to keep them in circulation. By 1940 the library had so many overcirculated, dog-eared, and soiled books that it incinerated 8,000—"a woeful tale of the Depression," the *Los Angeles Times* reported.[4]

By appealing for donations in newspapers and radio announcements, by mounting posters in libraries, stores, schools, and public transportation, public libraries desperately tried to make up for reduced budgets. During National Book Week in 1933, for example, Spokane, Washington, high school students brought books from home, and through an agreement with a bookstore traded seven *Peter Rabbit*s for Emily Post's *Etiquette* and three *Tarzan*s for Richard Byrd's *Little America*. Chicago sponsored "Give a Book Week"—if every child donated one book, an official told the *Tribune,* the library would collect 500,000. Because the campaign realized only 10,000, however, hundreds of children canvassed neighborhoods for additional donations one 1934 Saturday, when they collected 20,000.[5]

Despite these dire circumstances, US communities in 1930 supported 6,000 public libraries (more than double the number at the end of World War I) that circulated 240 million books to 20 million readers. Yet in 1932, 45 million Americans still had no access to public library services; 88 percent lived in rural America, half of those in the Southwest and Southeast. One library expert thought lack of "local initiative" was the cause and wondered if the United States should not follow the European example with "state control and aid in national library organizations."[6] Although he did not say so, in 1935 the Third Reich boasted that its 15,500 public libraries served 45.6 million Germans—one for every 3,000, a ratio seven times better than in the United States. Like black Americans in the South, however, German Jews had difficulty using them.

Through many Great Depression "alphabet soup" agencies, the federal government helped public libraries greatly in the 1930s. In 1936, for example, public libraries employed 9,000 National Youth Administration workers to supplement staff, repair books, and beautify library grounds. In some states federal money funded most services. Public libraries served 38 percent of North Carolinians in 1935, 85 percent in 1942. At the time, two-thirds of its public library employees were Works Progress Administration (WPA) workers, and 85 percent of its counties had WPA-funded bookmobile projects. Although the WPA also provided funds to purchase 56,408 books for the state's public libraries, the agency limited how the money could be spent—no more than five copies of a single title. The North Carolina Library Commission complained: "The ruling . . . works a hardship on the sections where separate service must be provided for the whites and the negroes."[7]

Between 1935 and 1941, the WPA gave $51,000,000 to build new libraries, renovate or repair 1,500 others, repair 100,000,000 books, and fund outreach projects in 400 counties. For the latter it purchased 250,000 books for 150 counties instituting bookmobile services, and employed 500 bookmobile supervisors and 200 drivers. The Denver Public Library used WPA funds to index Colorado newspapers, develop an outdoor library, compile bibliographies of newspapers and authors, wash children's books, and hire filing and clerical workers. The Brooklyn Public Library also hired WPA employees to erase marks left by "o-fillers"—patrons who filled in o's in library books (some drew faces in the o's, even adding ears); workers could not keep pace. At the St. Louis Public Library, in 1937 four WPA women erased pencil markings from 10,000 books.

The Kansas City (Kansas) Public Library used WPA funds to employ twenty-four women to take books to shut-ins. In the morning, they all picked up armloads at the library, then on foot, by streetcar, and by bus spent the day delivering and retrieving the volumes. Along with books they brought back stories—a boy with the broken back who learned how to make toy airplanes from the texts he selected, an old man who kept himself clean and shaven for his "sweetheart with the books," and old people who begged them to stay because they were lonely. "Surely," the *Kansas Library Bulletin* reasoned, "no finer social use could be made of libraries."[8]

The Boise (Idaho) Public Library used federal funds for outreach services to the Elks Convalescent Home and the Idaho Department of Welfare's Crippled Children's Program. "How gratifying it was to take a cart load of books into the Children's Ward, show them the picture books, and leave books for each to look at or read," reported one librarian. With additional public dollars, the Buffalo Public Library employed sixty-five people in 1932 to make scrapbooks for hospitalized children, mount pictures for schoolrooms, build shelves and library furniture, clean books, and repair the building and equipment. In 1934, the Santa Monica (California) Public Library used Public Works Adminstration (PWA) money to commission local artists to paint murals on library walls. At the Dayton Public Library, federal projects employed a hundred men for carpentry, plumbing, plastering, and sheet metal work that bought $30,000 worth of necessary repairs for $550.[9]

Oklahoma used rural free delivery to mail books to rural residents. "Nine friends read this last book you sent me," wrote one Oklahoman. "Thank you for making this possible for women of small towns." Kentucky used Federal Emergency Relief Administration (FERA) funds to hire four young women to deliver public library books by horseback to fifty-seven mountain schools and communities in Leslie County, a place so rural it had few roads connecting them. To get books to residents, librarians rode their horses along riverbeds. Starting at "Hell-Fer-Sartin Creek"—a "tortuous, twisting stream with a rocky bed and brush tangled banks"—the four split up at Devil's Jump Branch, each taking a different tributary. "They feel well repaid," the *Christian Science Monitor* reported, "when they see the smiles of the youngsters for whose sake they penetrate deep into the mountain vastnesses." Within four years 100 federally funded packhorse librarians were delivering books to rural Kentuckians. "Sometimes the literature is left for children to read to illiterate parents," the *Monitor* reported; "sometimes the librarian herself stops to read to a group."[10]

Next to book repairs, bookmobiles merited the most federal funding and occasioned the gratitude of millions. "Here comes the bookmobile" was the cry heard along Lafayette (Missouri) County roads as the truck made its regular stops. Women wanted bestsellers such as *Gone with the Wind* and "books that make the most of your life" like etiquette, home decoration, and fashion books. Men wanted mysteries and westerns. One thing surprised, however. The bookmobile librarian had recently acquired books on soil erosion and farm planning, but bookmobile patrons left them on the shelves. "When the men sit down at night after a long, hard day," she told a reporter, "they want to read something that will take their minds off their work." Children were the bookmobile's most enthusiastic supporters, swarming it even before it came to a complete stop. Boys wanted action ("Gimme one without any love in it," said an eleven-year-old); girls looked for heroines exercising independence and socially acceptable freedoms like those seen in *Sue Barton, Nurse* and *Peggy Covers London*. "Even on bitter cold days," the reporter noticed, bookmobile librarians "found

Kentucky WPA women on horseback carry books to "holler" residents, 1938. *National Archives photo no. 69-N-12782-C*

people eagerly waiting for books at the stations and schools, often having come miles through the snowdrifts to get them."[11]

By 1939, the WPA had funded 140 bookmobiles nationwide. When the Dayton Public Library bookmobile pulled up to the curb, assistants raised upper panels that covered books on both sides, then dropped lower panels to form counters. On display were 600 books; another 600 were inside. Drivers always parked with children's books on the curb side; adults perused titles from the street. In 1939 a Chicago Public branch librarian loaded her car with children's books and a folding table, then traveled to local playgrounds to set up an outdoor library. The experiment proved so successful that officials commissioned a book trailer. One mother publicly thanked the library. Her ten-year-old previously identified reading with school, something "necessary to be done but not enjoyed." Because the "library lady" visited his playground, "Bobbie is looking forward to reading more books than anyone else this summer."[12]

The bookmobile awaits patrons in a Louisiana bayou, 1938. *Courtesy of the Franklin D. Roosevelt Library, Hyde Park, New York*

In 1935 *Publishers Weekly* estimated that retail stores across the country had 50,000 of their own rental libraries. "Every bookstore and drug store runs a lending library," reported Norwegian librarian Wilhelm Munthe, "cigar stores, railway depots and ferry buildings also have them." Munthe could not figure out why the American public library had not put private lending libraries out of business, but the answer was simple. Many public libraries favoring best reading would not stock the popular novels most people wanted; rental libraries would. In 1935, Pittsburgh's Carnegie Library admitted that patrons who wanted commonplace fiction the library no longer purchased had gravitated to commercial lending libraries. To explain a circulation drop for 1935 the NYPL director cited among several reasons "the place the commercial rental library has come to play." Consistent with a professional imperative he inherited, he noted "the tendency with many commercial libraries to supply the cheaper sort of books, far below public library standards, ruinous to taste and morale of young and old."[13]

Nonetheless, many public libraries still offered rental collections. For a dime (which they kept), telegraph messenger boys home-delivered book rentals to New Rochelle (New York) Public Library borrowers. Worried when a state auditor questioned whether public libraries could charge fees, the Dayton Public Library substituted a "One Day Collection" from which patrons could take popular fiction for one day, but had to pay two cents a day thereafter. To maximize borrowing limits, people lined up Saturday evenings to check out books they did not have to return until Monday; nearly 40,000 books circulated this way in 1934. Other Ohio libraries adopted the "Dayton scheme."[14]

By 1935, forty-four urban public libraries had readers' advisor (RA) services largely consisting of annotated bibliographies on special topics that librarians compiled for individual readers. Their purpose was clear—"to educate the reader away from weak reading matter," a librarian explained in 1934. As a practice, however, this 1920s innovation had begun to fizzle. The Toledo Public Library director teased a 1936 American Library Association audience that because of the "rarified cultural atmosphere" RA services fostered, the average patron worried "the librarian will sneak up on him and submerge him in cultural reading before he has a chance to defend himself." These advisor services also lost momentum at the Chicago Public Library—too expensive in a bad economy, many complained. A 1938 ALA publication—*Helping the Reader toward Self-Education*—did not help. It classed readers by occupation, race, sex, and personality traits, the latter including the "Timid and Inferior-Feeling Person," the "Low Brow," and the "Criminal in the Making." Fifty years later RA experts Joyce G. Saricks and Nancy Brown marveled at the "moralistic, didactic tone" of 1930s readers' advisors. "It seems amazing to readers' advisors of today that librarians of the past could make the smug assumption that their reading suggestions would result in dramatic self-improvement in the reader."[15]

Youth received increased attention from public libraries during the Depression. In 1933, young adult librarian Margaret A. Edwards instituted "Y Work" at the Enoch Pratt Free Library in Baltimore. She believed that promoting world citizenship through reading constituted a core value of youth services and used carefully selected fiction to help young people "live with themselves as citizens of this country and to be at home in the world." Other public libraries repurposed space for young adults. East Orange (New Jersey) Public Library officials allowed youth to open the "Monkey Wrench Canteen" in a branch basement. Teenagers repainted walls, purchased overstuffed furniture, and installed a Coke bar. In 1940 the St. Paul (Minnesota) Public Library renovated a basement room into an informal room for youth. Teenagers gathered there to "discuss all kinds of problems," a librarian reported.[16]

In early 1945 a youth lounge opened on the third floor of the New York Public Library's Aguilar branch three nights weekly. Youth did most of the planning. "They already have selected the books for the shelves, popular novels, detective stories, westerns, war books, joke and quiz books, as well as magazines that are a novelty to the branch, such as moving picture magazines, radio, boxing and band leaders," the *Times* reported. "They will also select their own phonograph records and map out their own exhibits and entertainments." Not all agreed with this innovation, however. Some veteran branch librarians, mostly irritated with having to serve pesky teenagers, ran their libraries like a boarding school, one librarian recalled.[17] Memories created by these interactions undoubtedly fed negative stereotypes of "Marion the Librarian."

Despite the terrible economy, however, the *Washington Post* concluded in 1932 that the Depression "is good for the reading business." A daily newspaper sold to every third person, a monthly or weekly magazine to every eighth, and Americans annually bought two books per capita but read eight. Public libraries accounted for most of the difference. Other media seemed to have little effect on circulation. Between 1930 and 1935, when radio use increased 170 percent (70 percent of families owned one or more), and 9,700 theaters served millions of moviegoers weekly, public library circulation increased 27 percent. An analysis of 1930–1935 data from 150 variously sized public libraries revealed expenditures plunging in 1932 and 1933, then up slightly in 1935. During those same years, collection size, borrowers, and circulation all increased, peaking in 1932 and 1933. Adult circulation increased for nonfiction more than fiction, but juvenile circulation decreased as more school libraries opened.[18]

Many readers continued to mine public libraries for useful knowledge. In 1934 the *New York Times* detailed library patron success stories across the country—an elderly couple who learned how to become florists and opened a greenhouse; a woman who read chemistry books in an effort to invent an improved water softener. In 1939 a well-dressed man approached a Brookline (Massachusetts) librarian. "Possibly you remember a poor down-and-outer who used to come here . . . every day last winter to keep warm?" he asked. "I had lost my house, my land, everything I owned. This library was the only place I could come to keep from freezing." One day he read a gardening magazine soliciting an effective spray for certain insects. "Using the books and magazines in the library, I worked out a formula, got a man with some capital to back my project, and now I'm manufacturing the stuff in quantities." He then glanced into the reading room, where three unemployed men snoozed. "I just thought my story might encourage you to continue letting all sorts of people into the library without making them feel uncomfortable."[19]

Sometimes the quest for useful knowledge at the public library was controversial. "An outrage that such a thing would be permitted!" exclaimed a government official who found *The Bartender's Guide* on Camden (New Jersey) Public Library shelves in 1932. But his was a losing cause. Anticipating the repeal of the Eighteenth Amendment, that same year, grape growers Ernest and Julio Gallo decided to become winemakers. To learn how to make wine, Ernest visited the Modesto (California) Public Library. Gallo told the librarian what he had in mind, but she found nothing in the collection to help him. She then remembered old pamphlets in the basement. "Why don't you go down and see?" There Gallo found a pamphlet on fermentation and another on wine care—"exactly what we needed." It was, Gallo noted, the beginning of his knowledge about making commercial wine.[20]

Other useful knowledge was less controversial. In 1933 nineteen-year-old Woody Guthrie went to the Plano (Texas) Public Library "and scratched around in the books." He carried them home "by the armloads, on any subject. I wanted . . . something . . . that would turn me into a human being of some kind—free to work for my own self, and free to work for everybody." One day he discovered Kahlil Gibran's *The Prophet.* The book helped him articulate a philosophy of life later reflected in his musical lyrics. At the Lorain (Ohio) Public Library in 1941, a ten-year-old black girl "spent long, long hours reading," she later recalled. More than fifty years later library officials dedicated the Toni Morrison Reading Room in her honor. "I wanted there to be one place where," Morrison said at the 1995 ceremony, "you could come in and sit down on . . . comfortable chairs, in a quiet room and just spend . . . an hour or two with a book."[21]

At the Atlanta Public Library's Auburn branch, director Annie Watters bought books on Gandhi for the library's adult education discussion groups. At the time a young Martin Luther King Jr. came to the library several times each week. "He would walk up to the desk," she later recalled, "and look me straight in the eye." "Hello, Martin Luther," she responded, always calling him by his first and middle names; "what's on

your mind?" "Oh, nothing, particularly." For Watters, that was the cue
that King had learned a new "big word," and they then initiated a conversation in which King used the word repeatedly. Another game involved
poetry. Again, King would stand by the desk, waiting. "What's on your
mind, Martin Luther?" Watters asked. "For I dipped into the future, far
as the human eye could see," he responded. Watters immediately recognized the poem, and finished the verse: "For I dipped into the future, far
as the human eye could see; saw a vision of the world and the wonders
that would be." The Gandhi collection presented a problem, however,
because King was too young to check out adult books. To solve it, Watters
issued a library card to his father, then checked the books out on his
father's card. "He read every one of those [Gandhi] books that we had,"
she later recalled.[22]

Through their books, public libraries often transformed readers' lives.
Because she found no curricular attention to people of color at school,
nine-year-old Paule Marshall, daughter of Barbados immigrants, went
to her Brooklyn Public Library branch in 1938. There she found a book
by Paul Lawrence Dunbar, and turned to one of the poems. "Little
brown-baby wif spa'klin / eyes / Come to yo' pappy an' set on his knee."
The poem "spoke to me as nothing I had read before of the closeness,
the special relationship I had had with my father." Another poem read:
"Seen my lady home las' night / Jump back, honey, jump back. / Hel' huh
han' an' sque'z it tight." Marshall's breath quickened, she later said in an
interview. "It roused in me all kinds of delicious feelings and hopes." Her
interest piqued, she began to ask the white librarian for stories and poems
about "The Race" ("as it was put back then"), although "I did so at first
with a feeling of shame—the shame I and many others used to experience
in those days whenever the word 'Negro' or 'colored' came up." Years later
Marshall became a successful novelist, inspired, she said, by what she had
read at her branch library.[23]

In 1933, eleven-year-old Jade Snow Wong walked daily from her San
Francisco school to her basement home beneath her father's blue jeans
factory. On four of those days she "squeezed in a pleasure dividend for
myself"—she stopped at SFPL's North Beach branch, returned four
books she was allowed on the previous visit, and took out four more.
"I devoured a book a day," she recalled in her memoir. "They were my
escape, my easy teacher of the English language in various styles, my
window into other worlds." Chinese American adolescents who wanted

to get "up there" (their euphemism for gaining social status) used the branch heavily.[24]

In the 1930s—as news about book-burning events in Nazi Germany appeared in newspapers, as Chinese librarians appealed to American colleagues for help against the censorship practices of occupying Japanese forces—many librarians believed that they needed to fight censorship and cultivate intellectual freedom. In 1938, Forrest Spaulding of the Des Moines Public Library got his trustees to adopt a Library's Bill of Rights. A year later, in the midst of efforts across the nation (including at many public libraries) to ban John Steinbeck's *Grapes of Wrath* for profane language and perceived radical politics, the ALA adopted a "Library Bill of Rights" (LBR). It posited that librarians had a responsibility to fight censorship and thus embrace, at least in abstract democratic rhetoric, the defense of intellectual freedom as a professional imperative. Book selections should not be "influenced by the race or nationality or the political or religious views of the writers," opinions on all sides of an issue "should be represented fairly and adequately," and library building meeting rooms should be open to all groups engaged in useful cultural activities. The title suggested the force of law, but the language adopted in its principles carried only "should" statements that imposed no penalties for violations. A year later the ALA created a Committee on Intellectual Freedom to monitor censorship incidents in American libraries.[25]

But fissures in LBR rhetoric were obvious, if little discussed. For example, one librarian claimed his library had not banned *Grapes of Wrath*, "only refrained from buying it." Similarly, the ALA adopted the LBR during the presidency of Ralph Munn, who in the late 1930s refused to buy commonplace fiction for his Carnegie Library of Pittsburgh. His first vice-president was Essae Mae Culver of Louisiana, his second vice-president Donald Coney of Texas, both states that directly violated the LBR because they segregated and underfunded public library services to black Americans. Contrasts between professional rhetoric and library reality were evident elsewhere. At NYPL's 135th Street branch in Harlem, children's librarian Augusta Baker considered race prejudice a criterion for exclusion and began pulling titles, such as *Little Black Sambo*, that she thought were "racially insulting to Blacks" and depicted them as "servile buffoons." Ultimately, Baker judged only forty-one titles in her collection "acceptable." At Chicago's George Cleveland Hall branch, children's librarian Charlemae Hill Rollins found only thirty books in her collection without racial stereotypes she could recommend to black children. That Baker and Rollins could find only a few acceptable titles speaks volumes to racism's ability to root itself in the printed works public libraries had been handing over circulation desks to millions of children for half a century. And while some librarians issued bibliographies of "substitutes for unrecommended juveniles," three state library journals published Mary Root's updated bibliography of unacceptable series fiction—another LBR violation—between 1933 and 1944.[26]

Because patrons did not always agree on the stories they wanted their libraries to hold in their collections, acquisitions continued to be a process—sometimes public, more often not—that librarians negotiated between public demand, vocal members of their communities, and external pressures brought by distant experts, including, after 1939, the Library Bill of Rights. Some disputes were based on political ideology. In 1939, New Hyde Park (New York) public library trustees voted 13 to 2 to ban Anne Morrow Lindbergh's *Listen! the Wind*. Because her husband Charles had accepted a Nazi decoration, said one trustee, "I just don't believe our taxpayers should give money in book royalties to people like the Lindberghs." In 1932 a Cincinnatian charged that the public library did not have Theodore Dreiser's *An American Tragedy* because it was "an indictment of the capitalist system that permits millions to starve while a few parasites are committing the same crimes as under Louis XIV." The next day the director explained the library did not have *Tragedy* because it was "a bad book." Yet demand for *Mein Kampf* in New York public libraries was so strong in 1939 that each branch had more than fifty copies. A "demonstration of democracy," the Brooklyn Public Library director called it. In Chicago, a list of sixty waited for one of the library's twenty-three copies.[27]

When several community members objected to John Steinbeck's *Of Mice and Men*, the Fort Wayne Public Library destroyed all its copies. The library also refused to purchase *Grapes of Wrath*, instead referring patrons to commercial libraries. Some patrons protested. "Discussions of the book in local literature clubs, an editorial in the local newspaper, comments in the press, a book review by a professional book reviewer, radio broadcast references to it, and the knowledge that the Public Library would not buy it all added fuel to the controversy," a librarian noted. Although uncomfortable, the library was clearly in the middle of a public sphere debate. Some clergymen denounced the library's policy; others commended it. By year's end demand for the book had diminished, a librarian said. Perhaps more accurately, protesting readers simply gave up—an example of a bureaucracy outlasting public protest, one that occurred less than a year after the ALA approved its Library Bill of Rights. Within the year, however, the library reversed itself and purchased multiple copies of *Grapes of Wrath*; in 1940 it was the library's most circulated book.[28]

Great Depression reading practices—whether serious or harmless—were nonetheless embedded in social life. Examples of the value patrons placed on commonplace reading they obtained from local public libraries abound. In 1932, eleven-year-old Polish immigrant Jeanne S. Chall was profoundly moved by a popular novel about the daughter of a sugar beet farmer whose family moved to a new state. "Her pains were my pains," Chall later recalled, "for I too was struggling, as an immigrant . . . to adjust to my new world—to understand it and to become part of it. And the books I read from the public library made it possible for me to learn about my new world—through knowledge and through empathy with the struggles of others."[29]

Although a 1932 survey of 614 public libraries found appropriations averaged a 10 percent drop, how they reacted varied by size. Libraries with fewer than 10,000 volumes—those mostly run by nonprofessionals with little library training—reduced budgets 9 percent for "literary" fiction (defined in the survey as "Galsworthy, Dreiser"), 11 percent for "popular" fiction (defined as "mystery and adventure"). Libraries with over 200,000 volumes—those mostly run by library professionals—reduced expenditures for "literary" fiction by 14 percent, "popular" fiction by 50 percent.

While these patterns were obvious, they were not universal. On the one hand, the Fort Wayne Public Library reported in 1931 the demand for Tarzan books "is insistent." No matter, however, the library refused to stock them. Although Tarzan was not permitted in Fort Wayne's public library, he was allowed in New York's Bronx branches, where E. L. Doctorow pored over Burroughs's adventure stories. And in 1944 "tiny Miss Ruth"—always sporting a "friendly smile"—gave twelve-year-old John Updike permission to use the Reading (Pennsylvania) Public Library adult collection and check out whatever books he wanted, including Erle Stanley Gardner, Ellery Queen, and Agatha Christie, authors many professional librarians were convinced stunted intellectual growth.[30]

In 1940, journalist Dale Kramer set out to assess how small-town America fared twenty years after Sinclair Lewis's *Main Street* pilloried small-town values. Rather than return to Lewis's birthplace—Sauk Centre, Minnesota—he picked Sigourney, Iowa (population 2,000). Among institutions he analyzed was the Carnegie library. At night, high school students still crowded heavy oak tables, he noted, and although "armloads of books are carried home, . . . the library's presence has not resulted in an appreciation of contemporary literature." The library had one title each by Theodore Dreiser, Sherwood Anderson, and Ernest Hemingway (all three among the authors' less controversial works), but none by Erskine Caldwell, John Dos Passos, or William Faulkner. Willa Cather and Sinclair Lewis were well represented, although the former's *A Lost Lady* and the latter's *Elmer Gantry* were absent. *Grapes of Wrath* "created no problem—for the simple reason that, having spent its half-year budget, the library's board was not considering new books." Zane Grey dominated. Other popular authors included Gene Stratton-Porter, Edna Ferber, and Fannie Hurst. "Burroughs would undoubtedly fare well if the librarian had not some years ago taken a notion to censor him by the simple process of neglecting to reorder his books," Kramer reported.[31]

Readers often purchased books on their own because many libraries refused to buy them, including the wildly popular new Stratemeyer syndicate series, the Hardy Boys and Nancy Drew. By 1934 the syndicate had sold 45,000,000 books, outpacing Bibles two to one. "My first great reading experience was a Hardy Boys," novelist Chris Zenowich remembered. "I was home alone, terrified, and the idea that my imagination could scare me . . . it changed reading for me." As adolescents, Supreme Court justices Sandra Day O'Connor and Ruth Bader Ginsburg each read Nancy Drew; so did Betty Friedan and Gloria Steinem. As a Brooklyn twelve-year-old in 1936, Shirley Chisholm, who became the first black woman elected to Congress, dutifully followed her mother to the public library every other Saturday to check out her limit of three books. Because she found no Nancy Drew or Bobbsey Twins there, however, she received them as birthday and Christmas gifts. "I read every single Nancy Drew," said National Organization of Women president Karen DeCrow about her 1940s adolescent reading. "She had the kind of freedom that I wasn't allowed. She was an independent, together young woman."[32] Just as sensationalist authors E. D. E. N. Southworth and Mary J. Holmes gave mid-nineteenth-century female readers permission to choose their own husbands and control their own bodies, Nancy Drew showed mid-twentieth-century adolescent readers that they could—within culturally acceptable limits—be independent, intelligent, and female at the same time. Yet Nancy regularly made Mary Root's "Not Recommended" list.

Stratemeyer fan mail shows that readers engaged these stories in many ways, often accomplishing what librarians believed possible only with serious fiction. Some letter-writers were complimentary. After reading *Shipwrecked on Cannibal Island*, a Virginia reader wanted to know if the island was real and praised the author for accurately describing geography in that section of the world. Others criticized: "You could have done much better," wrote two girls after reading *Betty Gordon at Mystery Farm*. "It sounds as if you wrote it in ten minutes." One character was "stingy and treated his wife shabbily. . . . Uncle Dick never shows any affection toward Bobby, never scolds Betty, or hardly ever refuses her for anything," they argued. "Please get some new ideas."[33]

About the Don Sturdy series, a New York boy reported he "learned very much about animals, reptiles, and Indian customs," and as a result "I have pulled my geography mark . . . up from 70 percent to 95 percent." An eight-year-old California girl asked for more "Sturdy" books "to satisfy my insatiable love of thrilling and exciting adventure" (she acknowledged help with her spelling from her older sister), but "please emphatically" begged the author not to "make Mrs. Sally Sturdy and Ruth so weepy and weak." A Baltimore grandmother reported she and her grandson shared the Sturdy series, and although he was nine and capable of reading them himself he "enjoys them more when I read aloud to him and we hunt up the various places mentioned, discussing each chapter as we progress." A twelve-year-old Pennsylvania boy wrote: "I never used to read much until I read" a Sturdy book. "There is a lot of knowledge in your books about inventions and different lands."[34]

In none of this 1930s fan mail—much demonstrating series fiction's ability to inform, inspire, bond, entertain, socialize, empower, and educate—is there any reference to public libraries. At the fortieth anniversary of the Chicago Public Library building in 1937, the mayor called the civic institution "one of the city's most valuable agencies for molding the minds of young people toward good citizenship." As a youth, he said, he daily visited the library, where he read every Horatio Alger book on the shelves. "I got much of my ambition from those books." But when director Carl Roden followed the mayor to the podium, he had to admit: "Alger books were taken from the library shelves thirty years ago."[35]

Confronted with a library that would not stock the books they wanted to read, some youth showed impressive enterprise. In 1935 one Oklahoma City eleven-year-old started her own book club with 150 titles, charged its twenty members twenty-five cents to join and three cents a day to rent books. Mostly she stocked the Nancy Drew, Judy Bolton, Girl Aviators, and Little Colonel series. In Chicago, a fourteen-year-old started a library for "crippled children" by pasting comic strips into scrapbooks. She told a reporter that she got the idea after talking to a girl recently released from a hospital who "told me how terrible it was when you had to lie in bed with no visitors, sometimes no one to talk to, and nothing to read." Into her homemade books she pasted cartoon strips of Popeye, Superman, Bat-Man, and Little Annie Rooney. Both white and black children ("'cause we're both people," she said) could check out any book in her collection for two weeks, just like a public library.[36] The Chicago Public Library offered no similar services since it purchased no comic books.

Not all libraries followed Chicago's example, however. The Dayton Public Library's 266 percent circulation increase between 1927 and 1931 was because it met the demand for commonplace reading, particularly "detective, western, and love stories." In 1940, St. Louis Public Library director Charles Compton began a "Who Reads What" survey. A sixth-grader complimented the library on having True Comics, because "it tells about the war and all the heroes." Although most of his peers shunned comics, Compton contended they gave children history and current events in a form they "crave—with lurid colors, a small amount of text, and fast action." The previous year, his library had circulated 257 copies of nineteen different comics.[37]

And sometimes library experts just got it wrong. In 1945, famed NYPL children's librarian Anne Carroll Moore wrote E. B. White, whose *Stuart Little* she had just read in proofs. Don't publish it, she said. The book "was non-affirmative, inconclusive, unfit for children, and would harm its author if published." White thanked Moore for her comments but resolved to push forward. Once published, children's librarians gave *Stuart* a tepid reception. Millions of readers, however, loved him. "Like little springboks," children "can sail easily over the fence that separates reality from make-believe," White said. "A fence that can throw a librarian is nothing to a child."[38]

Although patrons and community groups continued to use public library spaces for productive purposes during the Great Depression, some library experts called for change. In *The American Public Library Building* (1941), authors Joseph L. Wheeler and Alfred M. Githens asserted that Carnegie buildings had been erected "during the period of pretentious display," and because most Carnegies included an auditorium used for community gatherings, librarians discovered "by bitter experience that such extraneous activities interfered with the real book service for which budgets were always too meager." Wilhelm Munthe agreed. "It is in the reading room that the greatest dissemination of information and knowledge takes place," he wrote in 1939. Lectures, exhibits, concerts, forums, and theatrical performances in library auditoriums "have in many instances weakened the influence of the library through dissipation of its energies." Like Wheeler and Githens, Munthe favored useful knowledge. Like many library leaders, he did not see that patrons who used public libraries often considered their architectural features and community spaces meaningful and life-changing.[39]

But Munthe, Wheeler, and Givens did not speak for all librarians. Unknowingly echoing an 1893 Woman's Library legacy, the Pasadena (California) Public Library director insisted a library should not "be a big, barnlike place" but more "like a home . . . a place where people will want to stay." Patrons welcomed the experience. "I may be in an ugly mood when I come, but the peace and serenity of this place have a magic effect," wrote an unemployed Cleveland Public Library patron in 1930. "Before I know it I feel right with the world and myself." Said a reporter in 1943: "Ask me when I enter the Concord [Massachusetts] Library, why I feel as if I were entering home, and I say it is because of the welcome, the air of freedom, the unspoken good will, and the comfort. There is a homemaker's hand in this."[40]

That Americans still wanted public libraries was evident—almost 800 more opened between 1930 and 1940, and none closed, even in this worst of times. In tiny Buhler, Kansas, a local women's club opened a new public library in an abandoned gas station in 1936. Armed with mops and hot water they drew from the neighboring barbershop, they cleaned the building, stocked it with 850 books, then paid a fellow member fifty cents to staff it two afternoons a week. On occasion, a motorist came "bustling into the library asking for five gallons of gas," the *Christian Science Monitor* reported, "and then stared in open-mouthed wonder at the first filling station he had ever seen filled with books." A Gretna (Nebraska) women's club started a library in another gas station with $835 collected from locals. By 1938 it was the pride of the community, open two afternoons and one evening per week and available for community meetings. Women's club members served as librarians without pay.[41]

Often demands on library space reflected patron daily needs during the Great Depression. "At times this branch is a combination day nursery, bath house (we found a little girl giving Saturday baths to her two small sisters), meeting place for loafers and refuge for the unemployed," reported a (SLPL) branch librarian in 1930. Eight years later she wrote: "We continue to function as a day nursery, old men's retreat, boys' and girls' club, and a public library." When a reporter toured Los Angeles Public Library branches in 1935, she noted that branches served different clienteles; "from Hollywood, where a young lady may come to borrow a book riding a scooter and attired in shorts, to the east side of town where little Japanese girls with very straight bobs mingle with aged Russian and Yiddish philosophers, the same story is true."[42]

As in previous generations librarians invented nicknames to stereotype certain kinds of users. "Item-snorters" manifested "a peculiar pastime of searching carefully through the daily prints in quest of news items at which to snort." Outside the Chicago Public Library a young Saul Bellow listened to "Facts-and-Figures Taylor," a black "virtuoso who entertained shouting crowds in Washington Park by reciting the statistics he had memorized" in the library. "Want to know what the steel industry exported in 1921?" he shouted to passersby. "You tell 'em, Facts-and-Figures!" they yelled back.[43] In 1935 an East Dallas branch librarian said the neighborhood loved its library not only because it was a place mothers brought their children for story hour and librarians greeted old folks cheerfully at the circulation desk, but also because "we were always interested in people's illnesses and their love affairs and their marriages and their children." Patrons treated like human beings rather than customers were grateful. "Human sympathy is the greatest gift the librarian can possibly give to people," the *Christian Science Monitor* observed in 1936.[44]

One particular marvel of melting pot evidence was NYPL's Chatham Square branch, not far from Chinatown, Little Italy, and substantial settlements of Irish, Greeks, Poles, and Czechs—the 1940 census counted forty different nationalities in its service area. "What's going on?" a *Christian Science Monitor* reporter asked a Chinese girl approaching the front door in 1941, her arm around the waist of an Irish American friend. It was storytelling hour, the girl responded. The reporter asked if she was allowed to enter. "Sure," interjected a German American boy. "Mrs. Alessios wants people to keep coming." Alison Alessios was a special person, the reporter wrote. With so many nationalities around her library, how did she cope? Shortly after she got the Chatham Square post, Alessios responded, she roamed the neighborhoods and discovered two

Chinese-language schools for second-generation Chinese children. After attending classes, she organized a Library Chinese Club. To get Chinese children together with Greek, Italian, and Irish children, Alessios relied on story hour, and in them she deliberately tried to grow cultural pride in children whose values were being pulled away from their parents by an educational system that celebrated white Western traditions. "Children and grown-ups who are encouraged to conserve and respect their native arts and traditions and given opportunity to pour them into the great crucible of American democracy will, it seems to me, have a vision of the true America which would be lacking in an education exclusively given over to our own history and customs."[45]

As public forums, libraries sometimes became sites for statements about race. Because whites complained about sharing toilets with blacks at Baltimore's Enoch Pratt Free Library, in 1934 the library opened separate "Colored Men" and "Colored Women" washrooms. "Pratt Library Stoops to Jim Crow," denounced the Baltimore *Afro-American*. In 1939 five black American youths staged a sit-in when they were refused service at the Alexandria (Virginia) Public Library. As a solution, city council members voted $2,500 for a colored branch. At the Negro Library in Greensboro, North Carolina, black citizens met in the early 1940s to plot ways to get the city to hire black police officers; their efforts were successful. When Durham, North Carolina, dedicated a black branch library in 1940, instead of singing the *Star Spangled Banner* at opening ceremonies participants sang the "Negro National Anthem," "Lift Every Voice and Sing."[46]

A 1935 federal survey showed that only 94 of 509 public libraries in 13 southern states served black Americans; half were in Kentucky, West Virginia, Texas, and North Carolina (where library officials had used federal funds to increase services to blacks). And in those systems black Americans were variously served. In 1940 New Orleans, for example, 329,130 whites had access to the public library's 273,683 volumes; 129,632 blacks had access to 14,697 volumes in the one branch open to them. Still, some progress was evident, but only when funded by outside sources. Between 1928 and 1935, demonstration projects supported by the Julius Rosenwald Foundation of Chicago helped extend public library services in the South to 114,237 whites and 140,459 blacks; they increased total book circulation to rural people by 592 percent, and to black southerners by 579 percent. In 1938, an Aberdeen, Mississippi, Rosenwald agent helped local blacks open a public library.[47]

While black branch libraries slowly increased their numbers in the South, branches in northern cities had to adjust to southern blacks who continued to stream into urban neighborhoods. In some cities public library services brought whites and blacks together. The Hartford (Connecticut) Public Library was especially proud of its interracial services. In 1941 it hired Spencer Shaw who, his white colleague Julia Moriarty reported, acquired materials that did "not hold the darker races up to ridicule" and crafted programs that informed black and white patrons of the unique contributions that black people made to American history, art, music, and literature.[48]

Because of neighborhood patterns in other northern cities, however, branches were de facto black. The Chicago Public Library's Hall branch, which opened in 1932, quickly became a community and cultural center for America's new black capital. Black librarian Vivian Harsh initiated a semi-monthly Book Review and Lecture Forum and organized the DuSable History Club; within a decade fifteen similar groups organized. During that time Richard Wright, Langston Hughes, Zora Neale Hurston, Arna Bontemps, Alain Locke, Katherine Dunham, and Margaret Walker all gave presentations. And while they were in residence, one teenage girl—who as a child listened to Charlemae Rollins read poems and stories about black people—frequently asked writers to assess her poetry. In 1950 that girl, Gwendolyn Brooks, won a Pulitzer Prize for Poetry.[49]

As NYPL's 135th Street branch prepared to occupy new quarters in Harlem in 1942, a *Christian Science Monitor* reporter visited. "We'll have a bang-up time when the building's opened," she overheard a boy say to a girl. "It's got a room for everything you want to do, and they're goin' to let you do it. Miss [Ernestine] Rose said it had to be big because it houses our Negro history, and that's awful big."[50] In that branch James Baldwin read voraciously in the 1930s. And there, one Saturday morning in 1939, little Audre Lorde "lay spread-eagled on the floor of the Children's Room like a furious little brown toad, screaming bloody murder" because her mother pinched her ear to keep her quiet. "Suddenly, I looked up, and there was a library lady standing over me. . . . From the floor where I was lying, Mrs. [Augusta] Baker seemed like yet another mile-high woman about to do me in. . . . 'Would you like to hear a story, little girl?'" Baker placed her on a stool and read *Madeline* and *Horton Hatches the Egg*. "I took the books from Mrs. Baker's hands after she finished reading, and traced the large black letters with my fingers, while I peered again at the beautiful bright colors of the pictures. . . . I said, quite loudly, for whoever was listening to hear, 'I want to read.'"[51]

In Chicago's Hall branch, NYPL's 135th Street branch, and Atlanta's Auburn branch, blacks had access to materials that treated them favorably. The Hall branch collection made possible a 1944 Negro History Week exhibit in the library's main building featuring "the gallantry and patriotism of Negroes in all of this country's wars," the *Tribune* reported. In 1945, NYPL hosted an exhibit supported by 135th Street branch collections titled "Races of Mankind." "Exhibit Serves to Debunk Myth of Race Superiority," the *New York Amsterdam News* headlined. Panels carried titles like "No Race Is Most Primitive," "Culture Is Not Inborn," and "Jews Are Not a Race." Thousands toured the exhibit, which traveled to public libraries in Brooklyn, Richmond, and Washington, DC, and to universities across the South.[52] Collections also corrected history. "Our increasing Negro public has shown us the weakness of many of the most respected books," an NYPL branch librarian reported in 1944. "We have found that many quite famous Negroes, such as Sojourner Truth, were omitted from the Dictionary of American Biography."[53] In most public libraries, however, blacks met the stereotypes that print perpetuated.

Patrons continued to use libraries to discuss questions in the public sphere. In 1932 the Des Moines Public Library sponsored forums on current affairs, and on alternate Sundays included Communist and Socialist groups. At Chicago's John Toman branch, local Czech Americans organized a forum series in 1931. A committee of seven (two "conservatives," two "radicals," and three "liberals," a librarian noted) ran the series for more than a decade. Topics discussed enabled community members to explore what it meant to be an American from different ideological perspectives. Not everyone was happy with the library's role as public forum, however. "Frankly, I have never felt that the Library was a place for open discussions of controversial subjects," Director Roden told his board in 1938.[54]

Libraries also helped determine what was acceptable public art. At the Des Moines Public Library patrons complained about four WPA-funded children's room murals in 1941. One depicted a lemon growing out of an acorn, which viewers interpreted as the artist's protest against real estate overdevelopment on the Des Moines River. The board decided it was "an unnecessary slur upon the state." A second depicted Indians at a feast. "We don't know exactly what it means," a librarian told the *Chicago Tribune*, but some children were frightened by "the grim expression on the face of the kneeling old woman." Another showed Indians driven from their homes by soldiers and settlers. "Children ordinarily like pictures of Indians," observed another librarian, "but they don't like this picture. The figures of the Indians are distorted and the whole scene is one of needless horror." The final panel also confused her. "It certainly doesn't depict our children's ancestors in a flattering light." When the murals were removed from the walls of the institution that gave birth to the Library Bill of Rights, the library community—locally and nationally—said nothing.[55] The episode confirmed that library walls were public spaces on which community cultural and, in this case, artistic values were on display.

On Chicago playgrounds in summer, 1932 children listened for a whistle, then gathered in the "Fairy Ring" to hear librarians tell stories. "All had a taste of what fun it is to 'see with your imagination,'" noted the *Christian Science Monitor*. In Boston, the library hired three seasoned storytellers for slum neighborhood branches. Every Friday night, hundreds gathered. "The poorer children . . . look forward all week" to their visit, a *CSM* reporter wrote in 1936. "Drab homes, ragged clothing, angry words, ugliness, neglect, physical hunger, vanish as they set out with the Red Cross Knight to fight a dragon, or crawl with Mogill into a wolves' cave, or sail with a seafaring kitten on the 'Roll and Go,' or pioneer in a wilderness with Susan and her doll Arabella."[56]

Other media continued to influence reader demand. Kentucky's packhorse librarians were constantly asked for *Gone with the Wind* and other bestsellers "holler" dwellers heard about on their radios. A 1938 survey showed "the tremendous influence of Hollywood on reading tastes." When a *David Copperfield* movie premiered in the mid-1930s, Cleveland libraries ordered 125 copies to supplement the 375 they already had; every one circulated the week after the movie opened, "and the rush extended to other Dickens books as well." The library also had bookmarks featuring the most recent popular movie and listing other library books relating to it. "The movies and the library seem to fit so much better than one would expect," a newspaper reporter noted.[57]

In 1930, Cleveland College offered educational programs on radio station WTAM; faculty routinely identified relevant books available at the public library. Anyone interested who lacked a radio could "listen in" on a radio in the library's lecture room. In 1938, the Cuyahoga (Ohio) County Public Library began a weekly "Book Caravan" radio program. Each featured a segment in which two women discussed personal problems also addressed by books from the library. By 1942 more than

200 public libraries sponsored such radio programs. In the 1930s, many NYPL branches hosted groups listening to the Metropolitan Opera on library radios. At the Ottendorfer branch, a "room has been made as attractive as possible, with curtains at the windows, pictures of opera singers and scenes from the opera on the book shelves, books about the opera and composers on the desk, and musical periodicals scattered about the room on tables." Usually, 75 to 100 people attended.[58]

At the Little Rock (Arkansas) Public Library, the "Music Coterie" presented concerts in the auditorium, and from the proceeds they purchased a phonograph and classical album collection. The Falls City (Nebraska) Public Library also developed a successful music department. In a town of 6,000 it circulated 400 donated classical records 2,173 times to clubs, teachers, students, and patrons in 1941. In 1940 the Quincy (Massachusetts) Public Library used PWA funds to erect a new wing dedicated to music recordings. Singer Marion Anderson and composers Schubert, Rimsky-Korsakoff, and Rossini were all represented (the latter's "William Tell Overture"—theme for the *Lone Ranger* radio program—was especially popular with children). In 1943 a reader criticized Windy City music lovers for "overlooking" Chicago Public Library Saturday-afternoon recorded music concerts.[59]

Before World War II, WPA workers had also converted a number of New York Public Library branch auditoriums into "little theatres." With federal funds the Fort Washington branch supported the "Fort Washington Players," and when funding dried up an amateur group established a permanent theater company "where unknown talent can be discovered." Although it did not have "the facilities to produce in the spectacular Broadway manner," a playbill explained, "we feel that this is . . . counter-balanced by the enthusiasm" of the players and the auditorium's "pleasantly personal atmosphere." Admission tickets consisted of the programs librarians stuck in books readers checked out. Other amateur groups also used the facility, and by 1941 the branch was one of the city's best venues for amateur productions. Patrons were never charged admission.[60]

At mid-decade several American public libraries started lending toys. In Newark, the library used National Youth Administration money to fund thirteen "toy library" stations. In the first half of 1936, the Los Angeles Public Library acquired 7,126 used toys, which it then circulated 21,610 times. Some toys were given away for "adoption" after a "probationary" period. "How's Rosalie this morning?" a librarian asked an eight-year-old girl pushing a baby buggy. "She's just fine, thank you," the girl answered. "Let's see, this must be the end of your six weeks' probation," the librarian remarked. "Well, Rosalie looks neat and happy. She's yours!" "Oh, thank you very, very much," the girl responded. "She's the first baby I ever had for my very own. I'll be awful good to her."[61] To a child from a poor family this was a significant lesson in civic responsibility for which she received a substantial reward.

"On December 7, 1941, we set up a radio at the front desk and tuned in at 1:30 for the President's message declaring war on Germany and Italy," a NYPL branch librarian reported. "Seventeen members of the public listened with absorbed attention, and rose to their feet as the message was followed by the playing of the national anthem. . . . The silence as the music ended was impressive; everyone was moved by the solemnity of the moment. A cross-section of our public was represented there—older and younger men, housewives, a boy in his teens, a German refugee and his wife, and to those who were present, that library setting will always be recalled with the memory of the event."

Like other civic institutions, World War II had significant impact on public libraries. Once the nation entered the war, federal relief funds largely disappeared, but the library community nonetheless mobilized to serve the nation's wartime needs.[62] With 10 million Americans inducted into the armed services and home front demands preoccupying those who stayed behind, reading room attendance at public libraries plummeted 50 percent. Before they left, however, many patrons said good-bye. To the librarians at NYPL's Chatham Square branch, one soon-to-be ensign remarked: "Wherever I go, whatever I do, I will remember this library and what I have learned here." An army draftee said: "It is as hard to part with the library as with my family." Many remaining behind for jobs created by the war effort also abandoned public libraries. To some, using them in the Depression symbolized free time unbecoming an employed person. One branch librarian reported "an avalanche of borrower's cards . . . shot over the desk" as owners joyfully proclaimed: "Here, I don't want it any more. I have a job."[63]

Less than two weeks after the attack on Pearl Harbor, the Los Angeles Public Library set up a Wartime Information Desk in the first-floor lobby that daily averaged 300 questions and 150 letters of inquiry. A section of books on war production activities, labeled "Defense Counter" before December 7, became "Victory Rack" thereafter. By December 14 every book on Japan in the Chicago Public Library and its forty-six branches was checked out, and all had long waiting lists. And in branch reference rooms patrons pored over material on air raid defense, military strategy, and international politics. In Detroit the Office of Civilian Defense designated the library's "War Information Center" the official place for information on the Red Cross, American Women's Voluntary Service, the United Service Organizations (USO), and the Visiting Nurses Association. The Winchester (Massachusetts) Public Library invited a butcher to the library to show housewives how by skillful carving they could make their meat go further. The East Orange (New Jersey) Public Library exhibited pictures of 125 local men drafted into the war. At the Detroit Public Library seamstresses showed patrons how to hang drapes to darken houses at night.[64]

In many cities, public libraries provided war factories with lunchtime bookmobile service. The Kalamazoo Public Library sponsored family nights for patrons with men and women in service, showing films on places they were stationed. Servicemen stationed around Boston regularly paged through the library's 250 papers for hometown news. The District of Columbia Public Library established a "Home Interests" room with information on decorating small living spaces occupied by women who came to Washington for war work. The Petworth branch was a favorite hangout for single women who gathered in front of "burning logs in the large fireplace" to listen to Sunday-afternoon "victrola concerts," which, the *Washington Post* said, removed "much of the edge of loneliness . . . for the Government girl."[65]

As European Jewish refugees began arriving in New York in the late 1930s, many showed up at NYPL branches. In 1940 a Seward Park librarian overheard one girl tell a friend about her family in Poland, "we don't hear from them any more." At the Hamilton Fish Park branch "one of our readers came to the desk crying" in 1945. "She had just learned that from her village in Poland only 16 out a population of 250 had survived," and all her relatives had perished. "The tragedy of the European Jews has affected our people deeply," a Hamilton Fish Park librarian noted, "and has awakened a new interest in the history of their race and the foundations of their culture. The impregnable position of the Library—being intolerant only of intolerance [she obviously did not speak for all public libraries]—gives the institution at this time a graciousness that is needed by many depressed people in the neighborhood."[66]

In 1943 the Buffalo Public Library collected 88,000 books for a nationwide Victory Book Campaign to provide reading material for servicemen.

It also established a "War Information Center" that identified all war agencies within the city and made accessible their many publications. Because employment in war-related industries required birth records or proof that parents were US residents at time of birth, the library provided old city directories to validate residency, enabling 3,650 people to get jobs. Honolulu's public library provided rooms and materials for servicemen stationed there to write letters home. The New York Public Library developed a bibliography on letter-writing for wives and sweethearts. "Here is what I want," said one wife holding a copy of Elizabeth Barrett Browning's love letters to her husband. "See, it says, 'Dearest and my beloved.'" In late 1943 librarians addressed 3,000 Christmas cards to patrons in the armed services. Many recipients thought they were overdue notices. "The thought peeved me no end," wrote one, "for I thought . . . this was carrying efficiency too far." All who responded, however, thanked librarians for their kindness.[67]

As in World War I some librarians saw opportunities to "elevate" reading tastes. By 1941 American public libraries had generally adjusted to standards of middlebrow literary tastes established in institutional cultures like the Book-of-the-Month Club and *Reader's Digest*, and then through filters like *Booklist* and *Fiction Catalog* mediated those tastes for local communities. Nonetheless, many librarians happily reported that popular fiction reading was down, serious reading up. "For the first time on record the library can report that the supply of mystery stories exceeds the demand," noted East Orange (New Jersey) public librarians in 1943. "This shows that our library detective experts are too busy fighting on the battle fronts or are working hard and long in war factories with no time left for this kind of reading."[68]

Because the federal government did not consider public libraries essential wartime services, however, wartime priorities effectively punished some library practices. Bookmobiles suffered most. At the Los Angeles Public Library, tires were a particular problem, as it was forced to cannibalize good tires from decommissioned vehicles to replace bald tires on those still in service. Patrons wrote hundreds of letters expressing anxiety at losing service, but the situation only grew worse with gas rationing. A "casualty of war," the *New York Times* called it when reporting the loss of East Bronx bookmobile services. Baltimore's Pratt Library dealt creatively with these restrictions. It purchased a horse-drawn wagon to continue services. "The children dearly loved Betty" the horse, said the librarian. "They petted her cautiously and often fell into arguments over her sex. "'Miss, ain't it a her?' was a frequent question."[69]

On May 11, 1943, more than a thousand people assembled on NYPL's front steps to commemorate the tenth anniversary of the 1933 Nazi book burning of 25,000 "un-German" books in Berlin. While flags flew at half-staff, actor Ralph Bellamy read from Stephen Vincent Benet's play *They Burned the Books* and actress Helen Hayes asked the crowd to donate more books to the Victory Book Campaign. Public libraries also became sites for political statements. At the Portsmouth (New Hampshire) Public Library someone ripped cards identifying materials on Germany from the card catalog. In Toledo, an indignant ten-year-old threw a volume of Japanese fairy tales on the floor and trampled it. In Pittsfield (Massachusetts) a patron systematically stole every book with Japanese pictures or with a Japanese title.[70]

Libraries also shared in wartime emotions. From NYPL's Staten Island branch, patrons had a view of the world's busiest harbor. There they watched troopships go out—"thousands of soldiers on their way overseas pass the library in camouflaged transports," the librarian reported. They also watched ships return and unload. "Hundreds of Army trucks, jeeps, and ambulances with the wounded, rolled past the library's windows in seemingly endless procession." For the branch, "the war was always with us." One woman whose husband went down on a torpedoed ship told an NYPL branch librarian that because library books sustained her and helped her "regain her balance, . . . this is my home." Another young woman told a branch librarian in 1944, "I just heard that my fiancé was killed in action. I am all confused. I want to read something that will help me take it."[71]

At the Seattle Public Library, an army enlistee forgot to return a book before being shipped overseas, and the overdue notice followed him to different places he was stationed. When it was returned with a seventh and final postmark, a handwritten note on the outside read: "Missing in action, 11-17-43." At the San Diego Public Library, heartbroken children's librarian Clara Breed watched Japanese American children turn in their library cards before being shipped with their families to internment camps—"a terrible injustice," she said. She accompanied many to the train station, and gave them self-addressed stamped postcards to write her. Some did, detailing their isolation and homesickness. She often answered, and sent books. One later recalled Breed's kindness. "One particular book, *Home for Elizabeth*," she said, "was especially important since the only home I had at the time was a stable."[72]

At war's end, patrons of NYPL's St. George branch watched the ships return loaded with veterans. The first time a ship sailed by without camouflage was so thrilling, the branch librarian reported, the library resumed an old custom of ringing four bells as big ships passed. Still, some public library experiences persisted. Despite booming guns on warships in the river, traffic honking on the streets, planes roaring overhead, and ambulances and patrol car sirens screaming throughout the city on a postwar Navy Day, "some people were still unconcernedly selecting books," the St. Agnes branch librarian noted.[73] This was a part of their lives they did not want to relinquish, no matter the outside world.

In 1945 the United States had 7,400 public libraries, including branches. Annual circulation was 35 million with 25 million registered borrowers. This constituted 33 percent of the population under twenty-one (40–45 percent of titles circulated were "juveniles"), 10 percent over twenty-one. Of that percentage there were more women than men, the better educated more than less educated, middle class more than lower or upper classes, single more than married, and white more than people of color. Fiction still accounted for two-thirds to three-fourths of total circulation.[74]

By 1945 two generations of Americans had experienced a Main Street Carnegie building as a public place where the community displayed its cultural values, where people gathered to connect and exchange pleasantries and points of view, and where appropriate social behaviors were modeled and learned. Sights, sounds, smells, and sensations experienced in these buildings were similar to all, yet each user took unique lessons from collections and services that were also heavily influenced by place and time. Readers still used the card catalog and indexes to mine the useful knowledge public libraries collected and organized, and, more often, found stories ignored in the Dewey Decimal Classification arranged alphabetically by author surname. In addition to these printed books, however, American public libraries continued to disseminate stories in other forms—storytelling, LP records, radio programs, musical events, art exhibits, club room meetings, and auditorium presentations. All helped cement the community, and for millions of Americans made the public library an integral part of their lives.

CHAPTER SEVEN

"Winning the Battles of Daily Life": 1945–1964

Without question, the most compelling issue that preoccupied the library profession in postwar America was censorship. To a great extent librarians invited this by passing the Library Bill of Rights, a self-assumed responsibility to defend intellectual freedom and oppose censorship. Dissensions quickly showed differences between professional rhetoric and the realities of library practice, however. At the 1948 American Library Association annual conference, for example, some librarians criticized several New York, California, and New Jersey public libraries that had banned *The Nation* for "anti-Catholic" articles. Paul Rice, reference division chief of the New York Public Library, articulated the profession's new party line. "Should copies of *The Nation* ever be removed from library shelves? Should libraries in the South fail to have current books on the race problem or novels on the problem that may be offensive to perhaps even a majority of their constituents? Should witch hunts for subversive books persuade librarians not to stock a book because it is friendly to Russia or a communistic idea? The answer to all these questions is, of course, an emphatic no."

At the conference, the ALA also revised Principle 3 of the Library Bill of Rights to read: "Censorship of books, urged or practiced by volunteer arbiters of morals or political opinion or by organizations that would establish a coercive concept of Americanism, must be challenged by libraries in maintenance of their responsibility to provide public information and enlightenment through the printed word." Unlike the other four principles, the text used "must" instead of "should." Still, the ALA refused to impose punishments for violations of Principle 3. (The "must" remained in the 1961 revision, but reverted back to "should" in the 1967 revision, and it has remained ever since.)

A conference proposal that libraries practicing censorship be placed on a blacklist and boycotted by the profession went nowhere. Another proposal setting up a commission to defend librarians who refused to censor and blacklist libraries who fired them met the same fate. Five years later the *Wilson Library Bulletin* published Lester Asheim's article,"Not Censorship, but Selection," which recommended that librarians approach selection positively, by looking for value, strength, and virtue, not negatively, by looking for anything morally or politically offensive. The phrase quickly became part of the profession's lexicon.[1]

But implementing the Library Bill of Rights was almost always messy, often impossible, and professional consensus beyond LBR rhetoric was hard to discern. As in previous generations, in postwar America public libraries had to address sexual censorship. Although in 1933 the Supreme Court judged James Joyce's *Ulysses* not obscene when considered as a whole by an average adult, lower courts often ruled more conservatively. So, when a Massachusetts court found Lillian Smith's *Strange Fruit* obscene in the 1940s, Bay State librarians pulled it. When a New York court found Edmund Wilson's *Memoirs of Hecate County* obscene, the New York Public Library told patrons that reserve requests would not be honored.[2]

In late 1948, a researcher visited eleven Boston-area public libraries to see whether they had Norman Mailer's *The Naked and the Dead* and Alfred Kinsey's *Sexual Behavior in the Human Male*, both bestsellers. Four had rejected Kinsey, five had refused Mailer. Only one had both titles on open shelves. Most others had them in an Inferno, and one restricted Kinsey to lawyers, ministers, teachers, social workers, police, and "others who need it for professional reasons." Six years later Kinsey published the equally popular *Sexual Behavior in the Human Female* (1954). Again, public libraries across the country treated this useful knowledge differently. Some placed Kinsey's books on open shelves, others sequestered them in Infernos, still others refused to buy them. To identify books like Kinsey's on a "controlled shelf," many libraries followed a practice inherited from previous generations by inserting in the subject catalog a card reading: "For Sex Education, See Librarian." Ever since, librarians and patrons have tittered over that phrase, now part of library folklore.[3]

When in 1956 Grace Metalious published *Peyton Place*, a steamy novel about the sexual lives of three women in a small New England town (it sold 6 million copies in two years), the Fort Wayne Public Library refused to buy it. "Book reviews indicated caution," said the library director. With constant pressure, however, the library gave in to public demand and purchased twenty copies that circulated immediately. Only one person complained. When the county attorney declared the book obscene shortly thereafter, however, the library withdrew all copies. Several patrons demanded it be reinstated, but the library refused. When reporting these incidents in its annual report, the library did not mention the Library Bill of Rights but did imply that with time the controversy might pass, as it had with *Grapes of Wrath* and Richard Wright's *Native Son*, now both on open shelves despite the fact that the library initially refused to purchase them.[4]

When Washington's airport bookstores stopped selling *Lady Chatterley's Lover* in 1959 (the US postmaster general ruled it unfit for distribution through the mails), the *Washington Post* investigated. The District's public library had an expurgated edition in its Inferno. In the nearby suburbs, the Montgomery and Prince Georges County (Maryland) libraries had a copy each, but public libraries in Fairfax, Arlington, and Alexandria (Virginia) had none. When the Montgomery County manager banned Henry Miller's *Tropic of Cancer* from local newsstands in 1961, he also ordered the book removed from county public libraries. The central library in Gaithersburg had five copies, but only for patrons over twenty-one; at the time all were circulating with a waiting list of twenty-five. Several Burbank, California, residents demanded their public library remove Henry Miller's *Tropic of Cancer* from its locked case and throw it away, but the director refused. "The public library owes a duty to every segment of the community to make available the books they want," he said. The book remained—in its locked case.[5]

Sometimes religious beliefs grounded censorship challenges. In Santa Ana, California, a patron checked out the bookmobile's copy of *The Last Temptation of Christ*—a novel by Nikos Kazantzakis many considered sacrilegious—renewed it once, and just as soon as she returned it a friend withdrew it and also renewed it. The librarian later learned they were part of group determined to keep it out of circulation. In Arcadia, California, thirty clergymen demanded it be withdrawn from the library. They did not want it "censored," a priest said; "we are asking in unison that it be removed, that's all." Trustees refused, however, noting that the Wilson Company's *Fiction Catalog* gave it two stars. Similar protests followed in Long Beach, Pasadena, Fullerton, and Newport Beach. In San Diego, several citizens complained that *Temptation* was pornographic, defamed Christ, and was "part of the Communist conspiracy to undermine religion and morals." Until communities began protesting, the board chair stated, the book largely sat on shelves. "Now there are long waiting lists in the library and all book stores here have been sold out." In Ashland, Wisconsin, a patron withdrew the book and gave it to his priest, who then forbade him to return it, saying it would be a mortal sin. "I'll have to return it to the librarian," the priest said, "and see that it's burned." The librarian did not burn the book, but he did remove it from circulation.[6]

Controversy about *Peyton Place, Tropic of Cancer, Lady Chatterley's Lover,* and *The Last Temptation of Christ* provided occasions for the public to use the library to moderate disputes about a community's acceptable literary center and come to some resolution. Solutions reached by compromise—which varied by community as each worked its way through local public institutions—satisfied no one entirely, including libraries, many of which violated Library Bill of Rights principles by their actions. The record suggests that most public libraries defaulted to the Inferno—a time-tested compromise between removal and open access. The process was often unpleasant and divisive, yet no blood was shed, no blows struck. "My feeing is we've had censorship for years in many facets of life," one Arcadia resident argued with impeccable logic. "If libraries didn't exert some censorship all the time, you could walk in and ask where the pornographic section is. . . . Try to find a nude girlie magazine in the library; that's censorship, as it should be."[7]

But largely out of sight another kind of subtle influence operated—one that not only complicates the simplistic "not censorship, but selection" phrase introduced into the profession's lexicon at mid-century, but also shows how public libraries function in negotiating a community's acceptable literary boundaries. To maximize sales after World War II, many publishers began issuing paperbacks with alluring covers, which merchants in the country's 100,000 newsstands then displayed on racks—covers out—to attract customers. Because of their suggestive covers, some people insisted such literature affected the nation's moral standards, some claimed it led to increased juvenile delinquency, some maintained these books were evidence of a Communist plot to take over the country, some argued all three. Several groups addressed this issue, including the National Organization for Decent Literature (NODL), a Catholic agency established in 1938 to conduct "a systematic campaign . . . against the publication and sale of lewd magazine and brochure literature." In the early 1950s, NODL focused on paperbacks and comic books and published lists of books it disapproved in its monthly, *The Priest*.

An analysis was made of 370 condemned yet highly popular titles listed in eleven issues of *The Priest* between January 1952 and January 1953. These titles were matched against *Booklist* citations and the collections of five small-town public libraries in the Midwest—Sauk Centre, Minnesota; Lexington, Michigan; Osage, Iowa; Rhinelander, Wisconsin; and Morris, Illinois. The results show how these libraries dealt with this literature.[8] Each semi-monthly *Booklist* reviewed twenty-five adult fiction titles, or 600 per year. Of the 370 *The Priest* considered objectionable, *Booklist* cites only seven in Volume 47 (September, 1950–August, 1951), the period during which most of the 370 were published. Thus, if librarians at these five institutions looked to *Booklist* for guidance, fewer than 2 percent of the titles NODL condemned were listed. That the libraries were selective is obvious. Other books by authors of NODL-condemned titles (such as John O'Hara, Erskine Caldwell, John Steinbeck, and William Faulkner) were well represented in the collections.

These data suggest that people in charge of mid-century heartland public library collections either agreed with or were intimidated by local NODL committees, which monitored newsstands and pressured their owners in all five small towns to rid the communities of these popular paperbacks, many of which sold in the millions. Since each library had at least one Catholic trustee, agreement is a more likely explanation than intimidation. In those few instances where libraries held condemned titles, libraries had purchased them as hardbounds before NODL condemned them as reissued paperbacks. That they subsequently refused to buy cheaper paperbacks should not be surprising. The library profession identified with that part of the publishing industry that favored hardbounds over the softcovers that newsstands and drugstores sold largely to working-class readers. Their preference for hardbounds gave public librarians another reason to say: "That kind of material is not allowed to get on the shelves."[9]

These kinds of challenges were not new to the library profession, but because of its more recently adopted position on intellectual freedom, political censorship efforts brought widespread challenges to public libraries after World War II. By that time many librarians embraced the Library Bill of Rights as a professional imperative, and as a result they found themselves at the nation's center stage when Wisconsin senator Joseph McCarthy capitalized on Cold War fears that communistic movements supported by the Soviet Union posed grave threats to American democracy. McCarthy accused many civic agencies and institutions of spreading Communism, and in particular he picked on libraries that the recently established United States Information Agency had located in US embassies abroad. When McCarthy claimed they had "30,000 communist books," the effects of his campaign rippled through the nation's library community.

Either to protect their jobs or because they agreed with McCarthy's goals, many librarians voluntarily withdrew controversial materials; others never acquired them. In a study for the California Library Association, Marjorie Fiske found that although they "expressed unequivocal freedom-to-read convictions," almost two-thirds of librarians she talked to knew of instances where a contested book or author was not purchased, and nearly one-fifth "habitually avoided buying any material . . . known to be controversial or which they believe might be controversial." Evidence strongly suggests librarians in other states acted no differently.[10]

Some librarians, however, fought McCarthyism on LBR principles. When the *Boston Herald* attacked the Boston Public Library for stocking books the *Herald* said promoted Communism, numerous citizens and a local Catholic newspaper joined librarians in a successful protest. And in response to pressure from a Senate committee to suppress "immoral books," the ALA's Intellectual Freedom Committee joined the American Book Publishers Council for a conference in 1953 and jointly issued a statement that insisted the "Freedom to Read" (as the statement was titled) was essential to democracy. A month later, President Eisenhower implored the Dartmouth College graduating class not to "be afraid to go in your library and read every book." Later that month, at the annual conference, the ALA president read a letter from Eisenhower encouraging librarians to resist book burners.

But librarians' occasional resistance to these pressures did not stop censorship activities. Most public libraries freely circulated books by conspiracy theorists supporting McCarthyism (e.g., Elizabeth Dilling's *Red Network*), but not always. For example, when an American Legionnaire wanted to donate *Seeds of Treason* (a partisan conservative analysis of the Alger Hiss trials) to the Brookline (Massachusetts) Public Library in 1950, librarians refused. The book was "prejudicial and biased," they told him, and cited reviews substantiating that conclusion. The Legionnaire had previously discovered the library did have *From Bryan to Stalin* by Communist Party leader William Z. Foster. "The more I thought about it the more it burned me up," he told a reporter. "Here we have kids fighting against the Communists in North Korea . . . and the public library was handing out such tripe as this while banning anti-communist books." He protested to library trustees; they ignored him.[11]

When a *Chicago Tribune* reporter covering the story called the Brookline Public Library's board chairman for a statement, he responded: "We won't be pressured into buying or circulating any book." To that the *Tribune* protested. "Earlier generations of Bostonians had the intellectual courage to examine their conscience, face unpleasant truths, and deal with them bravely. . . . This generation of softies and sycophants, lacking in patriotism and easily manipulated . . . shows how fast a society can rot." Under such pressure the board ultimately caved in and accepted *Seeds of Treason* as a donation. In selecting books, the chair said meekly, "we are . . . dependent upon the reviews."[12]

In 1951 Burbank (California) Public Library trustees asked the editors of *Alert*, an anti-Communist serial, to train librarians to detect Communist propaganda. It was not a witch hunt or book-burning campaign, one trustee said, but simply for citizens' benefit. Those trustees also encouraged the League of California Cities to establish a book screening organization to advise public library patrons on any book's subversive or immoral contents. The California Library Association immediately condemned the action as contrary to American traditions and "the goals of American librarianship." The Burbank trustees responded that they did not want to remove the books, only "identify" them.[13]

In 1953 a San Antonio housewife compiled a list of 574 books by authors many considered Communists or Communist sympathizers that she found on public library shelves. The mayor suggested the city "brand all Communist-written volumes in the library," while the city manager insisted "they should be burned instead of stamped." The idea was "foolish and ignorant," the *New York Times* protested. "Among the enemies of democracy are not only those who plot against it; there are also those who make it ridiculous." Letters to the *San Antonio News* ran 10 to 1 against branding. Ultimately the board refused to buckle; the books stayed on library shelves, unbranded. In 1953 the District of Columbia Public Library took another approach by issuing a bibliography titled *The Case against Communism.* "A library should have books both for and against Communism," said a DC librarian, "but I also believe that as an American institution it should take positive steps to give expression to American ideals and their conflict with the Communist ideology."[14]

In 1951 the ALA used Ford Foundation funds for an American Heritage Project that enabled public libraries to set up discussion groups reading texts about democracy. Margaret Monroe, NYPL adult services director, quickly assembled a program she believed demonstrated that the library was not only a place where ideas could be discussed freely but also a channel for addressing McCarthyist tensions in a civil manner. But programs funded by the American Heritage Project were run differently in southern public libraries, where all roads still led to race. In Georgia, for example, training sessions for librarians were segregated; in Mississippi, discussion groups were segregated.[15]

Although censorship actively engaged many public librarians after World War II, an analysis of efforts to integrate Jim Crow public libraries in the American South between 1946 and 1964 shows librarians across the country were mostly silent, and largely absent. Between 1954, when the US Supreme Court ruled in *Brown v. Board of Education* that "separate but equal" was no longer legal, and 1965, when Congress passed a Voting Rights Act, southern public libraries frequently became sites of racial protest, almost always initiated by black people and after 1960 almost always by young black people.

Sometimes integration occurred quietly. Before opening a new building in 1951, the Miami Public Library decided to desegregate when a local black preacher wrote the board: "Please do not force me to bring an injunction against the opening of this very beautiful library." An integrated library opened months later. In Newport News, Virginia, a local black citizen did bring suit against the public library. But on July 19, 1952, Newport News became the first Virginia public library to integrate. Rumor had it the decision was made to squelch the suit. In 1957 a black interior decorator entered the Purcelleville (Virginia) Public Library to borrow a book on French drapes. He was denied, trustees said, because "to lend him a book would not be in the spirit of the library's founders." The decorator threatened to sue. Days later trustees decided 7 to 5 not only to open the library to Purcelleville blacks but also to provide them with bookmobile service.[16]

Sometimes public library integration was a sop to give the appearance of local progress on desegregating public accommodations, while whites continued to resist integration of institutions (like schools) they considered more important. Sometimes court orders ended library segregation, but segregationist boards still resisted. In Talladega, Alabama, for example, a court order integrated its public library in 1962, but trustees decided to admit only people whose residency could be verified by a Talladega phone book listing. At the time, most blacks had no phone.[17]

Desegregation of public libraries was always painful, if not always violent or immediately successful. White southerners who defended black access to public libraries paid a price. In Bartlesville, Oklahoma, Ruth Brown—for thirty years the public library director—was fired in 1950 for circulating "Communist" magazines and newspapers like *The Nation, New Republic,* and *Soviet Today.* But these charges were a ruse for the primary reason she was dismissed—attempting to integrate the public library and the Bartlesville community by challenging local segregationist practices. In the mid-1950s, white Montgomery, Alabama, reference librarian Julliette Morgan wrote the newspaper about racism she saw on city buses. "Some bus drivers use the tone and manners of mule drivers in their treatment of Negro passengers. . . . Twice I have heard a certain driver, with high seniority, mutter audibly 'Black ape.'" Thereafter segregationists called her at the library and home, where she lived with her mother. "They threatened her. They harassed her. They insulted her with vulgar and obscene accusations," a *Pittsburgh Courier* columnist reported. The stress became so great "she could not sleep, she could not eat." When she died shortly thereafter, the columnist pronounced it "plain murder."[18] Brown's and Morgan's experiences had a chilling effect on white librarians sympathetic to integration elsewhere in the South.

Atlanta's experiences served as a harbinger for the rest of the South. To desegregate the library system, in 1959 the Atlanta Negro Voters League—which had organized at the Auburn branch and used it to register voters—joined with the branch's Friends of Libraries, the American

Veterans Committee, the Atlanta Council on Human Relations, and the Atlanta Urban League, to threaten suit. Mayor William B. Hartsfield, who as a young adult had educated himself in the Atlanta Public Library and who owed his election to 30,000 black voters, pushed the board to integrate. Because no law existed to prevent integration, the board buckled.[19]

In 1959, over Christmas break during his University of Illinois freshman year, Jesse Jackson went to the black branch in his hometown of Greenville, South Carolina. Because he could not find certain titles, the librarian wrote a note and sent him to the white main library. When Jackson walked through the rear entrance, several policemen were talking to the librarian, who took the note and remarked: "It'll take at least six days to get these books." "*Six* days?" Jackson responded. "Couldn't I just go back in the shelves and look for them . . . where nobody else would see me?" "You cannot have the books now. That's the way it is." "You heard what she said," remarked one policeman. Jackson stormed out the library's rear door, walked to the building's front, and looked up. "I just stared up at that 'Greenville Public Library,' and tears came to my eyes. I said to myself, 'That thing says public, and my father is a veteran and pays taxes.'" Angry and humiliated, he decided to take action. On a July Saturday afternoon Jackson and eight other students walked into the library and staged a sit-in. Although all were arrested for disorderly conduct, held in jail for forty-five minutes, and released on bail, their efforts proved successful. On September 15, 1960, the Greenville public library opened as an integrated facility.[20]

On March 27, 1961, nine NAACP Tougaloo College chapter members entered the Jackson, Mississippi, public library. Ten minutes later they were arrested for disturbing the peace; thirty-two hours later they were released on bail. For Jackson, NAACP Field Secretary Medgar Evers asserted, their action set the city's desegregation process in motion. When their cases were heard on April 21, more than 100 black Jacksonians began applauding as the students were escorted into the courthouse. As Evers described it, "Instantly, there was a call from some police officers saying 'get 'em out of here,' and it was then that hordes of policemen and two vicious dogs converged on Negro citizens only." A minister was bitten on the arm, an NAACP field secretary was struck on the back with billy clubs and on the head with a pistol, and an eighty-one-year-old man suffered a broken wrist. The defendants drew $100 fines and suspended sentences.[21]

In 1962 a black teenager filed a federal suit to desegregate the Montgomery, Alabama, public library. When the court ordered the library to desegregate, the trustees ordered all reading tables and chairs removed. The *Philadelphia Tribune* ridiculed "the idiocy of Montgomery white folk in their 'cut-off-the-nose-to-spite-the-face' move," but teased that a pleasant by-product "might be improved posture for the new reader who no longer can slouch in his chair or hunch over his book while reading." When city fathers in Albany, Georgia, closed libraries, parks, and public facilities in 1963 rather than obey a federal court order to integrate, the *Tribune* wondered whether the recently erected Berlin Wall was "more adverse to the cause of freedom" than what was happening to southern blacks. "Perhaps it is safer, or better politics, to condemn Communists in far-off places than it is to tackle un-American activities right on our doorsteps." Albany's city fathers integrated the library months later.[22] At no time during these years did the American Library Association file any amicus brief in federal cases involving the desegregation of public libraries (the ALA did file one for a *Tropic of Cancer* censorship case, in which it cited the Library Bill of Rights); during these years the association also allowed segregated libraries to hold full membership.

White officers carry out a black teenage girl who participated in a sit-in at the segregated Albany (Georgia) Carnegie Library, 1962. *Copyright Bettmann/Corbis/AP Images, ID 6207310241*

Blacks also experienced obstacles to integrated public library services in the North; here real estate redlining and complicit city governments all but guaranteed ghettoized neighborhoods in which branches, like Chicago's Hall and NYPL's 135th Street libraries, served almost entirely black populations. Black patrons often complained of the contents of children's books these branches contained. "There is rarely a book," one black mother wrote the *Washington Post* in 1946, "written exclusively on Negro children fit for any child to read." Others shared her sentiments. Books "were always full of picture perfect Sallys and Jacks in clinically uncluttered farmhouses or cottages, living neat, prescribed lives that bore little resemblance to our Black lives," recalled another, describing her 1950s childhood reading experiences in a northern public library. "Nowhere was there a portrayal of our Black and brown faces, or any suggestion of the warmth and spontaneity that filled our homes; no hint of the loving smells of sweet bread baking in the oven or the friendly and familiar scent of oilcloth-covered tables; nothing of the snap-and-dash style and wit of our language or the rhyming cadences of our voices on spring and summer evenings as we played limber-legged games that had been handed down to us for generations." A few children's librarians like Charlemae Hill Rollins and Augusta Baker pressed publishers to include more black experiences—with little success, however.[23]

But some obstacles to black use of public libraries in the North were cultural. In 1948, for example, young Walter Dean Myers—who as an adult became a successful children's author—was often harassed by older black boys when he carried books home from his NYPL branch library. "It was, they made it clear, not what boys did. . . . I began taking a brown paper bag to the library to bring my books home in." In Milwaukee, nine-year-old Oprah Winfrey read so much her mother worried she would begin thinking she was "better than the other kids." One day she caught Oprah reading in her apartment building hallway. "You're nothing but a something-something bookworm," she shouted. "Get your butt outside. . . . And I'm not taking you to no library!" In *Go Tell It on the Mountain*, James Baldwin places his chief protagonist in front of the New York Public Library. "He had never gone in because the building was so big . . . he would be lost and never find the book he wanted. And then everyone, all the white people inside, would know that he was not used to great buildings, or to many books, and they would look at him with pity."[24]

Despite the headlines that censorship challenges and desegregation efforts generated for American public libraries between 1946 and 1965, traditional library practices were not significantly altered. Reference desk services reflected patterns now generations old. In 1948, a reference librarian at a branch of the New York Public Library recalled "questions and readers ranging from the fearful sad-eyed mother seeking information" on Down's syndrome "to the cheerful Girl Scouts desiring identification of a mysterious insect whose body, in two neat parts, arrives at the library with the girls." One day "we had a Jewish mother with an only daughter about to marry a Catholic, who wanted to read anything which might be helpful in clarifying her thinking." Two years later a father sought South Carolina marriage laws because his teenage daughter had married without his consent. Prospective parents asked how to adopt a baby, and an indignant fifty-four-year-old mechanic wanted to know how to publish an account of rebuffs he experienced in finding a job "due solely to his age."[25]

Reference room irritations persisted. In 1946 Brooklyn public librarians were so annoyed at call-in questions from people playing radio quiz programs that they insisted patrons come to the library. But bringing them in brought its own problems. After one quiz, "the circulation room looked like a wheat field after the locusts," a librarian remarked. "Neither the Information Please experts, Dr. I.Q., nor Solomon himself," Kokomo, Indiana, reference librarians grumped, "could answer the myriad questions that test and torment" them. Sometimes an inability to answer reference questions led to unwanted results. At NYPL's Cathedral branch, a father of three asked a librarian in 1958 for a book on the "rhythm method of birth control." The library's copy was missing, the librarian said; so were other branch copies. "Months went by, with the man coming in every so often to ask" about his reserve. One day, however, he canceled it; his wife was pregnant. At the Enoch Pratt Free Library, "one man came in and told me he and his wife were not getting along sexually," noted a librarian. "I gave him books from the locked case." At NYPL's 96th Street branch in 1961 a patron asked a librarian: "I want to know how to take an enema." Because he was not satisfied with his pharmacist's instructions, "he plied me with detailed questions until there was nothing left to ask," then left.[26]

Overdue fines continued to perplex librarians and patrons. To enforce an ordinance fining patrons up to $200 for failure to return materials, in 1961 East Orange, New Jersey, police arrested six delinquents in post-midnight raids for books four or more months overdue. One delinquent told reporters that police came to his home in the wee hours, woke him, and although he produced the books, took him to the station. Because he could not make bail, he spent the night in jail. The arrests had immediate impact. "We're getting three times the usual rate" of returns, a librarian reported. Not many citizens were happy with the new policy, however; some readers turned in their library cards and said they would never be back. Yet, a week later, the library reported "hard core" delinquents had dwindled to seven.[27]

The story went national. "Booked for Bookkeeping," the *Christian Science Monitor* teased. "Don't panic," the *Washington Post* told readers with books overdue at the District of Columbia Public Library. "You will not be hustled away to jail before dawn"; the editorial also needled East Orange for actions "against an especially vicious and dangerous set of evil-doers." When a *Post* reporter checked with area libraries, he discovered Prince Georges County did not charge overdue fines. "I wish you would," patrons often told librarians. "Then I wouldn't feel so guilty." On Long Island, the Hicksville Public Library went to court to reach several hundred delinquents but dropped charges when those subpoenaed returned the books. In nearby Plainview, subpoenas brought in 95 percent of overdues.[28]

While the East Orange incident generated national attention, it also reminded readers across the country about civic responsibility. In Georgia, a breathless man ran into the Carroll-Heard Regional Library, dropped off books due that day, and as he ran out shouted: "My wife is in labor in my car and I'm on the way to [the] hospital. See you later!" At one NYPL branch a girl with a handful of pennies returned books for her brother, saying "He took these out a long time ago and overdid it."[29]

Public libraries still had rental shelves, but by the 1960s many had contracted with a subscription service vendor to supply these shelves with popular books, mostly fiction. The Winfield (Kansas) Public Library, for example, subscribed to a 150-book plan and charged five cents a day per title. "We fully expected our patrons to object to the higher rental fees," the librarian wrote, "but were pleasantly surprised when no objections were forthcoming. . . . The beauty of this plan is that we need to do no fiction buying and all of our money may be used for standard books."[30] "Standard books" was code for serious reading.

Community efforts to open new public libraries after World War II showed as much creativity as in previous generations. In 1947 folks in West Danville, Vermont, remodeled a 10 by 17 foot gas station into a public library. In Winchester, Kentucky, the Fine Arts Club hosted a dance that collected $1,661.71; residents donated 500 books and the state library matched them. All were housed in a courthouse room that immediately proved too small, so a construction company donated an old railroad car that the club renovated. "Now our library consists of 6,000 books," the president remarked in 1956. "We can't say much for the architecture, but we're pleased to know that some months our circulation goes over 18,000."[31]

Public libraries also adopted new technologies. In 1955 the Chicago Public Library got a Recordack circulation machine that photographed transaction records, greatly speeding the checkout process. "Thump, thump, thump" no longer signaled the end of a transaction in many public libraries, and the ink-stained pencil-mounted date stamp that had become a part of many female librarians' coiffures started to disappear. After libraries obtained diffusion-transfer reversal (Thermofax) and electrostatic (Xerox) copy machines in the late 1950s, patrons lined up—even though the NYPL reading room charged patrons thirty cents a page, then a substantial sum and higher than most other public libraries providing the service. Copy machines at LAPL would prevent "writer's cramp," the *Los Angeles Times* promised in 1955.[32]

In 1956, President Dwight Eisenhower signed the Library Services Act (LSA), the first federal legislation specifically intended to fund some library services. The bill made it to his desk mostly because southern state librarians convinced their representatives (many held crucial committee chairs) that passage would not curtail states' rights, since state library agencies determined how funds would be distributed. (For southern legislators a constant subtext in librarians' lobbying efforts was state agency ability to limit and control services to southern blacks.) With the appropriations, many states bought bookmobiles that traversed remote areas previously little served. At the time the act passed, 26 million Americans—most rural—had no public library services. Eight years later Congress revised the act to become the Library Services and Construction Act, specifically abolishing the rural restriction and making urban areas eligible for funds.

By that time bookmobiles had won the hearts of millions, rural and urban. "Yonder she comes!" children shouted when the Carroll-Heard

Regional Library bookmobile drove to sites in five West Georgia counties. On one occasion a nine-year-old returned a book his dog had shredded. "Shedding copious tears," the bookmobile librarian described, he placed it on the bookmobile desk. "It won't happen again, Miz Betty." Accidents do happen, Miz Betty reassured him, but since his mother paid for the book he could still check out others. Not until the boy confessed his "dog won't mess up anymore 'cause my mother runned over him and he's dead" did the librarian realize the reason he was crying. On another occasion two brothers announced the book they had checked out was "a goner." What happened? the librarian asked. They were on their way to school one morning, one explained, and went by their father's vat where he kept his mash. When his brother leaned over too far, the book fell in. "It was plumb ruint," they lamented.[33]

By 1960, 200 bookmobiles traveled rural roads to reach 1 million new patrons. "Hiram, come here quick," said one Kansas woman to her husband when a bookmobile pulled into her farmyard. "We're rich! We're rich!" "This bookmobile is a bright spot in our lives," acknowledged a New Mexico forest ranger's wife. "We live for the times it comes; we need the reading to keep us sane." A Louisiana patron said: "This is the best thing that's happened to us since gas!" Bookmobiles in Alaska were airplanes and mail boats, the state librarian explained. "Usually the pilot can land, but in bad weather the books are sometimes dropped from the plane." On one occasion a box of books fell into a river. People waiting there "got the box out immediately and wiped every book so . . . thoroughly that we would never have known anything had happened to them if we hadn't received their apologies for the damage."[34]

After the war many urban public librarians increased efforts to attract young adults. In 1945 the Santa Monica (California) Public Library converted a branch basement into a Young People's Room. "Teenagers gathered here for study and games. . . . A radio played constantly, and the room was staffed by a social worker rather than a librarian." The Chicago Public Library's teenage reading room had a radio and phonograph. Every Saturday night teens selected the music, which ranged from Tommy Dorsey to bebop.[35] In 1949, Brooklyn's Bedford branch contacted a gang caught vandalizing neighborhood property. The gang responded, and with librarians created a neighborhood headquarters for young adults with bebop, swing, and "sweet music" records, plus a youth newspaper and a drama group that met every Wednesday evening. "This is library service at its best," said one city official. That same year NYPL's Seward Park branch opened the Holladay Memorial Library for Young People in a donated house. Besides a Great Books course, discussion groups on foreign affairs, and a creative writing group that self-published its work in pamphlets, the Holladay House (as locals dubbed it) became a teen social center. A student council directed its activities. In 1961 the Dallas Public Library organized a Monday-night Young People's Jazz Series that played to standing-room-only audiences. "Did the project result in progress for the Library?" the librarian asked. "In publicity, yes; in humanizing the institution, yes; in stimulating circulation of books, yes; in inveigling non-library users into the library, yes."[36]

But the baby boomer generation also brought what librarians often called a "student invasion." Because high schools increasingly encouraged independent study but failed to provide the materials for it, public libraries often had to make up the difference as students flooded school systems. During Christmas vacation in 1960, for example, Newark (New Jersey) Public Library surveys showed 64 percent of users were high school and college students working on assignments. In 1962, surveys in Whittier, California, found an average of 500 high school students using the public library every Saturday.[37]

Often these large numbers of young people brought trouble. In the early 1960s, Owosso, Michigan, teens of both sexes began gathering at the public library and causing disturbances. The board's solution was to separate the teens by gender. During the school year the library allowed girls to study on Monday and Wednesday evenings, boys on Tuesday and Thursday evenings. The Santa Ana (California) Public Library required students to leave library cards at the front desk after 6 P.M. (if there were disturbances the library would then be able to identify the troublemakers) and sit in the reference room only when using reference materials. When a teen gang disturbed patrons by swearing in loud voices at the Bethesda (Maryland) Public Library in 1954, they were told not to return. The next evening gang members rode bicycles through the reading room, and in subsequent evenings hurled bricks through the front door. One night they tossed a homemade pipe bomb into the building, but it failed to explode. In 1957 the Brooklyn Public's Bushwick branch became a site for so much street crime the branch closed. "People were afraid to walk in the area after dark." By 1963, 13 percent of public libraries reported they had placed restrictions on services to high school students. The Great Neck (New York) Public Library even eliminated its youth department. As minority groups migrated into cities and white youth and their families moved into the suburbs in the 1950s, many urban libraries with young adult departments retreated into middle-class book services largely disconnected from the kinds of cultural texts the remaining minority neighborhood youths found relevant to their daily lives.[38]

Nonetheless, in postwar America public libraries continued to inspire, rescue, assimilate, and educate their young patrons. In Marshall, Texas, the public library "became a mecca for poor kids like me," Bill Moyers later recalled. "In books plucked from the shelves were stories that I have never forgotten: explorers whose adventures I could envy, heroes whose exploits I could admire, villains I could hiss." To escape a dysfunctional family environment, Nancy Pearl, a future author and librarian, spent most of her 1950s youth at a Detroit Public Library branch. "It's not too much of an exaggeration . . . to say that reading saved my life." When she reached Miami from Cuba after the 1959 revolution, thirteen-year-old Marcia Del Mar became a permanent fixture at the Miami Public Library. "All the employees there got to know me by my first name," she recalled after achieving fame as a television actress: "I forced myself to read voraciously." Within six months "I was beginning to understand what was said to me and also able to make myself understood."[39]

Sometimes, however, public libraries frustrated their patrons. In the 1950s one young man combed Evanston (Illinois) Public Library shelves, desperately searching for information that "might confirm an identity I was piecing together and accommodate a sexuality that fate seemed to have thrust on me." What he found were "grim psychiatric case studies—all bits of half-information to convey prevailing notions of homosexuality as sin, madness, or crime." His experience was typical, but not universal. When an adolescent girl visited the Miami (Florida) Public Library in the early 1960s to seek understanding about sexual feelings confusing her, she discovered homosexuality books on open shelves. "I read the passages that described 'mannish' wimmin with short, cropped hair. . . . And I thought to myself, 'That's me!'"[40]

And at mid-century the westerns, mysteries, and love stories Pittsburgh public library director Ralph Munn said had "little or no value except as entertainment" still averaged 70 percent of public library circulation. In 1948, the Carnegie Corporation funded a Public Library Inquiry (PLI) to analyze the public library's purpose and especially the "library faith" that grounded it. The project eventually led to seven books and five reports. In these publications the authors recommended that instead of supplying popular reading desired by large populations, public libraries should instead address the information needs of a smaller but more influential combination of serious readers, community leaders, and adult education students. In *The Library's Public,* author Bernard Berelson showed little understanding of why readers so highly valued the commonplace reading public libraries had been providing since 1854.[41]

The PLI also overlooked differences in reading behaviors. A bookmobile driver observed this during a 1950–1952 Demonstration Project of the Door-Kewaunee County (Wisconsin) Regional Library. He noticed that people on the region's south end and people on the north end read different popular authors. He also observed how readers constantly shared information about authors they read on their bookmobile visits. "We met our friends down there," one farmwoman recalled. "It was a social gathering."[42] Although PLI researchers concluded public libraries could do little to influence adult commonplace reading tastes, children were different. Surveys showed the public library supplied 67 percent of the "quality" books read by children, Berelson reported, and only 43 percent of "nonquality" books." Public libraries pushed for these "quality" books in guides like *Horn Book* and *Children's Catalog,* and except for many small public libraries run by nonprofessionals and a few sympathetic children's librarians staffing branches in urban systems, they continued to shun series fiction.

Not many librarians openly agreed with youth librarian Margaret C. Scoggin, who bravely claimed in 1947: "One reason for adult worry about young people's reading is our unwillingness to grant to young people a sense of discrimination between the valuable and the ephemeral in what they read." Nor did they agree with children's literature expert Mark Taylor, who observed in 1963: "Lists, commendations and damnations of children's books appear to be based solely upon personal criteria of literary quality from a strictly adult and subjective point of view." Instead, most seemed to fall behind literary standards set by children's library pioneer Anne Carroll Moore and her successors, whose "far-seeing vision of the *best*," one NYPL branch children's librarian insisted, "is none too good for the children of N.Y.C."[43]

Children obviously saw series fiction differently from adults. Months after her father died in 1963, nine-year-old Sonia Sotomayor buried herself in reading at her branch library and in the Bronx apartment she shared with her mother and brother. "Nancy Drew had a powerful hold on my imagination," she recalled. "Every night, when I'd finished reading and got into bed and closed my eyes, I would continue the story, with me in Nancy's shoes until I fell asleep." Her mind worked in ways similar to Nancy's, she discovered. "I was a keen observer and listener. I picked up on clues. I figured things out logically, and I enjoyed puzzles. I loved the clear focused feeling that came when I concentrated on solving a problem and everything else faded out." Her reading that summer, she later admitted, got her through this troubled time in her life. But she got the Nancy Drew books as gifts from her mother; her NYPL branch library did not stock them.[44]

Others also remembered librarians who tried to control their childhood reading. "I can remember having a fight with a librarian over a book," recalled one. "She said . . . it was for third graders and I wasn't. I was very stubborn and I read it." Another recalled her librarian continually used "her authority to bar me from certain books." Not a problem, however. "I merely asked the older girls to check them out for me." In 1949 a mother complained to the *Chicago Tribune* that her eight-year-old son—enamored of the *Wizard of Oz* film—wanted to read the fourteen Oz books millions had been reading for generations, but was shocked to discover the Chicago Public Library system did not have them. Apparently CPL librarians had determined that the yellow brick road would bypass Windy City libraries. Yet in tiny Lexington, Michigan (population 594 in 1950), the public library, run by a local high school graduate with over forty years of service in the post, had fifty-four Oz books on its shelves.

As with Nancy Drew and the Hardy Boys, many librarians still hated comics, wildly popular at mid-century. In 1948, Chicago Public Library officials attended a Chicago Recreation Commission meeting to discuss ways of "controlling objectionable comics." No comic books in the Charlotte (North Carolina) Public Library system, library officials assured local citizens in 1951. In the library children read "great classics . . . 'true' books—books that tell a story based on facts." In 1954, Santa Barbara, California, citizens initiated a public library fund-raising campaign for better children's books "to counteract the blight of objectionable comic books."[45] Comic book readers disagreed. "My comic book reading certainly led to other reading," recalled linguistics professor Stephen Krashen, a late-twentieth-century advocate of voluntary reading—"the most powerful tool we have in language education," he said. Comic books "opened up my imagination and gave me a large vocabulary," said Philippine American immigrant Sharon Cho. "Reading comics gave me a sense of being special."[46]

Like previous generations, communities connected and networked in the spaces their local public libraries provided. Between 1959 and 1967, for example, the Racine (Wisconsin) Public Library hosted 50,000 people for 2,000 meetings by groups like the Humane Society, the African Violet Society, the Garden Club, an investment club, and a hobby club. It also ran a weekly noon film program, book discussion groups for adults and youth, and lectures on "Contemporary Thought in Fiction" and "Art for the Home." A 1963 *Chicago Tribune* article titled "The Library Is for People" noted that "millions . . . come here—kids, executives, co-eds, housewives, scientists, and Skid Row bums. . . . They come here not just for books or facts, . . . but for invaluable help in winning the battles of daily life."[47] At one NYPL branch in 1957, patrons asked librarians to "translate" their doctors' prescriptions; at another a mother called for first-aid information because her son had sealed his eyelashes with chewing gum. In a 1960 report, one librarian noted her branch gave efficient service to its patrons even on days when "Jonathan was spanked in the Adult Room, . . . Lillian's wrist was caught in the swinging doors," a woman "insisted she was going to walk out the window," and a "little old lady left a puddle in the reference room."[48]

In 1952, Boy Scouts helped the Cedar Rapids Public Library move 12,000 books in three hours. In 1953, Boy and Girl Scouts began delivering Roselle Park (New Jersey) Public Library books to shut-ins. In Fitchburg, Massachusetts, a Youth Library Project mobilized 7,000 children to raise $10,000 for a library addition designed just for them. Younger children raised money from their parents by "remembering to hang up their nightclothes and clean their teeth," the *Christian Science Monitor* reported. Others sold seed, soap, and fishworms. Older children put on fashion shows and a Girl Scouts' circus, and others sold artwork and crafts they made. Eighteen speakers between fourth and twelfth grades addressed business groups, parent-teacher organizations, fraternal societies, and lodges. The Elks organized a city-wide paper drive and got fifty boys to pick up the paper. The library addition these efforts ultimately funded contained a 250-seat auditorium that showed motion pictures. In the garden outside, memorials recognized European cities where Nazis had destroyed books. A librarian told the *Monitor* the project was "uniting a city divided in its racial, religious and cultural background, and through the union they are building for a still greater unity in years to come."[49]

Public libraries still taught children proper social behavior—in many ways. At Savannah's black branch a janitor cracked a buggy whip if children got too loud. Shortly after the war the Atlanta Auburn branch director Annie McPheeters noticed young Maynard Jackson walk in with a "big brown paper bag in his hand." Maynard circled the children's room, selected books he wanted to read, and put them on the table next to his bag. When McPheeters heard paper rustling moments later, she found Maynard eating a lunch the bag contained. "We do not eat in the library," she said, and "we certainly do not eat when we are reading books." "Yes, Mrs. McPheeters," Maynard responded, and closed the bag. "Later," McPheeters recalled, "I would hear that bag opening again. . . . Maynard loved to eat while he was reading."[50] And because parents still considered public libraries safe destinations, libraries enabled youth to mask other behaviors. In a 1964 recording the Beach Boys sang about a teenager who told her "daddy" she was going to the library, then had "Fun, Fun, Fun" while driving his T-bird around town instead. My wife Shirl did this routinely as a 1960s teenager; her three sisters routinely covered for her.

But on occasion the secluded spaces public libraries provided also made inappropriate social behaviors possible. Some were discovered, and people punished. In 1953 Atlanta police installed two-way mirrors in the library men's restroom to apprehend gay men having sex; they arrested twenty in eight days. All were convicted, all had to promise never again to visit the library "on any occasion for any purpose." Some were secret, however, and not discovered. In the early 1950s, New York teenager Frank Conroy worked as a branch page. While shelving books one day he heard someone approach. "A girl. I could tell from her footsteps. She went directly to the next alcove without seeing me. A chair scraped. Papers rustled." Conroy's hormones kicked in. First he moved a few books to peer at her and "found a piece of her, neck to breast, in white cotton." He then moved other books to find her legs "primly crossed, although enough thigh showed to hold my interest." Again he changed position, this time to see her face. "Her eyes were shut tight, tear stained. . . . She wept, . . . her head nodding slowly. I recoiled from the peephole as if a needle had pierced my pupil."[51]

Like their parents, baby boomers found children's story hour staple fare in public libraries across the country—"just a part of our lives," recalled one Chicagoan of his 1950s experiences. Librarians' agendas for story hours varied, however. In 1948 the El Paso (Texas) Public Library's story hour aimed "to unite children of many backgrounds." On one occasion black high school students did a choral reading of *The Gingham Dog and the Calico Cat* for Anglo and Hispanic children. The *Christian Science Monitor* photographer who covered the event remarked that he had learned English "in this very manner by listening in Chicago parks to librarians holding story hours for children."[52]

By mid-century many urban public libraries that were located near business districts routinely conducted admission-free noontime activities, including book reviews and discussions, author interviews, and music recitals. Often these activities focused on special library exhibits on gardening, artwork, or international affairs. For example, the Boston Public Library sponsored a once-a-week "Books Sandwiched In" program from 12:20 to 12:45. In 1949 the Chicago Public Library hosted a lecture series on Wednesdays, noon-hour book talks on Thursdays, a film series titled "You and Your World" on Fridays, and on Saturdays chamber music concerts. In 1951 the Brooklyn Public Library opened its lobby for a chess expert to demonstrate moves that made him a world champion. Similarly, in 1953 the library's Flatbush branch opened a "Senior Citizens Room" where Friday-afternoon canasta and bridge games and Tuesday book discussions became staple fare. Attendees ranged in age from from sixty to eighty-eight.[53]

Postwar first-generation immigrants who used public libraries repeated the experiences of previous generations of immigrants going back to the mid–nineteenth century. In 1962 the Cambridge (Massachusetts) Public Library helped the Knights of Lithuania celebrate Lithuanian Independence Day (Lithuania was at the time under Soviet domination) by exhibiting Lithuanian paintings, needlecrafts, jewelry, and hand-carved icons. Knights donned native dress and answered questions. A recent immigrant who with her family used the library daily thought: "I belong here, and I'm appreciated." Library programs she attended "made you more respectful of other ethnic groups in the city." In 1946 NYPL's Hamilton Fish Park branch librarians welcomed refugees rescued from Nazi death camps who told of "harrowing experiences. They are constantly amazed at the marvel of a public library." A Seward Park branch librarian recalled when one small boy recognized an ex-soldier who had befriended him in a camp. "There was a very affecting reunion."[54]

After World War II San Francisco's Chinatown residents—whose families had lived in the Bay Area for generations—agitated to improve their neighborhood branch. They wanted books on Chinese history, but even more important, space for exhibits, meeting places, and programs to focus on Chinese culture. In 1956 they got it—a new building on Powell Street, with a small collection of Chinese books donated by local residents. Across the Bay junior high student Ben Fong-Torres used the Oakland Public Library as a welcome escape from the small apartment he, his parents, and four siblings called home. "The library was where I found America." Perhaps Ben was helped by seventeen-year-old Floyd Salas, Latino American library page, who, after finishing his work, made himself "scarce in the public stacks and read, everything from *Black Boy* to *Native Son* to *This Is My Beloved*. . . . The library is the most socially important structure that can be built," he concluded.[55]

Like disputes about what constituted acceptable reading in public libraries, disputes about what constituted acceptable art on public display there also required mediation. Resolutions varied, however. When a Boise, Idaho, resident objected to a partially nude mermaid on a public library mural in 1960, trustees decided to make no changes. To minimize the possibility of further complaints a Children's Librarian covered the mermaid with burlap. That brought more objections. To resolve the issue, however, one patron suggested keeping a plant in front of the semi-nude figure. Trustees who viewed the mural with the plant in place agreed. For years thereafter, hundreds of teenage boys with raging hormones peeked behind the plant.[56]

Much more public was the brouhaha at the Dallas Public Library when it opened a new building in 1955. Over the circulation desk hung a 10 by 24 foot screen by Henry Bertoia that consisted of metal shapes arranged on vertical bars. Many hated it. The mayor called it "a pile of junk"; the building architect said he might reimburse the library the $8,500 it cost and "throw it in the river." When the library removed it, newspaper columnists teased. "The mural of Bertoia will no longer annoia," wrote one. Ultimately, prominent Dallas citizens gave $8,500 to repurchase the piece and donated it to the library, which put it back over the circulation desk. As expected, the controversy brought many more into the library, just to see it.[57] A year later the library exhibited a Pablo Picasso painting. When patrons objected to this "Communist art," the library took it down. A library employee later explained that although the librarian hated to give in to this act of censorship, he needed trustee support to win staff raises. Another DPL art piece escaped controversy, however, because negotiation about it occurred outside the public eye. For the library lawn, officials commissioned a sculpture that, the artist promised, would depict "the hands of God supporting youth reaching for learning through the medium of literature." When initial drawings showed the youth nude, several shocked trustees "voted to put pants on that sculpture." When the 880-pound figure was unveiled six months later, the youth indeed sported pants.[58]

As new media developed, public libraries adapted. In postwar America, television especially worried librarians. In 1948, 172,000 families owned sets; twelve years later 90 percent of American homes had at least one. The effect of this new technology on public libraries showed in different ways. "I could not possibly have taken any book on that date," complained one NYPL patron protesting an overdue fine in 1951; "I had television by then." At the same time, however, television often became part of library services. In 1953, for example, when relatively few households had their own TV sets, 100 people watched Dwight Eisenhower's inauguration on a Brookline (Massachusetts) Public Library television set; the library also exhibited books, pamphlets, and displays to mark the occasion. On October 2, 1951, the Stamford (Connecticut) Public Library had its television tuned to the Giants-Dodgers baseball play-off game. By the fourth inning, the library had a "full house." As Bobby Thompson rounded third base after hitting the game-winning home run, Giants fans stood and cheered.[59]

And as in previous years, newer media had limited impact on the mix of choices public libraries provided. After noticing an uptick in circulation once people got used to television, the Queens Public Library decided in 1951: "Reading has survived in spite of the prophecies that television would supplant books." That same year the Erie (Pennsylvania) Public Library director stated: "Apparently television is no longer a threat or even serious competitor to books and library use." As the *New York Times* asserted, survey findings have refuted "the persistent assumption that the young book reader would be lost to television. A substantial majority of public libraries reported that children were actually reading more and not less."[60]

As places, public libraries created many opportunities for enterprising artists of all sorts. For example, after NYPL's 135th Street branch organized the American Negro Theater in the basement, it played host to struggling young actors like James Earl Jones. When the Cincinnati Public opened a piano room in 1955, among its first visitors was "Big Joe" Buskin, well-known blues pianist who regularly entered the room, closed the door, and then loudly played boogie-woogie music. Outside the room listening patrons tapped their feet. Because patrons had to sign a register to reserve the room, on June 7, 1955, twelve-year-old "Jimmy Levine" signed in pencil, and over eight visits the next eighteen months changed his signature to "J. Levine" and finally "James Levine." When he gave a concert for 150 children in the Children's Room in 1957 he had already performed as a soloist with the Cincinnati Symphony. Years later he became the music director of New York's Metropolitan Opera.[61]

In 1951 the Erie (Pennsylvania) Public Library opened its renovated art gallery—"unequalled in the city for exhibition purposes," the librarian boasted. Local artists regularly exhibited, and the Federation of Erie Artists held annual competitions. In 1951 the Santa Monica Public Library art gallery hosted its fifth annual exhibit of work by 400 local veterans that included more than 800 paintings, sculptures, drawings, illustrations, photographs, and crafts pieces. "Ever go to a Library to browse thru [*sic*] an art show?" asked the *Chicago Tribune* art critic in 1957. Exhibits changed monthly, and only Chicagoans' artwork was displayed. In 1953 a District of Columbia Public Library (DCPL) branch exhibited paintings by patients of an alcoholic rehabilitation program.[62]

When a Los Angeles art teacher asked her fifth- and sixth-graders in 1949 if they wanted to do a mural as a class project, all agreed. How about at the library? their teacher asked. Great idea, they thought, and settled on *Alice in Wonderland* as their theme. "They knelt in a hollow square, . . . each intent on the space before him," observed a reporter.

"With brush in hand they looked long and carefully before making a stroke. Some backed off and took sight with the brush to insure the right perspective, then backed off and looked again." The two murals they finished found space on the Wilshire branch children's room walls. "Next time I hope I can work on a table," said one at dedication ceremonies attended by proud parents, young artists, and city officials. "My knees sure got sore."[63]

Public library film services also increased, in part because of Carnegie Corporation funding in 1947. The results were obvious. The Portland, Oregon, public library bought 100 films in 1949 on many subjects. Churches borrowed *Life in Palestine* for group programs, the PTA showed films on raising and educating children, and the American Association of University Women borrowed films addressing racial and religious prejudices. Neighborhood groups used films, one patron reported, to keep children off the streets. In 1951, the Brooklyn Public Library showed *Pattern for Survival* and *You Can Beat the A-Bomb* in branch auditoriums; 339 showings drew 21,540 people. A 1952 survey showed that 114 American public libraries had circulated films for 48,000 showings to 3.7 million people the previous year.[64]

Between 1946 and 1964, American public librarians were even more successful at providing "the best reading for the greatest number at the least cost" than predecessor generations. As a profession they had also assumed responsibility to be advocates for intellectual freedom and to oppose censorship during this same period, but their tepid responses to black efforts to integrate Jim Crow public libraries in the American South showed that commitment was significantly circumscribed. Yet traditions persisted. Because of the voluntary nature of these civic institutions, patrons still largely determined for themselves what "best reading" was, and by force of demand they compelled libraries they did not have to use to supply it, and in some cases even to withdraw it from circulation. Patrons also participated in occasional public sphere disputes that libraries mediated to determine what was acceptable public art. During this period librarians adopted and implemented new technologies and incorporated new media into their services. And public libraries continued to serve their millions of patrons in multiple ways that librarians themselves often failed to recognize.

In 1963, 9,517 public libraries (including 3,376 branches) served 73 percent of the population (an increase of 30 percent from 1945). Between 1945 and 1963 circulation almost doubled to 657,705,000 books; juveniles accounted for 50 percent of that total.[65] Yet in many respects the more things changed in American public libraries the more they stayed the same. On November 22, 1963, a tenth-grader studying in the now deseg-regated Greenville (South Carolina) public library observed a nondescript woman walk up to the circulation desk and state loudly: "Somebody just shot the president!" "Just as vividly," he later recalled, "I can hear the immediate response: 'Shhhhhh!'"[66]

CHAPTER EIGHT

"An Individual Meaning to Each User": 1964–1980

After Lyndon Johnson succeeded to the presidency following John F. Kennedy's assassination in 1963, he quickly launched a major push for social legislation that resulted in the "Great Society." Besides Medicare, Congress also passed legislation funding libraries and librarianship, and reconfigured the Library Services Act into the Library Services and Construction Act (LSCA), thus opening up federal funding for public library buildings. Added to that mix was "War on Poverty" funding that urban public libraries tapped for outreach programs. Many called this period the second golden age of American public libraries, and with reason. In 1964 the United States had 9,517 public libraries (3,376 were branches). Sixteen years later, the country had 14,653 public libraries (including 5,936 branches), the population served had increased from 73 percent to 96 percent, and the number of books circulated was up from 657.7 million to nearly a billion. Because of the number of new school libraries funded by Great Society legislation, however, the percentage of circulation accounted for by juveniles dropped from 50 to 31 percent.[1]

From the beginning, the profession's lexicon had defined the kinds of information an evolving capitalist democracy favored, and Benjamin Franklin's "useful knowledge" had served well for nearly a century and a half, with Melvil Dewey's "best reading" serving for another century. With the advent of the computer in the mid–twentieth century, however, "best reading" gave way to "information"—although by that term librarians still largely meant the kinds of useful knowledge they had been acquiring and organizing for 250 years, which this new technology promised to store and retrieve much more rapidly and efficiently. In *Libraries of the Future* (1965), J. R. Licklider predicted automated "precognitive systems" harnessing "user-oriented" languages programmed into computers to facilitate search and retrieval of specific bits of information. In 1970 Alvin Toffler published *Future Shock*, which declared that in recent years computers had changed societies with dizzying speed; ten years later he published *The Third Wave*, which hypothesized that American political and social institutions were becoming obsolete as the country shifted to an information-based economy. Sandwiched between was Daniel Bell's *The Coming of Post-Industrial Society* (1973), which stated the economy had shifted primarily from the production of goods to the production of services heavily dependent on information and knowledge.

Library leaders across the country regularly cited futurists like Licklider, Toffler, and Bell to persuade colleagues that adopting newer information technologies was not only essential to the profession's future but also promised to raise its profile. Many started calling librarianship an "information profession"—some even *the* information profession—and the study of its practices an "information science." But like Licklider, Toffler, and Bell, like Franklin and Dewey, advocates for an "information science" largely overlooked the role of the library as a place and seldom analyzed commonplace reading. Nonetheless, many public librarians jumped on the bandwagon. "The public library as we know it is dead," insisted one library forecaster in 1980. "It just has not gone yet." The future of libraries, he declared, was tied to a technological revolution in computerized information.[2]

"Information and referral" (I&R) services became one manifestation of this push. In 1974 Brooklyn used $4.5 million in federal grants to set up "information centers" in fifty-five branches to dispense information about community services in city, state, federal, and private voluntary agencies. "Since TV and paperbacks, people don't come to libraries anymore to take out books," said the program director, who provided little evidence to back up his claim about book circulation. Others joined the I&R movement, including public libraries in Atlanta, Houston, and Cleveland. The Detroit Public Library called its I&R service "The Information Place" (TIP). The director acknowledged the community center role public libraries had historically played in assimilating millions of immigrants, but agreed with her Brooklyn colleague that because the paperback revolution had drained away "the traditional recreational reader, we can no longer just depend on popular reading as the principal adult service of the library."[3]

But like many other twentieth-century initiatives librarians had crafted to improve services addressing useful knowledge, I&R met with mixed success. Local newspaper publicity for the New York Public Library's Community Information File service created only brief public interest, one branch librarian noticed. Some librarians lamented that I&R advocates undervalued other library services. "Our librarians visit schools, put on puppet shows and story hours, help children with their homework, select materials for shut-ins, answer a wide range of questions and choose materials for our collections serving a wide variety of patrons," said one Los Angeles Public Library administrator in 1980. "Technology is but one tool. It takes a human being to comprehend and serve the complex needs of other human beings." And numbers continued to belie the rhetoric many used to prioritize I&R. In 1976, the ALA executive director reported that public library circulation had jumped 10 percent in the previous year, 40 percent since 1968. "People are reading more, not less," he said.[4]

As in previous generations, librarians adopted newer technologies to improve library efficiency and security. Many libraries adopted automatic scanners that read bar codes on patron cards to record borrowing transactions. When the patron returned the book, the system canceled the record. If the book was overdue, the system automatically generated a notice. By 1964 many libraries had also placed magnetic strips in books and periodicals that triggered alarms when patrons tried to clear turnstiles with unchecked items. At the Flint (Michigan) Public Library, however, baby strollers set off the alarms more frequently than transgressors. In Gary, Indiana, librarians magnetized newspaper rods because boys stole them to use as mock swords; in Levittown, New Jersey, the library magnetized its men's toilet key and never lost another.[5]

In Chicago, public librarians noticed damage to reference material increased as baby boomer students flooded branch libraries. At NYPL's Donnell branch, a mutilated reference book contained an unsigned note: "12/1/73. . . . Had to tear these pages out. All the copy machines were broken, the library was closing and my *mark* rested on this material. . . . Forgive me please?" As libraries added photocopy machines and reduced their cost per page, mutilation and theft diminished, but library security officers did not disappear. In 1970 the Los Angeles Public Library recovered $76,000 worth of stolen and overdue library materials. "Most cases are routine," a reporter noted, "but now and then the library dicks run across a real artist, a Willie Sutton in the world of the

Dewey Decimal." One thief stole single *Encyclopedia Britannica* volumes from separate branch libraries until he had a complete set. The best of the "library fuzz," the *Los Angeles Times* reported, was "Supersleuth" Jess Simpkins, who said "his principal occupational hazards are amorous ladies answering doors in the altogether."[6]

Some libraries imposed new rules to regulate behavior. In 1965, the Fort Wayne Public Library insisted that students wear shoes and socks in the Young Adult room. In 1969 the Chicago Public Library forebade patrons from exposing their toes while reading—"can't have toes all over the place," one official commented. "Feet disturb some people," said another. But Chicago contrasted with Laguna Beach, California, where many public library patrons walked about barefoot. Equal parts retirement haven, art colony, and hippie headquarters, Laguna Beach gave its library a unique patron base. At the copy machine one patron copied his palm "to send away for analysis." No one seemed to care about open toes.[7]

Veterans who had read paperbacks during World War II, baby boomers used to paperback racks at local newsstands and drugstores, and publishers transitioning from hardbound to hard- and paperbound all pressured librarians to change their attitudes toward paperback books. Many librarians acknowledged that they had to supply readers with the kinds of story containers they wanted. When the San Francisco Public Library installed a "Popular Library" of 5,000 paperbacks in 1970, the collection accounted for 19 percent of the main library's circulation. Rental collections for popular fiction persisted in public libraries, but not without protest. Richard Condon, author of the bestsellers *The Manchurian Candidate* and *An Infinity of Mirrors,* scorned the practice. He made ninety cents a copy from the sale of his books, he said; if libraries rented them, why not set aside one-third the fees collected as author compensation? To that an East Orange, New Jersey, public librarian responded: "Has he ever thought of . . . paying the libraries whose facilities he's used . . . insatiably?"[8]

In the early 1960s the "student invasion" occasioned by baby boomers—many now in high school—perplexed many librarians. The Whittier (California) Public Library director enumerated reasons students were overwhelming local public libraries: "Today's stimulating teaching methods, which require a student to do individual research in various types of books, magazines, pamphlets, and government documents instead of relying solely on the textbook for information on a specific topic; the post-Sputnik emphasis on academic studies; inadequate or non-existent school libraries, lack of training and parental supervision; and the World War II baby crop are some of the factors which have combined to cram our public libraries with teenagers every evening."[9]

Articles and letters to library press editors frequently cited problems youth created when they clustered there. Many librarians complained that their public libraries had become school annexes, and they dreaded the "swarm of beasts" that frequented their doors after school. To cope, some libraries refused to buy school textbooks. Others closed their doors to teenagers, or allowed them only to use well-monitored reference rooms. Because junior high school students had used the library as a gathering place, raced book trucks in the aisles, talked loudly, congregated at the front doors, and opened windows to let in their friends, in 1979 the Rutherford (New Jersey) Public Library banned students under tenth grade after 5 o'clock unless accompanied by a parent. "Students cannot be allowed to spoil . . . this haven of quiet and beauty for those who appreciate it," said the director.

For a few urban public library branches, student behaviors became so bad the only solution was closing them. In 1969, the NYPL Hunt's Point branch librarian recorded activities of local gangs. At various times of the day groups of fifteen to sixty-five young adults pushed furniture about as they consistently spoke in loud voices. They ripped down signs forbidding smoking, eating, and drinking, then engaged in the very behaviors the signs addressed. They tossed books on the floor whole shelves at a time, then trampled on the books while discarding chicken bones, used glue tubes, soda bottles, and cigarette butts into the mix. Many walked out of the library with an uncharged book, only to throw it into the gutter outside. "Gradually right under the eyes of staff the library became the center of a thriving narcotics trade . . . carried on quite openly," the librarian reported. "Brothers would walk in in progressive states of narcotic influence. They showed their puncture marks and bragged about them. . . . One small pasty-faced little boy . . . constantly came staggering in and fell asleep from . . . glue-sniffing." In 1969 NYPL closed the branch, ostensibly for painting and repairs. When it reopened months later, gangs continued to plague library services, but with less intensity. Only neighborhood gentrification in the next decade eliminated gang activities.[10]

As Great Society funding greatly increased the number of primary and secondary school libraries, public libraries paid less attention to young adults in the 1970s and in many cases abandoned youth services altogether. Although youth still used public libraries heavily (especially on Saturdays and Sundays, when school libraries were closed), library directors increasingly tended not to hire youth librarians to replace retirees. By 1980 most teen public library users instead found themselves served by generalist professionals.[11]

The public's love affair with bookmobiles continued, however, as Great Society funding accelerated their numbers and expanded their reach. With LSCA funds, the Los Angeles Public Library system funded bookmobiles into thirteen sites in South-Central and East Los Angeles. Once a week library employee Ben Thomas backed his eight-ton vehicle onto a patch of grass between laundry lines at a project housing 2,000 people on Watts's south side, then set up folding tables and opened the flaps on either side of the bookmobile to display fiction and paperbacks. Inside were another 3,000 volumes. Soon children from nearby schools showed up, browsed through Classic Comics the downtown library refused to buy with regular funding, and socialized with Thomas, whom they called "Baby Brother." Shortly thereafter, teenagers came and asked Baby Brother to start the concert. Thomas pulled out a phonograph, set up speakers, and the parking lot came alive with dancing. "The loudest library in Los Angeles is blaring its siren song again," wrote a reporter. "The young dancers are a visual come-on." One youth wandered into the bookmobile to check out a sports biography and apply for his first library card. "It is a noisy success," the columnist concluded, "broadcasting the clang of ideas where there used to be so many signs of silence."[12]

In Fresno County, California, LSCA funds supported a bookmobile to serve Mexican American farmworkers in the San Joaquin Valley in 1968. Patrons dubbed it La Biblioteca Ambulante; the library system staffed it with Spanish-speaking librarians. When a bookmobile pulled onto the Calhoun North School playground on Chicago's West Side in 1968 with music blaring from a loudspeaker, children quickly gathered. Out stepped a black librarian, who began telling a story to first-graders and Head Start children attending the school's summer classes. One seven-year-old wandered into the bookmobile. "Just look at it all," he exclaimed, then "roamed through a world of fairy tales, baseball, animals, and cowboys," a reporter noted. "Do I have to pay for it?" he asked. "I don't have any books at home." In 1972 the San Francisco Public Library started a "mediamobile" service. When the library canceled the service two years later because federal funds dried up, hundreds of affected older citizens in lower-income neighborhoods protested.[13]

In 1973, Orange County's Santiago Library System in California armed its "Outreach Bookmobile" with 3,000 Spanish and English paperbacks and pamphlets on subjects like Social Security and birth control, assigned it a multiracial bilingual staff, and regularly visited black and Mexican American neighborhoods and migrant labor camps. It also located book racks in community and recreation centers, free clinics, job training offices, and other places where people had to wait. To minorities raised in culturally isolated areas, the system's black director said, public libraries were perceived as a "white sanctuary" where they are "put off or lied to. . . . Books become something to fear and a library—a whole building filled with books—becomes terrifying." He was particularly proud of Spanish story hours drawing thousands of barrio children.[14]

In 1971 the Westminster (Maryland) Public Library initiated a program with 16 volunteers who took books to 6 area nursing homes housing 700 residents; 40 percent had no family to visit them. "The volunteers were terrific," said the program director. "They just took these people into their hearts, they took them to their homes for visits, out to different places. They saw that they got birthday and Christmas cards, because otherwise they wouldn't have had anything." Volunteers also benefited. "Some say it's depressing to go into a nursing home," said one, "but it's not when you can see you're making a difference, bringing joy to these people's lives." With the help of a $25,000 federal grant, the number of volunteers jumped to 125 by 1980 as the program worked through Meals on Wheels and added book delivery to the homebound. In the late 1960s the South Central Kansas Library System started Operation Whistle Stop with LSCA funds. Officials decorated a 20-foot truck with burlap walls, and armed with a puppet stage, film projector, 2 student summer employees and a driver made weekly visits to 34 rural towns. At each children and mothers swarmed the truck as soon as it stopped. "We must drive 15 miles one way to get to a library," one parent said. "How nice to have an armchair library at our fingertips."[15]

Many communities used War on Poverty funds to expand public library services to previously underserved populations. In 1969, the San Francisco Public Library (SFPL) announced federally funded cooperative initiatives with local agencies like New Careers, Neighborhood Youth Corps, and the Community Work Training Program. With help from the Neighborhood Arts Project it expanded the number of lectures, discussions, movies, dramas, and musicals it offered. At many events the Library also distributed paperbacks to encourage reading. It celebrated Negro History Week and

"War on Poverty" Head Start program, Queens Borough (NY) Public Library, 1965. *The Queens Borough Public Library, Archives, Queens Borough Public Library Photographs*

accelerated acquisition of minority materials, particularly works on the civil rights movement and books in Spanish, Tagalog, and Chinese.[16]

In 1977 Los Angeles city and county library systems set up a Chicano Resource Center in East Los Angeles with a bilingual staff to function as an information center and address questions dealing with Chicano history and culture. In Montebello, Norwalk, and Compton the county library operated LIBRE (Libraries Involved in Bilingual Education Reading) Centers to improve English reading and language skills. A year later 1,500 registered for tutoring classes, including a young Southeast Asian war bride who wanted to learn how to read a menu, a Mexican civil engineer looking to enter his profession in his new home, a recent Mexican high school immigrant who recognized his meager English-language skills would limit job promotion, and a Costa Rican grandmother who announced to her family, "You have all gone to school—now it is my turn."[17]

"War on Poverty" Head Start program, Queens Borough Public Library, Corona branch, 1965. *The Queens Borough Public Library, Archives, Queens Borough Public Library Photographs*

In the profession's lexicon, urban institutions that functioned as community centers were often referred to as "action libraries." As whites fled to the suburbs, branch libraries left behind adjusted to the demographics of newer populations. For a *Christian Science Monitor* article, Carolyn Ruffin contacted systems in Baltimore, Boston, Dallas, Detroit, New York, and Los Angeles, and noted most were working with other inner-city agencies. "Interviews with inner-city librarians indicate that library systems . . . are putting on more and more programs, discussions, film showings, exhibitions," Ruffin wrote: "Movies shown on the side of a van parked in a housing project. A trip to a Baltimore Orioles baseball game. Erle Stanley Gardner in Spanish. These things spell 'library' for an inner-city community."[18]

Because LAPL's Watts branch "represented the Establishment" before the 1968 riots, when African American Barbara Clark became librarian she used federal funds to turn it into a community center. For poor people, a public library needed to do more than circulate books, she insisted. New programs she initiated proved her point. Teenagers used the branch as a study hall, while preschoolers watched *Sesame Street* and *Electric Company* on the library's color television. To this mix of library services Clark added tricycle races for preschoolers, rock bands performing in the library's parking lot, and crochet classes for grandmothers. "We have discovered in working with children," she said, "that some who don't even talk in the classroom will read to us."[19]

Public libraries located in Hispanic neighborhoods had similar experiences. At one Los Angeles County Public Library, a Mexican American artist painted a twenty-foot mural of a brown man bursting his bonds. Another, located in a neighborhood lacking a movie theater, hosted a monthly film night and puppet shows put on by barrio children. Bookmobiles, often blaring music to announce their arrival, brought Chicano materials into the barrios; one drew 2,000 to Fiesta de los Barrios, organized by a Spanish-speaking librarian. At yet another the librarian hired a clown to circulate the neighborhood, hand out free books, and "like a ghetto pied piper" lead children to the library. "This was just one of the many moves to get poverty kids in where previously we had only elderly, middle class Anglo people, steeped in the tradition of shushing anyone who raised his voice above a whisper," said the librarian. "In the old, Anglo-Puritan way of doing things a child was threatened with severe punishment if a book was ruined. To a minority child, in what he already regarded as a hostile environment, this would inhibit his ever using library facilities."[20]

The Library Services and Construction Act also funded school bus trips to Chicago's Douglas branch. For children who seldom left their neighborhoods, the trip not only brought new experiences, a branch librarian reported in 1969, but they also refuted the old clichés about Douglas—that inner-city children were not interested in books, that they refused to read, and that their teachers and parents did not care. "This program not only exposed them to books," she observed, "it acquainted them with the neighborhood, it permitted them an opportunity to have something to talk about among themselves—books to take out—library cards (how to obtain one), . . . responsibility (getting books—returning them—holding on to your card)." Middle school students frequently requested books on black history, narcotics (especially marijuana), nursing as a career, birth control, and venereal disease.[21]

When the branch began sponsoring "listening hours" in 1970, teenagers specifically requested music by black artists. Schoolchildren attended lunchtime sing-a longs. The branch also hosted a young adult dance group practicing for a tour to the American South, local teenage singing groups, and Martin Luther King Jr. Mental Health Center meetings that dealt with mentally challenged children. A mothers' group sponsored by the Model Cities Program organized a day care center; another program took materials to schools, nearly tripling the branch's circulation rate. "It was not until we went to them that anyone became remotely interested" in the library, a branch librarian reported. And in 1970 library officials agreed to change the name of the branch honoring Stephen A. Douglas—a mid-nineteenth-century white politician who debated Abraham Lincoln and was ambivalent about slavery—to honoring Frederick Douglass, the late-nineteenth-century black abolitionist. In the early 1970s, however, funding for the busing program ceased. A study done six years later showed that white neighborhoods in Chicago received more and better services than black and Latino neighborhoods, in large part because the system still used culturally biased tradition-bound statistics focused on circulation, reference questions, and number of library cards issued to determine how to allocate resources.[22]

Librarians' perception of their profession's domain sometimes showed in discussions to expand public library services. For example, when a local community organization suggested in 1966 that the District of Columbia Public Library system use War on Poverty funds to create public programs for the poor, library officials balked, labeling them "gimmicks . . . infringing on recreation functions" that detracted from the library's "true" mission. The library instead needed to concentrate on activities that matched basic public library services, the director said. The two organizations "don't speak the same language," a *Washington Post* reporter wrote, "and can't get a joint program off the ground." Five years later, however, the system used federal funds to open three storefront libraries that not only housed color televisions but also circulated puzzles, games, records, art prints, viewmasters, and posters.[23]

Other public libraries were not so reluctant. In 1964 the New Haven (Connecticut) Public Library renovated an abandoned supermarket as a Library Neighborhood Center specifically designed to "bring economically and culturally deprived Negroes and whites together in a program that, for the time being at least, is necessarily focused more on neighborhood uplift than the reading of books," the *New York Times* reported.

Within months 1,100 patrons (the majority black) took part in 66 group activities. A mixed-race committee of neighborhood residents advised the center's director. In 1980, the San Diego Public Library sponsored an exhibit of *po dao*—embroidery art crafted by Hmong women recently arrived from Laos. None could speak English, but through interpreters they told a reporter they were grateful the library provided space to show their work. For all of them, it was the first time they had stepped into an American public library.[24]

In 1969 the Queens Public Library opened the Langston Hughes Community Library and Cultural Center in Corona. Local activists got the library to acquire a boarded-up storefront and pushed the project forward. The library hired a professional librarian to manage the new facility, but the rest of the staff came from the neighborhood. The library of 14,000 paperbacks and 400 records contained no card catalogs and charged no overdue fines. It offered English- and Spanish-language children's story hours; karate classes; poetry readings; Swahili lessons; journalism workshops that produced a neighborhood newspaper; a health, education, and welfare referral program; a job postings bulletin board; and civil service test review books. And from the Neighborhood Youth Corps the center hired fifteen "footmobilers" to carry books in knapsacks to neighborhood parks, beauty parlors, barbershops, and apartment stoops; they had authority to issue library cards and to check out the library books they were carrying.[25]

Often cultural traditions that American public librarians inherited from previous generations limited their ability to expand services to "the greatest number," but sometimes libraries overcame these traditions. For example, many Asian immigrants knew libraries only as places to store books. Cultural barriers like these may explain why the Los Angeles Public Library did not open a Chinatown branch until 1977. "Sharing books is a new concept for Chinese people," a Chinese American librarian noted. "They are used to buying their own books and newspapers." Yet the day it opened—Friends of the Library followed a Chinese tradition and lit firecrackers outside the front door to rid the building of evil spirits—every book was checked out.[26]

Sometimes, however, libraries could not overcome cultural barriers. From 600 interviews with California Mexican Americans in the late 1960s, one researcher found they were generally indifferent to public library services. The reasons were not hard to discern. At one branch Chicano teenagers reserved a meeting room for political discussions, but when officials discovered they had invited a controversial Chicano speaker, they withdrew permission. At another branch, teenagers asked for certain Chicano newspapers and periodicals. These too were denied; teenagers later learned that certain community leaders had objected to the materials because they contained foul language, criticized the American government, and called for political separatism. A second set of interviews yielded additional criticisms: "Why can't the library buy books about Chicanos?" adolescents asked. "Librarians won't buy any Chicano or Salsa music," a young Phoenix Chicano noticed. "I cannot talk to those librarians; they do not understand me," said a Texan woman who could speak only Spanish. "I do not speak English well and am afraid to go to the library, more from shame than fear or ignorance," added another.[27]

When federal funding dried up in the 1970s, many libraries tried to save outreach programs, but with mixed results. In most public library systems, funds continued to be allocated on the basis of circulation statistics. Because the Queens Public Library faced an 8 percent budget cut in 1975, the director decided to close the eleven branches with the lowest circulation. Not coincidentally, eight were in black neighborhoods. The proposal occasioned strong community protest and an NAACP racial discrimination suit. "Many residents . . . believe that circulation figures are not as important as community service," the *New York Times* reported. "They have become ideal meeting places for civic and youth groups." One branch director noted: "When you close the door here, you're closing a community out."[28]

Even without LSCA funding, however, public libraries brought people together in many ways and for many purposes. When the Vermillion (South Dakota) Public Library moved from an old Carnegie into a new building in 1978, a local farmer loaned the library his conveyor belt, and after books were placed in boxes scores of volunteers worked both ends and in the midst of a snowstorm hand-carried them to their new home.[29] In 1979, the Swissdale (Pennsylvania) Public Library hosted an all-day conference of women steelworkers to define a set of contract demands unique to their concerns that their male-dominated union was ignoring. In 1976 the Arcadia (California) Public Library showed the film "How to Say No to a Rapist," co-sponsored with the Junior Women's Club. In 1980 several Orange County branches hosted seminars on "Rape in the Suburbs" designed to provide counseling for rape victims, to encourage victims to report attacks, and to educate residents and police departments on methods of dealing with the issue.[30]

"Black is beautiful, and I want to show it," said a twenty-two-year-old Philadelphia photographer in 1969, as he stood before a collection of his work titled "Come On Down to Soulsville, U.S.A" that his local branch exhibited. In 1973 the Denver Public Library hosted a series of multicultural programs, including "Black Awareness" (3,735 attendees), "Viva Mejicano" (3,207), "Colorful Colorado" (1,912), "Problems of Biculturalism" (1,325), "Pioneers of Modern Painting" (1,267), and scholar-in-residence James Michener (350). That Michener drew the lowest numbers indicates how well Denver's outreach programs were connecting to marginalized groups.[31]

Sometimes public libraries brought people together to oppose library actions. When the San Francisco Public Library's Chinatown branch hours were cut in 1970, Chinese American teachers and community members protested so vigorously that system officials agreed to keep the branch open an extra night and renovate a downstairs room so students had a place to study. And for the first time—more than a century after Chinese Americans first settled in San Francisco—SFPL officials assigned a Chinese-speaking professional, Judy Yung, to develop a Chinese-language collection. With the aid of a citizens' advisory committee, she spent the next three years building a Chinese-language collection, doing community outreach, and developing library programs for senior citizens and non–English speakers. When Yung left in 1973, the branch used Community Block Development funds to hire more bilingual staff, build a community garden behind the library, and renovate the community room for neighborhood meetings and cultural events. Other libraries learned from San Francisco's experience.[32]

Elsewhere people used the public library as a place to make different kinds of statements. To show contempt for a recent ruling integrating the Clinton, Tennessee, high school, in 1965 one racist urinated on the steps of the public library, another recently integrated Clinton institution. Local authorities chased him out of town. Some previously segregated public library systems functioned as sites for racial reconciliation. During Negro History Week in 1970, for example, the now desegregated main Atlanta Public Library hosted two programs, one featuring the Booker T. Washington High School Modern Dancers, the other a local black folk artist. The week's theme was "The Fifteenth Amendment and Black America in the Country, 1870–1970." Also on exhibit were materials the Auburn branch struggled to collect when the system was segregated. Both blacks and whites attended the programs and reviewed the exhibits.[33]

In many communities public library spaces increased opportunities for local artists. In the new two-story-high main reading room of the South Huntington (New York) Public Library, bookshelves and tables mounted on lockable casters enabled librarians to clear the area quickly, and to lower the 16 by 16 foot lighting grid to create a theater in the round for Long Island's Arena Players and other traveling companies. "We owe just as much to taxpayers who want rich programming instead of bookcards," said one librarian in 1972; public libraries also had responsibilities to people "who won't want to know from a book." The American public library is "one of the few places where the independent film-maker can showcase his wares," noted a Phoenix Films vice president in 1968. "I cannot refrain from offering the view—not fully recognized by the library people . . .—that the public library is one of the most important resources on this continent for the growth of film culture," said another filmmaker.[34]

In Fort Lee, New Jersey, once the hub of the silent film industry, twice a year in the late 1970s the public library showed silent films it collected. "A lot of old-timers attend," said the librarian. "They call out the familiar streets, and they discuss their memories. Many of them, or their relatives, worked as extras in the silents." In the Record Library of NYPL's Donnell branch, an eighty-year-old nearly blind patron returned an album after listening to Mahler's Sixth Symphony. "It gives me *such* a lift—even at my age." A teenager who had just discovered a recording by a Spanish pop artist asked: "Got any more of these? This guy is Dominican—from my country. He is wonderful!"[35]

As people passed the Chicago Public Library's Washington Street entrance between 3 and 4 P.M. on August 20, 1969, they heard Parker High School students sing a capella and play progressive jazz, soul, and rock. Three years earlier the Gary (Indiana) Public Library had sponsored a local talent contest at which a group soon to be called the Jackson Five competed. Although they did not win, little Michael was an audience favorite. By the end of the 1970s the Eastern Shore Area Library in Salisbury, Maryland, sponsored a local high school rock band in its parking lot, and the Venice (California) Public Library sponsored a mariachi band on Cinco de Mayo. In Los Angeles Public Library, librarians at the Sylmar branch pushed back tables and chairs, laid down pads, and hosted a live exhibition of judo and karate in 1968. "Since the demonstration our books on self-defense have been circulating very well," said a librarian.

"When we're downtown," said one father to his children, "let's stop at the library and check out some birds." He was not joking. The Concord (New Hampshire) Public Library had just begun loaning specimens from its collection of 400 donated stuffed birds. For its summer reading program titled "Wildlife on the Prairie" the Henderson (Kansas) Public Library borrowed local zoo animals, including Blake the Snake and Yertle the Turtle, both of whom disliked the library's air-conditioned atmosphere and generally hid from children eager to pet them. Robert and Roberta Quail also avoided contact with humans, probably because they wanted to protect their two babies. Bambi the Fawn and Jim the Crow, on the other hand, loved the attention and welcomed petting. The latter cawed a greeting each time someone entered the children's room. Circulation rates were up from the previous summer.[36]

Like previous generations, the art public libraries displayed on their walls sometimes generated controversy. When the Chicago Public Library director viewed eight abstract paintings an artist did for the fine arts room in 1965, she had them removed. "Not censorship," she argued, "but a question of taste. . . . We felt the paintings would be the subject of snickers and much misinterpretation." "If this isn't censorship, I'd like to know what is," responded the artist. "Please understand," the director continued, "we recognize and defend the artist's right to paint anything he likes and to show it. . . . But in this case we felt the paintings were too suggestive for our public. Ours is an unsophisticated audience." With this statement she not only offended the artist, but insulted her patrons.[37]

Public libraries brought people together, but not always for cooperative purposes. When the Burbank (California) Human Relations Council (HRC) used the public library auditorium in 1964 to generate support for a housing act, a local citizen protested these were partisan political acts not suitable for a public building. In response the library director—ironically also chair of the California Library Association's Intellectual Freedom Committee—cited city rules and denied the HRC further use of the auditorium. It was "a tight rope to walk," he admitted to a reporter. Nowhere in the article did he or the reporter mention the Library Bill of Rights. When the American Civil Liberties Union (ACLU) later tested this rule by requesting use of the auditorium, the librarian denied them and later also denied requests from the American Association of University Women (AAUW), the local Homeowners Association (HA), and an American Field Service (AFS) local branch. Although the HRC and HA did not appeal, the AAUW and AFS did.

The city manager denied the former but granted the latter. In 1965 the city attorney reversed the AFS ruling, and also denied ACLU and HRC reconsideration requests. By that time the library director had also joined the Committee for Decent Publications, whose principal aim, the *Times* reported, was to obtain voluntary cooperation of newsstand owners not to sell questionable material to minors. He commended the committee for its moderate approach to preventing "pornographic materials from reaching juveniles." Again, he did not mention the LBR, which instructed him to fight censorship. Ultimately, the Burbank Public Library dropped its ban on political and religious meetings but redefined use for only library purposes or city-sponsored organizations. The ACLU did not qualify.[38]

The logically strained position in which the Burbank Public Library director found himself was in large part forced by rhetoric reflected in the library profession's elevated commitment to oppose censorship. In 1967 the American Library Association established an Office of Intellectual Freedom (OIF). From its beginning Director Judith Krug determined to make the Library Bill of Rights a professional imperative through an active program of publications, education, and public relations. By controlling the profession's conversation about censorship, she set the tone of its debate. "The library is the only true First Amendment institution in the country," she asserted from her perch—well entrenched in the ALA bureaucracy—in 1980. With little accountability to the public library community and no obligation to protect a budget against scenarios that would damage these institutions and hurt whole communities, she molded a professional ethos in which librarians who did not stand with her interpretations were perceived as failing their professional responsibilities. Yet she had no authority to enforce her will—lawyers and doctors can be barred from practice for breaches of ethics; librarians cannot. She therefore concentrated on engaging government agencies and organizations outside librarianship on censorship issues, but for the profession offered only opinions and unsubstantiated declarations from her OIF office.

For a profession eager to elevate its civic profile, however, her rhetoric was compelling. "The public library was justified on the Jeffersonian principle that a free, democratic society can survive only with an informed citizenry," an ALA president said in 1978. "The library serves this goal by providing information on all aspects of issues and by taking no stands. It is politically neutral and socially unbiased, and up to now freely accessible to all." To the *Los Angeles Times* he wrote: "The Library Bill of Rights and the Freedom to Read statements . . . guarantee that all sides of an issue will be presented in public libraries, and that no one's right to read anything in the library can be abridged."[39]

But this rhetoric masked reality (past and present), and actual public library practices showed that censorship issues consistently defied clichés echoed in the library faith. For example, in a late-1970s analysis of basic public library acquisition guides like *Booklist*, one researcher concluded that materials representing points of view outside dominant cultures were vastly underrepresented. In 1971 the OIF surveyed Midwest public librarians about several contested titles with sexual themes; 61 percent of respondents said people who wanted to read "erotic novels" like *The Carpetbaggers* "should buy their own and not expect to find them in a public library." When asked that same year if the LBR required public libraries to provide the pornography attracting huge audiences in the 1960s, Krug responded that patrons "probably should be able to get this kind of material in the library," but "people are too embarrassed or afraid to ask for it." In 1973, a *Los Angeles Times* story about censorship in public libraries quoted LBR Principle Two that libraries should present "all points of view concerning the problems and issues of our times." Doesn't it follow, then, a *Times* columnist asked, "that libraries should stock hard-core pornography and extreme left- and right-wing" literature?" Yet most did not, he observed. "Is this because they are avoiding conflict or because they think that different books could better serve communities?" He did not answer his own question.[40]

And when the US Supreme Court issued a 1973 decision in *Miller v. California* that recognized the power of local communities to determine for themselves what was obscene or pornographic to the average person, Krug complained that the "decision hit us right in the stomach." Just what is community, she wondered—state, city, neighborhood? The director of the Chicago Public Library also disagreed with the decision. "Literature is not a local thing," he argued, "but a national and universal activity. To narrow it down is bad."[41] Neither recognized public libraries as important platforms communities used to define local literary and cultural values, a role the Supreme Court decision merely reinforced, albeit without referencing these civic institutions. Public libraries did not stock pornography, but what constituted pornography was a decision each community made for itself. Imperfect and messy though the process was, the public library had been playing that role for generations.

Despite OIF pronouncements, public libraries addressed censorship issues differently at the local level. In 1965, the Los Angeles Public Library mounted an exhibit titled "Book Is a Four-Letter Word." In it were titles banned over the years, including works of Shakespeare, Lewis Carroll, Mark Twain, and Hans Christian Andersen—all canonical authors literary experts had endorsed by mid-century. More recent works by Henry Miller, Nicholas Kazantzakis, and J. D. Salinger, however—all variously banned by public libraries the previous decade yet applauded by literary experts as good literature—were absent from the exhibit. Although the system had copies of each, it labeled them "permission titles"—"very mature in outlook and very specific in descriptive areas, perhaps having to do with sex," one librarian told the *Los Angeles Times*—and printed red lines on book pockets to alert librarians they could be circulated only to adults. In 1971 another *Times* reporter noticed that county public libraries kept many books on sex education off regular shelves and required users to ask for them at the circulation desk. Administrators he interviewed acknowledged their staffs were "keenly aware of the standards of morality and other reading criteria in that community." At the Enoch Pratt Free Library librarians labeled controversial books "candidates for the cage."[42]

In 1967 Mount Pleasant (Iowa) Public Library trustees returned Elia Kazan's bestselling *The Arrangement* to the publisher with a scathing note about its unacceptability. The publisher immediately saw a publicity opportunity and offered free copies to all Mount Pleasant residents; 800 accepted, and the incident got a spot on Johnny Carson's *Tonight Show*. The librarian also reported that her bridge club read parts of the novel. "The dummy player, the one who sits out a round, would read it and gasp and gasp, 'I've never seen anything so raw.'" Still, the board refused to buckle. "They stuck to that resolve until the publicity faded and the incident was forgotten," a trustee's daughter later recalled.[43]

Another kind of censorship resolution occurred at the Virginia Beach (Virginia) Public Library when several Christian ministers, city councilmen, and scores of citizens protested *Our Own*, a local homosexual newspaper freely available on open shelves. When the library responded by placing it behind the counter, the American Civil Liberties Union (ACLU) filed suit. But pressure continued to remove it entirely. In the same 1980 election that carried Ronald Reagan into the White House, Virginia Beach citizens voted 48,217 to 13,694 that the library should not carry any publications depicting or advocating homosexual acts. The library quickly removed the newspaper from behind the counter. In 1973, 45 percent of Americans surveyed favored banning books on homosexuality from their local public library. Hostility toward gays in public libraries showed in other ways. In 1978 police arrested 105 men for homosexual solicitation in the Boston Public Library. Many librarians across the continent regarded this activity as part of a "problem patron" phenomenon, lumping gays with the homeless and mentally ill.[44]

Playboy was also a much-challenged serial. Justifications for not carrying it varied. The Arcadia (California) Public Library director said it was a magazine from which pictures were frequently stolen. The contents were not indexed, said another librarian. The Pasadena Public Library director did not stock *Playboy*, but was willing to get it on interlibrary loan. "We have to be selective," he said. One Northridge, California, teenager protested such treatment. "I highly resent the censorship placed upon people under 18," he wrote the *Los Angeles Times* in 1964, "in regard to what can and cannot be borrowed from the public libraries. This is a ridiculous attempt to shelter me, as well as others, from the facts of life."[45] In 1967, the Los Angeles Public Library refused to buy *Valley of the Dolls*, "not because of its treatment of alcoholism, sex, violence and drugs," the director said, but because "it is poorly done." Despite good reviews the Montgomery County (Maryland) Public Library system refused to buy Norman Mailer's *Why We Are in Vietnam* because, as one staff reviewer said, "This is such a poor book that I am not willing to inflict it on our borrowers." Although in nearby Prince Georges County citizens could find a copy in their public libraries, it was not available in the counties of Baltimore, Fairfax, Arlington, and Alexandria, and in the District of Columbia.[46]

When Clifton, New Jersey, erupted in controversy in late 1970 over sex education in schools, the public library did not escape scrutiny. A local councilman said he was "sickened" by passages in *The Sensuous Woman* and criticized the public library board for using taxpayer money to put it on library shelves. In a 5-to-4 decision the board agreed, and removed it. A local citizen then offered to donate a copy, but the board turned her down—"the book should not be available under any circumstances." After pressure from the New Jersey Library Association (NJLA), a year later the board allowed patrons to obtain the book through interlibrary loan. But NJLA persisted, insisting the library's citizen-based selection committee be disbanded and all selection responsibilities turned over to professional librarians. Clifton refused, so NJLA censured its library board members, but to no avail. The board was "prideful that we hadn't succumbed," said the president. "We felt they were inflicting their censorship when we're the ones who know the feelings of the city and the taxpayer." She was also proud to reject her librarian's request to subscribe to *Ms.* magazine—"salacious garbage," the mayor had called it.[47] In Clifton, the mediating process did not run smoothly, or quietly.

In 1965 the *Saturday Review of Books* carried an article titled "The All White World of Children's Books." In it the former president of the International Reading Association, Nancy Larrick, looked at 5,206 children's books issued by 63 publishers between 1962 and 1964, and found only 6.7 percent included one or more black people. "Integration may be the law of the land," she concluded, "but most of the books children see are all-white." Her article startled the world of children's literature, including a group of children's library experts who assumed primary responsibility for constructing that world, from which generations of public librarians had been making selections. Not all were startled, however. NYPL children's librarian Augusta Baker noted two years later: "Really fine books" portraying blacks positively were still scarce.[48]

In a 1972 *Redbook* article, black author Liz Gant lamented a childhood where children's books failed to represent non-white people. Parents, teachers, and librarians not only had a responsibility to make books available that fairly represented black people, she wrote, but also to make sure that a character like 'Little Black Sambo' never lives again."[49] Although the Boston Public Library never banned *Little Black Sambo*—it did not censor literature, one official explained—it did let copies "disappear from circulation," then failed to replace them. *Sambo* was no longer on District of Columbia Public Library shelves in 1973; too many black patrons remembered being referred to as "Black Sambo" by white classmates. The Chicago Public Library also withdrew *Sambo* in 1976 because it degraded black people, then replaced it and *Dr. Dolittle* with bowdlerized versions. The Detroit Public Library promised to buy no children's books containing passages that belittled racial or ethnic groups, but it refused to remove *The Oxford Book of Nursery Rhymes*, which contained the poem "Ten Little Niggers."[50]

While the 1960s civil rights movement brought attention to issues of race in children's books, the 1960s feminist movement profiled issues of gender. Linda Greenburg, a stay-at-home mom, became involved after reading a 1971 *Woman's Day* article titled "Miss Muffett Must Go: A Mother Strikes Back"; the article argued that "the feminine image" in children's literature was loaded with "stereotyped characters and outmoded situations . . . foisted upon small girls at an age when they are just beginning to formulate an idea of themselves and their worth."

214 PART OF OUR LIVES

Greenburg visited three Boston public libraries and found, as she wrote to the *Christian Science Monitor* in 1974, many books with girls as central characters, but none that placed them outside a patriarchal culture. So she asked for help from the librarians. "Here's one about a girl who wins a baseball game," said one. Greenburg noticed that the protagonist was mistakenly assumed to be a boy because she was wearing her brother's baseball gear, but once discovered to be a girl after hitting a home run she was then allowed to become a "manager" and thus serve the boys bats and bring them drinks. At the main library Greenburg was given a book about a duchess with fifteen children who fancied herself an intellectual. When she tried to bake a cake, however, she used so much yeast that the dough rose to an uncontrollable mass with the duchess precariously perched on top. "Children learn sex roles at a very early age," Greenburg concluded. "We cannot accurately measure to what extent the books we read to them contribute to this largely unconscious learning." She implored her readers not only to make children's librarians conscious of what was in their collections but also to get the offensive volumes removed. Some did. In the late 1970s several suggested that the Boston Public Library remove *Peter Rabbit* because Flopsy, Mopsy, and Cottontail—all girl bunnies—were well-behaved and placid compared to the intellectually curious Peter. The library ignored their request.[51]

Left unmentioned in librarians' responses to Larrick's and Greenburg's revelations were references to previous generations of children's librarians who had loyally followed the precept "not censorship, but selection," and by identifying what they thought the best reading actually promoted children's books in which systemic racism and patriarchy had been presented as a natural order. But librarians caught on quickly. By 1975 they were circulating selection lists for different age levels with titles like *Cinderella Comes Out of the Kitchen* and *Mary Is Not Contrary Anymore*. That did not necessarily make matters easier for professional librarians staffing public library children's rooms, however.

In 1975 a *Los Angeles Times* reporter interviewed a Pasadena children's librarian about non-sexist children's literature on the shelves. "Many feminist books are so self-conscious in making the point that they are not good literature, so we reject them," she said. She also felt the library needed to keep the classics, flawed though they were. "There is no burning purpose to get rid of all the sexist books in the library. . . . We will keep 'Dr. Doolittle' even though it's racist, because it's a classic. But we won't buy something current that is as racist." Always it was a balancing act. "In choosing books it's hard not to promote our own causes," she said, "but we do have the responsibility to have a quality collection of good literature. And since we are tax supported we have to buy what the public wants to read." She also recognized the power to choose that made libraries delightful for so many children. "You can make children aware the books are available but you can't push them down their throats. Librarians try not to . . . push kids in any direction but let them read what they want within limits."[52]

Like the Library Bill of Rights and the ALA's Office of Intellectual Freedom, the Council on Interracial Books for Children (CIBC)—formed as a nonprofit in 1965 to identify non-racist, non-sexist literature in its eight-times-per-year *Bulletin*—became yet another external player in librarians' local discussions about the best reading. It would not censor, CIBC reassured the public, only raise consciousness. The council set up workshops for children's book writers and publishers, and it identified consultants and resource specialists to increase awareness of racist and sexist subtleties still finding their way into children's books. When the CIBC declared in the late 1970s that *Mary Poppins* was still racist, some San Francisco Public Library branches banned it. "It's written from the old English view of the 'white man's burden' that is naturally offensive to minorities and others as well," explained a children's librarian after a parent learned it was gone. The action, she said, was not censorship. "Committee decisions are made only after very careful deliberation." In her mind, coming to a carefully considered committee decision made it selection, not censorship. Librarians "have the freedom to exercise their professional judgment and *not* buy such books," said a CIBC official in the SFPL's defense. "Developing criteria and guidelines for selecting bias-free books is not censorship. Americans . . . should join with all those who are working for a democratic society free of racism and sexism."[53]

Discussions about sex in children's literature did not diminish in the 1960s and 1970s. How public libraries dealt with the subject continued to vary from community to community. New York and Cleveland youth librarians developed a code; librarians should be wary of books that had an "episode" or "incident" (code words for "sex scene") in the narrative. "Sex is out in the open now," the *Los Angeles Times* argued in 1972, "at least at public libraries where in the past red-faced adolescents and shy parents had to ask the librarian for permission to obtain books on the subject." On the other hand, in 1972 several Louisiana and Pennsylvania public libraries whited out Mickey's pink nakedness in Maurice Sendak's

In the Night Kitchen for fear that patrons would object to the illustrations.[54] In those communities these libraries were probably right.

In the late 1970s the Fort Wayne Public Library labeled "Q" (for "questionable") any children's or young adult book containing sexual content. Here they followed *Kirkus Reviews*, which gave "Q" ratings for such books. But the library was more discriminating, a staff member explained, because "people in Fort Wayne can't stand books about masturbation or oral sex. . . . We try to 'Q' according to the morals and opinions and sensibilities of the community. . . . And these do change." Although violating a Library Bill of Rights principle regarding labeling, her solution nonetheless worked. Later, when the library removed restrictions on young adult nonfiction books addressing homosexuality, only one person complained. In 1976 the Niles (Illinois) Public Library moved Judy Blume's *Forever* to the adult section and refused to purchase William Burroughs's bestseller *Naked Lunch* because, a librarian said, "I felt we didn't need it." Said a library spokeswoman: "The librarian makes the selection not on the basis of personal preference but what the people in the community want. The same book may not be in every branch."[55]

Other titles also perplexed librarians. Some library systems struggled with *Sylvester and the Magic Pebble* (in which pigs portrayed policemen), *Mom, the Wolf Man, and Me* (told from the perspective of a girl whose mother never marries and whose boyfriend occasionally spends the night), and *Inner City Mother Goose* (which includes the verse "Jack be nimble / Jack be quick / Snap the blade and give it a flick"). Across the country these books drew protest; across the country librarians dealt with them in ways they determined their communities would find acceptable. In some the books were not purchased, in others they were purchased but restricted, in yet others they were placed on the open shelves.[56]

Librarians' attitudes toward popular fiction continued to shift from quiet hostility to tempered acceptance. A favorite bumper sticker intended to humanize their image in the 1970s read "Librarians Are Novel Lovers"—a message that might have offended some a generation earlier. But shifts did occur. When a new director took over at the Roanoke (Indiana) Public Library in 1979, she moved novels by Jacqueline Susann, Philip Roth, Vladimir Nabokov, and others—marked "X" if they used the words "hell" or "damn"—from the closed to the open shelf. "Funny thing is, soon as I did that, the books stopped circulating." On the other hand, she was highly irritated with "those darn Harlequin romances." Patrons "march in, check out 10 of them, and come back in the next week for 10 more." But the New York Public Library's Fort Washington branch considered itself "very fortunate to have someone . . . who brings in a shopping cart full of light romances every three or four months [to donate to the library]. This has kept our readers happy and has helped stretch our budget."[57]

"Not censorship, but selection" masked other traditional cultural and literary biases within the profession. Despite the fact that the ALA revised the Library Bill of Rights in 1967 to include "age" as another group having the right to access all public library collections, many children's and young adult librarians persisted in shunning series fiction. Those who did otherwise sometimes paid a price. For her first major acquisition as Rhinelander, Wisconsin, children's librarian in the mid-1970s, Kris Wendt, who read Nancy Drew as a child, purchased three complete sets of Nancy Drew, Hardy Boys, and Bobbsey Twins mysteries. Word of her transgressions spread quickly. Several months later a forceful colleague—"incensed that Rhinelander broke ranks to acquire such 'trash,' . . . accosted me in the ladies room during a regional children's services workshop. . . . Arms folded across her ample monobosom and glowering as though she would like to alphabetize my internal organs," she "cornered me against the sinks. In a voice like a silver dime she declared, 'You have lowered the standard of children's literature for the entire Wisconsin Valley!'" Wendt held her ground; Nancy stayed in the stacks, much to the delight of Rhinelander's children.[58]

Increasingly, Wendt's position found support elsewhere in the profession. When several Chicago Public branch librarians requested Nancys in 1976, the system's youth specialist refused. Nancy was not on the recommended list, in part because her narratives stereotyped East Indians, African Americans, Native Americans, Jews, janitors, and housekeepers. But the youth specialist was speaking for herself, not the system. Days later the library's director wrote the *Tribune*. "I have long been a supporter of . . . Nancy Drew and Hardy Boys books in public libraries—I read all of them in my own childhood." Chicago's librarians, he said, "were not *restricted* from ordering Nancy and the Hardy Boys." The year before, the NYPL had also reversed a position toward series fiction it had held for over six decades when it started buying Nancy, the Hardy Boys, and Bobbsey Twins. By that time the publisher had sold 60 million Nancy Drews, 50 million Hardy Boys, and 30 million Bobbsey Twins, and in 1975, annual sales averaged 5 million.[59]

Other less visible minority group patrons desperate for certain kinds of useful information quietly mined public library collections. Like previous generations of users, they defined "useful" in ways unique to their own lives, and like previous generations they found that public library collections sometimes met their information needs, sometimes not. At the San Francisco Public Library in the early 1970s, for example, a young city planner discovered *City of Night*, a novel about gay life. At first nervous about what he read, "I put it back on the shelf immediately," he recalled. "But then I went back and read whole chapters on my lunch hours. Just the fact that somebody had put it on the shelves . . . made the existence of gay people real for me." Other experiences were not so gratifying. Because she believed "libraries are the place where we can be most anonymous and delve deeply into areas we wish to uncover in secret, it was to the library I turned at fifteen [in 1969] to uncover the meaning of my lesbianism." What she found, however, "was not echoic of my own experience. Rather, those books frightened me and convinced me that this was not lesbianism I was experiencing but something else." The search itself may have been painful. Not until 1972 did the Library of Congress remove "see also" references from "homosexuality" and "lesbianism" to "sexual perversion." Four years later the LC introduced subject headings for "lesbians" and "homosexuals, male," which for the first time recognized them as classes of people.[60]

But satisfying the information needs of an LGBT minority population was not central to the agendas of the nation's public library leaders; this was obvious in the list of recommendations emanating from the first White House Conference on Library and Information Services held in 1980. Participants called for increased federal funding for new literacy programs; expanding programs for the handicapped, disadvantaged, and poverty-stricken ethnic and racial minorities; and a new assistant secretary for Library and Information Services in the US Department of Education. The recommendations worried the *Wall Street Journal*. Most, it editorialized, threatened to erode the kind of local support that marked public libraries "by wrapping its bounty in a blanket of centralized directions and decisions on how the money is to be spent."[61] Neither the *Journal* nor delegates at the conference asked why these programs were not being prioritized at the local level, where decisions by local people determined what services their public libraries provided. Because the conventions librarians inherited favored the kinds of useful knowledge now referred to as information, because they still undervalued or overlooked the importance that commonplace reading and public library spaces held for their patrons, library leaders consistently referred to programs they regarded as outside the profession's traditional domain as outreach that required funding beyond local revenues.

Between 1964 and 1980, American public libraries enjoyed substantial growth and a shifting profile. The nation noticed. "Libraries used to be little more than storehouses for books," wrote a *Wall Street Journal* reporter in 1975, "but in the 1960s a conviction grew among librarians that they ought to cultivate a broader public than the minority of citizens who came to borrow a book or to save a dime on a newspaper." He also quoted an *Atlanta Constitution* columnist about her library. "You wouldn't know the place. It's jumping night and day, and on Saturdays and Sundays it's like a fish fry." In 1980 *U.S. News & World Report* wrote: "America's 14,000 public libraries, once largely lenders of books, are becoming supermarkets of knowledge and information" with a broad array of "new" services.[62]

Although big numbers and expanded services drew national press attention, for most patrons it was what public libraries did for them as individuals that counted most—patrons like novelist Philip Roth, who in 1969 protested to the *New York Times* when Newark, New Jersey, threatened to close its public library to save money. He had used the library as a youth, he wrote, then enumerated the reasons he loved it. Most "compelling . . . was this idea of communal ownership, property held in common for the common good. Why I had to care for the books I borrowed, return them unscarred and on time, was because they weren't my property alone; *they were everybody's*. That idea had as much to do with civilizing me as any idea I was ever to come upon in the books themselves." But he also identified other lessons the place taught—"restraint, . . . solitude, privacy, silence, self-control," and especially the concept of order. "What trust it inspired . . . to decode the message on the catalogue cards; then to make it through the network of corridors and staircases into the stacks." He especially liked the sense of community reading a public library book brought—"with a local history of its own, a Newark family-tree of readers to which one's own name had now been added." Roth was one of thousands who protested. After "everyone got together—whites, blacks, rich, poor," a library official said, the city backed down.[63]

What public libraries did for individuals echoed in the comments of others. "The public library has an individual meaning to each user," an

NYPL branch librarian observed in 1968. "One boy who made the year memorable," wrote another in 1974, "is a slightly retarded teenager who can be *very* trying. He comes into the library often, is very persistent, and will not take 'no' for an answer to any request. . . . One day, he said to me: 'You know, you and me, it's not like I come in here and you're the librarian and I'm the customer. It's like we're partners.'"[64]

CHAPTER NINE

"Library Paste Is a Precious Part of Social Glue": 1981–2000

One day in 1993 a woman in her seventies approached Palm Springs (California) Public Library director Henry Weiss and introduced herself as Maggie Phelps. As a library patron for many years, she said, the library was "the only shrine" she knew. Because she was terminally ill, she wondered if her funeral could be held in her "shrine." Weiss not only said yes; he also visited her at a local hospice. There she handed him a numbered list of her most valued possessions. "Number one . . . was her Palm Springs Library Card." Days later she died. Funeral services took place on a Sunday. Maggie "would have been proud to know," Weiss said, "that the library opened briefly one Sunday, in her honor, for the first time since 1979."[1]

The love Maggie Phelps felt for her public library mirrored the emotions of millions of other public library patrons over the generations and was equally evident in the last two decades of the twentieth century. Although the nation's population had increased 70 percent between 1941 and 1982, during that same time period public library circulation rose 160 percent to more than a billion items. A 1994 survey showed 74 percent of three- to eight-year-olds had made at least one trip to the public library the previous year; forty years earlier fewer than 50 percent did. Given these numbers, it is little wonder that when the New York Public Library faced budget cuts in 1991 patrons inundated city hall with 25,000 protest letters—three times as many as those concerning other threatened departments.[2]

The number of public libraries increased, too, from 14,653 in 1980 to 16,298 in 2000. To get one, some people got very creative. In 1982 in

Elsinore, Utah (population 600), twelve-year-old Jason Hardman phoned the mayor every evening "until I drove him nuts. Finally, out of desperation from my continued harassment, he gave in. The city council, out of pity for the mayor, gave in also." In New Holland, Illinois (population 350), Dave Tibbs spearheaded an effort to transform the town jail into a library. Supporters turned cells into reading rooms (a sign marked "Crooks" directed visitors to the children's room) and kept the library open 24/7/365 on an honor system. Occasionally volunteers reshelved the books to keep them in order. To record transactions, patrons used a spiral notebook. "Pretty elaborate, isn't it?" chuckled Tibbs. "Book reternd," concluded one entry in a child's handwriting.[3]

Many communities also rebuilt, renovated, or replaced older libraries no longer capable of serving the needs of their increasingly diverse populations. When San Francisco opened its new public library building in 1996, the *New York Times* listed "the rainbow of San Francisco communities" that raised money for the $94 million library. "The library is not a cultural center," said the architect. "It is a multicultural center." US Poet Laureate Robert Hass called the interior "a marvel, . . . so deeply delicious you forget your previous ideas of what a library is." It contained a café; a garden terrace just off the children's room where people could have lunch and librarians could tell children stories; reading and research centers on gays and lesbians, Chinese, Filipinos, African Americans, and city history; a gallery; a meeting room funded by San Francisco's Latino community; a center for music and art; and an auditorium. "We have done something right," Hass concluded. "This library is going to be a place, especially for families, that it will simply be fun to go to and explore."[4]

As the entertainment and information industries introduced new forms of communications, the American public library responded. In 1990 libraries offered not only books and periodicals, films and recordings, but also videocassettes, compact discs, audio books, and sometimes even the playback equipment "readers" needed to access the stories these texts contained, now in more languages to match the increasingly diverse populations they served. In 1991 Los Angeles County began an Audio Express program consisting of 1,500 audio books. "The radio really doesn't take the pain out of commuting, and a book does," said one patron. "I listen to books on tape because I am not a good reader," a Baltimore cabbie and Enoch Pratt Free Library patron told a reporter in 1997. "It would probably have taken five of my lifetimes to read what I've heard on tape.

Ruth and Rose Hau, nine-year-old twin sisters, enjoy picture books at the Chinatown branch of the San Francisco Public Library, 1992. *Courtesy of the San Francisco History Center, San Francisco Public Library*

I started in 1988 with all the books I'd heard of but never read, what you'd call classics."[5]

Some public libraries initiated programs as welcome antidotes to perceived bad effects of modern communications technologies. In 1992 the East Baton Rouge (Louisiana) Parish Library began a "Prime Time" family reading program that twice a year gathered fifty grandparents, parents, and children willing to give up TV for an evening per week to discuss themes in assigned readings. While the library specifically targeted "at-risk families," they drew others, ranging from "people who had Ph.D. degrees to people who probably didn't have a high school diploma." In some cases children recognized an adult's limitations and provided help. "The pride they take in each other is remarkable," said the director. A subsequent analysis of the program's "at-risk" families showed half off welfare, and no child had failed a grade. "We can't take full credit," the director said, "but I think we've been a contributing factor."[6]

At the same time, however, some public libraries took advantage of the new opportunities cable television presented to develop their own programs. At the Beverly Hills (California) Public Library, Director Michael Cart interviewed famous authors in Los Angeles to promote books for a weekly show called *In Print* that he hosted on the city's cable station. By 1986 Cart's programs were on fifty stations in twenty cities. The show's intent, Cart said, "is to inspire [viewers] to leave the TV set and pay more attention to books." Not everyone agreed with the idea that public libraries should embrace non-print media. "There is a school of thought . . . that holds pop videos to be the sugary junk food that will attract patrons to the plainer intellectual nourishment of reading," editorialized the *Richmond Times-Dispatch* in 1990. "That's balderdash. . . . Librarians ought to reject the 'media center' claptrap, and get back to the basics of books."[7]

Other technologies improved library services. After 1980 online public access catalogs (OPACs) evolved into multifunction systems that allowed patrons not only to read bibliographical information on items held but also to identify whether titles were checked out. Within a decade telephone access systems enabled library patrons to identify the circulation status of individual items from remote sites, to request materials via electronic mail, and to reserve materials already in circulation. Computers connected readers to scores of new information databases and automated OPACs that identified materials across the country they could obtain via interlibrary loan. Circulation systems proved cost effective. Before installing a new system in 1982, the Orange County (California) Library employed forty people to type overdue notices. After installation, the system not only checked books in and out using a bar code and light pen but it also generated overdue notices. Gone was the "thump-thump-thump" of the date stamp, the "slrrr-thwack-slrr-clack" of card catalog drawers, both replaced by rapid-fire clicking on a computer keyboard and the responsive hum of printers.

Public libraries also offered new services. In 1982 Lake Bluff (Illinois) Public Library patrons could check out portable smoke alarms donated by the fire department. In 1993 the Rockingham (North Carolina) Public Library provided walkers to help senior citizens browse the shelves. In 1999 the Rockville (Connecticut) Public Library purchased handheld illuminated magnifiers for the visually handicapped. Some practices were unique, however. In California's Silverado Canyon, the Orange County Library's smallest library still attached notes to the collar of a dog who regularly visited to let its owner know her book had come in.[8]

The online revolution profoundly affected reference work. Although reference librarians continued to field "the dumbest questions on God's green earth" from "every kind of crank and eccentric and mouth-breather there is," as Garrison Keillor told a *Prairie Home Companion* audience in 1997 about his fictitious Lake Wobegon Public Library, in several libraries, database librarians set up appointments with patrons to help them tailor queries to terms that systems could process. Some information and referral services died for lack of funding; others converted manual systems into machine-readable databases and limped along. Yet reference service traditions persisted. In a 1982 *Globe* interview, a Boston Public reference librarian lamented calls to settle barroom disputes about things like the number of dimples on a golf ball. He and his colleagues answered questions cheerfully, he said, but they had little contact with people doing serious research. Rather, "it's the high school students and general public we spend most time with."[9]

When the nation experienced a recession in the early 1990s, the budget cuts it forced threatened libraries in poor black more than affluent white neighborhoods. For example, in 1991 the Omaha Public Library system decided to close a black neighborhood branch because the number of books circulated there was the lowest of the system's ten branches. "It hurts my heart," responded a sixteen-year-old who used the library daily. "It's like burying a member of the family," said an elderly woman. "Kids need a place to go to get them off the street," said a security guard. When Baltimore's Enoch Pratt system threatened to close a black branch in 1999, a Friends of the Library group complained: "The city just looks at the numbers, . . . but they won't look at what a library really means to a community."[10]

In 1990 library users protested loudly when the St. Petersburg (Florida) Public Library decided to close its James Weldon Johnson branch, located in a black neighborhood. "Some of the children come to the library to hide," the branch director told a reporter. "The gentler boys try to get away from the bad kids out on the street." Citizens mounted a petition drive to keep it open. "I was mother, I was teacher," said retiree Helen Edwards, who had directed the library for thirty-four years. "I fed them, helped them with homework, saw their report cards, even took them home at night." Mamie Brown, Edwards's successor, had become "a surrogate mother for a lot of these kids," said patrons conducting the petition drive. To justify the decision, however, the library's acting director cited conventional methods of measuring library impact. "It has the smallest staff, the lowest circulation, the least number of people visiting it," she said, "and the lowest amount of revenue coming out of it. . . . I understand a valid need for a place where kids can go, but that place doesn't need to be a full-service library."[11]

Political influence also affected how resources were allocated in bad economic times. In 1992 a *New York Times* reporter analyzed two Chicago working-class neighborhoods—Mount Greenwood (population 19,000, largely white) and Roseland (population 56,000, largely black). One institution the reporter used to measure difference was the branch library. Mount Greenwood whites were proud of their new branch, which boasted typewriting booths, computers, and compact discs and had opened the previous year with "the support of powerful officials." Roseland blacks did not have those connections, however. At Roseland the reporter observed children reading beneath walls of peeling paint, noticed the restrooms had no toilet paper or stall doors and only two librarians to monitor the entire building. Every week, patrons asked for computers and videotapes like those they had seen at other branch libraries. "The reason they're coming to us is because they don't have them at home," the librarian said.[12]

Budget cuts also threatened bookmobile services. "I feel I'm losing a friend," said one patron after learning in 1989 that Upper Darby (Pennsylvania) Township officials were canceling the service. "Oh God! Don't let them shut down the mobile library," shouted a senior apartment complex resident when San Diego Public Library budget cuts threatened bookmobile services that same year. "I forget my problems if I can just get into a book." A nursery school teacher worried about her preschool children. "The books I get from the bookmobile introduce a whole new world to them." Many library systems persisted in supporting bookmobile services, however. In 1995 people still gathered twice monthly around the bookmobile in tiny Dacada, Wisconsin. "They meet here, talk about their families and compare recipes," said the librarian. [13]

Some systems reallocated resources to start new services or improve an old one now serving new populations. In 1986 the Atlanta Public Library opened a library kiosk in a subway station. That same year the Wichita (Kansas) Public Library opened a branch in a local grocery store; within a year it ranked second in circulation among the system's nine branches. In 1987 the Santa Ana (California) Public Library began a "Children's Hispanic Bookmobile" service and stocked it with Spanish- and English-language materials. In 1989, 65 percent of the children who used the St. Paul (Minnesota) Public Library bookmobile were Asian immigrants. One mother of six regularly accompanied her children to the bookmobile to help them pick out easy-to-read titles; bookmobile librarians suspected she and her husband also benefited.[14]

In 1984 the Santa Fe Springs (California) Public Library conducted a Latino genealogy workshop. "I don't know who we are, what we did," said one participant, "but it's important for us to learn." Said another, "I want to know where I came from so I can tell my grandchildren." Because they believed young Marine Corps wives stationed at nearby Camp Pendleton needed parenting information, Oceanside (California) librarians crafted a new program at the base YMCA. "A lot of the wives are very, very young," said one librarian; most of them were from small towns "where everybody knew everybody. Here, on this large base, in this big town, they're nobody . . . and they're scared to death." Often their husbands were on six-month tours. One mother told a reporter she was pregnant with a third child while her four- and two-year-olds constantly fought. "I was really stressed out about it." A book the parenting program gave her "really helped me understand more about what they were going through," she reported. "I didn't want my children to have the bad childhood I grew up with."[15]

When the National Commission on Excellence in Education published *A Nation at Risk* in 1983, it largely ignored public libraries. Librarians complained. In response, the Department of Education issued *Alliance for Excellence: Librarians Respond to 'A Nation at Risk'* to address the oversight, but many librarians still groused: "Too little, too late." Nonetheless, the profession saw promising possibilities for libraries in scenarios pop-futurists predicted about the computer's ability to store and retrieve the useful information they had been handling for generations. In 1980 Alvin Toffler's *The Third Wave*—which said the United States was moving from an industrial to an information age—was on the bestseller list. By that time his *Future Shock* (1970)—which had popularized the term "information overload"—had sold 7 million copies in fifty languages. The library world listened closely. In *Toward Paperless Information Systems* (1978) F. Wilfrid Lancaster—boasting a background in the kind of information Benjamin Franklin had favored for his Library Company of Philadelphia centuries earlier—predicted that books would disappear as a basic feature of library service, and he expected the traditional library's "disembodiment" by the year 2000.

Other library professionals who also found the predictions of evangelists of information technology persuasive soon formed a priesthood of library and information science scholars to focus primarily on "information." Many predicted the imminent demise of the American public library. One expert said, "The profession of librarianship must separate itself from the institution of the library" and concentrate professional education on systems and technology emerging in new information environments that could organize information in new ways. Another insisted professional education had to incorporate "information science" to expand its base. "Libraries as we know them are on the way out," declared another in 1995. "We are destined to have libraries without halls or walls, libraries that lack stacks." And as these predictions seeped into public discourse, politicians saw opportunities. In the 1986 San Diego mayoral race, for example, one candidate said the city did not need a new public library building because the information it contained would eventually be stored on laser disks citizens could access from their home computers.[16]

Although several library forecasters predicted that public libraries would continue as community centers, most still overlooked the importance of commonplace reading, even in the midst of a national reading renaissance stimulated by tens of thousands of book clubs. Libraries across the nation hosted many of them. In 1996 the Southern Connecticut Library Council used National Endowment for the Humanities (NEH) funds to support book clubs in 140 public libraries. A reporter noted that clubs were not designed "for entertainment, but to hear the opinions of others and broaden their minds." But no one had a greater impact on public library book clubs than Oprah Winfrey. "I want to get the whole country reading again," she said, and regularly devoted portions of her daily television program to Oprah's Book Club. Once she identified a title, viewers flocked to local bookstores and public libraries to obtain a copy—a reaction known as the Oprah Effect.[17]

In response, many librarians began to openly advocate for commonplace reading. *Give 'Em What They Want!* read the title of a 1992 book authored by a Baltimore County Public Library (BCPL) committee and published by the ALA. "We are always somewhat bemused by librarians who underestimate, or at least misjudge, the tastes of the public they serve," wrote Director Charles W. Robinson in the preface. "Our users are very often quite different from the kind of people who become librarians, and placing value judgments on other people's interests and reading is certainly a violation of the intellectual freedom which librarians profess to hold so dear."[18]

Case in point—romances. At the Westville (Illinois) Public Library, romances constituted nearly half the library's 8,268 volumes, most donated by a local reader who brought in complete monthly lines after she finished them, the librarian said. Because the Dewey Decimal Classification ignored romance fiction, readers devised their own organization—"romances are shelved by publisher and author, and cross-indexed by publication date. Lists categorize the books according to trends and degree of sexual content." Within the Lincoln Trail Library System, Westville became the interlibrary loan source for romances. "Statistics ranked Westville very high in terms of circulation and community use among libraries," noted an official. The collection "might be the subject of derision, but in fact it has helped bolster the general collection."[19]

Across the country, patron demand for romances exercised similar pressures on public library collections. In 1981, romances accounted for 45 percent of all paperbacks sold. A decade later publishers were issuing 150 romance titles per month to 45 million readers, as annual sales approached $1 billion. Increasingly, however, women pushed back against the kind of romance novel bashing that dated back to the early nineteenth century. When an *Omaha World-Herald* columnist questioned the value of romances in 1996, for example, readers fired back. "I love romance because I can relate to the heroines, unlike the images portrayed by women's magazines or most movies," said one. Said another, "Romance is empowering and it's uplifting. . . . It makes us like women and expect more from men. Oops, maybe I've hit on a reason it's so maligned." "By far the better question," said a third, "is, Why, alone among all readers of commercial fiction, are those who read romances constantly challenged by such as you to defend their preference?"[20]

"Librarians have historically been a tough sell for romances, often relegating the well-worn 'silly' paperbacks, uncataloged, to a free-standing rack or donation shelf," a *Chicago Tribune* reporter wrote in 1998. "But buyers of library fiction have been forced to submit to the public's lust for romance." Many libraries increased purchases of romances, some sponsored romance book clubs, and the library press "now routinely features the once-snubbed genre." Said one librarian, "We've changed our tune. . . . We used to feel that [romance readers] were sheltered housewives, but we find that many businesswomen read them, and every kind of person, from grandmothers to young mothers."[21]

Young adult series fiction still met stiff resistance in certain quarters of the profession. In 1982 the *School Library Journal* editor complained about "taking trash lightly." The "current craze among paperback publishers to produce innocuous, interchangeable love stories for girls" was so upsetting she listed "Ten Commandments of Trash Novels" to discourage the purchase of "comic books, *Nancy Drew* (and company), . . . and the latest jag of love stories without consequences." "Perhaps the greatest menace" to children's literature in the 1980s, argued the children's book editor for *Booklist* in 1985, "is the series." Such series were "racist and sexist"—mere "junk food," claimed a Boulder (Colorado) children's librarian.[22]

Like romance novels, however, librarians increasingly buckled to public demand. When the new San Francisco Public Library opened in 1996, nine-year-old Thea Bosselmann wrote the *San Francisco Chronicle* she could find no Nancy Drews there. "They are a mystery series about a girl detective. . . . She is brave, smart, and never gives up. . . . My mom and lots of other people read them when they were little." Thea asked about Nancy, but was told by librarians that SFPL did not carry them. "They don't think it's good literature." When the *Chronicle* asked about this omission, the head of children's services replied: "Money is placed into materials that meet children's informational needs, expand their multicultural awareness and experiences, and that are of a higher literary quality." This brought many protests—most from mothers. "How delighted I was to meet a girl who wasn't afraid of danger, who didn't have to be rescued by some erstatz frog," said one. Said another: "We wanted to tell the librarians: Open your hearts and minds, then bring back that daring daughter of detection, that fearless fighter for right (not might), a role model for all girls who have been pushed aside by everyone from Prince Charming to Indiana Jones." Soon thereafter, SFPL acquired the series. By 1996, however, it was the exception. The Denver Public Library had been stocking Nancy for years—"our idea is to get a book in their hands and see what happens," said one children's librarian. So did the Louisville Public Library. "We want our kids to come and read. We can't be telling them what to read."[23]

Because of these shifting attitudes, many public librarians found it easier to acquire newer series late-twentieth-century young adults were reading by the millions like Baby-Sitters Club (about the experiences of a group of Connecticut middle school students who run a babysitting business), Goosebumps (a young adult horror fiction series), and Sweet Valley High (about California twin high school girls and their friends). In the Sweet Valley High books she got at a Los Angeles Public Library branch in the late 1980s Reyna Grande, recent Mexican immigrant from a dysfunctional family who later became an award-winning novelist, found much comfort. In the plots, she recalled, "there were no alcoholic fathers, no mothers who left you over and over, no fear of deportation."[24]

Sometimes library futurists who overlooked the values their patrons attached to reading paid a high price. For example, in 1996 the San Francisco Public Library director lost his job in part because of bad press over landfilling tens of thousands of books from "Old Main" that did not fit into a new building designed for the information age. "The New Main is a betrayal of what a public library is supposed to be about," complained one citizen. In a rush to embrace new technologies, he said, the library "left its soul behind."[25]

While the new information priesthood tended to look past library service priorities that patrons still used in convincing numbers, many librarians working the desks recognized that users benefited in their own ways from the reading and spaces the institutions provided. Like previous generations of public library users, immigrants remained a shining example. Among sympathetic librarians serving them was Estelle Friedman, who welcomed into her 125th Street NYPL branch new immigrants flooding the neighborhood that now included Russians, Chinese, Arabs, Dominicans, and Greeks. At the branch she provided immigration and citizenship materials, set up programs to recognize and share information about their diverse cultures, but at the same time created literacy classes to help them learn English.[26]

Newcomers to American shores between 1981 and 2000 generally found public libraries comfortable places not only to assimilate into their new environs but also inviting spaces to celebrate the cultures they represented. In 1990 the Broward County (Florida) Public Library sponsored activities for immigrant Filipinos, including a bamboo dance, art exhibits, and lectures on Filipino American contributions. "You have to admire a system that contributes so much to the common good with so little by way of expense," said an *India Currents* author about public libraries in 1992. In 1997 St. Paul (Minnesota) Public Library branches put up exhibits titled "The Fabric of Our Neighborhoods." Included were Hmong embroidery, black American quilts, and Latvian mittens. The library collected fabric from each and stitched them together into a community quilt that circulated the branches.[27]

Already twenty years old in 1997, the Queens Borough (New York) Public Library's "New Americans Program" sponsored many classes. In one a Chinese teacher explained to fifteen immigrants that American teenagers dated earlier than in other cultures. Other programs included a celebration of Indian culture, lectures to Turkish immigrants about domestic violence, and literacy lessons for Liberian Americans. "Libraries are a real magnet where immigrants can make connections," said an immigration official. In 1998 a recent Taiwanese immigrant trekked to the library twice a week with her ten- and thirteen-year-old boys. She pushed them to select only English books, and armed with her English-Cantonese dictionary, checked them for "no-good" words. "If they don't like books, I bring them back and get more." Every Thursday she attended English classes. "If I don't learn about American culture . . ., I could lose them," she said. "Thank God . . . for that precious library and its solicitous staff," said Felix Lopez of NYPL's 110th Street branch in 1981. "The library alone didn't get me from *el barrio* to the Yale Law School, but it sure helped."[28]

Because of traditions public libraries inherited, however, sometimes reaching out proved difficult. At the Corona (California) Public Library, for example, librarians met resistance in efforts to document local Hispanic culture (in 1996 they constituted 30 percent of Corona's population) for the city's forthcoming centennial. Hispanics had experienced segregation when using civic institutions for most of their lives, said a librarian, and that's why "they don't feel like they are a part of this." On the other hand, when Robert Gonzalez noticed in 1997 that the Redlands (California) Public Library's citrus industry historical collection covered men who owned the groves and ran packinghouses but ignored thousands of Mexican Americans who worked the fields and packed the boxes, he began collecting artifacts, photos, and scrapbooks, and conducting interviews. "No one made an active attempt to collect the history of the pickers and packers until now," he noted. The library planned to add the records Gonzalez generated to the collection. "This will wake up the old timers and enlighten the young," said a seventy-one-year-old interviewee. "It's important."[29]

In 1999 the Anaheim (California) Public Library used a $10,000 grant to fund a "Shades of Anaheim" project that began documenting the daily lives of the region's diverse communities. A retired welder brought his parents' marriage license after they fled the Mexican Revolution, along with a photo of the segregated Anaheim school he attended. "We are very proud Americans," he said. "Not Hispanics, not Latinos, but Americans—living the American dream." A Japanese American couple brought family scrapbooks. "I think maybe our photographs show all the things that people of Japanese descent gave to Anaheim . . . years ago," said the wife. When asked about his World War II internment and the discrimination he and his wife experienced looking for housing thereafter, however, the husband "looked down and shook his head."[30]

At one Los Angeles Public Library branch a Taiwanese immigrant regularly headed for Chinese-language materials. Although fluent in English, she told a reporter: "It helps relieve the feeling of homesickness when I can go to a place where the books and magazines are in Chinese and I can read about what's happening back home." But assimilation did not always go smoothly. In Monterey Park, California, where half the population had Asian heritage, some old-time Anglo residents worried. In 1988 the mayor dismissed three trustees who advocated acquiring foreign-language books. "We're losing our country," he told the *Los Angeles Times*. "They're taking our Western culture out and replacing it with eastern culture and Latin culture. . . . If their language is set up, all the rest will crumble."[31]

Native Americans often saw the public library as a white establishment. "I didn't use the library because I felt we didn't belong," said a California Native American. In 1987, however, the San Diego (California) County Library used a two-year grant to open nine reservation libraries. Because most library workers were from the reservation, patrons felt welcome. They told librarians they especially noticed a difference the library had made in the lives of their children, who did better in school. Librarians observed that adults read the newspaper, clipped coupons, and scanned ads for bargains. They favored romances and how-to books. Librarians also screened children's books for stereotypes. "We're not animals and we're not furniture or inanimate objects," said the librarian. She tossed a Disney ABC book in which a stereotyped "Indian" illustrated the letter "I." Very quickly, reservation libraries became community centers where people felt free to chat, drink coffee, and speak in normal tones.[32]

For black Americans, many public libraries that denied them service a generation earlier became sites of reconciliation. When the Hastings (Florida) Public Library director invited a black children's Bible study group to meet there in 1984, it became an "oasis of racial accord," the only place in the community that people of all colors were welcome, said a black pastor. That same year the Birmingham (Alabama) Public Library opened a civil rights archive, including the papers of Eugene (Bull) Connor, late city police commissioner who symbolized segregation in the 1960s by using dogs and fire hoses against demonstrators. The archives documented a history "we're proud to have moved away from," its black mayor said at dedication ceremonies.[33]

Because many public libraries began acquiring more stories young adults craved no matter their textual form, because young adults found the computers libraries supplied fascinating, and because many librarians started developing inviting and friendly spaces for them, a new generation of young people found public libraries to be welcoming places in the late twentieth century. In many urban areas public libraries assembled teen advisory councils to help redesign space, select materials, and implement relevant programs. In 1982, Fort Wayne's public library began a series that included school art exhibits, music concerts, craft programs, poetry contests, Dungeons and Dragons days, and term paper workshops. In 1991 *Los Angeles Times* reporters found one thirteen-year-old engrossed in a computer game called "Mortal Kombat" at LAPL's recently opened TeenScape Room, a seventeen-year-old reading the Japanese anime series "Dragonball," an eighteen-year-old thumbing through *MAD* magazine, and a high school senior reading Ray Bradbury's *Fahrenheit 451.* "I just like the atmosphere," said the *MAD* reader. "It's kind of like having your own library—for teenagers." In the previous year computer use in the room jumped 26 percent, circulation of materials 36 percent.[34]

The increased cultural diversity of many neighborhoods and cities across the country also brought shifts in the focus of American public library programs. "There is a hunger and need for this type of programming," observed a *San Antonio News-Record* reporter who watched standing-room-only crowds at a 1991 public library–sponsored lecture series titled "Mexico: Splendors of 30 Centuries." The success of the series not only "startled everyone involved with it and found the library system unprepared," the reporter concluded, but it also showed how important public library adult programming could be to local communities. In 1996 the *Pittsburgh Post-Gazette* urged readers to visit the Braddock Public Library, where Andrew Carnegie's first public library still brought people of all races together for shared activities of common interest. There one could observe black and white adults working with at-risk children of

In 1995, San Antonio (TX) opened a new public library building designed by the Mexican architect Ricardo Legorreta. As buildings, libraries have been objects of community pride throughout American public library history. *Photo courtesy of the San Antonio (TX) Public Library*

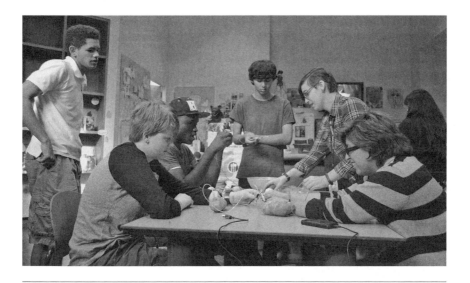

At the San Antonio (TX) Public Library, teenagers make simple circuits out of potatoes at one of the library's regularly scheduled "Tech Tuesdays" programs. *Photo courtesy of the San Antonio (TX) Public Library*

all colors to foster a love of reading they were convinced would improve children's futures.[35]

Some libraries initiated creative programs to address the needs of latchkey children who visited the library between the end of the school day and the time their working-class parents returned home from jobs. In 1989 several LAPL branch libraries started a "Grandparents and Books" program; more than 500 seniors volunteered to read to children after school. "I have a very good feeling when I go home," said one sixty-nine-year-old Chinatown volunteer reading to Chinese American children. "I'm getting back my culture, too." In 1993 LAPL started Homework Centers in six lower-income neighborhood branches to help latchkey children improve study skills. "My parents are always working," said one twelve-year-old Hispanic. "I can't always get help at home." Volunteer tutors—including high school seniors—also provided help. "I feel good when I'm able to help them because I was once in the same boat," said one. Latchkey children "know there is space reserved for them," said one librarian, "and that the library cares about them. They have a feeling of belonging."[36]

But as public places, libraries could also be dangerous to latchkey children, and many librarians worried. In 1988, after two Providence children were murdered and one Pawtucket child disappeared, the Cumberland (Rhode Island) Public Library asked parents not to leave children under twelve unsupervised at the library. In Long Beach, New York, unsupervised children under seven were sent home in a police car. In Boston, some men followed latchkey kids into library branches and attempted to seduce them. Latchkey children in some libraries witnessed unacceptable, even violent behavior. In a District of Columbia Public Library branch bathroom in 1989, a child found an unconscious woman with a needle hanging from her arm, and a man exposed himself to teenage girls. In 1998, a man raped a fifteen-year-old girl in the Newark Public Library restroom; four weeks later another man raped a sixteen-year-old girl in the stacks.[37] Libraries responded by beefing up security.

Problems brought by homeless people using public library spaces persisted. Solutions varied. In 1984 the Ann Arbor (Michigan) Public Library banned sleeping for more than ten minutes and smelly patrons with "extremely poor personal hygiene." In 1993 a homeless man sexually molested a mentally challenged nine-year-old girl at the Bloomington (Illinois) Public Library. "Last straw," said the director. He told department heads to cut enough from their budgets to hire security guards. But in 1991 a federal judge ruled the Morristown (New Jersey) Public Library had no right to bar a local homeless man from its facilities. "If we wish to shield our eyes and noses from the homeless, we should revoke their condition, not their library cards," he concluded.[38]

Political events (domestic and international) and social, cultural, and health issues that found prominent places in public discourse in the last two decades of the twentieth century also affected library programming. At the Bloomington (Illinois) Public Library, Planned Parenthood hosted a town meeting on abortion rights in 1992. Two years later an infertility support group organized there. In the Bronx's Melrose branch that same year the New York Black Women's Health Project sponsored a series of workshops, including "Love, Intimacy, and Sexual Health" (for HIV/AIDS prevention), "Sweet Sensations" (for safe sex and healthy relationships), and "Stress Prevention." In 1991 the Richmond (Virginia) Public Library hosted a program titled "Women and Human Rights Abuse" co-sponsored by Amnesty International and the YWCA Women's Advocacy Program. Angry at the treatment the US Senate accorded Anita Hill during confirmation hearings for Supreme Court Justice Clarence Thomas, local women organized a National Organization of Women chapter at the Hingham (Massachusetts) Public Library in 1991 "to raise awareness of women . . . and give them a place to go and talk about problems they are encountering in society and the workplace." Unity, a nonprofit group for battered women and their children, met in Baltimore County public libraries in 1992; across the country other Unity chapters did likewise. In 1999 the Orlando (Florida) Public Library hosted "Portraits of Courage," an exhibit documenting stories of local breast cancer survivors.[39]

Three years after Mothers against Drunk Driving organized nationally in 1980, Santa Ana, California, mothers met at the public library to establish a local chapter. In Bloomington, Illinois, people suffering from anorexia and bulimia organized a support group at their library. In 1992 puppeteers circulated Brooklyn's public libraries to teach children about the disabled. "I learned not to make fun of people who are disabled," said one ten-year-old. "It's not funny to make fun of retarded people," said a twelve-year-old.[40] In 1990, the Downey City (California) Public Library was among scores across the country hosting "Talking about Vietnam," a National Endowment for the Humanities–funded series. "Public libraries are the best institutions in which to discuss the war and its ramifications," the *Los Angeles Times* reported. Shortly after the United States attacked

Baghdad in 1991, the Placentia (California) Public Library began a series on "Gulf Arab States: Beyond Camels, Oil and the Sand Dunes." Said the librarian, "This is a cultural display. It's supposed to reflect the heritage, the social life of the region."[41]

Public libraries also participated in a national conversation revisiting the federal government's treatment of Japanese American citizens during World War II. In 1991 the Minneapolis Public Library hosted a program on "Nisei Women Remember: The Story of Japanese-American Evacuation and Internment." In 1999 the Salt Lake City Public Library was one of twenty hosting an exhibit, "A More Perfect Union: Japanese Americans and the United States Constitution." For six weeks patrons viewed photographs, documents, and a video showing the World War II experiences of 120,000 Japanese Americans who lost their property and were imprisoned in "relocation camps." A year later the Seattle Public Library scheduled "Relocation from the Camps: A Panel Discussion." Panelists included a federal official who relocated Japanese Americans, as well as several camp internees.[42]

New generations of local artists found public libraries welcome places to exhibit their work. "Art belongs in a public place," argued Livia Bury, founder of the Coral Springs (Florida) Artist-of-the-Month Program. She arranged 1986 exhibits at public libraries in Plantation and Fort Lauderdale, chaired the Broward Public Library Foundation's Art Acquisition Task Force, and served as art advisor to the Margate Public Library. "She's probably made us visible to the public, where we would have never done it on our own," said one artist. In Newington, Connecticut, one local artist—a Veterans Administration Medical Center cook—scheduled shows of his watercolors in the public library every three years because he did not have to worry about damage to the paintings, competing with other artists, or putting a price on his work, and he knew "plenty of people who use the library notice" them. In 1990, the Columbus (Nebraska) Public Library's gallery exhibited twenty works by a retired farmer whose paintings "helped me get through the frustrations of farming." At his first showing he said: "I'm really overwhelmed." And in 1999, over a century after being banned, *Bacchante and the Infant Faun* returned to the Boston Public Library. No longer considered a "monument to inebriety," the statue's return evidenced the shifting parameters of acceptable public art in Boston.[43]

In 1992 Naiad Press founder Barbara Grier sent books, periodicals, and memorabilia documenting American lesbian history to the San Francisco

Public Library's James C. Hormel Gay & Lesbian Center, established as a center for scholarship in gay and lesbian studies. Grier's materials represented the world's largest collection of lesbian letters, one expert reported. Although the library's foundation sought $1.6 million in contributions, by the time the center opened it had $2.8 million. "We are so hungry for a past and a future, and to do something positive and creative with our energies after fighting for survival," said its executive director, a lesbian.[44]

Not every public library effort to start a new service to meet a new information need was successful, however. When a St. Luke's Hospital AIDS Unit nurse contacted NYPL branch librarian Dean Sheehan about allowing her to check out multiple titles for her patients, hospital library volunteers refused to handle any books AIDS patients might have touched. What about a deposit collection the branch could bring directly to the hospital? Sheehan asked. The nurse loved the idea, so Sheehan visited the unit and talked with patients. With other librarians, he then assembled a collection of adult fiction by gay and lesbian authors. Weeks passed as his hospital contact did not return calls. When Sheehan finally

James C. Hormel Gay & Lesbian Center (opened in 1996), San Francisco Public Library.
Photo by author

reached her, she agreed to meet him so he could deliver the books. Upon his arrival, however, he was told she was on vacation, and because he was not allowed to enter the building he could not leave the deposit collection. The books never made it to St. Luke's. Elsewhere librarians were more successful. In 1989 the West Hollywood (California) Community Library opened the nation's first HIV Information Center, a project spearheaded by a community activist, himself infected. Through the Nebraska Library Commission that same year the Parents & Friends of Lesbians and Gays Cornhusker Inc. distributed eight-book sets on AIDS and gay issues to sixty-eight public libraries. "Accurate information is essential to combat prejudice," the group's president told the *Omaha World Herald*.[45]

In 1990, however, two Muscatine, Iowa, men complained about public library books dealing with homosexuality. "I don't think the taxpayer should be paying for this," said one. "It's immoral and unnatural." Eric Marcus, author of *The Male Couple's Guide to Living Together*—one of the books the men opposed—offered to donate a copy if someone objected to spending tax dollars for it. "People like them are always complaining that gay people are disgusting perverts," Marcus said. "When I come up with a book where I talk . . . about having responsible, supportive and productive relationships, I get slammed just the same." The librarian assured the *Omaha World-Herald* the complaining men could take their case to trustees but noted that the trustees believed "the patron has the right to chose what to check out," and on this issue the library is "getting incredibly fine support from the community."[46]

To bring national attention to this kind of public pressure to censor library materials, in 1982 the ALA's Office of Intellectual Freedom initiated Banned Books Week. In response, public libraries across the country mounted exhibits of books previously banned somewhere, sometime. Some questioned the premise, however. When he observed a 1985 Providence (Rhode Island) Public Library exhibit, a reporter noted one local incident in which public pressure forced the library to put a book on restricted shelves. That was not censorship, he maintained—parents exercised their right to free speech; the book was not banned. The exhibit was a failure, he said, because it "makes it appear as if all community involvement in library acquisition decisions verges on censorship." A Bloomington, Illinois, citizen asked: "Are public libraries funded by tax dollars? If so, what's the big beef if some of the bill-payers have a say in what they buy?" Thousands of books were published every year, she noted. "Whoever orders the books is censoring by choosing what they think is worth reading."[47]

These kinds of disagreements surfaced elsewhere, and citizen attempts to influence the acquisition and circulation of public library materials took many forms. At the Yorba Linda (California) Public Library in 1991, to keep them out of circulation one patron checked out all titles containing the word "devil"—"even those that had nothing to do with the devil," a librarian noted. At the Coquille (Illinois) Public Library, in 1994 someone used white correction fluid to blank out passages the person found offensive, and in the blank spaces entered ellipses. In 1998, a Baptist minister checked *Heather Has Two Mommies* and *Daddy's Roommate* out of the Wichita Falls (Texas) Public Library, gave the librarian a check for $54, and promised never to return them. When the local newspaper reported the story, patrons demanded the library reacquire the books. Sympathetic book lovers donated fifteen copies.[48]

Holding a Bible in his right hand and three issues of *Playboy* in his left, one man told a Fort Lauderdale, Florida, public librarian in 1984: "I am taking these out of the library in the name of Jesus Christ of Nazareth." Police arrested him shortly thereafter; they took one *Playboy* for evidence, and returned the other two to the library. Once released, however, the man returned to the library, took both a second time, and was not only arrested but also jailed. The Wellesley (Massachusetts) Public Library addressed resistance to *Playboy* differently. In 1995, the board voted to retain the magazine even after one parent complained that his nine-year-old boy had requested and received a copy. A year later, however, after two people opposed to the decision won seats on the board, the library canceled its *Playboy* subscription. "There are a lot of reasons why we would discontinue something," said the librarian, who denied she felt pressure. "If something got stolen a lot, we might not replace it. We might not buy something back because of lack of interest, and we might not purchase it because something comes along that we would feel would better serve the community." Besides, she told a reporter, "*Playboy* will still be available through a library-to-library borrowing system."[49]

Public libraries resolved these kinds of issues in different ways. When several Spartanburg, South Carolina, parents complained in 1990 that *Epaminondas and His Auntie* was demeaning to black people, library officials moved it to the adult section, where it was unlikely children would find it. When in 1996 someone at the Oak Lawn (Illinois) Public Library objected to Helga Fleischauer-Hardt's *Show Me!*, a sex education book with glossy pictures of nude prepubescent children that to many smacked of child pornography, the library shifted the book to its Inferno; so many people subsequently checked it out "the library's only copy literally fell apart." At the Bountiful (Utah) Public Library in 1992, however, one mother wanted books on how babies are born to help her explain the process to her six-year-old daughter. When she asked for a children's book about human reproduction the librarian said: "Follow me," then took her to a backroom where the library housed the materials she wanted. "Why are these books not kept on the shelves?" she asked. "Isn't this kind of suppression of information in the year 1992 shockingly backward?"[50] The book stayed in the Inferno.

That same year Madonna published *Sex*, largely a book of nude photos poorly bound with metal front and back covers. Within weeks it was a bestseller. "The book is sleazy trash," said the ALA's Office of Intellectual Freedom Director Judith Krug, but it "should be in every medium-sized library." Despite her "should," however, public libraries across the country had to find solutions acceptable to their communities, not the ALA's Office of Intellectual Freedom. Some libraries refused to buy it, for reasons ranging from too expensive to poorly bound; one librarian worried patrons might cut themselves on the covers. The Colorado Springs Library director—spearheading a bond issue for a new library building and facing strong opposition to the book—declared it "pornography" and thus not acceptable. The St. Joseph (Missouri) Library held public meetings, then purchased one copy. Like many others, the San Diego Public Library bought a copy but placed it in an Inferno. The Fort Wayne Public Library ordered two copies but put both in the Rare Books Room, where patrons had to request it. "I realize that this is a departure from our usual stance on access to books," the librarian said, and "runs contrary to ALA dogma." The local newspaper teased with a cartoon showing a librarian addressing a patron: "Yes, we have 'Sex,' . . . but unless you are prepared to prove you're on a scholarly mission and not some perverted leering maggot, it'll stay locked up in Rare Books, understood?"[51]

But in some communities even restricted access to certain titles was not acceptable. In 1992 only one of twenty-seven Orange County public libraries had a copy of *Daddy's Roommate*. "Librarians said there were several possible reasons for the book's virtual absence here," a reporter noted. "Some libraries said they had other children's books dealing with the same topic. Other libraries said that, with limited budgets, they can't buy as many books as they would like, yet all said they would not turn down a children's book simply because the topic is controversial." On the other hand, in 1993 the Dayton and Montgomery County (Ohio) Public Library board voted 7 to 0 to retain *Daddy's Roommate* and *Heather Has Two Mommies*, two of eight titles in its collection that addressed children with homosexual parents. "God will judge you!" yelled one protester at a public board meeting. One woman phoned in her support. She grew up in a gay household and wanted the books in her public library so her children could understand their gay grandmother. And at a 1995 Cleremont County (Ohio) Public Library meeting attended by 150 to discuss *The Advocate*—a gay periodical that drew petitions signed by 4,000 citizens asking that it be banned—Andrea Blankenmeyer walked slowly to the podium. Knowing all eyes were upon her, she choked with emotion: "I'm 19 years old and I'm gay. I only wish I had access to a magazine like *The Advocate* when I was younger. It would have made my life a lot easier." Ultimately, the library decided to leave *The Advocate* on the open shelf.[52]

In 1992 the San Francisco Public Library reaffirmed its right to display the gay rainbow flag over one of its branches despite challenges by local religious groups. That same year, however, the community showed its tolerance limits when sixty citizens protested use of Potrero branch rooms by a North American Man-Boy Love Association (NAMBLA) chapter. A dozen members, protesters noted, had been arrested on child molestation charges. "Witch hunt," said NAMBLA. "We're an open, public organization with nothing to hide." Library officials cited the Library Bill of Rights, and said they could not "flout constitutional free speech guarantees." But community pressure persisted, and a month later NAMBLA withdrew. Thus, concerned citizens used the library as place to force a resolution contrary to a Library Bill of Rights imperative.

Majority attitudes toward gays and lesbians varied from community to community and often demonstrated how differently public libraries responded to local challenges. Sometimes public libraries provided forums. In 1990 gay writers read from their works at NYPL's Mid-Manhattan branch. In 1998 the Broward County (Florida) Public Library showed a touring exhibit titled "Love Makes a Family: Living in Gay and Lesbian Families" that consisted of twenty photos—all annotated with interviews of their subjects—showing "families with gay and lesbian parents, grandparents, and teens."[53]

On the other hand, in 1995 the Fairfax County (Virginia) Public Library broke an eleven-year tradition and barred Gay History Month exhibits; critics said the exhibits were "unbalanced." Some protested, but to no avail. In 1996 Lancaster (Pennsylvania) Public Library trustees bowed to pressure from county commissioners to remove a local Pink Triangle Coalition exhibit recognizing well-known gay, lesbian, and bisexual artists and authors. Letters of support and protest quickly appeared in the newspaper. "When we turn away from a group of people that some (maybe even many) might object to, we shut down our minds to incoming information," said one writer. "That is not the job of a library." Even though one trustee resigned in protest, the board refused to reconsider its decision.[54]

But censorship challenges did not always focus on nudity and sexual issues—gay or straight. In 1992 the Palm Beach County (Florida) public library system refused to acquire two neo-Nazi publications requested by the local National Socialist White Workers Party. "I don't think a public library has an obligation to have propaganda that spreads fear and hate and violence in a community," said a library official. In Livingston, Texas, a local minister cried "censorship" when the public library refused his gift of *The God-Makers*, a book claiming Mormons practiced Satanic rituals. It did not meet selection standards, librarians said. Ultimately the library accepted the donation, but put it next to another book disputing its conclusions. With that the minister had no quarrel, but the experience, said a Fort Worth Pro-Family Forum official, showed flaws in routine library acquisition practices. "They scream censorship when we enter the selection process, but they've already gotten their ax in before parents ever know. . . . I feel it's totally improper for librarians to have the attitude, 'you furnish us the children and the money, and then by glory, keep your hands off.'"[55]

From Chicago, the ALA's Office of Intellectual Freedom watched, and frequently commented. In 1980 Krug criticized an effort by a Virginia minister to obtain the names of people who checked out copies of books by Harold Robbins, Phillip Roth, and Sidney Sheldon. "This sort of thing has a chilling effect on our ability to perform the duties for which we have been hired," she said. But the community took care of itself. When the minister asked for a community meeting, 200 packed the room "to denounce censorship." While Krug welcomed the result, the OIF showed a different position six years later when the Lebanon (Indiana) Public Library published the names of delinquent borrowers and titles they checked out in the local newspaper. Included were *Two Guys Notice Me . . . and Other Miracles, What Only a Mother Can Tell You about Having a Baby*, and *I Should Have Seen It Coming When the Rabbit Died*. Naturally, the list created a community "buzz," and when a reporter asked for comment, Krug replied: "Privacy protection does not apply to delinquent borrowers." Naming names "does what they want it to do . . . it brings the books back."[56]

Arguments about racism and sexism in children's books also carried over from previous decades. In the early 1980s, the San Francisco Public Library pulled *The Story of Ping* (1933) because its characters stereotyped Chinese. "It's scary," said Krug, by now the go-to person the nation's press contacted for comment on local public library censorship cases. "Everyone wants to protect the children. The problem is," she exaggerated, "they're going to be so protected they won't be able to function in the year 2000." A Council on Interracial Books for Children director disagreed. "Authors have the freedom to write racist and sexist books and publishers have the freedom to publish them," he insisted, "but librarians . . . have the freedom to exercise their professional judgment and *not* buy such books." "Convoluted logic," argued a *Los Angeles Times* letter-writer. "Censorship by any other name is still censorship!" said another.[57]

In 1982 public library systems in San Francisco, Milwaukee, and Chicago refused to acquire *Jake and Honeybunch Go to Heaven*, a Caldecott Award winner that depicted a black laborer and his mule after being killed by a freight train. The depiction of black heaven "would offend many people," said the Chicago Public Library's children's services librarian; "it reinforced many stereotypes." The publisher protested. "Librarians are deliberately keeping a widely acclaimed book by a major author-artist off their shelves in the name of morality." "Flaps over books are very temporary," said the SFPL director, "and 50 years from now this will be only a historical footnote." To this the publisher responded: "Fifty years from now, when [the SFPL librarian] is only a footnote, this book will still be enjoying a long, fruitful life in most of the libraries of America."[58] He was wrong in his prediction. In early 2013—thirty years later—WorldCat reported only 391 American public library systems—less than 5 percent of the total—held copies of *Jake*.

By far the greatest censorship disputes that affected libraries in the last years of the twentieth century concerned Internet filtering. The American Library Association's Office of Intellectual Freedom firmly opposed it.

Some librarians dutifully followed OIF's lead, most seemed to waffle, others resisted. "The Internet does present a unique situation for us," said one Contra Costa (California) County librarian. "Historically, everything in our collection is there because librarians selected it. . . . We obviously did not select the entire collection on the Internet."

Many outside the profession quickly challenged the OIF position. Just as they traditionally filtered printed materials, demanded a Washington, DC–based Family Research Council attorney, librarians needed to filter electronic information. "Electronic or print, pornography is not appropriate for children," she insisted. "Let's be practical," wrote a *Chicago Tribune* columnist. "Kids go to the library alone and have been doing so for years. Because this is a fact, libraries need to take some responsibility for protecting those who are underage." The right to view pornography "may be absolute in the home," reasoned the Denver *Rocky Mountain News*, "but the library is not anyone's home. It is a public place frequented by children, and civilized communities simply do not expose children to everything that any adult might hanker to see." Said one San Francisco parent, "I don't understand this, especially when there is software that blocks it."[59]

Despite OIF dictates, across the country public libraries began installing filters. "Some information sources are inappropriate for viewing in a public setting," the San Diego Public Library policy stated, and librarians had the right to end Internet sessions when such material was displayed. The Boston Public Library provided two kinds of Internet access, one in an unfiltered adult room, the other in a filtered children's room. The Oakland Park (Florida) Public Library did the same but located the adult computer in view of the circulation desk. If objectionable material popped up, a librarian would ask the user to clear the screen. The Austin (Texas) Public Library negotiated a "fragile compromise" by installing an unfiltered computer at each branch, locating it on a specially built recessed table, and allowing only patrons over eighteen to use it. At the Denver Public Library officials installed search engines in the computers in the library's children and adult sections that filtered out all but G-rated sites; in the adult section, however, users could opt out of the filters. When the Orange County (California) public library system installed a similar set of filters, a local columnist applauded: "Good for everybody . . . because it impinges on most people's rights hardly at all, while protecting the rights of parents and their children. And that's the sort of fair compromise that we—and the First Amendment—can all easily live with."[60]

But the situation in Minneapolis was unique. In February 2000, forty-seven public library staff members described to a local newspaper their working conditions around the fifty computer terminals they were required to monitor. In the last three years, one staff member said, male users obsessed with sex sites monopolized the terminals, and when reminded of their thirty-minute time limit (the only authority staff had to monitor their behavior) frequently responded with profanity. Several were masturbating when approached. In an article subsequently published in the feminist periodical *Off Our Backs,* reference librarian Wendy Adamson described in graphic detail the sickening images—including bestiality and sadomasochism—that staff saw on sites these men routinely viewed. But when they complained to administrators, she said, staff members were told that the library "supported unfettered access to information," and if they were "good librarians" they would follow the policy. Repeated complaints brought no change.

Three months later, however, convinced that the hard line the administration and the ALA's OIF took was actually forcing regular patrons from the library—"We were watching our users repeatedly assaulted by these images, . . . recoiling in horror," Adamson said, "and sometimes literally rushing out of the building"—twelve staff members filed a sexual harassment complaint with the Equal Employment Opportunity Commission (EEOC). Tolerating the environment, they concluded, "carried the message that we were willing to submit to sexual harassment which no other citizens would tolerate. . . . Too often, the problem is denied, glossed over, ignored, or simplistically addressed by ineffective official library policies, which wax poetic about the wealth of information available on the Internet, and the importance of making wise choices when we use it." Their EEOC complaint brought heavy criticism that demonstrated the rhetorical power the Library Bill of Rights had honed over decades. In the professional literature the women were portrayed as censors and professional traitors. From across the country, however, librarians who had endured similar experiences wrote supportive—but mostly private—messages.

A day after filing the complaint, the administration caved in and instituted a new policy. Each terminal had a sign indicating that it was illegal to display materials considered obscene by Minnesota law, and authorized security guards to enforce it. "In less than a week," Adamson reported, most sex site "users left the library, and have not been seen since. . . . At MPL, we succeeded in bringing a problem out into the open," but she also recognized that each public library had to find its own solution. Librarians had a "responsibility to take a part in the larger dialogue in a search for a variety of answers, rather than putting our collective heads in the sand and resolutely clinging to theoretical principles that may be doing more harm than good."[61]

Like the Infernos implemented in the nineteenth century, like the library reviewing media developed in the early twentieth, late-twentieth-century Internet filters offered a practical solution that communities could accept. They allowed public libraries to provide controlled access to controversial information, to respond to the sensitivities of local patrons, and at the same time to resolve local debates about what was acceptable information content in public library spaces. On December 21, 2000, President Bill Clinton signed the Children's Internet Protection Act requiring all libraries and schools receiving federal funds to filter material "harmful to minors." In 2002, the EEOC issued a preliminary ruling that Minneapolis Public Library employee exposure to pornographic Internet sites constituted "a hostile work environment." A year later the library settled the civil suit for $435,000.[62]

As the twenty-first century approached, many librarians reflected on their recent past. One remarked that Great Society legislation had helped public libraries develop computerized applications, provided funds for essential equipment, enabled communities to adjust their public library buildings to accommodate new hardware, established cooperative agreements that helped achieve computer-based resource sharing, and trained the personnel to operate and maintain the systems. While federal funds were a small portion of total funding, he wrote, they were nonetheless critical in the development of computerized applications."[63]

He was right—from his perspective. From behind the circulation and reference desks in the nation's public libraries that's what librarians seemed to notice most in the century's last two decades. The millions of Americans who stood in front of the desks, however, still saw them as places that transformed and enriched their everyday lives through services and collections. "Library paste," the *Los Angeles Times Book Review* editor wrote in 1983, "is a precious part of social glue." In 1988 a New York Human Resources Administration official told Fort Washington branch librarians that libraries were one of "the stable elements" in families he served and were instrumental in keeping them together. And like Maggie Phelps and so many other American public library users before her, in 1999 one very loyal patron gave voice to her feelings about the Queens Borough Public Library branch she used so often: "It has been such an important part of my life."[64]

CHAPTER TEN

Information, Reading, and Place: 2001–Present

Today, public library card catalogs have mostly disappeared, all replaced by online catalogs patrons can access from home computers, iPads, and mobile phones. At most public libraries circulation systems use bar codes that computers read to record transactions. Computers support most of the public library's basic routines. Because nearly all public libraries offer Internet access, computers link patrons to huge databases of information previously scattered in tens of thousands of reference books, newspapers, and periodicals. Printers spit out copies of the information users find there. LP recordings are mostly gone, and although some audiocassettes still tell books-on-tape stories to commuters driving cars built in the 1990s, increasingly CDs and DVDs are the new packages that carry these stories, including those in music and film.

At many public libraries children wear headphones attached to computer pods. Patrons harness interlibrary loan systems linking them to millions of books in libraries across the country. Some libraries lend Kindles loaded with e-books, another new textual form. Many libraries sport drive-up windows—both to drop off materials of all sorts and to pick up items patrons ordered online. The computers that thirty years earlier many predicted would cause the demise of the public library have actually made it more accessible. To librarians behind the circulation desk, it certainly feels like computers touch everything in library practice.

But public library traditions also endure. Sundays are still the busiest day of the week for most public libraries open that day. Sounds familiar to early-twentieth-century patrons—like the thumps and scuffles of children on their way to story hour who are often herded by adults urging

Young adults work together to hone their computer skills at one of the New York Public Library's "Tech Connect" classes. *Photo courtesy of the New York Public Library*

them to use their "library voice"—still rankle patrons who expect tiptoe silence. And many of the old smells remain. The aroma of old books in sober covers arranged on ordered shelves still hangs in the air. And in some public libraries a mixture of old clothes and unwashed bodies continues to create what one librarian called "the steam of the social soup."[1]

As in the nineteenth century, newspaper and periodical pages still rustle in reading rooms, and familiar sounds like the "thunk-slish" of books dropping and sliding across the circulation desk and the "whoosh-clang" of the outside depository station door persist as background noises. Patrons still read books at public libraries, but now often in comfortable chairs facing fireplaces and frequently while sipping cappuccino purchased from the library's coffee shop. Libraries still have straight-backed chairs tucked under sturdy oak desks—many showing a patina users find nostalgic, many sporting chewing gum decades old still stuck on their undersides. And users remain worried about overdue fines; one of Captain Chesley "Sully" Sullenberger's concerns after he landed US Airways Flight 1549 in New York's Hudson River in January 2009 was a Contra Costa (California) Public Library book he had aboard his plane. It might come back late, he told the library, perhaps even water damaged.

Many authorities still have questions about the value of public libraries. Most questions emanate from convictions trapped in blindered thinking about what a public library does for its community, supported by traditional public library statistics analysts have used for generations—for example, reference questions asked. Statistics show that the need for useful knowledge that public library reference services had prioritized for a century and a half diminished in the first decade of the twenty-first century. Between 1999 and 2008 reference transactions dropped 9 percent; when measured against numbers of visitors they dropped 24 percent. People in general, and public library users in particular, were finding their information on the Internet, at home.[2]

For budget-cutting politicians, this constituted an open invitation. In 2002 a Tacoma (Washington) *News Tribune* reporter quoted a city councilman who wanted to eliminate local public libraries because he considered them "somewhat of a dinosaur . . . too intensive on bricks and mortar." Fellow council members complimented the councilman for thinking "outside the box." After visiting Tacoma's public libraries, however, the reporter disagreed. "Let's think inside the box for a moment," he argued, "because it is inside those brick-and-mortar boxes where community lives. Tacoma's 10 libraries are the living rooms of 10 neighborhoods. They are places where latchkey kids can feel safe in the afternoons, where people without Internet access at home go online, where parents give their children the gift of reading."[3]

"Are Libraries Necessary, or a Waste of Tax Money?" a Chicago FOX News affiliate asked in a segment aired in 2010. "They eat up millions of your hard-earned tax dollars. . . . With the Internet and e-books, do we really need" public libraries? Chicago Public Library commissioner Mary Dempsey quickly answered that her institution served 12 million visitors a year through its 74 locations. In 2009 it circulated 10 million items, sponsored 3.8 million free one-hour Internet sessions, and provided safe places and homework assistance to tens of thousands of Chicago children whose public school system offered the nation's shortest school day.

In his widely cited *Bowling Alone: The Collapse and Revival of American Community* (2000), Robert D. Putnam failed to include the American public library in his analysis. Putnam had an epiphany several years later, however, when Dempsey invited him to visit her branch library system. "No longer a passive repository of books and information or an outpost of culture, quiet, and decorum in a noisy world," he observed, "the new library is an active and responsive part of the community and an agent of change." Putnam wrote as if these were recent developments, then added: "The Internet, which seems to threaten its reason for being, turns out to be one of the things that bring people to the library."[4]

Economists have tried to place dollar values on public libraries to show what returns taxpayers get for their investments. For every dollar of taxpayer money, one study showed, Indiana public libraries returned $2.38, Wisconsin $4, Vermont $5, and Florida $6.54. A University of Pennsylvania study analyzed the economic impact of the Free Library of Philadelphia in 2010 and found average real estate values of homes within a quarter mile of a branch higher by nearly $10,000, thus totaling $700 million more in home values that generated $19 million in property taxes, more than half the library's budget of $33 million. Add in the 6.5 million items circulated per year the study valued at $100 million, a reporter calculated, and it was easy to see that public libraries returned substantial amounts on the city's investment. Even that said nothing about the economic value of 3.2 million reference questions answered, the 1.2 million times Philadelphians used library computers, free lessons in computer literacy, after-school tutoring for latchkey kids, English as a second language classes for recent immigrants, and finally, those "hard to quantify intangibles—a safe and warm refuge, concerts and lectures, camaraderie. Even the most Scrooge-like conservative," the reporter wrote "would conclude Philadelphia should increase, not decrease, its investment in its public libraries."[5]

Perhaps because they are so difficult to measure, the Philadelphia study did not analyze reading and place per se. But if one defines reading broadly to include interaction not only with books (print and audio) but also music, art, film, and television programs now packaged in CDs and DVDs, on a national scale the reading evidenced in public library circulation statistics went up in the twenty-first century's first decade—way up. Although circulations per visit declined 5 percent between 1999 and 2008, the total number of items circulated went from 1.69 billion in 1999 to 2.28 billion in 2008, an increase of nearly 35 percent.[6]

And in a 2012 national survey of readers over sixteen, the Pew Research Center's Internet and American Life Project reported 78 percent had read a book the previous year, 58 percent had a library card, and 69 percent said the public library was important to them and their families. While these statistics certainly demonstrated increased public library use, even here surveyors could not move beyond conventional thinking to ask why reading stories was so important. Under "Reasons for

Reading" Pew provided four categories: "Read for Work/School" (54 percent checked this category), "Read to Keep Up with Current Events" (77 percent), "Read to Research Topics of Interest" (74 percent), and "Read for Pleasure" (79 percent). The taxonomy's first three categories clearly favored useful knowledge and gave those surveyed no opportunity to articulate ways they found "Read for Pleasure" fulfilling. Still, that category scored highest.[7]

Not only is reading in American public libraries up, but so is use of library space. Although librarians have counted noses for programs they hosted over the years and included those numbers in annual reports, not until 2004 were these statistics reported on a national level. The numbers show substantial growth. In 2008, the average US citizen in a library service area visited her local public library five times (1.5 million visits) compared to an average of 4.3 visits in 1999. Overall program attendance increased from 237.6 per thousand people in 2004 to 279.4 in 2008. And although the majority attended story hours (still a staple public library activity), the percentage of children's programs against the total declined from 81 percent in 2004 to 74 percent in 2008. Thus, in the twenty-first century's first decade, public libraries organized more public culture programs for more adults who increasingly used the library spaces in which these programs took place. In a 2013 Pew study, analysts found 85 percent of those surveyed regarded the meeting spaces public libraries provided to be important or very important, 93 percent appreciated their free events/activities, 95 percent liked their library's quiet study spaces for adults and children, and 95 percent enjoyed programs and classes for children and teens.[8]

Still, these numbers do not explain how users appropriated these public library spaces. Witness, for example, the scene in the Johnson County (Kansas) Library on September 11, 2001. "Patrons were exceptionally hushed and subdued, and the only ongoing noise was the low hum of CNN on a television . . . wheeled into a reading area for the day," reference librarian Stuart Hinds recalled. An elderly man asked about the location of the Twin Towers. "I retrieved a travel guide for New York City to pinpoint on a map exactly where they had stood." Without talking they both studied the map, "each of us silenced by the horrific events of the day, knowing that the towers depicted on the diagram—and the people inside—were no more. He then looked me in the eye, shook my hand, thanked me, and left the library." Assessing what happens in library places does not easily fit into statistical taxonomies documenting library use, yet anecdotes like this demonstrate that public libraries help build community in multiple ways.[9]

Other examples abound. In a Monticello (Iowa) Public Library alcove one morning in 2007, Michelle Obama, wife of presidential candidate Barack Obama and mother of two daughters, finished "a rousing reading" of *Olivia and the Missing Toy* to children sitting at her feet. She asked if they had questions. "The kids shake their heads no," wrote a reporter, "and look imploringly at their new friend for more." Obama was shown two additional titles—*Our National Anthem* ("the sort of red, white and blue book Lynne Cheney would write," the reporter said, "that an aspiring first lady would be expected to read") and *Skippyjon Jones*, story of a Siamese kitten with a Spanish accent. Obama chose the second. "Yip Yippee Yippito! It's the end of Alfredo Buzzito!" Obama read as she struggled with the words and the accent. "The kids go loco, rolling off their beanbags with belly-busting laughter." Obama laughed "pretty hard herself," but forged on, "hollering 'Holy Frijoles!' with great gusto." The kids did not care who she was, and were oblivious to the political cacophony surrounding them. They zoned on the story, and liked what they heard.[10]

Although reference statistics decreased between 1999 and 2008, patrons still found public libraries a hive of useful knowledge, but each patron defined what was useful knowledge in his or her own way. Again, examples abound. Shortly after giving birth prematurely to her first child in 2003, Amy Smith of Minneapolis began suffering postpartum depression. When her doctor prescribed antidepressants, she worried about taking them while breastfeeding. For answers, "I turned to the one resource I knew I could trust: my local library." There she did Internet searches and discovered the risks of not taking the antidepressant greatly outweighed the risks of taking it while breastfeeding. Even more important, however, she picked up Brooke Shields's *Down Came the Rain* (2005). It "really changed my way of thinking about and living with depression. . . . Her honesty about her feelings of hopelessness and desperation helped normalize what I was feeling," Smith said. "If Brooke Shields . . . could endure the same psychological challenges that I did post-baby and emerge even stronger for it, I could too."[11] Reading Shields's story empowered Smith as much as the information she got from her Internet search.

Perhaps the biggest "story" in American public library history since 1995 is J. K. Rowling's *Harry Potter*. What happened to Harry in libraries across the country reveals much about the power of reading that libraries provide and about the library as a place. Why was the Potter series so successful? They were books that did not patronize, writes Melissa Anelli in *Harry, a History,* books that treated their adolescent readers with respect. Anelli discovered many Potter readers used the Internet to form social connections, write fan fiction, and improve artistic skills by drawing Harry Potter characters and scenes. And because the fan fiction and art they shared online often received responses and reviews, they also learned constructive criticism. Media scholar Henry Jenkins sees *Harry Potter* as an excellent example of "convergence culture," a phenomenon in which the conversation about stories not only harnesses new technologies to play a major role in satisfying an innate desire for social connections but also provides a reading adventure that takes place outside the classroom, beyond adult control, and that children use to teach one another. Because his followers include adults and children, Harry Potter also becomes a space for intergenerational conversations in which adults often learn from their children.[12]

Across the country public libraries served as sites for the convergence culture Harry nurtured, where learning (albeit informal) was triggered by a set of activities. In 2000, nineteen children appeared for the second meeting of the Harry Potter Club at the Orange County (California) Public Library Taft branch. After whispering the correct password ("parselmouth") into the librarian's ear, they listened to her read from the latest Harry Potter novel and drew pictures of their favorite scenes. At the Las Virgenes branch, children attended a "Harry Potter Magic Show." The local magician asked Harry Potter trivia questions. "These kids raised their hands, 9-year-old kids, 7-year-old kids," said the branch librarian, "and they knew the answers." The New Britain (Connecticut) Public Library hosted "Harry Potter Night II—The First Year at Hogwarts," and encouraged fourth- to eighth-graders to wear their wizard wardrobes. On July 21, 2007, the Louisville Free Public Library held a Harry Potter House Party attended by 1,500 to celebrate the arrival of *Harry Potter and the Deathly Hallows.* Local media reported that the library's gathering appeared more demographically diverse than most other city events.[13]

But not everyone was happy with Harry Potter events and activities that public libraries hosted. In 2000, the Jacksonville (Florida) Public Library stopped giving a Hogwarts Certificate of Accomplishment for Completion of Term in Hogwarts School of Witchcraft and Wizardry when a parent complained about exposing her children to witchcraft.

A Harry Potter event at the Toledo-Lucas County Public Library in 2007 drew together people of both genders, and many races and ages, at the library. *Photo courtesy of Toledo-Lucas County Public Library*

That brought more reaction. One mother of three who read all the *Potter* books did not disagree with the library's decision but argued with the complaining parent. Her children learned valuable lessons about courage and morality from Potter stories. "You can select all the negative stuff you want, but overall it sends a very positive message to children," she said. "Even the Bible has a lot of different themes that are challenging for children. That doesn't mean we should keep them in a cocoon." In 2001, the Oskaloosa (Kansas) Public Library canceled a "Hogwarts class" for aspiring young witches and wizards because some parents thought the activity promoted demon worship.[14]

The public library's capacity to bring people together took other forms, most impossible to identify with statistical taxonomies and accountability measures public libraries use to assess value. For example, in 2005 the *Washington Post* carried an article by Eric Wee that focused on a DCPL branch in one of Washington's poorest neighborhoods. In it Wee reported that every Tuesday night a homeless man named Conrad Cheek Jr. entered the library and set up his chessboard on a children's room table. Wee immediately noticed a transformation. "No more ignored pleas, no averted glances. During the next hour, people will look him in the eye. They'll listen to his words. In this down-at-the-heels library he's the teacher." Among his students was nine-year-old Ali Osman. As Wee watched this interaction, Ali's mother explained that her son's confidence had soared after playing with Conrad, that he was now bragging to friends about being a chess player. "We owe it all to Mr. Conrad," his mother said. "We love him." Inside the library, Wee reported, "They call him Mr. Conrad."

Also frequenting this place were Jane and Doug Alspach, who seventeen years earlier moved to DC from Alexandria with newborn daughter Sarah to get away from gentrified neighborhoods. Unfortunately, Doug said, the neighborhood around them was becoming as homogeneous as the one they fled. Fewer places existed where people of different races, classes, and backgrounds mixed, he said, but the library was different. "It's one of the last outposts where a cross section of people still come together. It's where Sarah was reading in groups with kids from wealthy families and those who were just getting by. It's where they gathered on holidays for parties, where they caught up with neighbors during the weekly story times. And it's a place that remembers them." Wee also told of Catherine Stancil, a sixty-nine-year-old functionally illiterate grandmother who every Saturday came to the library to meet with a volunteer, thirty-year-old attorney Karen Dees. Although Dees worried she was not doing a good job, Catherine disagreed. Catherine, Wee reported, "had started to feel different about herself. Her shame is gone." Proudly, she told Wee, "Now I feel that I'm as good as you."[15]

On a 2008 summer trip I visited three Montana libraries to assess "library as place." At the Billings Public Library, I met with library staff and patrons to learn about several initiatives recently undertaken, among them an annual event called "Food for Thought: An Evening of Great Conversation" that encouraged the gathering of community and exchange of free thought (each table was hosted by a moderator expert in a particular subject); "Raging Flood Waters: Billings' Gloomiest Night" (an exhibit of a 1937 flood that devastated the town); a program called "Can We Talk? A Community Conversation" (a Humanities Montana activity to promote civil discourse); and "Project Homeless Connect," an annual one-day event to connect Billings's homeless and near-homeless population to resources that provide a "hand up and out of poverty."

At the Bozeman Public Library, I noticed a large community room just inside the front door—used for lots of purposes, I was told. At the time I was in the building about twenty toddlers were being read to by parents. When I peeked inside I met eighty-three-year-old Ray Bequet, a volunteer who read to and enjoyed the company of children nearly every day. "For some reason," he said, "my smile appeals to kids." What especially caught my eye, however, was the artwork and sculpture that adorned the building. Greeting me at the front door was an eight-foot bronze sculpture by a local artist depicting a youth holding a book riding on the back of a winged horse. Once inside, I looked up into the building's soaring heights to see suspended sculptures representing clouds done by another local artist and donated by the Friends of the Library. Adorning the walls of one very long hallway were decades-old framed posters of the Union Pacific Railroad, which had a huge influence on Bozeman history. And as I looked into the children's room, children's artwork plastered the walls. The library had won a 2003 Institute for Museum and Library Services National Award for Library Service for, among many other activities, working with the Montana Center for International Visitors to sponsor programs on Bangladeshi fabrics and Mongolian ecotourism, and shortly after 9/11 for sponsoring a program titled "What Is Islam?"

At the Flathead County Library in Kalispell I learned about a civic project titled "Principles of Civil Dialogue: Turning Strangers into Neighbors," designed to provide safe space in which people could discuss diverse opinions and respectfully disagree without shouting at each other. Meetings took place in the library—an active partner in the program since it began. What interested me most, however, was a series of incidents that occurred earlier that year. Because the library's assembly room was open to anyone in the community, library director Kim Crowley said, she did not hesitate to allow a local white supremacist group called Kalispell Christian Fellowship to show two films—Epic: The Story of the Waffen SS (which takes a positive spin on the Nazi war machine) and The Truth behind the Gates of Auschwitz, a Holocaust denial film. Predictably, local opponents rallied. At the first film showing, hundreds appeared with placards that read "No Neo-Nazis" and "No Hate in My Backyard." The second also drew hundreds with similar placards, some promoting peace, others denouncing hatred. "I only hate broccoli," read a local rabbi's sign. I asked Kim how she felt about these incidents: "Though the two groups disagreed (sometimes loudly and angrily), there were conversations going on everywhere. . . . And at the second one, I was thrilled to see 300 people at the library for an event! It was really great to see all the public discourse happening." Ironically, she noted, "both sides thanked me separately for allowing this to happen."[16]

Public library as place manifested itself in other ways in the twenty-first century's first decade. One mother said that for her homeschooled son, the Camano Island (Washington) Public Library was the place where he "crawled into an inflatable planetarium to 'stargaze,' . . . molded sculptures from recyclables, laughed at puppet shows, and not long after we studied insects, he ogled—but refused to engage with—a 'Bug Chef' who fried, sautéed, and baked bugs for a gawking group of elementary school-age kids," said his mother. "Never was a science unit so memorable! . . . The library has made homeschooling completely doable on a single wage-earner's salary." "It's not about the library material itself," noted one El Paso, Texas, public librarian in a moment of epiphany when a mother homeschooling her children confronted her about the explicitness of graphic images in Spanish *fotonovelas*. Instead, it was "about the tensions that arise when cultures (religious, ethnic, or other) meet" in the library. When several groups protested against Spanish *novellas* in the Denver Public Library in 2005, a *Denver Post* columnist predicted "the public library will get through the review of the content of these books and find a balance that works for the community."[17]

As an important community place, the public library continued to assimilate immigrants. Eight months after arriving from Baghdad in 2010, the Musa family began attending English and civics classes at the Hartford (Connecticut) Public Library's ten-year-old program to help immigrants. The Musas were among the 2,500 immigrants who participated annually. The entire family walked the half-mile to the library from their sparsely furnished apartment every Tuesday, Wednesday, and Thursday. The three youngest—thirteen, fourteen, and sixteen—enrolled in public schools. The nineteen-year-old and his mother were in beginners' classes, but the father had already advanced to the intermediate. "I want to learn English and get a job," he said. Every Tuesday in another library room, immigrant women from Somalia, Sri Lanka, Burma, Iran, Iraq, and Bosnia gathered in a sewing circle that three years earlier contributed a library exhibit titled "Weavings of War." Initially, the program director noted, many showed signs of post-traumatic stress disorder from wars they had fled. "When I first started working with them, they were very sad," she said. Once they got to know each other, however, "that feeling began to fade, at least for a few hours." "Everyone is so encouraging," said one Sri Lankan immigrant who watched an Iranian woman teach an Iraqi woman how to make intricate loops and knots with needle and thread. In broken English the three practiced new language skills. "I wait for Tuesdays," said the Sri Lankan.[18]

Public libraries continued to serve as places for reconciliation. In 2006 the widow of Michael Schwerner, who with fellow civil rights workers James Cheney and Andrew Goodman was killed by Ku Klux Klan members in Philadelphia, Mississippi, in 1964, donated a honorarium to the Neshoba County (Mississippi) Public Library's Collier-Mars Civil Rights Collection, established several years earlier by a multiracial Philadelphia coalition that led efforts to bring Edgar Ray Killen to trial and convict him in 2005 for his part in the murders. The collection was named for a black minister who bravely delivered Cheney's graveyard eulogy and a white woman who had immediately denounced the murders and as a result lost her local business. Where forty years earlier Mississippi public libraries were places that divided races, in Philadelphia it was now a place that brought them together.[19]

In the early twenty-first century public libraries still functioned as mediating sites for public debates about information resources containing sexual content. "Look at this book," said one Jessamine County (Kentucky) Public Library employee to a colleague in 2009 about Alan Moore's graphic novel *League of Extraordinary Gentlemen: Black Dossier.* "It's filthy and it's on hold for an eleven-year-old girl." "Well, okay," responded a colleague, "let's take it off hold." The two then effectively rendered it inaccessible by repeatedly checking it out. When administrators found out, they fired the employees. Days later the media caught the story, and what followed demonstrated the library's community mediating role. Local Christian groups mounted a protest and made their case through the local media. Petitions circulated, a television station interviewed the fired employees, and library officials weathered much public and private criticism. As a result, more than 100 community members attended a board meeting at which each speaker was given two minutes. Opinions for and against divided evenly. For the Jessamine County Public Library, the solution was predictable. "After researching how other libraries shelved graphic novels and after careful deliberation," officials wrote, "the library management decided to relocate the graphic novels to the adult and nonfiction sections." Many Library Bill of Rights absolutists saw this as "censorship"; local librarians saw it not only as a solution to a problem but also as an agreement balancing community interests.[20]

As public space open to all, however, public libraries also witnessed undesirable—sometimes even horrible—human behaviors. In 2004 serial killer Dennis Rader—who had taunted police with notes about the ten people he killed between 1974 and 1991 and referenced himself as the BTK ("Bind, Torture, Kill") Strangler—used Park City (Kansas) Community Library public-access computers to do research for a series of insolent communiqués he sent to local police. In 2011 a couple were caught having sex in the Charlotte Mecklenburg (North Carolina) Public Library children's department; fortunately no children were around.[21]

While librarians worked hard to shed many of the cultural biases inherited from previous centuries, some remained, including vestiges of systemic racism that continued to plague most Western cultural institutions. "Libraries are simply institutions that tell a story," said Winnebago tribal member and Huntington Park (California) Public Librarian Michael McLaughlin in a 2005 *Native American Times* article. "It is the community that decides what that story is and how it is told." To McLaughlin, it was clear that librarianship's practices placed Native Americans at a distinct disadvantage in the "story" public libraries told about them. For example, neither the Library of Congress nor the Dewey Decimal Classification "adequately addresses the histories and contemporary realities of American Indians." Neither had a category for "tribal sovereignty" that enjoyed equal status with other systems of government. Similarly, while Picasso and Monet were classified as "Art," Indian sand paintings, pottery, and basketry were classified "Crafts" or "Primitive Art," and while Protestantism and Catholicism found comfortable niches in "Religion," Indian spiritualism was found in "Mythology," "Folklore," and "Other Religion." "In short," McLaughlin concluded, "every American Indian perspective, accomplishment, or cultural belief, practice, or material product, according to these classification systems, is of a subordinate or inferior nature."[22]

Library practices reflecting homophobic community biases were more overt. At the Tahlequah (Oklahoma) Public Library in 2008, someone dropped a photocopy of a *Lambda Book Report* page of young adult reviews in the suggestion box. A note on the back read: "I'm not the only one who wants these. There are more of us than you may think, and we need these books!" Fearing community challenges, Tahlequah librarians chose not to select any. As he weathered a challenge to LGBT titles in 2007, Douglas County (Colorado) public librarian James La Rue heard from both sides. "To my mind the most touching stories were from gay people," he wrote, "many of whom reported trying to find books in the libraries of their youth about people like themselves—and in the absence of such books concluding that they must indeed be outcasts." La Rue was unlike generations of his professional predecessors, who once they recognized race and gender biases in their collections and services neglected to publicly acknowledge their institutional complicity; La Rue concluded: "The silence of our libraries on the topic, to my mind, had damaged lives."[23]

A study of Wisconsin gay men's book clubs validated La Rue's suspicions. All thirty-seven members interviewed said they mistrusted public libraries and did not want to shift club meetings to library space. "The majority of programs target children, families, and senior citizens," said one, "and none of that concerns me." Said another: "I think established [gay reading] groups would want to continue to select books to be discussed, rather than relying on a library staff member to create a list from books in their system. Do you think the Madison Public would order gay books for a gay reading group?" Author John Pruitt found many bibliographies and programming kits for book clubs that addressed race and ethnicity, but none that addressed sexual orientation. The Madison Public Library sponsored programs for American Indian Heritage Month and African American History Month, but not Gay and Lesbian Pride Month. Feeding their anxieties was "a popular concern about what is at stake if public libraries successfully define what and whose knowledge is of most worth to the larger community," Pruitt concluded. "Marginalizing particular discourses while valorizing others perpetuates the cultural dualisms of which public libraries profess to disapprove in their mission statements proclaiming inclusivity."[24] Pruitt knew the rhetoric; his research demonstrated it did not always match everyone's reality.

Lessons Learned

Increased funding for American public libraries will not necessarily result in a more informed citizenry. There, I did it—directly challenged the cornerstone of the narrative librarianship uses to justify support of these ubiquitous civic institutions. At the beginning of the twenty-first century communications scholars Michael X. Delli Carpini and Scott Keeter noted that the mean level of knowledge among Americans was about the same as fifty years earlier. In 1950, less than half (and in many cases less than a quarter) of the public could define key terms like "liberal," "conservative," or "primary elections"; recognize many of the individual and collective rights the Constitution guaranteed them; name public figures beyond the president or their state governor; identify candidate and party positions on contemporary political issues; knew national or local unemployment rates or the numbers of people living in poverty or without health insurance; or cite how much the federal government spent on defense, foreign aid, or social welfare. Half a century later they noted that despite increased use of the Internet these numbers had not improved. "The more I read and the more I listen," former Supreme Court justice Sandra Day O'Connor told an Idaho audience in 2013, "the more apparent it is that our society suffers from an alarming degree of public ignorance."[25]

If Americans care to be better informed, the 17,219 public library facilities available to them (up nearly 15 percent from 1980) will provide this information for free. And American public library history is certainly full of patron success stories proving that many did, including Thomas Edison, Hamlin Garland, Richard Wright, Martin Luther King Jr., Oprah Winfrey, Toni Morrison, and Sonia Sotomayor. Their stories are compelling. Still, if surveys are accurate about how poorly informed most Americans are, one has to wonder whether the public library's rhetoric as an institution essential to democracy holds up against this evidence. Yes, some of the 210 million Americans who visit a public library every year go there for the useful knowledge Benjamin Franklin thought so important. But more, many more, are apparently using—and loving—their public libraries for other purposes. To unearth reasons why, we have to expand our scope beyond information and incorporate the kind of public culture thinking that includes analysis of the reading public libraries provide and use of the library as a public place.

Because people do not have to use a public library, what patrons want—and, by *their* definition, what they need—gives them a power most other civic institutions deny them and forces public libraries to balance competing community needs. What a public library is—what I try to describe here—reflects these compromises. Since the mid–nineteenth century the American public library has been an essential public institution providing many kinds of informal but important learning experiences to millions of Americans. Where librarians and trustees humanized their spaces and services, they created one set of patron memories and loyalties. Where they exercised what mid-twentieth-century youth librarian Margaret Edwards called the "tyranny of petty authority" over patrons and prioritized professional agendas, they created another.[26] Varied memories and loyalties ranging on either side of this divide show up in recollections of the famous, the infamous, and the common people whose voices I researched for this book; all judged the American public library based on their own limited public library experiences. That explains why some lamented the loss of quiet in the "new" library—a complaint voiced by every generation of public library users since 1854—and others did not. Still, the vast majority of voices I found expressed love and loyalty for their public library.

Part of Our Lives shows that over time American public libraries multiplied, survived, and regularly prospered, in large part because they perpetuated practices or eventually embraced changes on which their users insisted. They have always been public places of performance where users displayed moral progress and achievement. From a "library in the life of the user" perspective, public libraries have put cultural participation on public display. They operated as a robust commons where members of the public discussed in a variety of ways issues that concerned them. They functioned as centripetal forces to craft a sense of community (local, state, and national) among disparate populations and to evolve community trust between its multicultural elements. They acted as key players in constructing group identity through the reading and places they provided. They started neighborhood conversations, mostly welcomed the recently arrived into their midst, and served as community anchors. Public libraries also functioned as sites where communities displayed the social harmony libraries helped generate. And for cultural minorities of all kinds, public libraries helped break the bonds of self-segregation. Some accepted newcomers and embraced commonplace reading more quickly than others; some developed community space more than others. Still, the evidence presented here shows what many accomplished, and thus identifies traditions heretofore seldom recognized, and therefore not much acknowledged in the profession's memory or its research. Yet my research also shows generations of users have an intuitive sense and personal memory of these contributions.

The public library's mediating traditions have been central to its existence and over the years have helped define the parameters of its community's acceptable cultural values. Public libraries make political statements all the time in their collections, services, decorations, and physical plant, but they do so within boundaries acceptable to local communities. On occasion, this mediating process goes public. When a public library appears to step outside the boundaries—displaying Bacchante at the Boston Public Library in 1895, acquiring *Grapes of Wrath* in 1940, resisting filters against Internet pornography sites in the 1990s—community members force conversation and compromise. Analysis of the solutions over time also demonstrates the shifting center in a community's public culture. Bacchante now stands boldly in the Boston Public Library's interior garden; *Grapes of Wrath* is now on the shelves of most public libraries; almost all public libraries have filters on computers accessible to children.

Because American public libraries function as public mediation stages for determining local cultural and literary values, librarians cannot comply absolutely with the Library Bill of Rights—a set of guidelines for what librarians "should" do, not what they "must" do. An absolutist perspective of the LBR places an impossible burden on public librarians, and at the same time it places the libraries employing them at risk for legal action, particularly sexual harassment lawsuits. In 2012, for example, the Birmingham (Alabama) Public Library reached a $150,000 out-of-court settlement brought by an employee arguing she was being forced to work in a sexually hostile environment. That the library press—serving a profession dedicated to free access to information—failed to report the settlement demonstrates the power this ideology has over librarianship.[27]

Do public librarians toe the party line and risk alienating large parts of their community by insisting on LBR compliance, or do they mediate public culture disputes for the community's greater benefit? I am not recommending that the profession abandon its opposition to censorship, only arguing that it modify its position to accommodate the library's traditional public role. If librarians represent the LBR's guidelines in the community's decision-making process, they will carry out their professional responsibilities by making it one of several perspectives the community considers. Under this scenario, the LBR's "should" is the correct word to use in this process, and no further professional representation is needed. At the same time, however, librarians must not be tagged as failures by fellow professionals if local decisions do not accord with the LBR. By mediating local disputes librarians are actually following a public library tradition with a much longer history than the Library Bill of Rights.

Through the public spaces they provide, public libraries have functioned as incubators for the kinds of social relationships that increased patrons' personal happiness. They have been places where Americans became aware of their interdependencies and interconnections. They stimulated the dynamism of diverse communities by both addressing and celebrating their diversity, but also by promoting a sense of belonging for those who thought of themselves as outsiders. Because they hold comfortable niches in public culture, they occupy places in the traditions and practices of multiple cultures that people have created for themselves and in which they form networks. And as public institutions, through their services and collections, American public libraries connect users to even larger communities (local, state, national, and international); a century ago this happened primarily through print; now it occurs through information systems like the Internet and the media. At the same time, however, because public libraries have little power to force acceptance of particular ideologies, they also allow individuals to develop alternative values and views.

Through the stories, songs, films, and videos they make available, public libraries provide social knowledge and models for ethical behavior that users appropriate for their everyday lives. Tools like stereopticons have disappeared, but the stories they contained remain a public library's stock-in-trade, albeit in newer packages, newer cultural forms. American public

"Food for Thought: An Evening of Great Conversation" is an annual event at the Billings (Montana) Public Library. Among those attending were foundation board member Heather Fink, Billings mayor Tom Hanel, and Superintendent of Schools Terry Bauch. *Photo courtesy of Jan Pierce and the Billings Public Library Foundation*

libraries also allow users to manifest cultural tastes that personalize the formation of morals and self-discipline, and within a larger cultural environment, they contain enough room for most people to be selective in the kinds of stories and cultural forms they want. Not all public library users become as successful as Sonia Sotomayor, but like her they experience the kinds of emotions and sentiments reading, hearing, and viewing provide to enhance life's good times and help weather the bad.

The American public library has been in a unique position to satisfy self-designed needs of multiple groups and at the same time help individuals make sense of their worlds in myriad ways. Although public libraries could never be all things to all people, the history presented here shows they have been more things to more people than most cultural authorities—including many librarians—have realized. After going through the data for this book from a bottom-up perspective, I come away with a new appreciation for this civic institution which, because it built a tremendous record of achievement serving people who used it in so many different ways, deserves much more credit than it has heretofore been given—this, despite the fact that as users pressured American public library services, collections, and spaces they often had to fight librarians' oppositions—some subtle, some not so subtle.

Nowhere in my research did I find evidence that public libraries fostered the major social movements that mark American history. In fact, public libraries often inhibited them (e.g., exhibiting systemic racism and sexism in children's literature until challenged in the 1960s; demonstrating systemic homophobia in public library collecting practices that are still being challenged as I finish this book) because these social movements threatened hegemonies built into the library systems and services that reflected community priorities. My research does demonstrate, however, that the changes American public libraries fostered for individuals constitutes their strongest bond with users. That's why telling their stories and seeing the library through their eyes is so important.

The American public library also stands as one of the few civic institutions resistant to centralizing tendencies that characterize the last hundred years. Although it has sought and accepted federal money (and made very good use of it), it has nonetheless resisted federal control. Because 85 percent of their funding comes from local taxation, public libraries are local organisms living within the social and cultural environments their communities create for them. No matter how hard the ALA's Office of Intellectual Freedom tries to protest what it calls censorious practices, the

American public library still makes decisions at the local level. And at that level it acts as a stage to mediate the parameters of local public culture to the satisfaction of most in a relatively peaceful, albeit sometimes messy way. That they do not perceive their public libraries as an appendage of big government may be another reason Americans love them so much.

Since the early twentieth century, every generation of librarians experiencing budget pressures has predicted disaster for—and in recent years even the demise of—the American public library. Yet *Part of Our Lives* clearly shows these predictions have little basis in history. Unless they violate a set of community standards they negotiated with patrons over the years, public libraries seldom lose much community support. Only in poor economic times—when most other public institutions suffer similarly—have public libraries lost substantial financial support. And in bad economic times public library use consistently increases. Thus, they are a solution—not a contributor—to other problems their communities experience. But that does not stop librarians from a birdsong that predicts disaster at every budget cycle—a birdsong that relies on replicating the rhetoric and reinforcing a stereotyped history, thus overlooking the primary experiences generations of public library users identify with these civic institutions. In many cases, librarians' lack of knowledge about their own history is evident from statements like: "Public libraries are not just warehouses of books anymore"—as if "warehousing books" has ever been their only purpose! For effect and contrast, journalists often parroted and reinforced this historically inaccurate statement by drawing on these stereotypes and their own limited public library experiences. If I had a dollar for every time I came across this kind of statement in my research I would probably make more than the royalties this book will generate.

As the book went to press I finished reading Susan Pinker's *The Village Effect: How Face-to-Face Contact Can Make Us Healthier, Happier, and Smarter* (2014). By harnessing research in the fast-developing field of social neuroscience, she finds that substantial benefits accrue to those who experience high levels of face-to-face contact, including improved vocabularies, an increased ability to empathize, a deeper sense of belonging, and—most important—a longer life span.[28] As I pondered her conclusions, I wondered if American public library users live longer, happier, and healthier lives than non-users, and if they do, why? Answering that question requires librarianship to expand its traditional focus on information in order to explore the community-building benefits of public library as place and the sociability that reading fosters.

My son Andy, reading to his son Teague, 2015. Teague picked out this library book because of an interest he and his dad shared in sports. He was fully capable of reading it, but preferred that his dad read it to him. *Photo by Jenelle Welling*

In his monumental *History of the American People*, Paul Johnson argues that US history addresses three fundamental questions. First, can the nation overcome injustices (like slavery) that existed at its origins and over time make amends for them? Second, can Americans construct a dynamic society by successfully mixing a collective desire to build a model community with often competing goals generated by personal ambition and an individual's will to acquire power and wealth? And third, has the republic the American people designed as a model to the rest of the world lived up to its bold claims?[29] While the jury is still out on the last, he notes, the answer to the first two is "yes." As the research for this book shows, the American public library has been a major—albeit largely unrecognized—player in effecting positive answers to the first two questions, and from the perspective of its users, it scores very well on the third. Measured against these three questions the American public library historically comes as close to "We the People" as any other publicly funded agency. And for $42 a year per citizen (in today's money), that's exceptional value for a civic institution that is still very much a "part of our lives."

Acknowledgments

My thanks go to the following:

The American Antiquarian Society, for a Grant-in-Aid in May 2010, that enabled me to research its rich collections for two weeks, and to its librarians (especially Elizabeth Pope), who were so gracious in helping me find materials;

The New York Public Library for a Short Term Fellowship in October 2011, and especially to Thomas Lannon of the NYPL Special Collections Room, who made sure I had all the NYPL branch materials I wanted in the three weeks I spent there;

Emory University's Manuscript, Archives and Rare Book Library for a Short Term Fellowship, October 2012, and especially Randall Burkett, who made my week-long stay so profitable;

The National Endowment for the Humanities, which gave me a Fellowship for University Teachers in 2008–2009 (one of eight designated that year by the NEH as a "We the People" Project);

Dean Larry Dennis of Florida State University's College of Communication and Information Studies, who agreed to match the NEH Fellowship so I had a complete year for nothing but research;

Librarians at the University of Wisconsin-Madison, and especially Michele Besant of the School of Library and Information Studies, where I screened thousands of public library annual reports that its collection contains;

Librarians at Florida State University, and especially the School of Information's Goldstein Library Director Pamala Doffek and her staff, many of whom helped this project in so many ways;

Librarians and archivists at the Library of Congress (where I spent weeks going through newspaper databases and several days going through the Papers of the National Association for the Advancement of Colored People in the Manuscripts Reading Room), the University of Illinois (where I consulted the American Library Association Archives), and the San Francisco Public Library and the Chicago Public Library (where I perused the unpublished reports of branch libraries);

Librarians at the Auburn Avenue Research Library on African American Culture in Atlanta, Georgia, who kindly copied and mailed to me a transcript of an Oral History Interview with Annie Watters McPheeters, longtime director of Atlanta's black public libraries;

Christine Pawley, who painstakingly went through an earlier draft of this book and gave wise counsel and advice that substantially improved it;

Leonard Kniffel, who read early chapters of the manuscript;

Charley Seavey, who gave me boxes of articles on American library history subjects he had gathered over the years that provided much detail for this study;

Chris Dodge, who compiled the index;

Publications and publishers listed in the "Notes" section for permission to "reuse" bits and pieces of previously published material;

Oxford University Press, the anonymous readers who carefully screened the manuscript for the Press, and especially my editor, Nancy Toff, who showed enormous patience with a sometimes fussy author and certainly made this into a better book;

Former students and colleagues with whom I've discussed ideas and conclusions that found their way into this book, and especially Doug Zweizig, who originally crafted the phrases "user in the life of the library" and "library in the life of the user" that convinced me to undertake a "people's history" of the American public library; and, finally,

My wife Shirl, who read through the entire manuscript with her usual critical eye, and with whom this year—on June 19, 2015—I am celebrating fifty years of marriage.

Notes

Where possible I have relied on original sources to enable patrons of American public libraries to tell their story in their own words. Because so many of those words occurred in annual reports and local newspapers, the list of abbreviations below covers the most commonly cited sources. Annual reports are referenced in notes as AR (year), Library, page numbers.

ABBREVIATIONS

Libraries and Archival Depositories

AAS   American Antiquarian Society
ALA   American Library Association
DCPL District of Columbia Public Library
LAPL Los Angeles Public Library
NYPL New York Public Library
SFPL San Francisco Public Library
SLPL St. Louis Public Library

Newspapers and Periodicals

CSM   *Christian Science Monitor*
CT   *Chicago Tribune*
LAT   *Los Angeles Times*
LJ   *Library Journal*
NYT   *New York Times*
WP   *Washington Post*

MANUSCRIPT COLLECTIONS

Bostwick Papers: Arthur Elmore Bostwick Papers, Humanities and Social Sciences Library, Manuscripts and Archives Division, New York Public Library

CPL Archives: Chicago Public Library Branch Reports, Douglass, 1957–1979, Special Collections, Chicago Public Library

McPheeters, Annie Watters. Transcript, Oral History Interview with Annie Watters McPheeters, Collection No. aarlohe 92-001, Auburn Avenue Research Library on African American Culture, Atlanta, GA

NAACP Papers: Papers of the National Association for the Advancement of Colored People, Manuscripts Reading Room, Library of Congress, Washington, DC

Newark Librariana, Letters: Box S, Newark Public Library Archives; New Jersey Room, Newark Public Library, Newark, New Jersey

NYPL Branch Archives: New York Public Library Archives, Record Group 8: Office of Branch Libraries, Branch Annual Reports, 1941–1985, including 125th Street, Chatham Square, Countee Cullen, Donnell, Fort Washington, Hamilton Fish Park, Harlem, Hunt's Point, Melrose, Muhlenberg, and Webster branches, Humanities and Social Sciences Library, Manuscripts and Archives Division, New York Public Library

Paschall Papers: Eliza Paschall Papers, Emory University, Manuscripts, Archives and Rare Books Library, Atlanta, GA

Stratemeyer Papers: Stratemeyer Syndicate Records, 1832–1984, Boxes 2 (Incoming, 1905), 3 (A-B, 1906), 20 (Outgoing, 1905), 56 & 57 (Fan Mail), and 276 (Tom Swift Fan Mail), Humanities and Social Sciences Library, Manuscripts and Archives Division, New York Public Library

PUBLIC LIBRARY ANNUAL REPORTS AND PUBLICATIONS CONSULTED

Atlanta Carnegie Library, Atlanta, GA, 1899–1916
Atlanta *Carnegie Library Bulletin*, Atlanta, GA, 1902–1922
Bangor Public Library, Bangor Maine, 1898–1932
Boston Public Library, 1877–1939
Boston Public Library *Monthly Bulletin*, 1871–1908
Boston Public Library Quarterly 1949–1960
Braddock (PA) Carnegie Public Library, 1909–1918
Bradford (PA) Public Library, 1902–1928
Brockton (MA) Public Library, 1894–1935
Brookline (MA) Public Library, 1870–1970
Public Library of Brookline Bulletin (1894–1898)
Brooklyn Public Library, 1881–1995
Buffalo (NY) Public Library, 1887–1971
Bulletin of the Salem [MA] *Public Library* (1891–1895)
Carnegie Library of Pittsburgh, 1897–1989
Cedar Rapids (IA) Public Library, 1896–1950
Charlotte Mecklenberg (NC) Public Library, 1948–1975
Cincinnati and Hamilton County Public Library, 1867–1971
Cleveland Public Library, 1884–2006
Clinton (IA) Public Library, 1905–1929
Council Bluffs (IA) Public Library, 1895–1936
Davenport (IA) Public Library, 1904–1958
Dayton Public Library, 1878–1949
Denver Public Library, 1895–1979
Des Moines Public Library, 1901–1927
Detroit Public Library, 1886–1930
District of Columbia Public Library, 1901–1970
Dover (NH) Public Library, 1888–1922
Dubuque (IA) Public Library, 1903–1921
East Chicago (IN) Public Library, 1925–1954
East Orange (NJ) Public Library, 1903–1965
Erie (PA) Public Library, 1899–1952
Fitchburg (MA) Public Library, *Bulletin of the Fitchburg Public Library* (1896)
Fort Wayne (IN) Public Library, 1907–1958
Galesburg (IL) Public Library, 1903–1922

Galveston (TX) Rosenberg Library, 1910–1919
Gloversville (NY) Public Library, 1882–1909
Hammond (IN) Public Library, 1929–1954
Hartford (CT) Public Library, 1839–1971
Indianapolis Public Library, 1874–1936
Jones Library (Amherst, MA), 1921–1954
Kansas City (MO) Public Library, 1904–1954
Lexington (KY) Public Library, 1905–1931
Lincoln (NE) Public Library, 1904–1965
Los Angeles Public Library, 1897–1973
Louisville Free Public Library, 1905–1931
Milwaukee Public Library, 1879–2007
Monthly Bulletin of the Providence [RI] *Public Library* (1895–1899)
Monthly Bulletin of the Free Public Library, New Bedford, Mass. (1909)
New York Public Library, 1897–1977
Bulletin of the New York Public Library
Osterhout Free Library Newsletter (Wilkes-Barre, PA), 1891–1902
Queens Borough Library, 1902–1995
Rockford (IL) Public Library, 1904–1953
St. Joseph (MO) Public Library, 1890–1922
St. Louis Public Library, 1873–1938
San Francisco Public Library, 1881–1968
Scranton (PA) Public Library, 1891–1923
Sedalia (MO) Public Library, 1896–1923
Tacoma (WA) Public Library, 1908–1952
Taunton (MA) Public Library, 1867–1908
Worcester [MA] *Library Bulletin* (1899–1903)
Worcester [MA Public Library] *Monthly Bulletin* (1899)

DATABASES RESEARCHED

APS Online, 1740–1940
America's Historical Newspapers, 1690–1922, Series 1–5
Alexander Street Press databases, including *Oral History Online; Manuscript Women's Letters and Diaries, 1750–1950; North American Immigrant Letters, Diaries, and Oral Histories; Black Thought and Culture; Social and Cultural History: Letters and Diaries*
Ethnic Newswatch to 2009
HarpWeek 1857–1912
Library of Congress: *Online Accessible Archives*
Library of Congress: *19th Century Newspapers*
Proquest Historical African American Newspapers (including *Chicago Defender* [1905–1975], *New York Amsterdam News* [1922–1993], *Baltimore Afro-American* [1893–1998], *Cleveland Call & Post* [1934–1991], *Los Angeles Sentinel* [1934–2005], *Atlanta Daily World* [1931–2003], *Norfolk Journal and Guide* [1921–2003], *Philadelphia Tribune* [1912–2001], and *Pittsburgh Courier* [1911–2002])
Proquest Historical Newspapers and Periodicals, 1850–2000
Readex Early American Newspapers, Series 1, 1690–1876
Readex U.S. Congressional Serial Set, 1817–1980

Bits and pieces of the narrative have appeared in previous publications, including the following:

"'I Only Hate Broccoli': The Library as Place in 21st Century America," *Proceedings of the International Conference Commemorating the 40th Anniversary of the Korean Society for Library and Information Science* (Seoul, South Korea: Korean Society for Library and Information Science, 2010): 203–212.

"Library as Place," *North Carolina Libraries*, 63 (Fall/Winter, 2005): 76–81.

"Out of Sight, Out of Mind: Why Don't We Have Any Schools of Library and Reading Studies?" *Journal of Education for Library and Information Science* 38 (Fall, 1997): 314–326.

Main Street Public Library: Community Places and Reading Spaces in the Rural Heartland, 1865–1956 (Iowa City, IA: University of Iowa Press, 2011).

"Tunnel Vision and Blind Spots: What the Past Tells Us about the Present: Reflections on the 20th Century History of American Librarianship," *Library Quarterly* 69 (January, 1999): 1–37.

INTRODUCTION

1. Herbert Hadad, "Helping a Library Celebrate," *NYT*, March 27, 1994; Danna Sue Walker, "Helmerich Award Author Lauds Libraries," *Tulsa World*, December 11, 1995; Kurt Vonnegut, *A Man without a Country* (New York: Seven Stories Press, 2005), p. 103.

2. "Library Services in the Digital Age," Pew Internet & American Life Project, January 22, 2013, http://libraries.pewinternet.org/2013/01/22/Librar-services/; "Pew Study: Parents Love Libraries," *American Libraries* 44 (2013): 11.

3. "Public Libraries in the United States Survey: Fiscal Year 2011" (Washington: Institute for Museum and Library Services, June 2014), 6–8; http://www.ala.org/research/sites/ala.org.research/files/content/initiatives/pilftas/2011_20; "Public Libraries in the United States Survey: Fiscal Year 2012" (Washington: Institute for Museum and Library Services, December, 2014), 5-14 6–8. http://www.ala.org/research/sites/ala.org.research/files/content/initiatives/pilftas/2011_2012%20PLFTAS%20Key%20Findings.pdf; David Vinjamuri,"Why Public Libraries Matter: And How They Can Do More," http://www.forbes.com/sites/davidvinjamuri/2013/01/16/why-public-libraries-matter-and-how-they-can-do-more/.

4. Redmond Kathleen Molz and Phyllis Dain, *Civic Space/Cyberspace: The American Public Library in the Information Age* (Cambridge, MA: MIT Press, 1999), pp. ix, 122.

5. Andrew Piper, *Book Was There: Reading in Electronic Times* (Chicago: University of Chicago Press, 2012), p. 132. See also Howard Zinn, *A People's History of the United States* (New York: Harper & Row, 1980).

6. "Seeger's Heavy Reading," *NYT*, February 9, 2014. The book Seeger mentioned is Ernest Thompson Seton, *Rolf in the Woods: The Adventures of a Boy Scout with Indian Quonab and Little Dog Skookum* (Garden City, NY: Doubleday, Page, 1911).

7. "Oprah on 'the Fire for Reading' at the AAP," *Publishers Weekly*, 250 (2003): 16; Marilyn Johnson, "A Life in Books," *Life* (September, 1997): 44.

8. "Annual Report, Epiphany Branch, 1982," Box 4, NYPL Branch Archives.

CHAPTER ONE

1. Margaret Barton Korty, "Benjamin Franklin and Eighteenth-Century American Libraries," *Transactions of the American Philosophical Society* 55 (1965): 8.

2. Jesse Shera, *Foundations of the Public Library: The Origins of the Public Library Movement in New England, 1629–1855* (Chicago: University of Chicago Press, 1949), pp. 11, 39, 50.

3. James Green, "Subscription Libraries and Commercial Circulating Libraries in Colonial Philadelphia and New York," in Thomas Augst and Kenneth Carpenter (eds.), *Institutions of Reading: The Social Life of Libraries in the United States* (Amherst: University of Massachusetts Press, 2007), p. 54; Shera, *Foundations*, p. 31.

4. John Bigelow (ed.), *The Complete Works of Benjamin Franklin*, Vol. 1 (New York: G. P. Putnam's Sons, 1887), p. 167. See also Jonathan Lyons, *The Society for Useful Knowledge: How Benjamin Franklin and Friends Brought the Enlightenment to America* (New York: Bloomsbury Press, 2013).

5. Shera, *Foundations*, p. 32; Cotton Mather, "A Father's Resolutions," http://www.spurgeon. org/-phil/mather/resolvd.htm.

6. Wilmarth S. Lewis, "Preface," in Marcus A. McCorrison (ed.), *The 1764 Catalogue of the Redwood Library Company at Newport, Rhode Island* (New Haven, CT: Yale University Press, 1965), pp. ix–xi.

7. Shera, *Foundations*, p. 119.

8. David Hall, "Books and Reading in Eighteenth-Century America," in Cary Carson, Ronald Hoffman, and Peter J. Albert (eds.), *Of Consuming Interests: The Style of Life in the Eighteenth* Century (Charlottesville: University Press of Virginia, 1994), p. 371.

9. James D. Hart, *The Popular Book: A History of America's Literary Taste* (New York: Oxford University Press, 1950), p. 54.

10. Elizabeth Carroll Reilly and David D. Hall, "Part Four. Modalities of Reading," in Hugh Amory and David D. Hall (eds.), *A History of the Book in America*, Volume 1: *The Colonial Book in the Atlantic World* (Cambridge: Cambridge University Press, 2000), p. 410 (volume hereafter cited as *HBA 1*).

11. Ross W. Beales and James M. Green, "Libraries and Their Users," in *HBA 1*, p. 402.

12. *Public Libraries in the United States of America: Part I: 1876 Report* (Washington, DC: Government Printing Office, 1876), p. xvi (hereafter cited as *1876 Report*).

13. James Raven, "Social Libraries and Library Societies in Eighteenth-Century America," in Augst and Carpenter (eds.), *Institutions of Reading*, pp. 24–52; Shera, *Foundations*, p. 119.

14. Richard R. John, "Expanding the Realm of Communication," in Robert A. Gross and Mary Kelley (eds.), *A History of the Book in America*, Volume 2: *An Extensive Republic: Print, Culture, and Society in the New Nation, 1790–1840* (Chapel Hill: University of North Carolina Press, 2010), p. 213 (volume hereafter cited as *HBA 2*). See also Robert A. Gross, "Reading for An Extensive Republic," in *HBA 2*, p. 518.

15. Haynes McMullen, "The Founding of Social and Public Libraries in Ohio, Indiana, and Illinois through 1850," *University of Illinois Library School Occasional Papers* 51 (1958): 3–4; Kenneth E. Carpenter, "Libraries," in *HBA 2*, pp. 274, 279; Paul Johnson, *A History of the American People* (New York: HarperCollins, 1998), p. 406.

16. Shera, *Foundations,* pp. 70–71. See also Thaddeus Mason Harris, *A Selected Catalogue of Some of the Most Esteemed Publications in the English Language to Form a Society Library, with an Introduction upon the Choice of Books* (Boston: I. Thomas & E.T. Andrews, 1793).

17. Shera, *Foundations*, p. 61; Horace Scudder, "Public Libraries a Hundred Years Ago," *1876 Report*, p. 10.

18. Royall Tyler, *The Algerine Captive; or, The Life and Adventurers of Doctor Updike Underhill* (Walpole, NH: 1797), pp. 4–7, quoted in Thomas Augst, "Faith in Reading: Public Libraries, Liberalism, and the Civil Religion," in Augst and Carpenter (eds.), *Institutions of Reading*, pp. 156–157.

19. Shera, *Foundations*, pp. 121–122; 127; Hart, *The Popular Book*, p. 66; David Kaser, *A Book for a Sixpence: The Circulating Library in America* (Pittsburgh: Beta Phi Mu, 1980), p. 118; and Elisabeth B. Nichols, "Female Readers and Printed Authority in the Early Republic," in Barbara Ryan and Amy M. Thomas (eds.), *Reading Acts: U.S. Readers' Interactions with Literature, 1800–1950* (Knoxville, TN: University of Tennessee Press, 2002), pp. 13.

20. Gross, "Reading for An Extensive Republic," in *HBA 2*, pp. 536–537; and Nichols, "Female Readers and Printed Authority in the Early Republic," pp. 4, 8, 16; Hart, *The Popular Book*, p. 91.

21. Kaser, *A Book for a Sixpence*, pp. 67, 118; Shera, *Foundations*, p. 139.

22. Timothy Jacobson, *Knowledge for Generations: Wiley and the Global Publishing Industry, 1807–2007* (Hoboken, NJ: John Wiley, 2007), p. 25; Gross, "Reading for an Extensive Republic," *HBA 2*, p. 532; William J. Gilmore, *Reading Becomes a Necessity of Life: Material and Cultural Life in Rural New England, 1780–1835* (Knoxville, TN: University of Tennessee Press, 1989).

23. S. B. Cutler, "The Coonskin Library," *Publications of Ohio State Archives and Historical Society* 26 (1917): 58–77.

24. Tom Glynn, "Books for a Reformed Republic: The Apprentices' Library of New York City, 1820–1865," *Libraries & Culture* 34 (1999): 353–354; Katherine Wolff, *Culture Club: The Curious History of the Boston Athenaeum* (Boston: University of Massachusetts Press, 2009), pp. 53, 87, 89; Carpenter, "Libraries," *HBA 2*, p. 277.

25. Shera, *Foundations*, pp. 158–165.

26. Thomas Jefferson, *The Writings*, Vol. 15 (Washington, DC: Thomas Jefferson Memorial Association, 1903), p. 166; Gillian Silverman, *Bodies and Books: Reading and the Fantasy of Communion in Nineteenth Century America* (Philadelphia: University of Pennsylvania Press, 2012), p. 27; Edwin Hubbell Chapin, *Duties of Young Women* (1848; repr. Boston: G. P. Putnam's Sons, 1856), pp. 81, 83; Hart, *The Popular Book*, p. 104.

27. Silverman, *Bodies and Books*, p. 33.

28. Elizabeth Barnes, "Novels," *HBA 2*, p. 444.

29. Thomas Augst, *The Clerk's Tale: Young Men and Moral Life in Nineteenth-Century America* (Chicago: University of Chicago Press, 2003), p. 170; Wolff, *Culture Club*, p. 49.

30. "Mercantile Library Association of St. Louis," *Western Journal of Agriculture, Manufacturers, Mechanic Arts, and Internal Improvements* 5 (1850): 6; Adam Arenson, "Libraries in Public before the Age of Public Libraries: Interpreting the Furnishings and Design of Athenaeums and Other 'Social Libraries,' 1800–1860," in John E. Buschman and Gloria J. Leckie (eds.), *The Library as Place: History, Community, Culture* (Westport, CT: Libraries Unlimited, 2007), pp. 41–60.

31. "Lectures and Lecturing," *New York Evangelist*, March 20, 1856; Carpenter, "Libraries," *HBA 2*, p. 283; Lloyd Pratt, "Speech, Print, and Reform on Nantucket," in Scott E. Casper, Jeffrey D. Groves, Stephen W. Nissenbaum, and Michael Winship (eds.), *A History of the Book in America, Volume 3: The Industrial Book, 1840–1880* (Chapel Hill: University of North Carolina Press, 2007), pp. 392–393.

32. "The Athenaeum," *Boston News Letter & City Record*, February 26, 1826.

33. George Ticknor, *Life, Letters, and Journals*, Vol. I (Boston: Houghton Mifflin, 1909), p. 371; Wolff, *Culture Club*, pp. 98, 106, 112.

34. Roger W. Moss, "The Athenaeum of Philadelphia," in Richard Wendorf (ed.), *America's Membership Libraries* (New Castle, DE: Oak Knoll Press, 2007), p. 135; Inez Shor Cohen, "The Mechanics' Institute of San Francisco," in Wendorf (ed.), *America's Membership Libraries*, pp. 265–266; Austin Baxter Keep, *The History of the New York Society Library* (New York: New York Society Library, 1908), pp. 401, 420–421.

35. Augst, *Clerk's Tale*, p. 203; Shera, *Foundations*, pp. 109, 239; Keep, *The History of the New York Society Library*, p. 188.

36. Nina Baym, *Novels, Readers, and Reviewers: Responses to Fiction in Antebellum America* (Ithaca, NY: Cornell University Press, 1984), pp. 47–54; 194; Randy F. Nelson (ed.), *An Almanac of American Letters* (Los Altos, CA: William Kaufmann, 1981), p. 146; James L. Machor, *Reading Fiction in Antebellum America: Informed Response and Reception Histories, 1820–1865* (Baltimore: Johns Hopkins University Press, 2011), p. 171.

37. Barbara Sicherman, *Well-Read Lives; How Books Inspired a Generation of American Women* (Chapel Hill: University of North Carolina Press, 2010), p. 2; Jane Tompkins, *Sensational Designs: The Cultural Work of American Fiction, 1790–1860* (New York: Oxford University Press, 1985), p. 124.

38. Mary Kelley, "Reading Women/Women Reading: The Making of Learned Women in Antebellum America," in Ryan and Thomas (eds.), *Reading Acts*, pp. 54–55, pp. 61–62, 64.

39. Frank Luther Mott, *Golden Multitudes: The Story of Best Sellers in the United States* (New York: Macmillan, 1947), pp. 63, 98; Hart, *The Popular Book*, pp. 49–50; Scott Casper, "Biography," in *HBA 2*, p. 458.

40. Gross, "Reading for An Extensive Republic," in *HBA 2*, p. 527; Kelley, "Reading Women/Women Reading," *Reading Acts*, p. 70.

41. Dorothy B. Parker, "The Organized Educational Activities of Negro Literary Societies, 1828–1846," *Journal of Negro Education* 5 (October, 1936): 561.

42. Elizabeth McHenry, "'An Association of Kindred Spirits': Black Readers and Their Reading Rooms," in Augst and Carpenter (eds.), *Institutions of Reading*, pp. 102, 105, 107, 116, 118.

43. F. B. Perkins, "Young Men's Mercantile Libraries," *1876 Report*, pp. 379, 381–382, 383–385.

44. Quoted in David Paul Nord, "Benevolent Books: Printing, Religion, and Reform," in *HBA 2*, pp. 235–236.

45. "Free Town Libraries," *Common School Journal* 13 (1852): 302.

46. C. C. Jewett, "Libraries of the United States," *Stryker's American Register and Magazine* (1851): 388.

47. Christopher Gray, "Streetscapes: The Old Astor Library," *NYT*, February 10, 2002.

48. Michael H. Harris, "Ticknor, George (1791–1871)," in Bohdan S. Wynar (ed.), *Dictionary of American Library Biography* (Littleton, CO: Libraries Unlimited, 1978), p. 515.

49. City Document No. 37 is extensively quoted in Walter M. Whitehill, *Boston Public Library: A Centennial History* (Cambridge, MA: Harvard University Press, 1956), pp. 27–34.

50. Whitehill, *Boston Public Library*, p. 35.

51. George Ticknor, *Life, Letters, and Journals*, Vol. II (Boston: Houghton Mifflin, 1909), p. 303.

CHAPTER TWO

1. Walter M. Whitehill, *Boston Public Library: A Centennial History* (Cambridge, MA: Harvard University Press, 1956), Chapter 3.

2. "The Public Library," *Boston Evening Transcript*, March 18, 1854; "Public Library," *Boston Evening Transcript*, March 21, 1854; "The Public Library," *Boston Evening Transcript*, May 3, 1854; "The Public Library," *Independent* 6 (1854): 280; "The Boston Public Library," *Gleason's Pictorial Drawing-Room Companion* 7 (1854): 157; "The City Library," *Christian Watchman and Reflector* 35 (1854): 202.

3. "The Public Library," *Boston Evening Transcript*, April 25, 1855; "The Public Library," *Boston Evening Transcript*, June 8, 1855; "The Ceremonies at the Public Library," *Boston Evening Transcript*, January 2, 1858; "Cornerstone of the Public Library Building," *Boston Evening Transcript*, September 17, 1855; "The Dedication," *Boston Post*, January 2, 1858; "Dedication of Public Library Building," *Boston Saturday Evening Gazette*, January 9, 1858; "New Public Library, Boston," *Ballou's Pictorial Drawing-Room Companion* 9 (1855): 252; "The Public Library of Boston," *The American Journal of Education* 7 (1859): 252–267; "The Experiment of Free Libraries," *The Round Table: A Saturday Review of Politics, Finance, Literature, Society* 6 (1867): 392; Horace G. Wadlin, *The Public Library of the City of Boston: A History* (Boston: Boston Public Library, 1911), p. 67.

4. Whitehill, *Boston Public Library*, p. 70.

5. "A Model Library," *The Round Table: A Saturday Review of Politics, Finance, Literature and Society* 3 (1866): 377; Whitehill, *Boston Public Library*, pp. 72–73.

6. "The Boston Public Library," *Appletons' Journal of Literature, Science and Art*, 6 (1871): 629; "Boston Public Library," in *Public Libraries in the United States of America: Part I: 1876 Report* (Washington, DC: Government Printing Office, 1876), p. 868. Hereafter cited as *1876 Report*.

7. "The Boston Public Library," *Appletons' Journal of Literature, Science and Art*, 6 (1871): 629.

8. Wadlin, *The Public Library of the City of Boston*, p. 109; "Increased Use of the Library," *Bulletin of the Public Library of the City of Boston* No. 15 (1870): 276; "Increased Use of the Library," No. 29 (April, 1874): 246; "The *Literary World* notes . . .," [San Francisco] *Daily Evening Bulletin*, July 17, 1871.

9. "The Public Library," *Boston Daily Advertiser*, November 12, 1869; "Strolls About Town," *Boston Saturday Evening Gazette*, June 5, 1858; "Public Library," *Boston Saturday Evening Gazette*, September 4, 1858; "An Offensive Class of Writers," *American Publishers' Circular and Literary Gazette* 4 (1858): 609.

10. "Letters to the Editor," *Boston Advertiser*, October 2, 1866; Frank B. Woodford, *Parnassus on Main Street: A History of the Detroit Public Library* (Detroit: Wayne State University Press, 1965), p. 32.

11. "The Boston Public Library," *Appletons' Journal of Literature, Science and Art*, 6 (1871): 629.
12. "A Bad Spell," *Pomeroy's Democrat*, September 29, 1872.
13. Barbara Sicherman, "Reading and Middle Class Identity in Victorian America," in Barbara Ryan and Amy M. Thomas (eds.), *Reading Acts: U.S. Readers' Interactions with Literature, 1800-1950* (Knoxville: University of Tennessee Press, 2002), p. 149; Paul Israel, *Edison: A Life of Invention* (New York: John Wiley, 1998), p. 37; "A Night with Edison," *Scribner's Monthly* 17 (1878): 88.
14. "The Public Library," *CT*, December 31, 1872; "The Library Dedication To-Day," *CT*, January 1, 1873; Annual Report (AR) (1873), Cincinnati Public Library, p. 21.
15. Barbara Sicherman, "Ideologies and Practices of Reading," in Scott E. Casper, Jeffrey D. Groves, Stephen W. Nissenbaum, & Michael Winship (eds.), *A History of the Book in America, Volume 3: The Industrial Book, 1840–1880* (Chapel Hill: University of North Carolina Press, 2007), pp. 283–288. Volume hereafter cited as *HBA 3*.
16. Janice Radway, "Interpretive Communities and Variable Literacies: The Function of Romance Reading," *Daedelus* 113 (Summer, 1984): 54; Jane Greer, "'Ornaments, Tools, or Friends': Literary Reading at the Bryn Mawr Summer School for Women Workers, 1921–1938," in *Reading Acts*, p. 18; Thomas Augst, "Introduction," in Thomas Augst and Kenneth Carpenter (eds.), *Institutions of Reading: The Social Life of Libraries in the United States* (Amherst, MA: University of Massachusetts Press, 2007), pp. 4–5; and Thomas Augst, "Faith in Reading," in *Institutions of Reading*, p. 53.
17. AR (1874), St. Louis Public School Library, pp. 12–15.
18. Henry Ward Beecher, "The Strange Woman," in *Lectures to Young Men, on Various Important Subjects* (New York: Derby & Jackson, 1857), pp. 210–211; Silverman, *Bodies and Books*, p. 31.
19. *Bulletin of the Public Library of the City of Boston* 1 (1867), front cover.
20. Winsor quote in Whitehill, *Boston Public Library*, p. 84.
21. "A Word about Public Libraries," *Springfield* [MA] *Weekly Republican*, August 22, 1863; Whitehill, *Boston Public Library*, p. 84.
22. "An article in the Nation . . . ," *Galveston* [TX] *Tri-Weekly News*, July 22, 1872; "Latest News Items," *San Francisco Bulletin*, July 22, 1872; "The Public Library," *Cincinnati Daily Gazette*, July 31, 1872.
23. AR (1873), Cincinnati Public Library, p. 20; "City News," *Cincinnati Daily Gazette*, April 15, 1868; "The Public Library," *Cincinnati Daily Gazette*, December 9, 1870; "Home News," *Cincinnati Daily Gazette*, March 15, 1871; "Germanism and the Library," *Cincinnati Daily Gazette*, June 29, 1871; "We Learn through the Catholic Telegraph . . . ," *Cincinnati Daily Gazette*, May 15, 1873; "The Catholics and the Rev. Vickers," *Cincinnati Daily Gazette*, December 4, 1873.
24. "What the People Read," *The Literary World* 4 (1874): 153; "Public Libraries and Fiction," *The Literary World* 4 (1874): 169.
25. "Public Libraries and Fiction," *The Literary World* 6 (1875): 48; "An Open Letter . . . ," *Boston Globe*, June 5, 1874.
26. "Editor's Table," *Appletons' Journal of Literature, Science and Art* 12 (1874): 121.
27. "A Good Example," *Friends' Review: A Religious and Miscellaneous Journal* 27 (1874): 599; Mary T. Shumway, *The Groton Public Library* (pamphlet found in AAS collections), p. 5; "Cranium Cultivators," [Chicago] *Sunday Times*, October 4, 1874; "The Chicago Public Library," *CT*, October 21, 1874; "Local Letters," *CT*, December 23, 1875.
28. "Public Library: A List of New Books," *Indianapolis Sentinel*, March 27, 1875; "The Mission of the Public Library," *Indianapolis Sentinel*, May 1, 1873; AR (1874), Indianapolis Public Library, pp. 10, 13, 14, 17.
29. "A Bad Book," [San Francisco] *Daily Evening Bulletin*, August 19, 1867; John G. Moulton, "Money Spent for Fiction Is Well Spent," *Boston Globe*, July 12, 1914; C.A.G., "Books and Boys," *Christian Union* 9 (1874): 135.
30. Susan S. Williams, "Authors and Literary Authorship," in *HBA 3*, p. 106; "Juvenile Reading," *Oliver Optic's Magazine*, 17 (1875): 477.

31. Sicherman, "Reading and Middle Class Identity in Victorian America," in *Reading Acts*, p. 146; Marlene Deahl Merrill (ed.), *Growing Up in Boston's Gilded Age: The Journal of Alice Stone Blackwell, 1872–1874* (New Haven, CT: Yale University Press, 1990), pp. 2–3, 12, 14, 67.

32. Barbara Hochman, *Uncle Tom's Cabin and the Reading Revolution: Race, Literacy, Childhood, and Fiction, 1851–1911* (Chapel Hill, NC: University of North Carolina Press, 2011), pp. 87, 128; Joan D. Hedrick, *Harriet Beecher Stowe: A Life* (New York: Oxford University Press, 1994), p. 232.

33. C. H. Cramer, *Open Shelves and Open Minds: A History of the Cleveland Public Library* (Cleveland: Press of Case Western Reserve University, 1972), p. 21; "Public Library Rules," *Cincinnati Daily Gazette*, August 22, 1874; "Home News," *Cincinnati Daily Gazette*, November 28, 1872.

34. "Branch Libraries," *CT*, January 12, 1873; "Cranium Cultivators," [Chicago] *Sunday Times*, October 4, 1874; "Chicago Loves Fiction," [Chicago] *Sunday Times*, November 8, 1874.

35. Clarence E. Sheerman, *The Providence Public Library: An Experiment in Enlightenment* (Providence, RI: Privately Printed, 1937), p. 26; "$1,000,000: Public Library of Kentucky" (flyer found in AAS collections).

36. "The Public Library," *Daily Cleveland Herald*, November 10, 1869; "Local Letters," *CT*, January 2, 1875.

37. "Light Literature," *CT*, February 7, 1875; "Local Letters," *CT*, February 9, 1875.

38. "Local Letters," *CT*, July 11, 1875; "In the Common Council . . .," [Chicago] *Inter Ocean*, July 7, 1875.

39. "A Public Library," *CT*, October 7, 1870; "The Microscope in Public Libraries," *CT*, May 7, 1871; "The Free Public Library and the Scandinavian Literature," *CT*, January 13, 1872; "A Public Library Building," *CT*, January 28, 1872.

40. "A Catholic Issue," [Chicago] *Sunday Times*, May 3, 1874; "Our Big Humbug," [Chicago] *Sunday Times*, May 10, 1874; "The Battle of the Books," *CT*, May 4, 1874; "Local Letters," *CT*, May 5, 1874.

41. "John Green and the Free Public Library, Worcester, Mass.," *American Journal of Education* 32 (1863): 605; Wilhelm Munthe, *American Librarianship from a European Angle: An Attempt as an Evaluation of Policies and Activities* (Chicago: American Library Association, 1939), p. 51; "Need of Public Libraries," *New York Observer and Chronicle*, September 19, 1867.

42. M. Field Fowler, *Protest and Remonstrance: Against Opening the Doors of the Public Library, Boston, on the Lord's Day* (Boston: Rockwell & Rollins, 1867); "Speech of Alderman Nash," *The Liberator*, December 30, 1864; and "Sunday—The Public Library &c." *Boston Investigator*, January 4, 1865.

43. *A Report by the Rev. William R. Huntington of Worcester, Mass., on the Expediency of Opening a Free Public Library in That City on Sunday* (Boston: Alfred Mudge & Son, 1873); *1876 Report*, p. xx; and AR (1874), Indianapolis Public Library, pp. 10, 13, 14, 17.

44. Samuel Swett Green, *The Public Library Movement in the United States, 1853–1893* (Boston: Boston Book Co., 1913), p. 12. See also Wayne A. Wiegand, *Politics of an Emerging Profession: The American Library Association, 1876–1917* (Westport, CT: Greenwood, 1986), Chapter 1.

45. "Libraries," *Appletons' Journal of Literature, Science, and Art* 11 (1874): 606.

46. Reuben A. Guild, "Bibliography as a Science," *American Library Journal* 1 (1876): 67–69.

47. Wayne A. Wiegand, "The 'Amherst Method': The Origins of the Dewey Decimal Classification Scheme," *Libraries & Culture* 33 (1998): 175–194; Margaret A. Edwards, *The Fair Garden and the Swarm of Beasts: The Library and the Young Adult* (Chicago: American Library Association, 2002), p. 67.

48. "People and Things," [Chicago] *Inter Ocean*, August 27, 1877.

49. *1876 Report*, pp. 820–822.

50. William F. Poole, "Some Popular Objections to Public Libraries," *American Library Journal*, 1 (1876): 45–51; F. B. Perkins, "I.—On Professorships of Books and Reading," *1876 Report*, pp. 231, 235, 237, 238.

CHAPTER THREE

1. Paul Johnson, *A History of the American People* (New York: HarperCollins, 1998), pp. 596–597; 672.

2. Samuel Swett Green, *The Public Library Movement in the United States, 1853–1893* (Boston: Boston Book Co., 1913), p. 1; Robert H. Wiebe, *The Search for Order 1877–1920* (New York: Hill and Wang, 1967).

3. Wayne A. Wiegand, *Irrepressible Reformer: A Biography of Melvil Dewey* (Chicago: American Library Association, 1996), Chapter 4.

4. Joy Lichtenstein, "Recollections of the Early San Francisco Public Library," *California Library Bulletin* 11 (1950): 165–166.

5. "The Average Length of Time Required to Get a Book," *Cincinnati Daily Gazette*, December 23, 1878; "The Public Library," *Cincinnati Daily Gazette*, May 17, 1878; "The Public Library," *CT*, January 19, 1878; "The Public Library," *CT*, January 23, 1878; "A Disgusted Lady," [Chicago] *Inter Ocean*, November 21, 1879; "To the Editor," *St. Paul* [MN] *Daily News*, May 2, 1889.

6. Margaret A. Edwards, *The Fair Garden and the Swarm of Beasts: The Library and the Young Adult* (Chicago: American Library Association, 2002), p. 78; Mary E. Root, "American Past in Children's Work," *LJ* 71 (1946): 548; Letter to the Editor, *LJ* 6 (1881): 259–261.

7. Annual Report (AR) (1881), Milwaukee Public Library, p. 17; Gerri Flanzreich, "The Library Bureau and Office Technology," *Libraries & Culture* 28 (1993): 405–409; Klaus Musmann, *Technological Innovations in Libraries, 1860–1960* (Westport, CT: Greenwood Press, 1993), p. 63; "A Library Adhesive at Last!" *LJ* 18 (1893): 453.

8. "Duluth Public Library," *Duluth* [MN] *News-Tribune*, March 8, 1891; Charles A. Seavey and Caroline F. Sloat, "The Government as Publisher," in Carl F. Kaestle and Janice A. Radway (eds.), *The History of the Book in America, Volume 4: Print in Motion; The Expansion of Publishing and Reading in the United States, 1880–1940* (Chapel Hill: University of North Carolina Press, 2009), pp. 260–275.

9. Hamlin Garland, *Son of the Middle Border* (New York: Macmillan, 1917), p. 322; "Library Workers Recall Days When $13 a Month Was Salary," *CSM*, December 16, 1926; Richard O'Connor, *Jack London: A Biography* (Boston: Little, Brown, 1964), pp. 37–39; Marjorie Barrows, "The Child Reader," *Philadelphia Tribune*, March 16, 1933.

10. "The Public Library," *Milwaukee Daily Sentinel*, July 16, 1878; "The Catholic Telegraph Says . . .," *Cincinnati Daily Gazette*, April 15, 1881; "A Roman Catholic Member . . .," *Cincinnati Daily Gazette* December 26, 1879; "Public Library," *CT*, December 14, 1879; "A Political Bigot," *CT*, December 15, 1879; "Discrimination Alleged," *CT*, December 17, 1879; "Fanatic or Bigot?" *CT*, December 18, 1879; "Bigot or Fanatic?" *CT*, December 19, 1879; and "Public Library," *CT*, December 28, 1879.

11. "What Our Boys and Girls Are Reading," *New Hampshire Sentinel*, November 13, 1879.

12. William Kite, "Fiction in Public Libraries," *LJ* 1 (1877): 278; J. P. Quincy, "Free Libraries," *Public Libraries in the United States of America: Part I: 1876 Report* (Washington, DC: Government Printing Office, 1876), p. 396.

13. "Novel Readers," *Boston Daily Globe*, March 9, 1879; AR (1880), Boston Public Library, p. 22; "What the People Read," *Milwaukee Sentinel*, September 13, 1879.

14. C. H. Shinn, "Evil Literature," *Californian and Overland Monthly* 6 (1882): 442–447.

15. "The Classification of People Who Use the Library," *Cincinnati Daily Gazette*, April 17, 1876.

16. "The Public Library and Its Choice of Books," *Boston Daily Advertiser*, February 12, 1878.

17. James M. Hubbard, "Fiction and Public Libraries," *International Review* 10 (1881): 168–172.

18. "The Public Library," *Boston Daily Advertiser*, May 14, 1881; "Novels in the Boston Library," *Springfield* [MA] *Republican*, August 11, 1881; "Hubbard's Hubbub," *Boston Daily Globe*, August 20, 1881; "Notes," *Bulletin of the Boston Public Library* 5 (1882): 60.

19. "Novels and the Public Library," *Cincinnati Daily Gazette*, March 18, 1881; "On Library and Other Literature," *The Friend* 55 (1881): 50; Harriet D. Palmer, "A Question Concerning Our Public Libraries," *Overland Monthly and Out West Magazine* 2 (December, 1883): 592; "Fiction

and Public Libraries," *Worcester Daily Spy*, February 3, 1881; "Books and Books," *Northern Christian Advocate* 50 (1881): 4; "Moral Literature," *The Critic* 1 (1881): 192.

20. "Novel Reading," [Chicago] *Inter Ocean*, August 11, 1881; "Trash or Literature?" [Chicago] *Inter Ocean*, August 12, 1881; "Light Novel Reading," [Chicago] *Inter Ocean*, August 23, 1881; "The Public Library Loafer," *Wisconsin State Journal*, July 9, 1886.

21. A.L.A. Cooperation Committee, "Report on Exclusion," *LJ* 7 (1882): 28; "A Library Black List," *WP*, March 1, 1882; "A Glimpse into Boston's 'Inferno,'" *CT*, March 18, 1882.

22. AR (1882), Boston Public Library, pp. 17–19; "According to a writer . . . ," *Boston Daily Advertiser*, June 11, 1885; "Might Offend Prudes and Hypocrites," *Boston Daily Globe*, June 9, 1885; "Naughty Books: How the Boston Public Library Keeps Them Out of Sight," *Rocky Mountain News*, August 6, 1888.

23. "The Annual Report of the Trustees . . . ," *Congregationalist* 33 (1882): 5; "Library Censorship," *Cincinnati Daily Gazette*, March 18, 1882.

24. "Persons and Things," *New Haven* [CT] *Register*, February 13, 1882; "A Library Black List," *WP*, March 13, 1882.

25. Garland, *Son of the Middle Border*, pp. 259–263, 266.

26. Susan Belasco, "The Cultural Work of National Magazines," in Scott E. Casper, Jeffrey D. Groves, Stephen W. Nissenbaum, & Michael Winship (eds.), *A History of the Book in America, Volume 3: The Industrial Book, 1840–1880* (Chapel Hill: University of North Carolina Press, 2007) p. 269; "Leaves of Grass," *CT*, September 12, 1884; "Leaves of Grass," *CT*, September 14, 1884.

27. "Huckleberry Finn," *Kansas City Star*, March 18, 1885. Under same heading were stories also carried in *Worcester* [MA] *Daily Spy*, March 22, 1885; *Springfield* [MA] *Republican*, March 22, 1885; *San Francisco Bulletin*, March 28, 1885; and *St. Louis Globe-Democrat* March 17, 1885. See also Barbara Hochman, *Uncle Tom's Cabin and the Reading Revolution: Race, Literacy, Childhood, and Fiction, 1851–1911* (Chapel Hill: University of North Carolina Press, 2011), pp. 244, 249.

28. Mary E. S. Root, "An American Past in Children's Work" *LJ* 70 (1946): 550; Green, *Public Library Movement*, p. 115.

29. Shelley G. McNamara, "Early Public Library Work with Children," *Top of the News* 43 (1986): 62; Root, "An American Past in Children's Work," p. 548; "The Dime Novel Cure," *Michigan Farmer* 16 (1885): 7; "The Dime Novel Cure," *Detroit Free Press*, April 12, 1885.

30. "Vox Populi," *LAT*, February 27, 1889; Amanda B. Harris, "The Kind of Books That Children Should Not Read," *Christian Union* 36 (1887): 325; "What Do People Read?" [Portland] *Oregonian*, August 9, 1891.

31. Caroline M. Hewins, "How Library Work with Children Has Grown in Hartford and Connecticut," in Alice Hazeltine (ed.), *Library Work with Children* (New York: H. W. Wilson, 1917): 48; AR (1891), Hartford (CT) Public Library, p. 5.

32. Garland, *Son of the Middle Border*, pp. 92–93; Sherwood Anderson, *A Storyteller's Story* (New York: Grove Press, 1951), pp. 155, 221; Theodore Dreiser, *Dawn: A History of Myself* (New York: H. Liveright, 1931), p. 198.

33. James D. Hart, *The Popular Book: A History of America's Literary Taste* (New York: Oxford University Press, 1950), p. 153; Michael Denning, *Mechanic Accents: Dime Novels and Working-Class Culture in America* (New York: Verso, 1987), pp. 3, 207–208, 212.

34. "The True Reason Why . . . ," *Philadelphia Inquirer*, January 5, 1892; "The Hub's Objection to Puck," *Omaha World Herald*, January 6, 1892; "Judge and Puck," *Boston Journal*, January 25, 1892; "Book Chat," [Sacramento] *Themis*, February 20, 1892; and "What Puck Thinks of It," *Boston Daily Globe*, January 13, 1892.

35. Richard J. Chaisson, "Building Is One for the Books: In Petersham, 'Library' Is a Word That Was Written in Stone," [Worcester, MA] *Telegram & Gazette*, November 24, 1991.

36. "Our Public Library," *Boston Daily Globe*, May 15, 1887; "In English, Not Latin," *Haverhill* [MA] *Bulletin*, December 1, 1888.

37. *The Buffalo Library and Its Building* (Buffalo: *Buffalo Morning Express*, 1887), p. 20.

38. Arline A. Fleming, "Its Back Pages Are Rich in History: Peace Dale Library Celebration to Mark 95th Anniversary of Its Opening," *Providence* [RI] *Journal*, October 1, 1986; "Public Library Lectures," *St. Louis Republic*, January 20, 1889; AR (1891), SLPL, pp. 20–21.

39. "Among the Books," *Detroit Free Press*, November 17, 1889; "Caloric vs. Literature," *Detroit Free Press*, July 20, 1890; "Literary Cranks," *St. Louis Globe-Democrat*, April 8, 1887; "Library Cranks," *Christian Union* 36 (1887): 212.

40. "As to Convenience in Public Libraries," *Cincinnati Daily Gazette*, December 11, 1878; "Filthy Condition of the Public Library," *CT*, January 9, 1879; "The Public Library," *CT*, November 21, 1880; "The Public Library Reading Room," *CT*, November 24, 1880; "Library Habitues," [Chicago] *Inter Ocean*, January 7, 1887.

41. "Books for All People," *CT*, March 16, 1891.

42. "The Exhibition in the Art Room of the Public Library," *Cincinnati Daily Gazette*, May 14, 1878; "Chess and Checkers in the Public Library," *LAT*, September 26, 1882; "Useful and Ornamental," *Macon* [GA] *Telegraph and Messenger*, September 21, 1877; "Caught Up In the City," *Macon* [GA] *Telegraph and Messenger*, March 27, 1886; "City and Suburban News," *Macon* [GA] *Telegraph and Messenger*, August 15, 1890; "Bill Arp on Macon," *Macon* [GA] *Telegraph and Messenger*, November 9, 1880; "Library Art Show," *Macon* [GA] *Telegraph and Messenger*, June 21, 1882.

43. "The Confederate Fair," *Macon* [GA] *Telegraph and Messenger*, January 9, 1890; "Pictures at the Library," *Worcester* [MA] *Daily Spy*, August 30, 1891; "New Pictures at the Library," *Worcester* [MA] *Daily Spy*, April 20, 1892; "To Establish a Public Library," *WP*, June 20, 1891.

44. Frederick M. Crunden, *The Function of a Public Library and Its Value to a Community* (St. Louis: Nixon-Jones Printing, 1884), pp. 15–16.

45. "Troublesome People," *Boston Daily Globe*, July 16, 1888; Goldie Tuvin Stone, *My Caravan of Years: An Autobiography* (New York: Bloch Publishing, 1945), pp. 88–91.

46. L. H. Robbins, "The Rediscovery of the Public Library," *NYT*, June 12, 1932; Salome Cutler Fairchild, "What American Libraries Are Doing for Children and Young People," *Library Association Record* 5 (1903): 543; Fannette H. Thomas, "Early Appearances of Children's Reading Rooms in Public Libraries," *Journal of Youth Services* 4 (1990): 81–85; John Parsons, "First Children's Room," *LJ* 34 (1909): 552.

47. "Loud Swearing," *Wheeling* [WV] *Daily Register*, June 16, 1877; "Loafers Crowd the Avenue," *Milwaukee Journal*, October 12, 1885; "The Tramps Who Make . . .," *Indianapolis Sentinel*, January 16, 1877; "A Study of Cranks," *Rocky Mountain News*, August 12, 1888; "Among Books," *Brooklyn Daily Eagle*, September 21, 1888; "Loungers among Books," *CT*, February 10, 1889; Tessa Kelso, "Some Economical Features of Public Libraries," *The Arena* 42 (1893): 709.

48. "The Public Library," *CT*, February 27, 1876; "Aldermen vs. Public Library," *CT*, March 6, 1876; "I Propose," *CT*, March 19, 1876; "I Propose," *CT*, March 26, 1876; "Letters from the People," *CT*, April 5, 1876.

CHAPTER FOUR

1. Wayne A. Wiegand, "Catalog of 'A.L.A.' Library (1893): Origins of a Genre," in Delmas Williams et al. (eds.), *For the Good of the Order: Essays in Honor of Edward G. Holley* (Greenwich, CT: JAI Press, 1994), pp. 237–254.

2. Jennie June Croly, "Women in Club Life," *Frank Leslie's Popular Monthly* 50 (1900): 18. See also Sarah Wadsworth and Wayne A. Wiegand, *Right Here I See My Own Books: The Woman's Building Library at the World's Columbian Exposition* (Boston: University of Massachusetts Press, 2012).

3. Harry S. Truman, "Me and Libraries," *College and Research Libraries* 19 (1958): 99–103; Fred Howard, *Wilbur and Orville: A Biography of the Wright Brothers* (New York: Alfred A. Knopf, 1987), p. 28; Wendy Leopold, "Bus Put Librarian on Right Track," *CT*, February 7, 1990.

4. Annual Report (AR) (1909), St. Joseph (MO) Public Library, p. 14.

5. AR (1905), Louisville Public Library, pp. 26, 33; AR (1917), Sedalia (MO) Public Library, n.p; AR (1915), Clinton (IA) Public Library, p. 14; "A Model Library," *Boston Globe*, February 15, 1894.

6. Data taken from database created for Wayne A. Wiegand, *Main Street Public Library: Community Places and Reading Spaces in the Rural Heartland, 1876–1956* (Iowa City, IA: University of Iowa Press, 2011).

7. AR (1903), St. Joseph Public Library, p. 16; AR (1908), Bradford (PA) Public Library, pp. 16–17.

8. "Libraries for Men," *The Independent*, 58 (1905): 1374.

9. "A Library League," *Minneapolis Journal*, August 3, 1897; E. A. Birge, "The Effect of the 'Two-Book System' on Circulation," *LJ* 23 (1898): 93–101; AR (1907), Louisville Free Public Library, pp. 54–55; Eudora Welty, *One Writer's Beginnings* (Cambridge, MA: Harvard University Press, 1983), pp. 29–30.

10. AR (1908) SLPL, p. 53; AR (1900) Kansas City (MO) Public Library, pp. 15–16.

11. "Letter to the Editor," *Boston Globe*, May 1, 1895; "The Public Library," *LAT*, September 8, 1897; "Can't Display Figure," *Macon* [GA] *Daily Telegraph*, July 28, 1912.

12. *Dedication of the Tompkins County Public Library and the Finger Lakes Library System Headquarters, April 20, 1969* (copy in Library of Congress collections), pp. 21–22.

13. "At the Public Library," *Columbus* [GA] *Daily Enquirer*, February 24, 1903; Grace Louis Phillips, "The Books Read by the Children of the Ghetto," *World's Work* 6 (1903): 3475.

14. "Old Books Laundered," *CT*, June 5, 1904; "Some Queer Bookmarks," *Detroit Free Press*, June 11, 1899.

15. AR (1908), SLPL, p. 53; AR (1900), Kansas City (MO) Public Library, pp. 15–16; "Need More Books at the Library," *Kansas City Star*, February 1, 1900; AR (1912), Cleveland Public Library, p. 49; "Work for the Blind," *Bulletin of the New York Public Library* 18 (1914): 260–261; Ramon Jaen, "The New York Public Library: An Impression," *Bulletin of the New York Public Library* 20 (1916): 5.

16. Sarah Comstock, "Byways of Library Work," *Outlook* 72 (1914): 200; Mary E. Lee, "The Traveling Library," *Ohio Farmer* 96 (1899): 491; "Michigan Travelling Library," *Detroit Free Press*, July 9, 1900; Jessie M. Good, "The Traveling Library as a Civilizing Force," *The Chautauquan* 36 (1902): 65; "Take to Books," *Brooklyn Eagle*, February 11, 1900; "Want More Book Deliveries," *CT*, December 10, 1902; AR (1907), LAPL, pp. 37–38, 76.

17. Lutie E. Stearns, "Reading for the Young," AR (1894), Milwaukee Public Library, pp. 80–81; Bishop Hurst, "The Children in the Library," *Christian Advocate* 73 (1898): 1857; AR (1897), Free Library, Pratt Institute (NY), p. 11; Adele M. Fasick, "Moore, Anne Carroll (1871–1961)," in Bohdan S. Wynar (ed.), *Dictionary of American Library Biography* (Littleton, CO: Libraries Unlimited, Inc., 1978), **pp. 368–371**; Mary Ellka Dousman, "Children's Department," *LJ* 21 (1896): 406; Dousman, "The Children's Room of the Milwaukee Public Library," *LJ* 23 (1898): 664; "Even the Babies," *Boston Daily Advertiser*, November 8, 1897; "Saturday Story Hour at the Library," *San Jose* [CA] *Mercury Herald*, November 30, 1913.

18. AR (1902), Carnegie Library of Pittsburgh, pp. 24–26; AR (1890), Carnegie Library of Pittsburgh, p. 6; Fannie S. Bissell, "What the Libraries Are Doing for the Children," *Outlook* 70 (1902): 420; "The Home Library" (Kansas City Public Library) *Public Library Quarterly* 3 (1903): 50–51; William Byron Forbush, "The Public Library as a Philanthropy for Children," *Congregationalist and Christian World* 47 (1902): 754; AR (1897), Cleveland Public Library, pp. 21–22; AR (1899), Cleveland Public Library, pp. 57–61; AR (1905), Cleveland Public Library, p. 48; AR (1911), Cleveland Public Library, pp. 61–63; Frances Jenkins Olcott, "Books and Reading," *St. Nicholas* 26 (1899): 1049; Linda A. Eastman, "The Children's Library League," *Congregationalist* 84 (1899): 870; AR (1914), SLPL, pp. 89–90; Elizabeth L. Foote, "The Children's Home Library Movement," *Outlook* 57 (1897): 172.

19. AR (1894), Milwaukee Public Library, p. 22; "Books and Children," *Milwaukee Journal*, July 3, 1894.

20. W. E. B. Du Bois, "The Opening of the Library," *Independent* 54 (1902): 809.

21. AR (1905), Louisville Public Library, p. 26; (1910), p. 37; Matthew Battles, *Library: An Unquiet History* (New York: W.W. Norton, 2009), pp. 33–34; Paul M. Culp Jr., "Carnegie Libraries of Texas: The Past Still Present," *Texas Libraries* 43 (1981): 81–96; Paul M. Culp Jr., "Carnegie Libraries: The Past No Longer Present," *Texas Libraries* 43 (1981): 132–144; Margaret I. Nichols, "Lillian Gunter: County Librarian," *Texas Libraries* 39 (1977): 138.

22. "Discrimination Alleged," *Boston Journal*, December 19, 1895; "Public Library Attacked," *St. Louis Republic*, June 2, 1896; "Public Library Denounced," *Milwaukee Journal*, June 3, 1896; "Denounces Libraries," *WP*, July 17, 1907; "Catholics and Libraries," *Atlanta Constitution*, April 18, 1901.

23. "The 'Catholic Literature' List in the Present Number," *Monthly Bulletin of the Providence Public Library* 4 (1898): 147–148; *Catalogue of Catholic Books in Milwaukee Public Library* (Milwaukee: Milwaukee Council No. 524, Knights of Columbus, 1904), p. 3; AR (1905), Cedar Rapids Public Library, p. 11; AR (1910), SLPL, p. 41.

24. "It Has Just Fallen Out . . .," [Olympia, WA] *Morning Olympian*, August 1, 1905; "Huckleberry Finn Banned," *Salt Lake City Telegram*, August 11, 1902; "Rough on Iowa Boys," *WP*, December 22, 1904; "Twain's Books Barred," WP, March 27, 1906; "Some Views of the Laity," *Omaha World Herald*, August 24, 1902; "Mark Twain to the World-Herald," *Omaha World Herald*, August 31, 1902; "Reading for the Boys," *Omaha World Herald*, September 14, 1902; "Two of Twain's Books Placed under Ban," *Philadelphia Inquirer*, March 27, 1906; "It Is Almost a Pity . . .," *Tucson Citizen*, March 31, 1906; "Any Other Public Library Board . . .," *Wilkes-Barre* [PA] *Times*, April 3, 1906; "Mark Twain Scores Some Individuals," [Columbia, SC] *State*, September 8, 1902; "Mark Twain's Retort Courteous," *Lucifer the Light-Bearer* 6 (1902): 292; "Children's Taste in Reading," *Youth's Companion* 79 (1905): 326.

25. "Suppressed in Boston," *LAT*, November 29, 1896; "Decameron and Rabelais Are Kept in 'Inferno,'" *Boston Journal*, November 29, 1903.

26. AR (1906), LAPL, pp. 44, 60; "Library Bars the Jungle," *CT*, June 30, 1906; "Success Assured," *Duluth* [MN] *News-Tribune*, May 21, 1906; "The St. Paul Public Library Board . . .," *Duluth* [MN] *News-Tribune*, July 4, 1906; "By barring Upton Sinclair's . . .," *Tucson Citizen*, August 1, 1906; "New Book Is on Forbidden List," *Grand Forks* [ND] *Herald*, September 12, 1908; "New Books Are Barred," *Detroit Free Press*, September 13, 1908; "Bars Giddy Books from Her Shelves," *Detroit Free Press*, July 22, 1910.

27. "'World' and 'Journal' Shut Out," *New Haven* [CT] *Register*, February 26, 1897; "Let the Good Work Go On," *Life* 29 (1897): 230, 310; "Bandon Papers Balk," [Portland] *Oregonian*, April 23, 1913; "Mr. U'Ren and Menace," [Portland] *Oregonian*, August 23, 1914; "Library Is Criticised," *Duluth* [MN] *News Tribune*, November 5, 1911.

28. "Southern Books Needed," *Columbus* [GA] *Daily Enquirer*, July 23, 1899; "It Is Removed," *Boston Globe*, June 5, 1905; "'Burn Book' Is GAR Cry," *Boston Journal*, June 7, 1905.

29. "Fiction Song," *LJ* 15 (1890): 325. It is likely the lyrics were structured to fit "Titwillow" from Gilbert and Sullivan's *The Mikado* (1885).

30. Howard L. Rann, "Curbstone Sketches—The Library," *Idaho Statesman*, July 9, 1912; "Are Public Libraries Filled with Trashy Novels?" *Current Opinion* 49 (1915): 422; AR (1901), Cedar Rapids Public Library, pp. 6–7; John Cotton Dana, *A Library Primer*, 4th ed. (Chicago: Library Bureau, 1906), p. 42.

31. Helen Haines, "Books of 1896—II," *LJ* 22 (1897): 140; AR (1916), Boston Public Library, p. 31; "Are Public Libraries Filled with Trashy Novels?" *Current Opinion* 49 (1915): 422.

32. John Cotton Dana, "Fiction-Readers and the Libraries," *Outlook* 74 (1903): 512.

33. Barbara Ryan, "'A Real Basis from Which to Judge'; Fan Mail to Gene Stratton-Porter," in Barbara Ryan and Amy M. Thomas (eds.), *Reading Acts: U.S. Readers' Interactions with Literature, 1800-1950* (Knoxville, TN: University of Tennessee Press, 2002), pp. 171, 174.

34. Edith Dickson, "Notes in a Country Library," *Independent* 46 (1894): 5.

35. "Libraries and Novels," *The Literary World* 30 (1899): 296; AR (1899), Boston Public Library, p. 34; "A Bulletin in the Boston Public Library . . .," [Philadelphia] *North American*, August 28, 1897; Herbert Small, *Handbook of the New Public Library in Boston* (Boston: Curtis and Company, 1895), pp. 32–33, 42–44, 48–49; Ethel McClintock May, "Reading Is an Incident

at the Boston Library," *Atlanta Constitution*, November 18, 1900; "We Read Few Novels," *Milwaukee Sentinel*, April 18, 1897; "Answers," *Kansas City Star*, April 23, 1910; "Disheartening Books," *NYT*, November 19, 1898; "Within the Sphere of Letters," *Springfield* [MA] *Republican*, September 5, 1897; AR (1897), St. Joseph (MO) Public Library, p. 6; "Fiction Fiends," *Nation* 64 (1897): 258–259.

36. George Harris Healey, "Recollections," *Dedication of the Tompkins County Public Library and the Finger Lakes Library System Headquarters, April 20, 1969* (copy in Library of Congress collections), pp. 21–22.

37. AR (1904), Atlanta Public Library, No. 5, n.p.; "Boys' Books under Ban," *Macon* [GA] *Daily Telegraph*, March 19, 1911; "Gotham Readers Like Trashy Book," *CT*, March 19, 1911; Bella Spewack, *Streets: A Memoir of the Lower East Side* (New York: Feminist Press, 1995), pp. 54–55.

38. Carl B. Roden, "Library Extension in Chicago," *The Child in the City* (Chicago: Department of Social Investigation/Chicago School of Civics and Philanthropy, 1912), p. 393; Franklin K. Mathiews, "Blowing Out the Boy's Brains," *Outlook* 108 (1914): 652; "Literary Censorship," *Omaha World Herald*, May 30, 1897.

39. "Fiction in Public Libraries," *Current Literature* 22 (1897): 21; "Books Harmful to Children," *NYT*, August 20, 1898; "The Value of a Public Library," [Portland] *Oregonian*, November 1, 1898; "Passing Judgment on Fiction," *Boston Journal*, February 28, 1901; "An Enemy to Novels," *Atlanta Constitution*, December 30, 1900; "Barring Horatio Alger's Books," *Detroit Free Press*, August 10, 1907.

40. Edward Stratemeyer to W. F. Gregory, February 19, 1901; Gregory to Stratemeyer, February 21, 1901; Weldon J. Cobb to Edward Stratemeyer, October 13, 1906, all in Box 2, Incoming Correspondence, Stratemeyer Papers; Stratemeyer to James Seymour, April 23, 1901, Newark Librariana, Letters: Box S, New Public Library Archives; "Indignant Ouida," *The Christian Recorder*, February 21, 1895; "A Librarian Makes a Protest and a Plea," *NYT*, October 3, 1915; "Standards in Juvenile Literature," *NYT*, October 17, 1915.

41. William F. Nolan, *Hammett: A Life at the Edge* (New York: Congdon & Weed, 1983), pp. 5–6; Zora Neale Hurston, *Dust Tracks on a Road: The Restored Text Established by the Library of America* (New York: J. B. Lippincott, 1942), pp. 124–125; Bob Thomas, *Walt Disney: An American Original* (New York: Simon and Schuster, 1976), p. 36; "Alger's Books May Be Restored to Library," *Boston Journal*, August 8, 1907; "Barring Horatio Alger's Books," *Detroit Free Press*, August 10, 1907; "Bar Noted Writer's Books," *CT*, August 8, 1907, "Say His Books Are Too Sensational," *Salt Lake Telegram*, August 8, 1907.

42. "Library Entrance a Place of Beauty," *CSM*, January 18, 1913; "New Home for Books," *CT*, February 21, 1897; "Chicago's New Public Library," *CT*, September 11, 1897; Susan G. Larkin, *Top Cats: The Life and Times of the New York Public Library Lions* (San Francisco: Pomegranate, 2006).

43. AR (1912), Braddock (PA) Public Library, p. 18; AR (1914), Braddock (PA) Public Library, p. 15; AR (1916), Braddock (PA) Public Library, pp. 14, 16.

44. Abigail Van Slyck, *Free to All: Carnegie Libraries & American Culture, 1880–1920* (Chicago: University of Chicago Press, 1995), pp. 221–223 (six designs on pp. 38–39); "Letter to the Editor," *Brooklyn Eagle*, September 2, 1901; Gratia Countryman, "The Library as Social Centre," *Public Libraries* 11 (1906): 5.

45. "Opposes Carnegie Library," *NYT*, November 16, 1899; "Refuses It," *Biloxi* [MS] *Daily Herald*, November 17, 1899; David T. Javersak, " 'One Place on This Great Green Planet Where Andrew Carnegie Can't Get a Monument with His Money,' " *West Virginia History* 41 (1979): 7–19. See also Robert Sidney Martin (ed.), *Carnegie Denied: Communities Rejecting Carnegie Library Construction Grants, 1898–1925* (Westport, CT: Greenwood Press, 1993).

46. Lansing R. Robinson, "Don't Kick on Carnegie," *Duluth* [MN] *News Tribune*, September 28, 1902.

47. "Report for November," *Bulletin of the New York Public Library* 14 (1910): 733–734; Jeffrey A. Kroessler, *Lighting the Way: The Centennial History of the Queens Borough Public Library, 1896–1996* (Virginia Beach, VA: Donning Company, 1996), pp. 22–23, 59, 61, 78, 82, 83.

48. AR (1911), SLPL, pp. 44–45; AR (1913), SLPL, p. 82; AR (1917), SLPL, pp. 71, 72, 81, 87, 91–92, 115–117.

49. "Seats Placed on Lawn of Carnegie Library," *Fort Worth Star-Telegram*, August 6, 1911; "Here and There" [Baltimore] *Sun*, September 3, 1900; "Libraries in Parks," *Outlook* 66 (1900): 187; "A Library in a Garden," *The Youth's Companion* 74 (1900): 482; "Good Use for Roofs," *WP*, May 1, 1910; "First Public Library Roof Garden Opened in New York," *CSM*, May 4, 1910.

50. "Pamphlet for Dedication Ceremony of the Eastern Colored Branch, January 28–30, 1914," in Library of Congress Collections. See also "Colored Department, Louisville Free Public Library" (1927), Library of Congress Collections.

51. Mary Antin, *The Promised Land* (Boston: Houghton Mifflin, 1912), p. 341.

52. AR (1899), Boston Public Library, pp. 31–32; "Russian Readers at the Public Library," *Boston Globe*, May 16, 1904; "Homesick Men from Many Cities Meet in This Room," *Kansas City Star*, February 24, 1907; "Seekers after Knowledge," *Kansas City Star*, August 28, 1912.

53. "Ways of the Newspaper Girl," *Boston Globe*, September 29, 1901; "Boston's Free Papers," *Boston Globe*, November 24, 1901; "A Chicago Vignette," *Duluth* [MN] *News-Tribune*, March 4, 1896.

54. AR (1915), Milwaukee Public Library, p. 16; Van Slyck, *Free to All*, p. 99; "Newspaper Rack Defended by Librarians," *CSM*, January 7, 1915; "Tramps Stole the Soap," *Boston Globe*, May 23, 1895; AR (1908), Cleveland Public Library, pp. 39–40; "Scum of the Earth, Said Mr. Follin," *Detroit Free Press*, May 8, 1903.

55. Welty, *One Writer's Beginnings*, pp. 29–30; AR (1917), SLPL, p. 96; "Molested Little Girl," *San Jose* [CA] *Mercury Herald*, September 29, 1914; "Objects to Coughing," *LAT*, April 8, 1899.

56. "Dirty Hands Banned," *LAT*, August 18, 1900; Mary Wright Plummer, "The Work for Children in Free Libraries," *LJ* 22 (1897): 683; Mary Denson Pretlow, "The Opening Day—and After—in a Children's Library," *LJ* 33 (1908): 179; Arthur E. Bostwick, "The Joys of Librarianship," *Bulletin of the New York Public Library* 21 (1918): 12.

57. "Public Library to Serve Eats," *Duluth* [MN] *News Tribune*, January 14, 1917; "Libraries and Librarians," *CSM*, March 29, 1916.

58. Frederick M. Crunden, "The Public Library and Civic Improvement," *The Chautauquan* 43 (1906): 335; Larry Grove, *Dallas Public Library: The First 75 Years* (Dallas: Dallas Public Library, 1977), pp. 36, 37–39; AR (1906), Clinton (IA) Public Library, pp. 12–13; AR (1909), Cedar Rapids Public Library, pp. 7–9; "Art in New York Library Attracts Thousands Daily," *CSM*, June 10, 1911.

59. "Sends His Own Scalp as a Curio," *Omaha World Herald*, April 28, 1900; e-mail, Judith Brick to author, January 14, 2011; "The Perry Museum," *Perry* [OK] *Republican*, November 16, 1916; "Carnegie Public Library," *Perry* [OK] *Republican*, November 23, 1916. See also under same title *Perry* [OK] *Republican*, November 30, 1916; *Perry* [OK] *Republican*, December 14, 1916; *Perry* [OK] *Republican*, December 21, 1916; *Perry* [OK] *Republican*, December 28, 1916; *Perry* [OK] *Republican*, January 4, 1917; *Perry* [OK] *Republican*, February 1, 1917; *Perry* [OK] *Republican*, February 8, 1917; *Perry* [OK] *Republican*, February 15, 1917.

60. Eva Nelson, *The History of the St. Cloud Public Library, 1865–1975* (St. Cloud, MN: Friends of the Library, 1975), pp. 110–125; "Marion Flower Show a Beautiful Display," [Columbia, SC] *State*, May 2, 1910; Barbara Krasner, *The Kearny Public Library and Its Town: A Pictorial History* (Virginia Beach, VA: Donning, 2007), p. 43; AR (1912), Cleveland Public Library, p. 78.

61. "Twenty Thousand New York Suffragettes on Parade," [San Jose, CA] *Evening News*, May 3, 1913; "Antis Planning War on Suffrage Sisters," *Columbus* [GA] *Enquirer-Sun*, April 17, 1913; "Large Audience Will Hear Miss Gordon on Equal Suffrage," *Columbus* [GA] *Enquirer-Sun*, November 21, 1913; "Anti-Suffrage Speaker to Be Heard in Butte," *Anaconda* [MT] *Standard*, November 19, 1914; "Eastern Suffragists Sunday in Portland," *Idaho Statesman*, May 1, 1916; "The Modern Woman, XXVII—Women Librarians," *Fort Worth* [TX] *Star-Telegram*, April 21, 1913.

62. "Macon County Vets Hold Annual Reunion," *Charlotte* [NC] *Observer*, October 3, 1916; "Fitting Tribute to Robert E. Lee," *Columbus* [GA] *Enquirer-Sun*, January 20, 1915; "Lee Birthday Program Will Be Staged at Library," *Columbus* [GA] *Enquirer-Sun*, January 17, 1917;

"Story-Telling Hour Today to Be Devoted to Lincoln," *Anaconda* [MT] *Standard*, February 10, 1917; "Tell Aliens Story of Abraham Lincoln," *Duluth* [MN] *News-Tribune*, February 10, 1917; "Children Hail Flag in Public Library," *Pawtucket* [RI] *Times*, February 12, 1917; "Lincoln Lecture," *Pawtucket* [RI] *Times*, February 11, 1918; *Vacation Visits to Our Public Library* (Greensboro, NC: *Greensboro Daily Record*, 1911), pp. 10–11, 22.

63. Orpha Maud Peters, *The Gary Public Library, 1907–1944* (Gary, IN: Gary Public Library, 1945), p. 12; AR (1915), DCPL, pp. 62–64.

64. "Cold Shoulder Is Given Apollo," *Bellingham* [WA] *Herald*, April 7, 1909; "St. Gaudens Shocks Boston," [Chicago] *Inter Ocean*, February 10, 1894; "All Seeking Shocks," *Boston Globe*, April 15, 1894; "Fear the Nude," *Boston Globe*, August 5, 1896; "She Is Gone," *Boston Globe*, June 17, 1897; "The Religious Press," *New York Evangelist* 67 (1897): 16; "Our Public Library," *Boston Daily Advertiser*, October 14, 1896; "Plumb-Line Penographs," *Lucifer, The Light-Bearer* 13 (1896): 2.

65. Margaret Sanger, *My Fight for Birth Control* (Elmsford, NY: Maxwell Reprint, 1969), p. 146; "Socialist Tells of His Belief," *Salt Lake Telegram*, March 19, 1907; "Theorists Lock Horns in Debate," *Duluth* [MN] *News-Tribune*, March 23, 1908; AR (1917), SLPL, pp. 85, 92.

66. Malcolm G. Wyer, "Right Reading in Childhood," *Iowa Library Quarterly* 5 (1911): 181; AR (1915), Cleveland Public Library, p. 45; "The Evanston (Ill.) Public Library . . .," *Miami Herald*, August 17, 1915; Sherman Peer, *The First Hundred Years: A History of the Cornell Public Library, Ithaca, New York, and the Cornell Library Association, 1864–1964* (Library of Congress Collections), pp. 46–47; AR (1909), Cincinnati Public Library, p. 21; "News of Public Library," [Portland] *Oregonian*, November 7, 1909.

67. AR (1909), Cedar Rapids Public Library, pp. 7–9; Purd B. Wright, *Historical Sketch of the Kansas City Public Library, 1911–1936* (Kansas City: Privately Printed, 1937), pp. 35, 67; Mabel Newhard, "The Use of the Victrola in the Virginia (Minn.) Public Library," *Wisconsin Library Bulletin* 10 (1914): 76; "Victrola Concert at Public Library," *Grand Forks* [ND] *Daily Herald*, February 6, 1916; "Libraries and Librarians," *CSM*, May 10, 1916; "Libraries and Librarians," *CSM*, June 14, 1916; "Library Will Add Music to Its Equipment," *Hobart* [OK] *Daily Republican*, September 2, 1916; "100 Attend Concert," *Duluth* [MN] *News-Tribune*, December 18, 1916.

68. "The Day of Public Libraries," *WP*, April 22, 1900; "Public Libraries in America," *LAT*, June 11, 1900.

69. Douglas A. Galbi, "Book Circulation per U.S. Public Library User since 1856," *Public Library Quarterly* 27 (2008): 356; *Statistical Abstract of the United States, 1917* (Washington, DC: Government Printing Office, 1918), p. 831.

70. Arthur E. Bostwick, *The American Public Library* (New York: Appleton 1910), pp. 1–2, 19.

CHAPTER FIVE

1. "Pawtucket Women to Work for Soldiers," *Pawtucket* [RI] *Times*, November 13, 1914; "Readers Demand Books on Peace," *Duluth* [MN] *News-Tribune*, May 11, 1915; "Kaiser's Portrait, Gift to Roosevelt, Destroyed by Mob," *Philadelphia Inquirer*, July 29, 1918; "Follow the War by the Map," *Kansas City Star*, July 9, 1916; Annual Report (AR) (1916), Detroit Public Library, p. 6.

2. William Howard Brett, "The Round Table," *Cleveland Public Library Staff Newsletter* (1917): 7; "There Will Be a Better Atmosphere . . .," [Portland] *Oregonian*, August 16, 1918; "Pro-German Books in Public Libraries," *CSM*, January 3, 1918; "Many Books Barred from Army Reading" *NYT*, September 1, 1918; "Carnegie Library Bars Hearst's Publications," *LAT*, July 17, 1918; "Redlands Library and Lodge Bar Out Hearst," *Fort Wayne* [IN] *News Sentinel*, July 19, 1918; "Bar Hearst Newspapers from Cincinnati Schools," *Fort Wayne* [IN] *News*, May 31, 1918; "To Remove German Books," *Fort Wayne* [IN] *News*, September 25, 1918; "Shuts Out Hearst Papers," *NYT*, June 1, 1918; "Hearst Barred in Cincinnati," *LAT*, June 2, 1918; "The Fulton Library and the Star," *Kansas City Star*, June 14, 1918; "The Star in the War," *Kansas City Star*, June 17, 1918; "A New York View of Fulton," *Kansas City Star*, June 26, 1918.

3. "Library Retains German Books," *CSM*, August 9, 1918; "Editorial," *Belleville* [IL] *News Democrat*, May 7, 1918.

4. "Food Conservation Posters by School Children at Library," *Dallas Morning News*, April 10, 1918; "'Lighter Reading Aids Book Sales, Librarian Finds," *CSM*, November 6, 1936; AR (1918), Carnegie Library of Pittsburgh, p. 52.

5. AR (1925), Cleveland Public Library, pp. 28; 94–95; AR (1921), Galesburg (IL) Public Library, pp. 4–5; AR (1922), Cedar Rapids Public Library, p. 7.

6. Isabella M. Cooper (ed.), *A.L.A. Catalog, 1926: An Annotated Basic List of 10,000 Books* (Chicago: American Library Association, 1926), pp. 120–121.

7. AR (1926), Brookline (MA) Public Library, pp. 304–306.

8. "Best Seller Sleuths," [San Jose] *Evening News*, January 17, 1921; Bel Kaufman, "The Liberry," *NYT*, July 23, 1976; Douglas A. Galbi, "Book Circulation per U.S. Public Library User since 1856," *Public Library Quarterly* 27 (2008): 356.

9. "In the Library," *Columbus* [GA] *Ledger*, March 16, 1919; "Librarians and Soft-Shell Crabs," *Outlook* 138 (1924): 196.

10. A. J. Badger, "The Story of a Book Detective," *LAT*, September 8, 1929.

11. George Bobinski, *Carnegie Libraries: Their History and Impact on American Public Library Development* (Chicago: American Library Association, 1969), p. 192; "6,516 Public Libraries in U.S. and Canada," *CT*, July 10, 1926; "Circulating Libraries Carried by Gas Boats," *San Jose* [CA] *Mercury News*, March 15, 1918; "Canneries Appreciate Magazines," *Daily Alaska Dispatch*, May 7, 1918; "Traveling Library Is Popular with Laborers," *Aberdeen* [SD] *News*, June 19, 1922; Kim Briggeman, "Boxcar Library That Served Lumberjacks on Display at Fort Missoula Museum," *Missoulian* [MT], August 30, 2013.

12. Louisiana Library Commission, *Report on the Louisiana Library Demonstration, 1925–1930* (New York: League of Library Commissions, 1931), pp. 57–59; rural North Carolina resident quoted in Walter M. High III, "A History of the Durham Public Library, 1895–1940," *North Carolina Libraries* 34 (1977): 41.

13. "Evanston's Library on Wheels," *CT*, June 24, 1920; "A Really Circulating Library," *Independent*, 104 (1920): 309; "Pushcart Brings Books to South End Readers," *Boston Globe*, July 22, 1925; "Work with Schools: Report of the Director, 1927," *Bulletin of the New York Public Library* 32 (1928): 315; "Work with Children: Extension, Report of the Director, 1928," *Bulletin of the New York Public Library* 33 (1929): 422–423.

14. "A New Form of Library Service," *Outlook* 134 (1920): 205; *Sioux City Public Library Hospital Service, October, 1925* (Sioux City, IA: Star Printing, 1925); Catherine Poyas Walker, "Women Librarians Make Success of Profession," *Atlanta Constitution*, February 19, 1922; AR (1925), Cleveland Public Library, p. 69.

15. Sam W. Small, "Looking and Listening," *Atlanta Constitution*, December 9, 1928; "Letter to the Editor," [Columbia, SC] *State*, June 22, 1919.

16. "The Library," *CSM*, February 3, 1926. The following are in the NAACP Papers: "Memorandum on Efforts to Establish Segregated Training School for Librarians," August 25, 1925; Walter F. White (NAACP Assistant Secretary) to ALA President Charles F. D. Beldon, August 28, 1925; White to Frederick Keppel (Carnegie Corp. President), August 29, 1925; Box C-204, NAACP Papers.

17. "Negro Branch Library," *CSM*, August 13, 1918; Julia Collier Harris, "A Library for Negroes," *Kansas City Star*, July 7, 1921.

18. Richard Wright, *Black Boy: A Record of Childhood and Youth* (New York: Harper & Brothers, 1937), pp. 214–217, 224.

19. AR (1929), Cleveland Public Library, pp. 68–70; AR (1930), pp. 63–67; AR (1929), Buffalo Public Library, p. 14.

20. AR (1922), Milwaukee Public Library, pp. 14–16.

21. AR (1921), DCPL, pp. 17–18; AR (1926), Des Moines Public Library, p. 13; AR (1927), Davenport Public Library, pp. 18–19; AR (1928), Cedar Rapids Public Library, p. 8; "Book Characters Come to Life," *LAT*, November 20, 1929.

22. Kathleen M'Laughlin, "Mental Diets Now Selected by Librarians," *CT*, December 31, 1929; William S. Learned, *The American Public Library and the Diffusion of Knowledge* (New York: Carnegie Corporation of New York, 1924), pp. 6, 7, 11, 13.

23. AR (1922), Milwaukee Public Library, pp. 17–18; "The Library," *CSM*, March 10, 1926; AR (1927), LAPL, pp. 27–28; Carl L. Cannon, "Broadcasting Books," *Bookman* 68 (1929): 563; AR (1929), Buffalo Public Library, pp. 14–15; AR (1928), Boston Public Library, p. 62.

24. "To the Editor," *NYT*, May 29, 1926; AR (1929), Brooklyn Public Library, p. 30.

25. Deirdre Carmody, "Library Restores Periodical Room's Splendor," *NYT*, April 6, 1983; John J. Murphy, "Historical Essay," in Willa Cather, *Death Comes for the Archbishop* (Lincoln, NE: University of Nebraska Press, 1999), pp. 352–352; http://americanlibrariesmagazine.org/news/ala/tahlequa-public-library-designated-literary-landmark-altaff-honor-wilson-rawls.

26. "Library Shy on Dictionaries in Puzzles Craze," *LAT*, December 23, 1924; "Dictionary Is Worn Ragged in New Craze," *LAT*, January 18, 1925; "Time Limit on Dictionary," *NYT*, December 23, 1924; "Letters," *CSM*, October 7, 1918; "Books on Home Brews Asked," *Duluth* [MN] *News-Tribune*, August 24, 1919.

27. John Cotton Dana, "Public Libraries as Censors," *Bookman* 49 (1919): 147; "Hits Ban on Frank Books," *LAT*, April 30, 1924; Paul Johnson, *A History of the American People* (New York: HarperCollins, 1998), p. 719.

28. "Customs Censorship," *LAT*, June 23, 1929; Jennie M. Flexner, *Circulation Work in Public Libraries* (Chicago: American Library Association, 1927), p. 122.

29. AR (1927), LAPL, p. 27; "In Our Own Library," *CT*, May 15, 1927; "Library Censorship," *CT*, May 21, 1927; "Censorship," *CT*, September 18, 1927; "Library Censors Shunt Racy Novels to 'Purgatory Shelf,'" *Duluth* [MN] *News Tribune*, September 26, 1920.

30. "Library Bars Ford Weekly," *NYT*, February 26, 1921; "Ban on Ford Sheet," *NYT*, February 27, 1921; "Won't Bar Ford's Paper," *NYT*, March 28, 1921; "Public Libraries and Ford Weekly," *CSM*, March 8, 1921; "Library Censors and Ford Weekly," *CSM*, March 15, 1921; "Ford Paper Is Not to Be Barred," *CSM*, March 29, 1921.

31. "Darwin Works Are in Demand," *Lexington* [KY] *Herald*, February 5, 1922; "Evolution Books Eagerly Sought Now," *Atlanta Constitution*, September 17, 1925; "Little Demand in City for Books on Evolution," *Boston Globe*, July 14, 1925; William Cole, "The Heart of the New York Public Library . . .," *NYT*, March 26, 1972.

32. "Wants Dictionary Out of Library," *Charlotte* [NC] *News*, September 2, 1922; "More 'Seeing' Red," *Atlanta Constitution*, September 8, 1922; William Hale Thompson, "Are We Victims of British Propaganda? 1—Patrons and Propagandists," *Forum* 79 (1928): 503.

33. "Thompson Starts Hunt in Libraries," *CT*, October 21, 1927; "Find John Bull Is the Founder of Our Library," *CT*, October 23, 1927.

34. "Four 'British' Books Seized in Chicago," *CT*, October 27, 1927; "Library Chiefs Chide Mayor for Book 'War,'" *CT*, November 1, 1927; "Plans Chicago Fire for British Books," *NYT*, October 22, 1927; "Thompson Stirs Jeers and Praise," *NYT*, October 30, 1927; "Mr. Thompson's Little British War," *Independent* 119 (1927): 444.

35. "Learned Anarchy in Public Library," *Pawtucket* [RI] *Times*, December 5, 1919; "Syndicalists Posting Literature in Library," *LAT*, November 14, 1919; "'Red' Literature in Public Library," *LAT*, December 13, 1920; "Prosecutor to Press Charges," *Salt Lake Telegram*, November 14, 1919; "Liquor Recipes Censored," *Salt Lake Telegram*, January 21, 1920.

36. Corinne Bacon (comp.), *Standard Catalog Series: Fiction Catalog* (New York: H.W. Wilson, 1931), pp. 11–12.

37. AR (1919), LAPL, p. 32; "New Library Rule Helpful," *Grand Forks* [ND] *Herald*, June 25, 1921; Annual Report, 1923, Seward Park, Box 1, NYPL Branch Archives.

38. AR (1920), LAPL, pp. 24–25; AR (1926), SLPL, pp. 75–76; "The Roundup," *Albuquerque Morning Journal*, May 22, 1922.

39. AR (1929), Detroit Public Library, pp. 6, 12; AR (1921), LAPL, pp. 26.

40. AR (1919), Detroit Public Library, p. 9; AR (1921), LAPL, pp. 26–27.

41. Marjorie Nicolson, "The Professor and the Detective," *Atlantic Monthly* 143 (1929): 483–493; Barbara Ryan, "'A Real Basis from Which to Judge,'" in Barbara Ryan and Amy M. Thomas (eds.), *Reading Acts: U.S. Readers' Interactions with Literature, 1800–1950* (Knoxville, TN: University of Tennessee Press, 2002) p. 161.

42. Jane Greer, "'Ornaments, Tools, or Friends': Literary Reading at the Bryn Mawr Summer School for Women Workers, 1921–1933," in *Reading Acts*, pp. 179, 182, 189, 191, 193, 194–5.

43. Jennifer Parchesky, "'You Make Us Articulate': Reading, Education, and Community in Dorothy Canfield's Middlebrow America," in *Reading Acts*, pp. 231, 238, 239–240, 245, 246.

44. "Saturday Book Marketing," *CSM*, June 13, 1924.

45. Kathleen Chamberlain, "'Wise Censorship,' Cultural Authority and the Scorning of Juvenile Series, Books, 1890–1940," in Lydia Cushman and Deirdre Johnson (eds.), *Scorned Literature: Essays on the History and Criticism of Popular Mass-Produced Fiction in America* (Westport, CT: Greenwood Press, 2002), pp. 187–211; "Not for Boys and Girls," *Wisconsin Library Bulletin* 22 (1927): 95–96; *Library News & Notes* 9 (1928): 61; *Library News & Notes* 10 (1929): 102.

46. Ernest F. Ayres, "Not to Be Circulated?" *Wilson Bulletin* 3 (1929): 528–529.

47. Isaac Asimov, *In Memory Yet Green: The Autobiography of Isaac Asimov* (Garden City, NY: Doubleday), pp. 89, 90; Isaac Asimov, "The Library Book," in *The Best Mysteries of Isaac Asimov* (Garden City, NY: Doubleday, 1986), p. 261; Jerry Griswold, "Young Reagan's Reading," *NYT*, August 30, 1981; Arthur Bartlett Maurice, "Chronicle and Comment," *Salt Lake Telegram*, July 30, 1922; "Review of the 'Dime Novel,'" *CSM*, August 19, 1922; Edmund Lester Pearson, "Beadle's Dime Novels," *Independent*, 109 (1922): 37.

48. "Because of the Absence of Crime . . . ," *Wyoming State Tribune*, February 10, 1921; "Police Station Is Library," *Salt Lake Telegram*, October 23, 1921; http://heritage.wisconsin-libraries.org/2009/03/railroad-car-library.html; Helen Hooven Santmyer, *Ohio Town* (New York: Harper & Row, 1984), p. 187.

49. James O'Donnell Bennett, "Whole Town of Book Lovers on Illinois Prairie," *CT*, July 30, 1926; "Noontime Browsing in Boston Library's Courtyard," *CSM*, July 11, 1924; "Courtyard of Boston Public Library Has Become Open-Air Reading Room," *Boston Globe*, July 27, 1924; "Librarian Finds Readers' Choice Widespread," *Idaho Statesman*, December 9, 1922.

50. AR (1925), Detroit Public Library, pp. 6–7; AR (1920), LAPL, pp. 35–36; AR (1922), LAPL, pp. 11–12; AR (1920), Cleveland Public Library, p. 13.

51. James Bond, "Louisville Negroes and the Public Library System," *Philadelphia Tribune*, August 4, 1927; Lillian Taylor Wright, "Thomas Fountain Blue, Pioneer Librarian, 1866–1935," Master's thesis, Atlanta University, 1955, p. 27.

52. Isabel Wilkerson, *The Warmth of Other Suns: The Epic Story of America's Great Migration* (New York: Random House, 2010), p. 181; AR (1921), Cleveland Public Library, p. 28; AR (1922), Cleveland Public Library, p. 23; AR (1925), Cleveland Public Library, pp. 57–58; AR (1926), Cleveland Public Library, pp. 65–66; AR (1928), Cleveland Public Library, p. 49; AR (1929), Cleveland Public Library, p. 44.

53. AR (1920), Carnegie Library of Pittsburgh, p. 39; AR (1925), Carnegie Library of Pittsburgh, pp. 1–12; AR (1929), Carnegie Library of Pittsburgh, p. 13.

54. "Chisholm's Clubs, Lodges, and Societies," *Duluth* [MN] *News-Tribune*, July 18, 1920; "Public Library to Stage Smoker," *Duluth* [MN] *News-Tribune*, December 1, 1919; AR (1920), LAPL, pp. 35–36.

55. "Library Allows Many Privileges to Men," *San Jose* [CA] *Mercury Herald*, August 20, 1920; "Silence Kept in Library by Tact and Vigilance," *NYT*, October 25, 1925; "Library's Ban on Shirtsleeves Upheld," *NYT*, July 24, 1926.

56. "Romance Not Dead in Small Downtown Park," *Fort Worth* [TX] *Star-Telegram*, October 8, 1922; Anthony Balas, "Why Men Read," *CT*, March 3, 1927; "Library Lights Start All-Night Vigils to Discourage 'Spooners' on the Terrace," *NYT*, April 7, 1925;

Timothy Jacobson, *Knowledge for Generations: Wiley and the Global Publishing Industry, 1807–2007* (Hoboken, NJ: John Wiley, 2007), p. 135.

57. "Someone Ought to Call Attention . . .," *Duluth* [MN] *News-Tribune*, December 8, 1918; "Forbidden," [Biloxi, MS] *Daily Herald*, February 3, 1921; AR (1926), SLPL, p. 30.

58. "Aliens and the Public Library," *CSM*, August 11, 1922; "Citizenship through Libraries," *NYT*, October 8, 1928.

59. AR (1922), SLPL, pp. 94–95; AR (1921), Cleveland Public Library, pp. 25; 27; AR (1925), Cleveland Public Library, pp. 58–59; AR (1928), Cleveland Public Library, p. 48.

60. AR (1929), Denver Public Library, pp. 13–14.

61. "Barrooms to Be Used for Reading Room," *Duluth* [MN] *News-Tribune*, April 4, 1920; "No Substitute for Abolished Saloon Has Been Offered," *Anaconda* [MT] *Standard*, January 13, 1919; "City Now Flooded," *Macon* [GA] *Weekly Telegraph*, September 15, 1919; Florence M. Jumonville, "Books along the Bayous: Reading Materials for Two Centuries of Rural Louisianans," in Robert S. Freeman and David M. Hovde (eds.), *Libraries to the People: Histories of Outreach* (Jefferson, NC: McFarland, 2003), p. 21; "Public Library Will Be Closed Wednesday," *Belleville* [IL] *News Democrat*, February 11, 1919; "Holiday at Library," *San Jose* [CA] *Mercury Herald*, February 11, 1919; "Georgia Day Celebration This Evening at the Public Library," *Columbus* [GA] *Ledger*, February 14, 1919; "Lee's Anniversary," *Columbus* [GA] *Ledger*, January 19, 1920.

62. Jeffrey A. Kroessler, *Lighting the Way: The Centennial History of the Queens Borough Public Library, 1896–1996* (Virginia Beach, VA: The Donning Company Publishers, 1996), p. 23; "Cupid's Nudity Shocked," *Pueblo* [CO] *Chieftain*, February 5, 1919.

63. AR (1920), Boston Public Library, p. 35.

64. Jack D. Hess, "Childhood Memories of Books, Libraries and Librarians," *Top of the News* 43 (1986): 88; "Story Telling Hour Makes a Hit with the Kiddies," *Duluth* [MN] *News-Tribune*, July 13, 1919; AR (1923), Carnegie Library of Pittsburgh, p. 9.

65. Raymund F. Wood, "The Traveling Libraries of California," *News Notes of California Libraries* 71 (1976): 48; "Milwaukee Sets Up Bird 'Lunch Rooms,'" *CSM*, February 11, 1928.

66. Louise B. Caccamise, *Echoes of Yesterday: A History of the DeLand Area Public Library, 1912–1995* (New Smyrna Beach, FL: Luthers, 1995), p. 140.

67. AR (1927), Des Moines Public Library, p. 21; "Canned Music Libraries," *Anaconda* [MT] *Standard*, August 7, 1921.

68. AR (1919), SLPL, p. 57; "Librarian Finds Readers' Choice Widespread," *Idaho Statesman*, December 9, 1922; AR (1929), Brooklyn Public Library, p. 31; Ronald F. Sigler, "A Rationale for the Film as a Public Library Resource and Service," *Library Trends* 27 (1978): 11–12.

69. "Radio Supersedes Books?" *LAT*, July 2, 1922; *A Survey of Libraries in the United States*, Volume 3 (Chicago: American Library Association, 1926), p. 215; "Radio Association to Meet at Library," *Salt Lake Telegram*, February 1, 1921; AR (1926), Buffalo Public Library, p. 19; AR (1928), Cincinnati Public Library, p. 10; "Public Library Aided by Radio," *CSM*, December 30, 1924.

70. AR (1920), Cincinnati Public Library, pp. 17–18; AR (1928), Cleveland Public Library, p. 57; "Chevy Chase Library Has Fashion Review," *WP*, March 24, 1928.

71. Nathaniel T. Kidder, *The First Sixty Years of the Milton Public Library, 1870–1931* (Milton, MA: Privately Printed, 1932), p. 92; Paul Weingarten, "United Cow Town Trying to Rescue 'City's Cultural Soul,'" *CT*, August 15, 1990; "Pictures Now Lent Like Library Books," *CSM*, April 10, 1929; *The Long Beach Public Library: How It Serves the Community* (Long Beach, CA: Long Beach *Telegram*, 1919), p. 1.

72. AR (1926), Denver Public Library, p. 3; "Books Are Known in the Twentieth Century," *Kansas City Star*, December 29, 1922.

73. AR (1927), Bangor (ME) Public Library, p. 14; Arthur E. Bostwick, "The Socialization of the Library," *The Bookman* 51 (1920): 668.

74. John Cotton Dana, "The Librarian's Business," *NYT*, October 4, 1926.

CHAPTER SIX

1. "Report of the Director, 1938," *Bulletin of the New York Public Library* 43 (1949): 227, 237.
2. Paul Johnson, *A History of the American People* (New York: HarperCollins, 1998), p. 743.
3. "Library Depressions," *NYT*, June 3, 1932; David Morris, "All Hail the PUBLIC Library," http://www.onthecommons.org/all-hail-public-library; "Public Library Halts Purchase of New Books," *CT*, June 18, 1931; Carl Roden, "The Library in Hard Times," *LJ* 56 (1931): 984–987; Annual Report (AR) (1934), Brooklyn Public Library, p. 19; "Report of the Director, 1934," *Bulletin of the New York Public Library* 39 (1934): 276, 279; "Shelves Fill Up as Books Return," *CSM*, October 19, 1932.
4. AR (1935), LAPL, p. 39; Margaret K. McElderry, "Remarkable Women: Anne Carroll Moore & Company," *School Library Journal* 38 (1992): 159, 160.
5. "Citizens Help Library Situation," *CSM*, May 6, 1933; "Gift of Books Will Replenish Library Stocks," *CT*, November 15, 1933; "School Children Will Collect Books to Aid Public Library Drive," *CT*, March 23, 1934; "30,000 Volumes Given to Public Library in First Week of Drive," *CT*, March 26, 1934.
6. "Citizens Help Library Situation," *CSM*, May 6, 1933; "U.S. Libraries Declared Inadequate," *CSM*, August 30, 1939; Wilhelm Munthe, *American Librarianship from a European Angle: An Attempt at an Evaluation of Policies and Activities* (Chicago: American Library Association, 1939), p. 16.
7. Edward Barrett Stanford, *Library Extension under the WPA* (Chicago: University of Chicago Press, 1944), pp. 50, 96–97; Elaine van Oesen, "Public Library Extension in North Carolina and the WPA," *North Carolina Historical Review* 29 (1952): 387.
8. AR (1936), Denver Public Library, pp. 5–7; "'O-Fillers' Please Stop," *NYT*, June 14, 1945; AR (1938), SLPL, p. 19; "Books to Shut-ins," *Kansas Library Bulletin* 6 (1937): 6–7.
9. Kathleen R. Hodges (ed.), *A Light in the Window of Idaho: Boise's Public Library, 1895–1995* (Boise, ID: Friends of the Boise Public Library, 1995), pp. 66–67; AR (1933), Buffalo Public Library, pp. 24–27; Ellen Braby and Janet Hunt, *The Santa Monica Public Library, 1890–1990* (Santa Monica, CA: Santa Monica Public Library, 1990), pp. 19–22, 47, 50; AR (1935), Dayton Public Library, p. 37.
10. Ranya Ducker Finchum and Allen Finchum, "Not Gone with the Wind: Libraries in Oklahoma in the 1930s," *Libraries & the Cultural Record* 46 (2011): 290; "Pack Horse Library in the Hills," *CSM*, September 3, 1935; Marjorie Schuler, "By Mail, Pack Horse, and Wagon, Books Reach Village and Farm," *CSM*, April 4, 1939.
11. "Here Comes the Bookmobile!" *Kansas City Star*, May 19, 1940.
12. "Library Takes to the Trail," *CSM*, November 14, 1939; AR (1931), Dayton Public Library, pp. 7–8; "Build Trailer Library for Children," *CT*, July 13, 1939; "Letter to the Editor," *CT*, June 23, 1940.
13. Munthe, *American Librarianship from a European Angle*, p. 46; AR (1935), Carnegie Library of Pittsburgh, p. 5; "Report of the Director, 1935," *Bulletin of the New York Public Library* 40 (1936): 222; Kathleen M. Rassuli and Stanley C. Hollander, "Revolving, Not Revolutionary Books: The History of Rental Libraries until 1960," *Journal of Macromarketing* 21 (2001): 125.
14. "Messengers Speed Books to New Rochelle Readers," *NYT*, March 23, 1936; "Library Service," *CSM*, April 29, 1936; AR (1935), Dayton Public Library, p. 24.
15. "Library Service," *WP*, April 29, 1934; "Stresses Demand for 'Hard' Books," *NYT*, May 13, 1936; Eric Novotny, "'Bricks without Straw': Economic Hardship and Innovation in the Chicago Public Library during the Great Depression," *Libraries & the Cultural Record* 46 (2011): 266; Joyce G. Saricks and Nancy Brown, *Readers' Advisory Service in the Public Library* (Chicago: American Library Association, 1989), p. 5; John Chancellor, Miriam D. Tompkins, and Hazel I. Medway, *Helping the Reader toward Self-Education* (Chicago: American Library Association, 1938).
16. Margaret Root Zahler, "Is Attracting the Public to Good Books," *CSM*, May 28, 1940; AR (1944), East Orange (NJ) Free Public Library, p. 6.

17. Dorothea Kahn, "To Change the Subject: Children's Library, 1943 Style," *CSM*, June 24, 1943; "Youths of Public Library Branch in Harlem Will Open Their Own Clubhouse Tonight," *NYT*, April 4, 1945; Miriam Braverman, *Youth, Society, and the Public Library* (Chicago: American Library Association, 1978), pp. 33–34, 124.

18. "Depression Booms Library," *WP*, April 24, 1932; Louis Round Wilson, *The Geography of Reading: A Study of the Distribution and Status of Libraries in the United States* (Chicago: University of Chicago Press, 1938), pp. 32–33, 191–192, 252, 257, 263; "Libraries as Civic Centers," *CSM*, July 29, 1936; Margaret M. Herdman, "The Public Library in the Depression" (Ph.D. diss., University of Chicago, 1941), pp. 1–6, 68–70.

19. L. H. Robbins, "The Rediscovery of the Public Library," *NYT*, June 12, 1932; "America Carries On with the Library's Aid," *NYT*, May 20, 1934; "Public Library," *CSM*, August 16, 1939.

20. "Jersey Dry Leader Would Ban Liquor Recipes from Library," *NYT*, March 11, 1932; Ernest and Julio Gallo, *Ernest and Julio: Our Story* (New York: Times Books, 1994), pp. 55–56.

21. Woody Guthrie, *Bound for Glory* (New York: E.P. Dutton, 1943), p. 226; Joe Klein, *Woody Guthrie: A Life* (New York: Alfred A. Knopf, 1980), pp. 68, 69; http://www.lorain.lib.oh.us/author_biography.

22. Transcript, Oral History Interview with Annie Watters McPheeters, Collection No. aarlohe 92–001, Auburn Avenue Research Library on African American Culture, Atlanta, GA, pp. 54–56.

23. Steven Gilbar (ed.), *The Open Door: When Writers First Learned to Read* (Boston: David R. Godine, 1989), pp. 105–106.

24. Jade Snow Wong, "A Repository of Treasures," in Timothy Jacobson, *Knowledge for Generations: Wiley and the Global Publishing Industry, 1807–2007* (Hoboken, NJ: John Wiley, 2007), p. 215; Judy Yung, "History of the Chinatown Branch Library," June 11, 2011, copy in possession of author.

25. Louise S. Robbins, *Censorship and the American Library: The American Library Association's Response to Threats to Intellectual Freedom, 1939–1969* (Westport, CT: Greenwood Press, 1996), Chapter 1.

26. Stanley Kunitz, "That Library Serves Best . . .," *Wilson Library Bulletin* 13 (1939): 314; "Libraries Held Vital to Democracy," *CSM*, June 3, 1940; Lucia Mouat, "How to Screen Children's Books for Prejudice," *CSM*, February 26, 1979; Cathy Chance, "Sambo's under Fire," *New York Amsterdam News*, September 15, 1979; "Substitutes for Unrecommended Juveniles," *LJ* 57 (1932): 391; "Not for Boys and Girls," *Wisconsin Library Bulletin* 29 (1933): 175; "Not for Boys and Girls," *Michigan Libraries* 10 (1944): 17–18; "Not for Boys and Girls," *Iowa Library Quarterly* 14 (1944): 178–185.

27. Doris Lockerman, "1914 and Today: Reading Tastes Show a Change," *CT*, October 11, 1939; "Anne Lindbergh's New Book Banned by Long Island Library," *LAT*, January 7, 1939; John Fleischman, *Free & Public: One Hundred and Fifty Years of the Public Library of Cincinnati and Hamilton County, 1853–2003* (Cincinnati: Orange Frazer Press, 2003), p. 83; "Hitler's Book Rises in Demand at Library," *NYT*, January 12, 1939; "'Mein Kampf' in Demand," *CSM*, January 12, 1939.

28. "Libraries Resist Censoring of Book Shelves," *CSM*, January 3, 1939; AR (1940), Fort Wayne Public Library, p. 29.

29. "Jeanne S. Chall, "The Impact of Public Libraries in Children," in Edward G. Doyle, *A Commemorative History of the Cambridge Public Library* (Cambridge, MA: Cambridge Public Library, 1989), pp. 102–103.

30. Douglas Waples, Leon Carnovsky, and William M. Randall, "The Public Library in the Depression," *Library Quarterly* 2 (1932): 328–330; Lila Hanft, "Public Libraries Are as Important as the Military, Says E. L. Doctorow," *Cleveland Jewish News* 96 (2005): 77; John Updike, *Odd Jobs: Essays and Criticism* (New York: Alfred A. Knopf, 1991), pp. 837–838.

31. Dale Kramer, "Main Street in 1940: Sigourney, Iowa," *Forum and Century* 53 (1940): 166.

32. "For It Was Indeed He," *Fortune* 9 (1934): 86; Kim Winship, "Faithful Readers," *Syracuse New Times*, March 10, 1993; Judith Hennessee, *Betty Friedan: Her Life* (New York: Random House,

1999), p. 12; Sandra Day O'Connor and H. Alan Day, *Lazy B: Growing Up on a Cattle Ranch in the American Southwest* (New York: Random House, 2002), p. 229; Sydney Ladensohn, *Gloria Steinem: Her Passions, Politics, and Mystique* (Secaucus, NJ: Barol Publishing Group, 1997), p. 26; Shirley Chisholm, *Unbought and Unbossed* (Boston: Houghton Mifflin, 1970), p. 19; Carolyn Stewart Dyer and Nancy Tillman Romalov (eds.), *Rediscovering Nancy Drew* (Iowa City, IA: University of Iowa Press, 1995), pp. 98, 102.

33. S. G. Reid to "Fenworth Moore," June 11, 1933; Shirley Beman and Shirley Levine to "Miss Alice B. Emerson," August 17, 1931; Robert McIntyre to "Mr. Appleton," October 1, 1930, "Incoming Fan Mail," all in Box 56, Stratemeyer Papers.

34. Mary Vernon Charnley to "Mr. Appleton," n.d.; Lillie M. Nickerson to "Mr. Appleton," May 15, 1933; Joseph Schroth to "Sir," January 1, 1932, "Incoming Fan Mail," all in Box 56, Stratemeyer Papers.

35. "Mayor's Secret of Success: Read Horatio Alger," *CT*, October 10, 1937.

36. "'Little Women's Library' Shows Huge Success," *WP*, March 3, 1935; "Little Cripples Find a Friend in Girl of 14," *CT*, September 8, 1940.

37. AR (1931), Dayton Public Library, pp. 9–11; Charles H. Compton, *Twenty-Five Crucial Years of the St. Louis Public Library, 1927 to 1952* (St. Louis: St. Louis Public Library, 1953), pp. 151, 157.

38. E. B. White, "The Librarian Said It Was Bad for Children," *NYT*, March 6, 1966.

39. Joseph L. Wheeler and Alfred M. Githens, *The American Public Library Building: Its Planning and Design with Special Reference to Its Administration and Service* (New York: Charles Scribner's Sons, 1941), pp. 1–4, 7, 9; Munthe, *American Librarianship from a European Angle*, pp. 52–53, 56.

40. Agnes Rush Burr, "An Unique Civic Institution, and the Woman Who Evolved It," *LAT*, October 10, 1930; T. Morris Longstreth, "Report on a Small Town Library," *CSM*, August 19, 1943; C. H. Cramer, *Open Shelves and Open Minds: A History of the Cleveland Public Library* (Cleveland: Press of Case Western Reserve University, 1972), p. 167.

41. "Where There's a Will There's a Way," *Kansas Library Bulletin* 6 (1937): 8; "Nebraska Women Turn Gas Station into Library," *CSM*, June 26, 1940.

42. AR (1930), SLPL, pp. 70–71; AR (1938), SLPL, p. 23; Elsie Madison, "Chaos Taught Us to Read," *LAT*, September 8, 1935.

43. Michael Kane, "Peculiar Pastimes," *Life* 103 (1936): 15; Saul Bellow, "Facts That Put Fancy to Flight," *NYT*, February 11, 1962.

44. Michael V. Hazel, *The Dallas Public Library: Celebrating a Century of Service, 1901-2001* (Denton: University of North Texas Press, 2001), pp. 74–75; "Survey Shows Book Lending Is Only Part of Library Work," *CSM*, February 25, 1936.

45. Helen Johnson Keyes, "Where Library Brings Forty Nationalities Together," *CSM*, October 18, 1941.

46. "Pratt Library Stoops to Jim Crow," [Baltimore] *Afro-American*, May 19, 1934; Matt Spengler, Eddie Becker, and Julian Bond, *Out of Obscurity: The Story of the 1939 Alexandria Library Sit-In* (Spring Lake, MI: River Bend Productions, 1999); Helen Snow, *The Greensboro Public Library: The First 100 Years* (Greensboro, NC: Donning Company, 2003), pp. 43–44; Janice A. Radway, "The Library as Place, Collection, or Service: Promoting Book Circulation in Durham, North Carolina, and at the Book-of-the-Month Club, 1925–1945," in Thomas Augst and Kenneth Carpenter (eds.), *Institutions of Reading: The Social Life of Libraries in the United States* (Amherst: University of Massachusetts Press, 2007), pp. 262–263.

47. Tommie Dora Barker, *Libraries of the South: A Report on Developments, 1930–1935* (Chicago: American Library Association, 1936), pp. 35–36, 199–201; Louis Round Wilson, "The Role of the Library in the Southeast in Peace and War," *Social Forces* 21 (1943): 464; "Free Library," *New York Amsterdam News*, September 3, 1938; R. L. Duffus, *Our Starving Libraries: Studies in Ten American Communities during the Depression Years* (Boston: Houghton Mifflin, 1933), p. 70.

48. Julia Moriarty, "Library Service to Negroes," AR (1943), Hartford Public Library, pp. 16–19.

49. Roy Petty, "Library Gets Grant to Restore Its Black Writers' Collection," *CT*, January 22, 1970; Emily Guss, "Cultural Record Keepers: Vivian G. Harsh Collection of Afro-American History

and Literature, Carter G. Woodson Regional Library, Chicago Public Library," *Libraries & the Cultural Record* 45 (2010): 360–361; Anne Meis Knupfer, *The Chicago Black Renaissance and Women's Activism* (Urbana: University of Illinois Press, 2006), p. 63.

50. Helen Johnson Keyes, "The Negro's Niche in American History," *CSM*, May 2, 1942; "Interview of Baker, Augusta, 1911–1988," May 7, 1989, in *Speaking of History: The Words of South Carolina Librarians*, http://asp6new.alexanderstreet.com/orhi/orhi.result.words.asap?word=public+library &narrator=age&birth.

51. David Leeming, *James Baldwin: A Biography* (New York: Henry Holt, 1994), pp. 13, 22–23; Audre Lorde, *Zami: A New Spelling of My Name* (Trumansburg, NY: Crossing Press, 1982), pp. 22–23.

52. "Library Exhibit Portrays Role of Negro in U.S.," *CT*, February 15, 1944; "Exhibit Serves to Debunk Myth of Race Superiority," *New York Amsterdam News*, February 10, 1945.

53. Ellen Tarry, "'Inspired,' Is the World of Augusta Braxton Baker, Children's Librarian," *New York Amsterdam News*, August 29, 1942; "Annual Report, 1943, George Bruce Branch," Box 7, NYPL Branch Archives.

54. Evelyn Geller, *Forbidden Books in American Public Libraries, 1876–1939: A Study in Cultural Change* (Westport, CT: Greenwood Press, 1984), p. 152; Joyce M. Latham, "'A Liberal and a Dignified Approach,' The John Toman Branch of the Chicago Public Library and the Making of Americans, 1927–1940," in Christine Pawley and Louise Robbins (eds.), *Libraries and Print Culture* (Madison, WI: University of Wisconsin Press, 2012), pp. 111–128; Novotny, "Bricks without Straw," p. 270.

55. Seymour Korman, "Children Scared by WPA Mural in an Iowa Library," *CT*, January 11, 1941.

56. C. S., "The Story-Telling Hour," *CSM*, September 19, 1932; "When It's Time for Story Hour," *CSM*, April 30, 1936.

57. Marion Humble, *Rural America Reads: A Study of Rural Library Service* (New York: American Association for Adult Education, 1938), pp. 29, 61–62; George Gallup, "The Favorite Books of Americans," *NYT*, January 15, 1939; "The Librarian Provides a Preview," *CSM*, April 16, 1936; Louise Pendry, "From Movies to Books," *CSM*, October 27, 1936.

58. AR (1930), Cleveland Public Library, p. 26; *A Brief History of the Cuyahoga County Public Library, 1923–1998* (Cleveland: Cuyahoga County Public Library, 1998), pp. 9–10; Judith-Ellen Brown, "Meet Your Public Library," *CSM*, July 11, 1942; "Report of the Director, 1937," *Bulletin of the New York Public Library* 42 (1938): 214, 217, 225.

59. Shirley Schuette and Nathania K. Sawyer, *From Carnegie to Cyberspace: 100 Years at the Central Arkansas Library System* (Little Rock, AR: Butler Center Books, 2010), p. 46; "Circulating Records," *NYT*, September 14, 1941; "New Music Room Is Opened at Public Library in Quincy," *CSM*, April 26, 1940; "Letter to the Editor," *CT*, November 30, 1943.

60. "Report of the Director, 1939," *Bulletin of the New York Public Library* 44 (1940): 235; "Annual Report, 1946," Fort Washington Branch, Box 3, NYPL Branch Archives. Playbills in Box 2.

61. Barbara Miller, "Have You a Card for the Toy Library?" *LAT*, August 30, 1936.

62. "Annual Report, 1941, Riverside Branch," Box 11, NYPL Branch Archives.

63. "Reading Is Halved in Public Libraries," *NYT*, July 8, 1943; "Annual Reports, Chatham Branch Library, 1942," Box 1; "Informal & Annual Reports, Children's Room, 1942," Fort Washington Branch Records, Box 4; "Annual Report, 1941," Fordham, Library Center, Box 4; "Seward Park Branch Library Report," Box 3, NYPL Branch Papers.

64. AR (1942), LAPL, p. 4; "Reading Habits Changed by War," *LAT*, March 2, 1942; George Weinstein, "Libraries Go Modern," LAT September 16, 1945; "Library Maps, Charts in Great Demand," *CT*, December 16, 1941; "Have You a Query about War Activity?" *CSM*, April 4, 1942; AR (1943), East Orange Free Public Library, pp. 4–5; Bernice Stevens, "The Library Leaves Its Ivory Tower," *CSM*, June 19, 1943.

65. "Public Library Has New Place in War World," *WP*, October 11, 1942; "Government Girls Find Relaxation in Reading," *WP*, January 17, 1943; "Library's War Reading Room Opens Tuesday," *WP*, May 3, 1942.

66. "Seward Park Branch Report," Box 3; "Annual Report, 1945, Hamilton Fish Branch Library," Box 7, NYPL Branch Archives; *"No More Books": The New York Public Library in 1938* (New York: New York Public Library, 1939), pp. 8–9.

67. AR (1942), Buffalo Public Library, pp. 9–13; "Honolulu Library Does Major War Job," *CSM*, May 13, 1944; "'Sweet' War Letters—N.Y. Library Aids," *NYT*, March 5, 1943; "Library Getting Replies from Overseas to Christmas Cards for Former Readers," *NYT*, January 13, 1944.

68. AR (1943), East Orange (NJ) Public Library, pp. 4–5.

69. "Thinning Tires Cause Headaches for Librarian," *LAT*, October 11, 1942; "Library Book Wagon a Casualty of War," *NYT*, September 14, 1944; Margaret A. Edwards, *The Fair Garden and the Swarm of Beasts: The Library and the Young Adult* (Chicago: American Library Association, 2002), p. 43.

70. "Book Burning Marked by 1,000 at Library," *NYT*, May 11, 1943; "Libraries Report Reading Changes," *NYT*, December 27, 1943; "Public Found Reading Less but Demand Is for Quality," *CSM*, December 28, 1943.

71. "Annual Report, 1946, St. George Branch," Box 11; "Annual Report, 1941, Muhlenberg Branch," Box 10; "Annual Report, 1944, Ottendorfer Branch," Box 10, NYPL Branch Archives.

72. "Librarians Are Regularly Asked Silly Questions," *Seattle Post-Intelligencer*, September 17, 1991; Jim Okerblom, "Clara Estelle Breed: 'Library Lady' Who Guided City's Modern System," *San Diego Union-Tribune*, September 10, 1994.

73. "Annual Report, 1946, St. George Branch," Box 11; "Annual Report, 1945, St. Agnes Branch," Box 11, NYPL Branch Archives.

74. US Office of Education, Library Service Division, *Public Library Statistics, 1944–45* (Washington, DC: Government Printing Office, 1946); Douglas A. Galbi, "Book Circulation per U.S. Public Library User since 1856," *Public Library Quarterly* 27 (2008): 356.

CHAPTER SEVEN

1. Benjamin Fine, "Rising Censorship of Books Assailed," *NYT*, June 15, 1948; Benjamin Fine, "Librarians Plan Censorship Fight," *NYT*, June 16, 1948; "Nation Magazine Ordered Banned in Bay State Colleges," *CSM*, July 16, 1948; Toni Samek, *Intellectual Freedom and Social Responsibility in American Librarianship, 1967–1974* (Jefferson, NC: McFarland, 2001), pp. 148–151; Lester Asheim, "Not Censorship, but Selection," *Wilson Library Bulletin* 28 (1953): 63–67.

2. "Boston's Moral Decay," *CT*, October 3, 1950.

3. Roger P. Bristol, "It Takes Courage to Stock 'Taboos,'" *LJ* 74 (1949): 261–263; Martha Cornog and Timothy Perper (eds.), *For Sex Education, See Librarian: A Guide to Issues and Resources* (Westport, CT: Greenwood, 1996).

4. Annual Report (AR) (1957), Fort Wayne (IN) Public Library, pp. 39–40.

5. "No Censorship, Says Librarian," *WP*, June 13, 1958; "County Lays Library Ban on 'Tropic,'" *WP*, October 21, 1961; "Experts Present Diverse Views at Obscenity Trial of 'Tropic,'" *WP*, October 30, 1962; "Fight for Free Speech a Duty, Says Librarian," *LAT*, April 8, 1962.

6. Eleanor Frances Brown, *Bookmobiles and Bookmobile Service* (Metuchen, NJ: Scarecrow Press, 1967), p. 76; Bob Sherlock, "Row Erupts in Arcadia over Book Termed 'Blasphemous,'" *LAT*, November 29, 1962; "Long Beach Rejects Ban on 'Blasphemous' Novel," *LAT*, December 5, 1962; "Clergy Panel on Disputed Book Denied," *LAT*, January 31, 1963; "Library Bars Novel Assailed by Priest," *NYT*, April 13, 1963.

7. Bob Sherlock, "Public Splits on Book Removal," *LAT*, January 24, 1963.

8. For a deeper analysis of these collections over time, see Wayne A. Wiegand, *Main Street Public Library: Community Places and Reading Spaces in the Rural Heartland, 1876–1956* (Iowa City, IA: University of Iowa Press, 2011), Chapter 5.

9. Laura J. Miller, *Reluctant Capitalists: Bookselling and the Culture of Consumption* (Chicago: University of Chicago Press, 2006), pp. 27–28, 34–35; Carl F. Kaestle and Janice A. Radway, "A Framework for the History of Publishing and Reading in the United States, 1880–1940," in Carl F. Kaestle and Janice A. Radway (eds.), *The History of the Book in America, Volume 4: Print in Motion; The Expansion of Publishing and Reading in the United States, 1880–1940* (Chapel Hill: University of North Carolina Press, 2009), pp. 7–21.

10. Marjorie Fiske, *Book Selection and Censorship: A Study of School and Public Libraries in California* (Berkeley: University of California Press, 1959), pp. 64–65. See also Louise S. Robbins, *Censorship and the American Library: The American Library Association's Response to Threats to Intellectual Freedom, 1939–1969* (Westport, CT: Greenwood Press, 1996), p. 103.

11. William Fulton, "Library Favors Commie Books in Boston Area," *CT*, September 29, 1950.

12. "Library Stocks Anti-Red Book after Dispute," *CT*, October 14, 1950.

13. "Burbank Pushes Proposal to Screen Library Books," *LAT*, September 18, 1951; "Book Labeling Proposal Sponsors to Push Fight," *LAT*, October 7, 1951.

14. "Branding of Books Stirs Texas Battle," *NYT*, June 7, 1953; "Books in San Antonio," *NYT*, June 8, 1953; Stanley Walker, "'Book Branding'—A Case History," *NYT*, July 12, 1953; Gerald Ashford, "Texas 'Book-Branding' Issue Slumbers," *WP*, July 19, 1953; "Library Plans Anti-Red Book Reading List," *WP*, June 14, 1953.

15. Jean Preer, "The American Heritage Project: Librarians and the Democratic Tradition in the Early Cold War," *Libraries and Culture* 28 (1993): 165–188.

16. Isaac R. Barfield, "A History of the Miami Public Library, Miami, Florida" (Master's thesis, Atlanta University, 1958), p. 31; "File Suit against Library Practices," *Philadelphia Tribune*, August 12, 1950; "Library Admits Negro," *NYT*, March 23, 1957.

17. "Civil Rights Roundup," *Philadelphia Tribune*, February 27, 1960; Jeffrey A. Turner, *Sitting In and Speaking Out: Student Movements in the American South, 1960–1970* (Athens: University of Georgia Press, 2010), p. 77.

18. Louise S. Robbins, "Racism and Censorship in Cold War Oklahoma: The Case of Ruth W. Brown and the Bartlesville Public Library," *Southwestern Historical Quarterly*, 100 (July, 1996): 19–46; P. L. Prattis, "Plain Murder," *Pittsburgh Courier*, January 18, 1958.

19. "Joseph H. Baird, "Atlanta Library Integrates," *CSM*, May 26, 1959.

20. Marshall Frady, *Jesse: The Life and Pilgrimage of Jesse Jackson* (New York: Random House, 1996), pp. 130–135; "Library Opens at Greenville as Integrated," [Columbia, SC] *State*, September 20, 1960.

21. Myrlie Evers-Williams and Manning Marable (eds.), *The Autobiography of Medgar Evers: A Hero's Life and Legacy Revealed through His Writings, Letters, and Speeches* (New York: Basic Books, 2005), pp. 228–229.

22. "Montgomery Library Sued," *Philadelphia Tribune*, May 1, 1962; "New Jim Crow Law May Wipe Out 'Slouching' in Alabama Libraries," *Philadelphia Tribune*, August 25, 1962; Martin Luther King Jr., "The Solid Wall Cracks," *New York Amsterdam News*, April 13, 1963.

23. Mable Haden Todd, "Negro Reading Matter," *WP*, April 23, 1946; Liz Gant, "'That One's Me!'—New Books for Black Children That Mirror Their World," *Redbook Magazine* 139 (1972): 52–57.

24. Walter Dean Myers, *Bad Boy: A Memoir* (New York: HarperCollins, 2001), pp. 51–52; Marilyn Johnson and Dana Fineman, "Oprah Winfrey: A Life in Books," *Life* 9 (1997): 44; James Baldwin, *Go Tell It on the Mountain* (New York: Doubleday, 1953), p. 41.

25. Winifred Gambrill, "Annual Report, January 1947–June, 1948"; "Annual Report, 1949–50," both in Fort Washington Branch Library Records, Box 3, NYPL Branch Archives.

26. "Librarians, Fed Up with Role of Quiz Kids, Ban Phone Calls Inspired by Radio Queries," *NYT*, September 28, 1946; "Libraries Post Answers to Radio Quiz Programs," *NYT*, September 30, 1946; McCandlish Phillips, "About New York," *NYT*, September 28, 1956; Leonard B. Felkey, *Books along the Wildcat: History of the Kokomo-Howard Co. Public Library* (Kokomo, IN: Library, 1990), p. 201; Miriam Braverman, *Youth, Society, and the Public Library* (Chicago: American Library Association, 1978), p. 161; "Annual Report, Cathedral Branch Library, 1958–1959," Box 1; "Annual Report, 1960–1961, 96th Street Branch," Box 10, NYPL Branch Archives.

27. "Six Jailed, Fined for Keeping Library Books," *LAT*, February 9, 1961.
28. "Overdue Library Books Stream in Wake of Arrests," *CT*, February 11, 1961; "Borrowers Swamp Militant Librarian with 'Lost' Books," *NYT*, February 11, 1961; "Library in East Orange Cuts Delinquencies to 7," *NYT*, February 18, 1961; "Overdue Books Elude Collector for Library," *NYT*, July 18, 1961; "L.I. Library to Take Delinquents to Court," *NYT*, July 26, 1961; "Subpoenas Bring In L.I. Library's Books," *NYT*, October 14, 1962; "Booked for Bookkeeping," *CSM*, February 11, 1961; "5000 Books Flood Library, All Late," *WP*, February 16, 1961.
29. Edith Foster, *Yonder She Comes! A Once Told Li'bry Tale* (Bremen, GA: Gateway, 1985), p. 201; "Annual Report, 1951–1952," Fort Washington Branch Library, Box 3; "Annual Reports, Bloomingdale Branch Library, 1963–1964," Box 1, NYPL Branch Archives.
30. AR (1947), Queens Public Library, p. 22; "Commercial Lending Library Adapted to Public Library Use in Winfield," *Kansas Library Bulletin* 19 (1950): 30.
31. Patricia W. Belding, *Where the Books Are: The History and Architecture of Vermont's Public Libraries with Photos and Anecdotes* (Barre, VT: Potash Brook, 1996), p. 24; Quentin R. Howard, "We Now Have a Library!" *CSM*, November 13, 1956.
32. "Librarians Please Note!" *CSM*, March 17, 1955; David R. Francis, "Radio Due to Swap Library 'Books,'" *CSM*, October 20, 1960; "Library Photo Service," *NYT*, February 18, 1955; "Library to Supply Copying Service," *LAT*, February 7, 1961.
33. Foster, *Yonder She Comes! A Once Told Li'bry Tale*, pp. 64, 194, 197.
34. Edward G. Holley, *The Library Services and Construction Act* (Greenwich, CT: JAI Press, 1983), p. 18; John G. Lorenz, "Library Services Act—the First Three Years," *ALA Bulletin* 55 (1960): 18; "U.S. Library Act Called a Success," *NYT*, November 16, 1958.
35. Ellen Braby and Janet Hunt, *The Santa Monica Public Library, 1890–1900* (Santa Monica, CA: Santa Monica Public Library, 1990), p. 30; Sheila John Daly, "Library Goes Modern: It Has Teen-Age Room," *CT*, March 17, 1949.
36. Seward Park Branch Records, Box 1, NYPL Branch Archives; Michael V. Hazel, *The Dallas Public Library: Celebrating a Century of Service, 1901–2001* (Denton: University of North Texas Press, 2001), pp. 116–117; "Youth Gang Transformed to Public-Spirited Group," *New York Amsterdam News*, May 28, 1949.
37. Fred M. Hechinger, "No Place to Read," *NYT*, April 21, 1963; Ed Ainsworth, "Teachers Assist in Public Library," *LAT*, March 22, 1962; "'Youth Library' Opens," *NYT*, October 15, 1949.
38. "Youths Cite Urgent Need of Libraries," *WP*, March 6, 1961; "County Juveniles Plague Library before Bombing," *WP*, June 11, 1954; "Vandalism Hits a Library," *NYT*, August 1, 1957; Braverman, *Youth, Society, and the Public Library*, p. 187.
39. Bill Moyers, "Foreword," in Robert Dawson, *The Public Library: A Photographic Essay* (New York: Princeton Architectural Press, 2014), p. 6; Nancy Pearl, *Book Lust: Recommended Reading for Every Mood, Moment, and Reason* (Seattle: Sasquatch Books, 2003), pp. ix–x; Marcia Del Mar, *A Cuban Story* (Winston-Salem, NC: John F. Blair, 1979), pp. 106–107.
40. Gail Pool, "Gay Literature Has Carved a Niche for Itself," *San Diego Union*, December 15, 1991; Cal Gough and Ellen Greenblatt, "Services to Gay and Lesbian Patrons: Examining the Myths," *LJ* 117 (1992): 59; Jean Latz Griffin, "Library a Source of Pride to Gays," *CT*, April 17, 1991.
41. Ralph Munn, "The Library of the Future," *Carnegie Magazine* 24 (1950): 186–189; AR (1949), Carnegie Library of Pittsburgh, p. 7; Bernard Berelson, *The Library's Public* (New York: Columbia University Press, 1949), pp. 64–65, 68, 83, 86.
42. Christine Pawley, *Reading Places: Literacy, Democracy, and the Public Library in Cold War America* (Amherst: University of Massachusetts Press, 2010), pp. 28, 177, 202–203, 244, 251, 278.
43. Margaret C. Scoggin, "Teenager and Librarian: A Meeting Place," *NYT*, November 16, 1947; Mark Taylor, "Young Should Be Free to Choose Reading," *LAT*, November 10, 1963; "Informal & Annual Reports, Children's Room, 1956–1957," Box 4, Fort Washington Branch Records, NYPL Branch Archives.
44. Sonia Sotomayor, *My Beloved World* (New York: Alfred A. Knopf, 2013), p. 47; Sotomayor to author, March 25, 2013.

45. Carol Tilley, "Seducing the Innocent: Fredric Wertham and the Falsifications That Helped Condemn Comics," *Information & Culture* 47 (2012): 387; "Comic Books Cost U.S. More Than Textbooks," *WP*, March 2, 1955; "Chicago Girds for Attack on Comics," *CSM*, October 22, 1948; AR (1951), Public Library of Charlotte and Mecklenburg County (NC), p. 9; "Move against Comics," *LAT*, September 7, 1954.

46. Margaret C. Scoggin, "Teen-Ager and Librarian: A Meeting Place," *NYT*, November 16, 1947; Nadine Rosenthal, *Speaking of Reading* (Portsmouth, NH: Heinemann, 1995), pp. 52–54, 179–180.

47. *The Racine Public Library after 10 Years, 1958–1968* (Racine, WI: Racine Public Library, 1968), pp. 2–5; Ridgely Hunt, "The Library Is for the People," *CT*, July 14, 1963.

48. AR (1957), Brooklyn Public Library, n.p.; AR (1958), Brooklyn Public Library, n.p.; "Annual Report, 1958–59, Hamilton Grange Branch"; "Annual Report 1959–60, Hamilton Grange Branch," both in Box 8, NYPL Branch Archives.

49. *Cedar Rapids Public Library: The First Hundred Years* (Cedar Rapids, IA: Cedar Rapids Library Foundation, 1996), p. 46; "Shut-ins Will Get Books," *NYT*, February 8, 1953; "Pupils Shun Movies and Gum to Build Fitchburg Library," *CSM*, July 9, 1947.

50. Lon Dickerson and Patricia Gloyd, "Money Matters: How Community Spirit—and Dollars—Are Saving Savannah's Carnegies," *American Libraries* 30 (1999): 30–31; Transcript, Oral History Interview with Annie Watters McPheeters, Collection No. aarlohe 92-001, Auburn Avenue Research Library on African American Culture, Atlanta, GA, pp. 57–58.

51. Frank Conroy, *Stop-Time* (New York: Viking Press, 1965), pp. 145–146; John Howard, "The Library, the Park, and the Pervert: Public Space and Homosexual Encounter in Post–World War II Atlanta," *Radical History Review* 62 (1995): 171, 172.

52. Lela Cole Kitson, "Library Story Hours Unite Children of Many Backgrounds," *CSM*, November 13, 1948; Jodi S. Cohen, "For Readers, This Is Heaven," *CT*, August 2, 1998.

53. "Library Concerts," *CT*, January 2, 1949; "Library Begins 10th Series of Free Lectures," *CT*, October 2, 1949; "Library Noon Hour," *CSM*, January 8, 1949; AR (1951), Brooklyn Public Library, n.p.; "Own Library Room Delights Oldsters," *NYT*, January 12, 1953.

54. Edward G. Doyle, *A Commemorative History of the Cambridge Public Library* (Cambridge, MA: Cambridge Public Library, 1989), pp. 55–56; "Annual Report, 1945, Hamilton Fish Branch"; "Annual Report, 1946, Hamilton Fish Branch," both in Box 7; Seward Park Reports, Box 1; "Annual Report, 1956–1957, Mott Haven Branch," Box 9, NYPL Branch Archives.

55. Judy Yung, "History of the Chinatown Branch Library," June 11, 2011, copy in possession of author; Ben Fong-Torres, "An Escape into America," in Timothy Jacobson, *Knowledge for Generations: Wiley and the Global Publishing Industry, 1807–2007* (Hoboken, NJ: John Wiley, 2007), p. 187; Floyd Salas, "Cathedral," in *Knowledge for Generations*, p. 114.

56. Kathleen R. Hodges (ed.), *A Light in the Window of Idaho: Boise's Public Library, 1895–1995* (Boise, ID: Friends of the Boise Public Library, 1995), pp. 94–95.

57. Larry Grove, *Dallas Public Library: The First 75 Years* (Dallas: Dallas Public Library, 1977), pp. 76–81.

58. Hazel, *The Dallas Public Library*, p. 108.

59. "Annual Report, 1951–1952," Box 3, Fort Washington Branch Library, NYPL Branch Archives; AR (1953), Brookline (MA) Public Library, p. 77; "Library Offers Play-Off," *NYT*, October 3, 1951.

60. AR (1951), Queens Borough Public Library, p. 27; AR (1951), Erie (PA) Public Library, p. 1; "TV Fails to Stint Reading of Nation," *NYT*, June 28, 1951.

61. "Interview of Baker, Augusta, 1911–1988," May 7, 1989, in *Speaking of History: The Words of South Carolina Librarians*, http://asp6new.alexanderstreet.com/orhi/orhi.result.words.asap?word=public+library&narrator=age&birth.; John Fleischman, *Free & Public: One Hundred and Fifty Years of the Public Library of Cincinnati and Hamilton County, 1853–2003* (Cincinnati: Orange Frazer Press, 2003), pp. 77, 107.

62. AR (1951), Erie (PA) Public Library, p. 9; "Bay Display of Ex-GI Art Wins Praise," *LAT*, June 24, 1951; Edith Weigle, "Ever Go to a Library to Browse Thru an Art Show?" *CT*, August 11, 1957; "Paintings by Alcoholics Exhibited at Library," *WP*, February 12, 1953.

63. "Grammar Students Paint Mural as Gratitude Gift to Library," *LAT*, October 23, 1949.
64. Ronald F. Sigler, "A Rationale for the Film as a Public Library Resource and Service," *Library Trends* 27 (1978): 16–17; Dorothy Reed, "Public Library Lends Movies," *CSM*, April 16, 1949; AR (1951), Brooklyn Public Library, n.p.
65. Douglas A. Galbi, "Book Circulation per U.S. Public Library User since 1856," *Public Library Quarterly* 27 (2008): 3.
66. "Pro-Soviet Books Ripped," *NYT*, June 2, 1946; AR (1947), Brooklyn Public Library, p. 13; e-mail, Dennis Moore to author, January 27, 2010.

CHAPTER EIGHT

1. Douglas A. Galbi, "Book Circulation per U.S. Public Library User since 1856," *Public Library Quarterly* 27 (2008): 356.
2. J. R. Licklider, *Libraries of the Future* (Cambridge, MA: MIT Press, 1965); Alvin Toffler, *Future Shock* (New York: Bantam Books, 1970); Alvin Toffler, *The Third Wave* (New York: Morrow, 1980); Daniel Bell, *Coming of Post-Industrial Society* (New York: Basic Books, 1973); Ursula Vils, "Computers Come to Libraries," *LAT*, July 17, 1980.
3. Mary Breasted, "Brooklyn Libraries Will Set Up Information Centers," *NYT*, May 21, 1974; "New Information Center to Keep Brooklyn in Touch," *New York Amsterdam News*, November 27, 1976; Mary Knoblauch, "Clara Jones Fights for Libraries' Vital Role," *CT*, July 19, 1976.
4. "Annual Report, 1976/77," Box 2, Dongan Hills Branch Library, NYPL Branch Archives; Helen Mochedlover, Letter to the Editor, *LAT*, July 27, 1980; Richard J. Cattani, "TV Not Pre-empting Books," *CSM*, October 23, 1978.
5. Lucia Mouat, "Libraries Gain in Crime Fight," *CSM*, April 19, 1966; Bob Cromie, "Bugging the Books Cuts Library Thefts," *CT*, January 26, 1972.
6. Edward Hawley, "Librarians Relate Woes of Dealing with Students," *CT*, September 20, 1964; "Annual Report, 1973/74," Donnell Learning Center, Box 3, NYPL Branch Archives; Barbara Isenberg, "Library Gumshoes Relentlessly Pursue Their Overdue Prey," *LAT*, September 28, 1970.
7. Dawne Slater-Putt, *Beyond Books: Allen County's Public Library History, 1895-1995* (Fort Wayne, IN: Allen County Public Library, 1995), p. 126; Patricia Krizmis, "Bare Toes Are Taboo in Chicago Library," *CT*, August 23, 1969; Lael Morgan, "Astrology to Zen at Laguna: Library Mirrors Novel Community," *LAT*, March 24, 1970.
8. Eleanor T. Smith, "In the Library There's Now a Place for Paperbacks," *NYT*, January 5, 1964; Mark Taylor, "Teen-Agers Increase Paperback Market," *LAT*, September 19, 1965; "Author Infuriated over Library Book Renting," *LAT*, October 11, 1964.
9. Alan L. Gansberg, "Library Restricting Students," *NYT*, January 21, 1979.
10. "Annual Report, 1968–69, Hunt's Point Branch," Box 8; 1970 Annual Report, Seward Park Branch Records, Box 1, NYPL Branch Archives.
11. Gloria F. Teel, Letter to the Editor, *LAT*, March 13, 1964; Ramon Geremia, "Libraries Ponder Automation," *WP*, April 4, 1965; Margaret A. Edwards, *The Fair Garden and the Swarm of Beasts: The Library and the Young Adult* (Chicago: American Library Association, 2002), p. 81; Miriam Braverman, *Youth, Society, and the Public Library* (Chicago: American Library Association, 1978), pp. 1–2.
12. Art Seidenbaum, "The Loudest Library in Voluminous Los Angeles," *LAT*, May 13, 1968.
13. Patricia Krizmis, "Traveling Van Brings Library to W. Side Kids," *CT*, July 2, 1968; AR (1972), SFPL, pp. 9–10; AR (1974), pp. 7–8.
14. Marjie Driscoll, "Books Put on Wheels to Reach Minorities," *LAT*, January 24, 1973.
15. Ellie Baublitz, "Founder of Nursing Home Bookmobile Still Volunteers," [Baltimore] *Sun*, April 14, 1991; Judy Roepka, "Pied Pipers of SCKLIS Captivate Small Towns," *Kansas Library Bulletin* 40 (1972): 15–17; Shirley Schuette and Nathania K. Sawyer, *From Carnegie to Cyberspace: 100 Years at the Central Arkansas Library System* (Little Rock, AR: Butler Center

Books, 2010), p. 68; Edward G. Doyle, *A Commemorative History of the Cambridge Public Library* (Cambridge, MA: Cambridge Public Library, 1989), pp. 55–56.

16. AR (1969), SFPL, pp. 3–4.
17. Deborah Cipolla, "Books Only a Part of Library Services," *LAT*, March 15, 1977; Keith Takahashi, "Reading Treated as a Survival Skill," *LAT*, November 9, 1978.
18. Carolyn F. Ruffin, "The Not-So-Silent Inner-City Branch Library," *CSM*, September 4, 1968; "Outreach in the Inner City Makes Library 'For Real,'" *CSM*, September 6, 1968.
19. Ursula Vils, "Making a Joyful Noise in the Library," *LAT*, January 24, 1973; "Annual Report, 1980," Box 3, Fort Washington Branch Records, NYPL Branch Archives.
20. Richard Vasquez, "Libraries Lure Barrio Youth," *LAT*, May 11, 1970; "Quiet Is Not for Libraries," *LAT*, May 15, 1970; Richard Vasquez, "Libraries Seek to Lure Youths from Barrio," *LAT*, May 17, 1970; Ursula Vils, "Librarian's Chores Branching Out," *LAT*, December 30, 1971.
21. Annual Report (1969), Douglass Branch, CPL Archives.
22. Annual Report (1970); (1972), Douglass Branch, CPL Archives; "Board Renames Library Branch for Abolitionist," *CT*, August 30, 1970; "Libraries Are Better in White Areas: Study," *CT*, August 7, 1978.
23. Jean R. Hailey, "Library, UPO Both War on Poverty, but Can't Get Together on Joint Plans," *WP*, February 14, 1966; Jean R. Hailey, "Library Reaches Into Ghetto," *WP*, March 11, 1971.
24. Richard H. Parke, "Old Supermarket in New Haven Now a Library Culture Center," *NYT*, September 13, 1964; Elise Miller, "Hmong Tribeswomen Strive to Keep Embroidery Art Alive," *LAT*, June 9, 1980.
25. Barbara Campbell, "Mural Depicting Birth of a Library Returned Home," *NYT*, March 21, 1971; Jeffrey A. Kroessler, *Lighting the Way: The Centennial History of the Queens Borough Public Library, 1896-1996* (Virginia Beach, VA: The Donning Company Publishers, 1996), pp. 40–41.
26. Gerald Faris, "Dream Is Near for Chinatown," *LAT*, October 3, 1982; Keith Love, "Chinatown Library Speaks Volumes," *LAT*, April 19, 1983; Bob Williams, "Language Becomes Less of a Barrier as Collections Grow; Libraries Expanding Services to Asians," *LAT*, September 14, 1986.
27. Robert P. Haro, "One-Man Survey: How Mexican-Americans View Libraries," *Wilson Library Bulletin* 44 (1970): 736–742; Robert P. Haro, *Developing Library and Information Services for Americans of Hispanic Origin* (Metuchen, NJ: Scarecrow Press, 1981), pp. 93–96.
28. David S. Richwine, "11 Queens Libraries Kept Open by Protests," *NYT*, November 2, 1975; "NAACP Files Class Suit against Queens Library," *New York Amsterdam News*, November 26, 1975; "Suit against Library Gains Support," *New York Amsterdam News*, December 3, 1975.
29. Stephen K. Ward, *Women and Wine: The Making of the Vermillion Public Library in a Man's World, 1903–2003* (Vermillion, SD: Vermillion Public Library, 2004), pp. 58–59.
30. "Women, Steelworkers to Initiate Contract Fight," *New Pittsburgh Courier*, December 1, 1979; Ulish Carter, "Film on Rape to Be Shown," *LAT*, July 4, 1976; "'Rape in the Suburbs' Is Topic of Friday Library Seminar," *LAT*, January 10, 1980.
31. Lawrence M. Geller, "Photographer Mounts 'Soulville' Exhibit in Columbia Ave. Library," *Philadelphia Tribune*, May 17, 1969; AR (1973), Denver Public Library, n.p.
32. Judy Yung, "History of the Chinatown Branch Library," June 11, 2011, copy in possession of author; AR (1970), SFPL, p. 4.
33. "White Citizens Council; Battle of Clinton," *Pittsburgh Courier*, September 25, 1965; "Discrimination Charges Lodged against Library," [Cleveland] *Call and Post*, February 22, 1969; "Negro History Week Observed at Library," *Atlanta Daily World*, January 30, 1970.
34. Ronald F. Sigler, "A Rationale for the Film as a Public Library Resource and Service," *Library Trends* 27 (1978): 23; Laurie Johnston, "For L.I. Libraries More Than Just Books," *NYT*, May 14, 1972.
35. Mildred Jailer, "Libraries Are Shelving Their Musty Past," *NYT*, May 7, 1978; "Annual Report, 1972/73," Box 3, Donnell Learning Center Branch Library Reports, NYPL Branch Archives.
36. Irene Powers, "Library Goes Pop," *CT*, August 19, 1969; Lisa Bornstein, "Jacksonland, Ind.," *Philadelphia Tribune*, May 1, 1994; Kathleen W. Craver, "Social Trends in American Young Adult Library Service, 1960-1969," *Journal of Library History* 23 (Winter, 1988): 30; Roy J. Harris Jr.,

"L.A. Public Library Changing Image to Attract Teen-agers," *LAT*, August 5, 1968; Junivee Black, "Animals Liven Reading Program," *Kansas Library Bulletin* 40 (1970): 28–29.

37. "Library Throws Out Art as 'Suggestive,'" *CT*, December 7, 1965.

38. Lee Austin, "Politics Ruled Out at Burbank Library," *LAT*, April 5, 1964; Walt Secor, "ACLU Chapter to Test Library Rules Change," *LAT*, May 23, 1965; Walt Secor, "ACLU Denied Use of Library for Meetings," *LAT*, June 8, 1965; "ACLU Not Alone in Denial, Librarian Says," *LAT*, June 13, 1965; "One Group Granted Use of Library," *LAT*, June 17, 1965; "Burbank City Attorney Backs Library Meeting Restrictions," *LAT*, July 13, 1965; "Library Chief to Aid Decent Literature Unit," *LAT*, June 28, 1965; Walt Secor, "Burbank Drops Ban on Political, Religious Meetings in City Parks," *LAT*, October 10, 1967.

39. "Calls for Banning of Library Books Rise Sharply since Reagan Victory," *NYT*, December 11, 1980; Russell Shank, "The Greenback Curtain Is Threatening America's Libraries," *CSM*, August 21, 1978; Russell Shank, Letter to the Editor, *LAT*, October 14, 1978.

40. Judith Serebnik, "Book Reviews and the Selection of Potentially Controversial Books in Public Libraries," *Library Quarterly* 51 (1981): 390–409; "Pornography Flops in Public Libraries," *LAT*, January 10, 1971; Ed Fishbein, "Schools, Libraries Still Pressed to Censor Material," *LAT*, January 8, 1973.

41. Richard Whittingham, "Libraries Face the Vigilantes," *CT*, September 10, 1973; Daniel Egler, "No Book-Banning in Libraries Here," *CT*, February 21, 1974.

42. "Censorship Can Use Four-Letter Weapons," *LAT*, November 14, 1965; Ed Fishbein, "Schools, Libraries Still Pressed to Censor Material," *LAT*, January 8, 1973; Herman Wong, "The Library: Image Takes on 'Now' Look," *LAT*, July 18, 1971; Braverman, *Youth, Society and the Public Library*, p. 191.

43. "Kathryn Prestidge, "One of Those Not So Hideous Stories of a Book Challenge," in Valerie Nye and Kathy Barco (eds.), *True Stories of Censorship Battles* (Chicago: American Library Association, 2012), p. 129; "Publisher Retaliates for Book Banning," *LJ* 92 (1967): 2103; Peter Khiss, "A Library in Iowa Bans Kazan Book," *Newsletter on Intellectual Freedom* 16 (1967): 51.

44. "ACLU Wants Library to Restore Gays' Paper," *WP*, September 21, 1980; "Vote Ousts Gay Paper in Va. Beach Library," *WP*, November 6, 1980; Robert D. Putnam, *Bowling Alone: The Collapse and Revival of American Community* (New York: Simon & Schuster, 2000), p. 352; "Police Crack Down on Gays at Boston Public Library," *LJ* 103 (1978): 1012.

45. Mike Ward, "Centerfolds Don't Last on Library Shelf," *LAT*, July 11, 1976; David Berke, Letter to the Editor, *LAT*, March 30, 1964.

46. "Montgomery Library Bars Mailer's Viet Book," *WP*, October 25, 1967; "Libraries Call Book by Mailer 'Worthless,'" *WP*, October 30, 1967.

47. Walter H. Waggoner, "Sex Controversy Upsets 'Old-Fashioned' Clifton," *NYT*, November 27, 1970; Walter Wells, "A Tale of Censure and 'Censorship' Weaves a Tangled Course at Clifton Library," *NYT*, May 13, 1973.

48. Nancy Larrick, "The All-White World of Children's Books," *Saturday Review* 48 (September 11, 1965): 63–65+.

49. Liz Gant, "'That One's Me!'—New Books for Black Children That Mirror Their World," *Redbook Magazine* 139 (1972): 52–57.

50. Brian Melley, "Character That Demeans Blacks Is Back," *Philadelphia Tribune*, December 27, 1996; Joan Zyda, "Only One Book Banned Here," *CT*, January 13, 1976; "Refuse Purge," *Pittsburgh Courier*, December 18, 1965.

51. Marion Meade, "Miss Muffett Must Go," *Woman's Day* 34 (1971): 64–65; Linda Greenburg, "Sexism Found in Preschool Books," *CSM*, July 10, 1974; Barbara Burtof, "The Hidden Bias in Children's Books," *Boston Globe*, January 19, 1980.

52. Theodore G. Striphas, *The Late Age of Print: Everyday Book Culture from Consumerism to Control* (New York: Columbia University Press, 2009), p. 138; Alice McAllister, "Library Fights Sex-Stereotyping in Kids' Books," *CSM*, January 22, 1975; Sue Avery, "Sharks Outpull Nonsexist Reading," *LAT*, September 4, 1975.

53. James P. Murray, "Publishers Have a Few Good Words . . .,"*New York Amsterdam News*, March 1, 1975; Philip Hager, "'Mary Poppins' Banned in S.F.," *LAT*, October 7, 1980; Bradford Chambers, "'Banning' Books to Save Our Children: Is It Censorship to Act against Racial and Sex Bias?" *LAT*, October 24, 1980.

54. Braverman, *Youth, Society, and the Public Library*, p. 245; Sue Avery, "Libraries Admit It: Sex Exists," *LAT*, June 29, 1972; Henry Raymont, "Fig Leafs for Children Irk Librarians," *NYT*, June 27, 1972.

55. Slater-Putt, *Beyond Books*, p. 235; Carol Oppenheim, "Black Parents Ask New Trier East to Expel Huck Finn," *CT*, May 16, 1976; Patricia Brumback, Letter to the Editor, *CT*, June 2, 1976.

56. Myra MacPherson, "Who's Afraid of the Big Bad Books?" *WP*, February 11, 1973; Jack Nelson, "Controversial Books: The Banners and the Banned," *LAT*, March 4, 1973.

57. "X-rated Reading in Small-Town Indiana," *CT*, September 21, 1980; "Annual Report, 1979–1980," Box 3, Fort Washington Branch Library, NYPL Branch Archives.

58. Kris Wendt, "Reading between the Lines," *Rhinelander* [WI] *Daily News*, June 1, 2003.

59. Roger B. May, "Nancy Drew and Kin Still Surmount Scrapes—and Critics' Slurs," *Wall Street Journal*, January 15, 1975; David L. Reich, Letter to the Editor, *CT*, September 21, 1976.

60. Victoria A. Brownworth, "The Art of Reading: Do You Know Where Your Books Are?" *Lambda Rising Book Report* 2 (1990): 12.

61. Lena Williams, "American Libraries: A World Far beyond Books," *NYT*, August 21, 1988; "Diffusions of Knowledge," *Wall Street Journal*, January 14, 1980.

62. John J. Ryan, "With a Little Luck, You May Even Find Books in the Library," *Wall Street Journal*, May 7, 1975; "New Libraries: Lots More Than Just Books," *U.S. News & World Report* 88 (1980): 68.

63. Philip Roth, "Reflections on the Death of a Library," *NYT*, March 1, 1969; Ellen Hoffman, "Library 'Silence' Signs Can't Quiet City Clamor," *WP*, August 24,1969.

64. Seward Park Branch Records, Box 1, NYPL Branch Archives.

CHAPTER NINE

1. Henry Weiss, *At Sunrise: The History of the Palm Springs Public Library* (Palm Springs, CA: Palm Springs Public Library, 1999), p. 104.

2. "Rapid Rise Found in Use of Public Libraries," *NYT*, July 31, 1983; Nate Hobbs, "Book Smart," [Memphis] *Commercial Appeal*, December 6, 1996; Don Singleton, "This Favorite Branch Could Get Cut Down," *New York Daily News*, May 7, 1991.

3. Colman McCarthy, "A Citizen's Right to Know, and His Right to a Library," *WP*, August 1, 1982; "Small Town Jail Puts 'Booking' in a Different Light," *CT*, September 2, 1985.

4. Herbert Muschamp, "Room for Imagination in a Temple of Reason," *NYT*, May 12, 1996; Robert Hass, "A Poet Visits the New Main Library," *San Francisco Examiner*, April 14, 1996; Judy Yung, "History of the Chinatown Branch Library," June 11, 2011, copy in possession of author.

5. Betinna Boxall, "Library Can Provide a Moving Experience for Bookish Drivers," *LAT*, December 1, 1991.

6. Danny Heitman, "Read to Succeed: Library Program Gathers Families around Books," [Baton Rouge, LA] *Advocate*, November 6, 1996.

7. Jeff Burbank, "Librarian's Weekly Cable TV Show Is One for the Books in 20 States," *LAT*, September 7, 1986; Dan Rodricks, "Cabbie 'Reads' Classics behind the Wheel," [Baltimore] *Sun*, February 10, 1997; "Books, Videos, and Libraries," *Richmond* [VA] *Times-Dispatch*, January 8, 1990.

8. Doug Brown, "How Far Should Libraries Go to Balance the Books?" *LAT*, August 4, 1982; Patricia Tennison, "Thanks to the Library, Fire Protection Can Follow 'Em Anywhere," *CT*, October 6, 1982; "Rockingham Libraries Have Rolling Walkers for Patrons," [Greensboro,

NC] *News Record*, November 26, 1993; "Magnifiers Offered for Library Patrons," *Hartford Courant*, November 17, 1999.

9. Richard Higgins, "Word for Librarians—Longanimity: Patiently Spend Time Cracking Obscure Conundrums," *LAT*, December 17, 1982; Tatanya Eckstrand (comp.), *The Librarian's Book of Quotes* (Chicago: American Library Association, 2009), p. 19.

10. Julia McCord, "Final Pages Turned for Kellom Library," *Omaha World-Herald*, February 17, 1991; Rafael Alvarez, "A Day in the Life of a Neighborhood Library Branch; Patrons Fear Loss of Gardenville Site," [Baltimore] *Sun*, May 3, 1993.

11. Jacquin Sanders, "Library Has Nook or Cranny for Everyone," *St. Petersburg* [FL] *Times*, August 25, 1988; Elijah Gosier, "'It'll Be Terrible' if Library Closes," *St. Petersburg* [FL] *Times*, April 15, 1990.

12. Isabel Wilkerson, "Black Neighborhood Faces White World With Bitterness," *NYT*, June 22, 1992.

13. Sheri Johnson, "Budget May Spell End to Bookmobile," [San Diego] *Tribune* June 28, 1989.

14. Elaine Hardy, "A Timeline of Important Events in George Public Library History," *Georgia Library Quarterly* 45 (Summer, 2008): 16; Mike Madden, "Bread, Bananas, Biographies: Supermarket Library Puts Books Where People Gather," *USA Today*, June 5, 1996; Anne Davis, "The Bookmobile Still Rolls On," *Milwaukee Journal Sentinel*, July 19, 1995; "Santa Ana Library Will Open a Hispanic Bookmobile," *LAT*, November 21, 1987; Jean Hopfensperger, "Asian Students Swarm St. Paul Libraries," [Minneapolis] *Star Tribune*, February 1, 1989.

15. Melinda Burns, "20 Latinos Pursue Their Family Roots in Genealogy Class," *LAT*, February 2, 1984; Jane Clifford, "Oceanside Library Branches Out into Parenting Center," *San Diego Union*, April 12, 1990.

16. F. Wilfrid Lancaster, *Toward Paperless Information Systems* (New York: Academic Press, 1978); Robert S. Taylor, "Reminiscing about the Future: Professional Education and the Information Environment," *LJ* 104 (1979): 1871–1875; Michael K. Buckland, "Library Education—Meeting the Needs of the Future," *Catholic Library World* 50 (1979): 424–426; Talat S. Halman, "From Babylon to Cyberspace," *American Libraries* 26 (1995): 895; Richard Louv, "High-Tech Libraries Will Rise amid Crumbling Books," *San Diego Union*, January 11, 1987.

17. Carolyn Moreau, "Library Book Clubs: Just Don't Be Quiet," *Hartford Courant*, May 5, 1996; Theodore G. Striphas, *The Late Age of Print: Everyday Book Culture from Consumerism to Control* (New York: Columbia University Press, 2009), p. 113.

18. Blue Ribbon Committee. Baltimore County Public Library, *Give 'Em What They Want!* (Chicago: American Library Association, 1992), pp. 5–6.

19. "Written Romance in the Stacks," *NYT*, March 30, 1983.

20. Jim Spencer, "The Color of Passion Is Mostly White," *CT*, October 27, 1983; John Keenan, "Fans Defend Romances," *Omaha World-Herald*, November 4, 1996.

21. Nancy Bearden Henderson, "Publishers Need More Romance—Novels, That Is," *CT*, June 16, 1998.

22. Lillian Gerhardt, "Taking Trash Lightly," *School Library Journal* 28 (1982): 5; Betsy Hearne, "Children's Books: Bad Children's Books Drive Out Good," *NYT*, February 3, 1985; "Hardy Boys: Racist, Sexist?" *Philadelphia Tribune*, June 7, 1991.

23. Thea Bosselmann, "Letter to the Editor," *San Francisco Chronicle*, May 6, 1996; "Library Snubs Nancy Drew," *San Francisco Chronicle*, May 7, 1996; Ruth Sherman, *"Nancy Drew's* Library Comeback: Hard Questions in Hard Times for Our Free Public Libraries," *San Francisco Examiner*, June 12, 1996.

24. Karen Macherson, "Series Books Keep Kids Turning the Pages: It's an Old Formula That Works Today," *Seattle Post-Intelligencer*, August 22, 1996; Reyna Grande, *The Distance between Us* (New York: Atria Books, 2012), p. 241; Matea Gold, "Fearless Heroines," *LAT*, February 18, 1997.

25. William F. Birdsall, *The Myth of the Electronic Library* (Westport, CT: Greenwood Press, 1994); Kenneth E. Dowlin and Eleanor Shapiro, "The Centrality of Communities to the Future of

Major Pubic Libraries," *Daedalus* 125 (1996): 173–190; Mary Curtis, "Libraries Write New Chapter," *LAT,* February 1, 1997.

26. Annual Reports, 125th Street Branch Reports, Box 1, NYPL Branch Archives.
27. Janine Sieja, "Libraries Explore New Ways to Serve Ethnic Diversity," [Fort Lauderdale] *Sun Sentinel,* May 21, 1990; Arvind Kumar, "Unsung Wonder," [San Jose, CA] *India Currents* 6 (April 30, 1992): 6; Lourdes Medrano Leslie, "Common Thread," [Minneapolis] *Star Tribune,* October 7, 1997.
28. Emily Wax, "Library Takes a Page from Real Life," *Newsday,* November 16, 1997; Blaine Harden, "America as a Brand New Book, Waiting to Be Cracked Open," *LAT,* May 3, 1998; Felix Lopez, "To the Editor," *NYT,* July 7, 1981.
29. Valeria Godines, "Hispanic Past Still Mostly Unseen," [Riverside, CA] *Press-Enterprise,* February 4, 1996; Valeria Godines, "History Records the Forgotten," [Riverside, CA] *Press-Enterprise,* March 16, 1997.
30. Kate Folmar, "Hidden Hues of History," *LAT,* June 28, 1999.
31. Xiwen Zhang, "The Anti-Affirmative Action Movement in California: Implications for Public Library Services to Asian Immigrants," in Susan Luevano-Molina (ed.), *Immigrant Politics and the Public Library* (Westport, CT: Greenwood Press, 2001), p. 115.
32. Carmen Valencia, "At Reservation Libraries, the Aim Is to Be Friendly," *San Diego Union,* May 19, 1990.
33. Nancy J. Levine, George V. Minton, Sandie A. Stratton, Sharon Cleland, and Belinda Delzell, "Florida Classroom: Tea Sets, Tractors, T-1 Lines: The Survival of a Small Town Library: The Hastings, Branch Library, Hastings, Florida," *Florida Historical Quarterly* 88 (2009): 259; Dale Russakoff, "Relations Changing Rapidly in Segregation's Old Citadel," *WP,* September 16, 1984.
34. Dawne Slater-Putt, *Beyond Books: Allen County's Public Library History, 1895-1995* (Fort Wayne, IN: Allen County Public Library, 1995), p. 128; Bobby Cuza and Ann L. Kim, "Reading: The ABC's of Helping Youngsters Achieve Literacy," *LAT,* October 24, 1999.
35. Michael Greenburg, "Can the Library Handle Success?" *San Antonio Express-News,* February 10, 1991; "Celebrating History Can Be an Economic Engine for the Region," *Pittsburgh Post-Gazette,* May 26, 1996.
36. Sue Corrales, "Reluctant Libraries Become Sites for Children on Summer Vacation," *LAT,* July 21, 1985; Bettina Boxall, "Many Happy Endings; Library 'Grandparents' Teach Children Joys of Reading," *LAT,* September 11, 1996; Stephanie Stassel, "People for Kids," *LAT,* March 12, 1993; Jocelyn Y. Stewart, "Libraries Shelve Old Image," *LAT,* May 12, 1997.
37. "Library Bans Unsupervised Tots," *Providence* [RI] *Journal,* January 26, 1988; Marla Williams, "Libraries That Have a Problem," [Fort Lauderdale] *Sun Sentinel,* February 23, 1988; "Annual Report, 1987," Box 3, Fort Washington Branch, NYPL Branch Archives; Chris Spolar, "D.C.'s Problems Spill in Libraries' Hushed Realm," *WP,* June 8, 1989; "Man Charged in Rape of Girl at Library," *NYT,* June 20, 1998.
38. "Library Sets Rules Barring Sleeping or Smelly Patrons," *WP,* November 22, 1984; "New Library Code Issue in Ann Arbor," *NYT,* December 2, 1984; Robert Hanley, "Libraries Can't Ban the Homeless, U.S. Court in Newark Rules," *NYT,* May 23, 1991; Stacey Freedenthal, "Dozens of Homeless Find Cool, Comfortable Haven at Downtown Library," *Houston Chronicle,* August 2, 1987; Kevin Anderson, "Sex Assault Has Library Looking to Add Security," [Peoria, IL] *Journal Star,* July 8, 1993.
39. "Abortion Rights Meeting Planned," [Bloomington, IL] *Pantagraph,* July 4, 1992; "Infertility Group Forms," [Bloomington, IL] *Pantagraph,* October 21, 1994; "Workshop on Love, Intimacy, and Sexual Health," *New York Amsterdam News,* March 7, 1992; "Amnesty Chapter to Hold Discussion," *Richmond* [VA] *Times-Dispatch,* May 25, 1991; Sandy Coleman, "Hill Controversy Spurs Formation of NOW Chapter," *Boston Globe,* December 1, 1991; Mary Gail Hare, "Abused Women Get 'Unity,'" [Baltimore] *Sun,* December 22, 1992; Mary Ann Castronovo Fusco, "For Battered Women," *NYT,* August 18, 1999; Anita Hardin, "Exhibit Spotlights Breast Cancer Stories," *Orlando Sentinel,* September 25, 1999.

40. "MADD to Meet in Santa Ana," *LAT*, May 5, 1983; "Anorexia Group Forming," [Bloomington, IL] *Pantagraph*, December 23, 1992; Risa Cherry, "Different Isn't Bad, 'Disabled' Puppets Teach Kids," *Newsday*, August 18, 1992.

41. Malinda Reinke, "American Constitution Replica Popular Item in Library at Delray," [Fort Lauderdale] *Sun Sentinel*, August 24, 1987; "Humanities Grant Supports Series about Vietnam War at Downey Library," *LAT*, September 23, 1990; Ted Johnson, "$10,000 Awarded for Arab Culture Series," *LAT*, August 15, 1991.

42. "WWII Series at Library to Focus on Japanese Internment," [St. Paul, MN] *Asian Pages*, 2 (1991): 14; "Japanese-Americans in Utah to Mark 'Day of Remembrance,'" *Salt Lake Tribune*, February 2, 1998; David Quigg, "'Day of Remembrance' Events Mark Internment of Japanese Americans," [Tacoma, WA] *News Tribune*, February 18, 1999.

43. Lourdes Rodriguez-Florido, "Art Connoisseur Brings Her Love to Libraries," [Fort Lauderdale] *Sun Sentinel*, April 3, 1986; Jane E. Dee, "Library Cultivates Local Talent with Exhibit of Floral Paintings," *Hartford Courant*, October 2, 1996; "Farmer Kept Painting on Back Burner," *Omaha World-Herald*, September 23, 1990; "Nude Statue Returns to Site of Its Banning," *Orlando Sentinel*, May 21, 1999.

44. David Tuller, "Gay, Lesbian Archive Planned for New Library," *San Francisco Chronicle*, October 4, 1993; Victoria A. Brownworth, "In Remembrance: Barbara Grier," http://www.lambdaliterary.org/features/rem/11/11/in-remembrance-barbara-grier/; David W. Dunlap, "Making a Home for Gay History and Awareness," *NYT*, March 13, 1996.

45. "Annual Reports, Columbia Branch, 1988," Box 1, NYPL Branch Archives; Myrna Oliver, "Public Awareness," *LAT*, April 17, 1989; "Libraries Given Books on AIDS, Gay Issues," *Omaha World Herald*, June 8, 1989.

46. "Books on Homosexuality Spark Dispute," *Omaha World Herald*, July 11, 1990.

47. Elliott Krieger, "Exhibit on Censorship Skirts the Real Issues," *Providence* [RI] *Journal*, March 24, 1985; Judy Laberge, Letter to the Editor, [Bloomington, IL] *Pentagraph*, October 3, 1990.

48. Dianne Klein, "Checking Out Provocative Books," *LAT*, August 25, 1991; "Secretive Censor Defacing Books," *CT*, May 22, 1994; "After Protest by Pastor, Interest in Gay Books at Library Grows," *NYT*, May 24, 1998.

49. "Fla. Man Took Playboys Religiously, Police Say," *Philadelphia Daily News*, August 30, 1984; Doreen Vigue, "Wellesley Library Drops Playboy," *Boston Globe*, June 9, 1996.

50. John Farina, "San Diego Library Keeps Controversy on Shelves," *San Diego Tribune*, August 31, 1990; Patricia Davis Szymczak, "Oak Lawn Censorship Tiff Is Back," *CT*, June 24, 1990; William Booker, "Letter to the Editor," *Seattle Times*, August 21, 1985; Anna Bennett, "Letter to the Editor," *Salt Lake Tribune*, June 21, 1992.

51. Peter Kendall, "Madonna's Book Makes Controversy Vogue at Libraries," *CT*, December 13, 1992; Warren Epstein, "Library to Mark Madonna Book: Return to Sender," *Colorado Springs Gazette-Telegraph*, October 23, 1992; Ronald W. Powell, "Library to Limit Use of Madonna's Nude Photo Book," *San Diego Union-Tribune*, November 14, 1992; Slater-Putt, *Beyond Books*, pp. 237–238.

52. Tony Saavedra, " Daddy's Roommate in Few OC Libraries," *Orange County* [CA] *Register*, September 25, 1992; Benjamin Kline, "Library Rejects Book Ban," *Dayton Daily News*, December 16, 1993; Len Penix, "150 Attend 5-Hour Meeting on Drive to Ban Gay Magazine," *Cincinnati Post*, February 14, 1995; Len Penix, "Library Plan Would Hide Magazine Covers," *Cincinnati Post*, March 14, 1995; Laurie Petrie, "Library Won't Ban Magazine," *Cincinnati Post*, April 11, 1995.

53. Dan Levy, "S. F. Library Board Oks Gay Flag," *San Francisco Chronicle*, October 7, 1992; Dan Levy, "Outrage at Potrero Library," *San Francisco Chronicle*, January 16, 1992; "S.F. Library Board Endorses New Policy on Public Meetings," *San Francisco Chronicle*, February 6, 1992; "Pedophile Group Rips Media 'Witch Hunt,'" *Las Vegas Review-Journal*, January 21, 1992; "Frisco Man-Boy Sex Group Blasted: Parents Want Organization Booted from Public Library," *San Antonio Express-News*, January 17, 1992; "Gay Writers to Finish a Series of Readings," *NYT*, June 1, 1990; Melissa L. Salus, "Gay Family Life Shown in Photo Show," [Fort Lauderdale] *Sun Sentinel*, June 28, 1998.

54. "Libraries Bar Gay-Pride Display," *Washington Times*, May 18, 1995; Laura Korach Howell, "Puzzled by Uproar over Library Window Display," [Lancaster, PA] *Intelligencer Journal*, December 24, 1996; Tom Knapp, "Library Board Member Resigns amid Controversy over Display," [Lancaster, PA] *Intelligencer Journal*, March 1, 1997.

55. Larry Barszewski, "County Library Chief Rejects Request for Nazi Publications," [Fort Lauderdale] *Sun Sentinel*, November 18, 1992; Cindy Horswell, " 'Bad Words' in Books Making Some Local Parents See Fiery Red," *Houston Chronicle*, December 21, 1986.

56. "Calls for Banning of Library Books Rise Sharply since Reagan Victory," *CT*, December 11, 1980; Blaine Harden, " 'Shocked' Va. Preacher Trying to Ban 'Hard-Core Porn' from Town's Library," *WP*, December 15, 1980; Shirley A. Wiegand, *Library Records: A Retention and Confidentiality Guide* (Westport, CT: Greenwood Press, 1994), p. 141.

57. Torri Minton, "Sonoma Parents Call for Sensitivity Training," *San Francisco Chronicle*, March 22, 1995; Bradford Chambers, " 'Banning' Books to Save Our Children: Is It Censorship to Act against Racial and Sex Bias?" *LAT*, October 24, 1980; "Letters to the Editor," *LAT*, November 6, 1980.

58. Edwin McDowell, "Publishing: When Book Is Ruled Out by Library," *NYT*, January 21, 1983; Barbara Brotman, "Librarians Hit 'Black Heaven' Book as Racist," *CT*, January 27, 1982.

59. Heidy Hartley, "Checking Out *Hustler* at the Library," *CT*, May 18, 1997; "Porn and a Public Library; The Issue," *Denver Rocky Mountain News*, November 18, 1998.

60. Meita Marie Garza, "Group Aims to Make Libraries 'Family-Friendly,' " *CT*, May 25, 1997; Katie Hafner, "Library Grapples with Internet Freedom," *NYT*, October 15, 1998; Claire Martin, "Library No Web of Sex," *Denver Post*, September 11, 2000; Gordon Dillow, "Thumbs Up on Library Porn Filters," *Orange County* [CA] *Register*, September 12, 2000.

61. Wendy Adamson, "Sex in the City: What Happened at the Minneapolis Public Library," *Off Our Backs* 32 (2002): 28–31.

62. http://safelibraries.blogspot.com/2012/08/SexuallyHarrassedLibrarianGets150K.html.

63. Don Sager, "In Retrospect: Public Library Service during the Past Fifty Years," *Public Libraries* 35 (1996): 167.

64. "Annual Report, 1988," Box 3, Fort Washington Branch, NYPL Branch Archives; Art Seidenbaum, "A Reading on the State of Our Libraries," *LAT*, June 26, 1983; Sheila McKenna, "A New Chapter in Volunteerism," *Newsday*, October 12, 1999.

CHAPTER TEN

1. Tatanya Eckstrand (comp.), *The Librarian's Book of Quotes* (Chicago: American Library Association, 2009), p. 59.

2. David Tyckoson, "Everyday Library History: An Overdue Book Tale," *LHRT Newsletter* 11 (2011): 3; *Library and Book Trade Almanac*, 56th ed. (New York: Information Today, 2001), pp. 404–405, 407–411.

3. Peter Callaghan, "Councilman's Plan to Cut City Libraries Is Far from Courageous," [Tacoma, WA] *News Tribune*, October 1, 2002.

4. David Morris, "All Hail the PUBLIC Library," http://www.onthecommons.org/all-hail-public-library; Robert D. Putnam and Lewis M. Feldstein, "Branch Libraries: The Heartbeat of the Community," in Robert D. Putnam and Lewis M. Feldstein (eds.), *Better Together: Restoring the American Community* (New York: Simon and Schuster, 2003), p. 35.

5. Morris, "All Hail the PUBLIC Library."

6. "Service Trends in US. Public Libraries, 1997–2007," Institute for Museum and Library Service, Research Brief No. 1, December, 2009, p. 1.

7. Carolyn Miller Kristen Percell and Lee Rainie, "Reading Habits in Different Communities," http://libraries.pewinternet.org/2012/12/20/reading-habits-in-different-communities.

8. "Library Services in the Digital Age," Pew Internet and American Life Project, January 22, 2013, http://libraries.pewinternet.org/2013/01/22/Library-services/.

9. E-mail, Stuart Hinds to author, May 15, 2013.

10. Rebecca Traister, "Michelle Obama Gets Real," http://www.salon.com/news/feature/2007/11/28/Michelle_obama/.

11. Annemarie Conte, "The Library Made Me Healthier," *Woman's Day* 72 (March, 2009): 48.

12. Melissa Anelli, *Harry, A History: A True Story of a Boy Wizard, His Fans, and Life inside the Harry Potter Phenomenon* (New York: Pocket Books, 2008), pp. 66, 92, 119, 121, 126; Henry Jenkins, *Convergence Culture: Where Old and New Media Collide* (New York: New York University Press, 2006), pp. 182, 185, 186, 206, 216.

13. Ann L. Kim, "The Secret Key to Harry Potter: A Library Card," *LAT*, July 12, 2000; Jenifer Ragland, "Harry Potter Books Realize a Fantasy for Librarians," *LAT*, July 20, 2000; "Harry Potter Night at Library," *Hartford Courant*, July 22, 2000; "Libraries Welcome Harry Potter Novel," *LJ* 128 (2003): 16; Jennifer Burek Pierce, "Harry's Last Hurrah," *American Libraries* 38 (2007): 79.

14. "'Witchcraft' Certificates Disappear," *Orlando Sentinel*, September 13, 2000; P. Douglas Filaroski, "Popular Children's Book Has Parents' Guard Up," *Florida Times Union*, September 13, 2000; "The Leaky Cauldron," June 13, 2001, http://www.the-leaky-cauldron.org/MTarchives/00071.html.

15. Eric L. Wee, "Shelf Life," *Washington Post Magazine*, July 31, 2005.

16. Kim Crowley, personal communication with author, July 29, 2010.

17. Karen Schmidt, "The Library Saved Me Money! A World of Learning," *Woman's Day* 73 (March, 2010): 20; Alisa C. Gonzalez, "Vixens, Banditos, and Finding Common Ground," in Valerie Nye and Kathy Barco (eds.), *True Stories of Censorship Battles* (Chicago: American Library Association, 2012), pp. 25–29; Reggie Rivers, "The Duty of a Public Library," *Denver Post*, August 19, 2005.

18. Mark Spencer, "Hartford Library's 'The American Place' Program Helps Refugees, Immigrants," *Hartford Courant*, October 29, 2010.

19. "Schwerner's Widow Donates to Phila. Library," *Deep South Jewish Voice* 16 (2006): 20.

20. Ron Critchfield and David M. Powell, "Well-Intentioned Censorship Is Still Censorship: The Challenge of Public Library Employees," in Nye and Barco, *True Stories*, pp. 8–13.

21. Paul Hawkins, "A Serial Killer Visits the Library," in Nye and Barco, *True Stories*, p. 134; "Couple Caught Having Sex at Library," *Charlotte* [NC] *Observer*, April 13, 2011.

22. Michael McLaughlin, "The Need for American Indian Librarians," *Native American Times* 11 (October 21, 2005): 8.

23. James La Rue, "Uncle Bobby's Wedding," in Nye and Barco, *True Stories*, p. 113.

24. John Pruitt, "Gay Men's Book Clubs versus Wisconsin Public Libraries: Political Perceptions in the Absence of Dialogue," *Library Quarterly* 80 (2010): 121–141.

25. Michael X. Delli Carpini and Scott Keeter, "The Internet and an Informed Citizenry," http://repository,upenn.edu/asc.papers/2, p. 135; Michael X. Delli Carpini, "An Overview of the State of Citizens' Knowledge about Politics," http://repository.upenn.edu/asc.papers/53, p. 29; "Retired Justice Sandra Day O'Connor, in Boise, Laments 'Alarming Degree of Public Ignorance,'" *Idaho Statesman*, September 6, 2013.

26. Margaret A. Edwards, *The Fair Garden and the Swarm of Beasts: The Library and the Young Adult* (Chicago: American Library Association, 2002), p. 78.

27. http://safelibraries.blogspot.com/2012/08/SexuallyHarrassedLibrarianGets150K.html; Kent Faulk, "Birmingham and Library Board Settle Sexually Hostile Workplace Lawsuit," *Birmingham* [AL] *News*, April 19, 2012.

28. Susan Pinker, *The Village Effect: How Face-to-Face Contact Can Make Us Healthier, Happier, and Smarter* (New York: Spiegel & Grau, 2014).

29. Paul Johnson, *A History of the American People* (New York: HarperCollins, 1998), p. 3.

Index

Page numbers in *italic* refer to illustrations.